THE HEAVENS
ARE OPEN

THE HEAVENS ARE OPEN

The 1992 Sperry Symposium
on the Doctrine and Covenants
and Church History

Deseret Book Company
Salt Lake City, Utah

Library of Congress Cataloging-in-Publication Data.

Sperry Symposium (21st : 1992 : Brigham Young University)
    The heavens are open : the 1992 Sperry Symposium on the Doctrine
and Covenants / compiled by Byron R. Merrill . . . [et al.].
      p.   cm.
    Papers presented at the twenty-first annual symposium held on
Sept. 26, 1992, sponsored by Brigham Young University and the LDS
Church Educational System.
    Includes bibliographical references and index.
    ISBN 0-87579-741-5
    1. Doctrine and Covenants—Congresses.   2. Church of Jesus Christ
of Latter-day Saints—Doctrines—Congresses.   3. Mormon Church—
Doctrines—Congresses.   I. Merrill, Byron R.   II. Title.
BX8628.S72   1992
289.3'2—dc20   93-16876
                                                                        CIP

Printed in the United States of America

10   9   8   7   6   5   4   3   2   1

CONTENTS

PREFACE

President Ezra Taft Benson has borne testimony of the Doctrine and Covenants in these words:

"The Book of Mormon brings men to Christ. The Doctrine and Covenants brings men to Christ's kingdom, even The Church of Jesus Christ of Latter-day Saints, 'the only true and living church upon the face of the whole earth.' (D&C 1:30.) I know that.

"The Book of Mormon is the keystone of our religion, and the Doctrine and Covenants is the capstone, with continuing latter-day revelation" (*A Witness and a Warning: A Modern-day Prophet Testifies of the Book of Mormon* [Salt Lake City: Deseret Book Co., 1988], pp. 30–31).

He also stated: "The Author of the Doctrine and Covenants is the Lord Jesus Christ. . . . [It] is unique among the standard works of the Church . . . in that it is a modern book of scripture" (*Ensign*, Jan. 1993, p. 2).

That "unique" volume is compiled from revelations of the Lord to the Prophet Joseph Smith, Jr., and to his successors in the presidency of the Church. It records the words of "the only living and true God" (D&C 20:19), given through living prophets to a living Church. The Lord has declared that in conjunction with the Book of Mormon and continuing revelation, the Doctrine and Covenants "shall bring to light the true points of my doctrine" (D&C 10:62), upon which his Church and kingdom is founded in the latter days. He has further declared that his promises contained in this sacred volume "shall all be fulfilled, whether by mine own voice or by the voice of my servants, it is the same" (D&C 1:38).

Brigham Young University and the LDS Church Educational System were pleased to sponsor the twenty-first annual Sidney B. Sperry Symposium on 26 September 1992. The theme of the symposium was "The Heavens Are Open." This present volume contains presentations selected from those given at the symposium. Though the authors have sought to be in harmony with Church doctrine, their remarks represent their own ideas and are not necessarily those of the Church Educational System, Brigham Young University, or The Church of Jesus Christ of Latter-day Saints.

These presentations focus on the Doctrine and Covenants and the continuing stream of revelation that directs the Lord's work on the earth. They discuss topics ranging from historical insights on Zion's Camp and the early mission of the Twelve Apostles to prophecies of the last days. Subjects are as panoramic as the restoration of all things or as specific as Joseph Smith's poetic rendition of Section 76. Each bears witness to the fulfillment of the Lord's promise to reveal his will "by mine own voice out of the heavens" (D&C 84:42). Truly, the heavens are open.

BYU Religious Education Special Lectures Committee
Byron R. Merrill
Brent L. Top
David R. Seely
Vern D. Sommerfeldt

THE AUTHENTIC THEOLOGY

Bruce C. Hafen

Brigham Young University

A friend of mine is a successful physician and a stake president who lives with his family in the southeastern part of the country. He and his wife enrolled several of their children in an academically strong Christian school, where their children were among the school's best and most popular students. Not long ago, because of the fears of other parents who were convinced that Mormons are not Christians, the school required these parents to withdraw their children permanently. Another friend, who is a community-oriented priesthood leader in a West Coast city, recently applied for membership in an interdenominational organization of local Christian religious leaders. He was told that a Mormon would fit more appropriately with the city's association for non-Christian religions.

A substantial part of these puzzling attitudes can be attributed to widespread and erroneous perceptions about Latter-day Saint doctrines concerning the atonement and the grace of Christ. *Newsweek* magazine put it this way a few years ago in an article entitled "What Mormons Believe": "Unlike orthodox Christians, Mormons believe that men are born free of sin and earn their way to godhood by the proper exercise of free will, rather than through the grace of Jesus Christ. Thus Jesus' suffering and death in the Mormon view were brotherly acts of compassion, but they do not atone for the sins of others. For this reason, Mormons do not include the cross in their iconography nor do they place much emphasis on Easter."[1]

I find massive irony in these profoundly mistaken impressions, for it is my thesis that the Restoration through Joseph Smith actually made the atonement and the grace of Jesus Christ relevant and accessible to individuals in a way that traditional Protestant and Catholic doctrines have simply been unable to do. And this has occurred at a time when the contemporary society is literally starving with spiritual hunger.

I wish to introduce this thesis by telling you about a recent book from Yale University Press, called *Heaven: A History*, in which two historians, Colleen McDannell and Bernhard Lang, trace both popular and religious beliefs about the concept of heaven throughout the centuries of Western history. McDannell and Lang say they chose to study this subject because "it reflects a deep and profound longing in Christianity to move beyond this life and to experience more fully the divine. The ways in which people imagine heaven tell us how they understand themselves, their families, their society, and their God." Indeed, these authors regard their subject as "a key to [understanding] our Western culture."[2]

Their study concludes with an assessment of heaven in twentieth-century Christianity, which is characterized by two major findings: first, 71 percent of modern Americans believe "there is a heaven where people who have led good lives are eternally rewarded." Significantly, the proportion of the population who hold this belief is about the same today as it was in 1952.[3] Thus, in attitudes toward topics ranging from cemeteries to love songs, people from all Christian denominations still express their instinctive belief in "the eternal nature of love and the hope for heavenly reunion," especially with their family members.[4] These popular sentiments echo Emily Dickinson's from a century ago that the " 'Life that is to be' will be 'a Residence too plain / Unless in my Redeemer's Face / I recognize your own.' "[5]

This yearning for eternal forms of belonging reflects attitudes not only about human relationships but also about relationships with God. For example, a 1983 survey reported in a prominent Catholic publication revealed that many American Catholics "want to 'hug God' when they arrive in heaven." McDannell and Lang note that this response echoes "the hopes of earlier generations: God will be a personal character willing to be hugged, individuals will retain their personalities, families will reunite, and earthly activities will continue."[6]

When I first read about this widespread hunger to "hug God," my knowledge of gospel teachings on that sacred subject made me feel like Alma of old: "O that I were an angel, and could have the wish of mine heart" (Alma 29:1), to let these thousands of hopeful people know the glad tidings of the Restoration, to tell them the Lord's words to Joseph and Oliver, "Be faithful and diligent in keeping the commandments of God, and I will encircle thee in the arms of my love" (D&C 6:20). Or as Mormon wrote, "that this people . . . might have been clasped in the arms of Jesus" (Mormon 5:11).

With that tender perspective in mind, let us consider now the second and more sobering finding about the idea of heaven in twentieth-century America. After first describing the surprising strength of today's personal beliefs in a real heaven, McDannell and Lang observe that the mainline Christian churches offer no serious theological response to the natural intuition of their members. Rather, individuals' "ideas about what happens after death are only popular sentiments and are not integrated in Protestant and Catholic theological systems."[7] Modern Christian theology seems to assume that its earlier ideas about immortality are no longer socially relevant and, besides, are too speculative to be acceptable to contemporary scholarship. "For some of the most prominent Protestant and Catholic theologians of this century, heavenly life — if heaven exists at all — cannot be described by reason, revelation, or poetic imagination."[8]

But then these two historians make a further observation. They note one "major exception" to their generalization regarding today's theological vacuum among Christians about heaven, namely, "the theology of The Church of Jesus Christ of Latter-day Saints."[9] They then summarize in respectful and knowledgeable terms a range of LDS teachings from eternal marriage and genealogy to ordinances for the dead. They conclude that "the understanding of life after death in the LDS church is the clearest [known] example of the continuation of the modern heaven into the twentieth century."[10] I note here that I first became aware of this book in a conversation with the religion editor of *Newsweek* magazine when he said to me, "I see where the Mormons got some nice play in the new book on heaven out of Yale."

I find it poignant that so many people would instinctively yearn for a sense of genuine belonging in everlasting relationships of loving, intimate meaning not only with other people but also with God. How sad and ironic, then, that today's Christian theology offers no serious response to these deeply felt needs. If McDannell and Lang are correct that this "deep and profound longing in Christianity" is a key to understanding Western culture, then Western culture is a theological wasteland scorched with loneliness and alienation. Perhaps these are the days of which Amos spoke, days of "a famine in the land, not a famine of bread, nor a thirst for water, but of hearing the words of the Lord: and they shall wander from sea to sea, . . . they shall run to and fro to seek the word of the Lord, and shall not find it" (Amos 8:11–12).

Despite this virtual absence of theological support, many Americans dream of a heaven where families are reunited and where God himself might welcome them in a divine embrace. The Restoration offers these people not only the hope of such an embrace but a full understanding of its meaning, which offers the promise of "peace in this world, and eternal life in the world to come" (D&C 59:23). For being clasped in the arms of Jesus symbolizes the fulfillment of his atonement in our individual lives, here as well as in heaven, becoming literally "at one" with him, belonging to him, as he will to us.

The theological foundation for this fulfillment touches upon several major doctrines, including the Fall, the Atonement, salvation, the nature of man, grace, and repentance. Without probing all of these doctrines, I want to suggest that just as the Restoration offers the most complete and satisfying available theology about heaven, so does the Restoration also fill a similar — and more substantial — theological void about the atonement of Jesus Christ. Moreover, the Restoration teaches of Christ's mission in a way that lets his life and his death speak to our most profound human needs in everyday life, just as an understanding of heaven fulfills our hopes for the life after death. There is an answer to the doubt and fear that plague the modern wasteland. To borrow a phrase from Robert Browning, there is an answer to the passionate longing of the heart for fullness. That answer is in the teachings of the Restoration about our relationship with the Savior.

This bold assertion of the Restoration's revolutionary implications for Christianity's most central doctrine finds strong support in the work of a noted scholar on the Protestant Reformation, John Dillenberger. In a 1978 essay comparing Martin Luther with Joseph Smith on the question of grace and works, Dillenberger commented on Mormonism's doctrinal uniqueness: "Mormonism brought understanding to what had become an untenable problem within evangelicalism: how to reconcile the new power of humanity with the negative inherited views of humanity, without abandoning the necessity of grace." In this way, "perhaps Mormonism . . . is the authentic American theology, for the self-reliance of revivalist fundamentalist groups stood in marked contrast to their inherited conception of the misery of humanity."[11]

To explore the meaning of Professor Dillenberger's provocative observation, we must take a brief journey through the history of certain ideas in Western civilization. Any sketch of this kind runs the risk of being simplistic, but sometimes even a few headlines from history can provide needed perspective. Ever since the fourth century A.D., the teachings of traditional Christianity regarding man's nature and the role of Christ's grace have begun with the assumption that each person born since the fall of Adam and Eve has an inherently evil nature. According to Catholic teachings, this effect of original sin can be overcome only by the grace of Christ as that is dispensed through the official sacraments of the church. Standard Protestant theology on this subject is even more pessimistic about the uncontrollable nature of humankind's inherent evil, yet its primary departure from Catholic doctrine is its claim that the source of grace is not in church sacraments but only in the unearned gift that God may choose to bestow, at his option alone, directly upon an elect few. Let us consider the historical origin of these major premises for so much Christian reasoning.

Leading Christian scholars commonly acknowledge, as BYU's Stephen Robinson has pointed out, that by the fourth century, Christianity's basic doctrines had undergone a "radical change from the theology of the New Testament Church."[12] The extent of this change is illustrated by the *Harvard Theological Review's* recent publication of an excellent article by BYU's David Paulsen, which documents that "ordinary Christians for at least the first three centuries" after Christ believed that God had a body.[13] Brother Paulsen shows that beginning in the fourth century, Christianity gradually abandoned its belief in God's physical body, because that idea was unacceptable to the Greek philosophy that pervaded the Roman empire. This change erected one of the first conceptual barriers against human identification with a personal God. That the *Harvard Theological Review* considers this evidence of the Great Apostasy to be worthy of serious treatment by a BYU scholar is, like *Heaven: A History,* an encouraging sign that as we thoughtfully remove whatever bushels conceal the Restoration's light, Latter-day Saint perspectives can and will play a legitimate part in "restoring" the Restoration to its rightful place in the otherwise impoverished conversations of today's thoughtful people.

Another significant doctrinal change during and after the fourth century was the widespread acceptance of Saint Augustine's views about man's fallen and evil nature, which has had a profound effect on Christianity's understanding of both the need for and the meaning of the atonement and the grace of Christ. In another candid acknowledgment of the Great Apostasy, Princeton religious scholar Elaine Pagels's recent book, *Adam, Eve, and the Serpent,* describes in some detail how Augustine's highly original "teaching on 'original sin' became the center of [the] western Christian tradition, displacing, or at least wholly recasting, all previous views of creation and free will."[14] Augustine's reasoning began with his despair over his perceived inability to control the way his body responded to sexual stimuli. He finally concluded that all human seed is infected with the contaminated seed of Adam, thereby transmitting to each human person Adam's fallen nature. And in his view "no human power" could remedy this inborn human failure, but only the power of Christ, who was fathered without mortal seed. As a result, only the Church and its clergy could bestow God's grace by administering "to sick and suffering humanity the life-giving medication of the sacraments."[15] I infer from this logic that the Catholic doctrine of transubstantiation, whereby sacramental bread and wine are believed to be literally transformed into the flesh and blood of Christ, is the only way, under materialistic Augustinian thinking, to achieve a gradual, physical conversion of a fallen part of the body of Adam into a redeemed member of the body of Christ.

Professor Pagels's research shows that Augustine's ideas were a radical departure from both the moral freedom taught by the Old Testament and the ideas of free will and personal responsibility that had prevailed among Christians since the time of Christ. Given Augustine's heretical "decision to abandon his predecessors' emphasis on free will,"[16] she asks, why were his views embraced rather than condemned by the Christian leadership? One answer must be that Augustine's writings demonstrated great intellectual power. But Pagels found a further explanation in historical and political reality. The Roman emperor Constantine had accepted Christianity and declared it the official religion of the vast Roman empire not long before Augustine began writing. Augustine's views offered a perfect justification for the assertion of both governmental and religious power over a pluralistic and unruly population: because people by their fallen nature could not govern themselves, they required the help of a powerful state as well as a forceful church structure. Thus Augustine's theology of the Fall made "the uneasy alliance between the Catholic churches and [the] imperial power [of the Roman state] not only justifiable but necessary."[17] This political imperative moved Augustinian doctrine "into the center of Western history," surpassing the influence "of any other church father." From then on, it was heresy to teach the earlier Christian view of human freedom, which had once been "so widely regarded as the heart of the Christian gospel."[18]

In the centuries that followed, the church of the Middle Ages erected an elaborate structure of both doctrine and practice on the foundation of Augustine's assumptions about man's evil nature. This structure included the monastic orders. By the time of Martin Luther in fifteenth- and sixteenth-century Germany, the Church's influence was waning and the former Roman empire had fragmented into many nationalistic states that looked to their own interests rather than to Rome for leadership. New political, economic, and intellectual forces had emerged that would make the Renaissance into one of Western history's greatest watersheds. Nevertheless, Augustine's notion of natural human depravity was about to be reinforced in the life of Martin Luther as the linchpin of Christian theology.

Himself an Augustinian monk, Luther struggled with his personal weaknesses in an ordeal very similar to Augustine's. He tried in vain to satisfy his desperate need for grace through the church's sacraments.

Eleven hundred years earlier, Augustine had found guidance in Paul's New Testament letters, which Augustine interpreted as denying human will. Luther looked to those same sources and accepted Augustine's major premise about man's evil nature and utter incapacity.[19] He then launched the Reformation era by concluding (along with his other criticisms of the Catholic church) that God bestows undeserved grace not through church sacraments but directly on chosen individuals, removing any need for the church as an intermediary. Luther thus, perhaps unintentionally, broke the Catholic church's control over the sources of grace, thereby permanently undermining the church's social and political authority. In another echo of Augustine's experience, Luther's theology provided a rationale for the claims of potent new political forces throughout Europe that sought to overthrow rather than to sustain centralized authoritarian structures. Luther was courageous and articulate, but, as had happened with Augustine, a historic need gave wings to his thought that its religious merit alone might not have warranted.

John Calvin, Luther's contemporary, soon developed a complete doctrine of predestination based on Luther's idea that God alone chooses the individuals on whom he bestows the gift of grace, regardless of what they deserve or even what they prefer. The American Puritans later drew heavily on Calvinism, emphasizing the belief that when one is chosen by God to receive his grace, one's life will spontaneously reflect such fruits of the Spirit as goodness and material success. Because being "elected" by God to receive grace was a totally private experience, the urge to show that one had been chosen paradoxically provided considerable incentive for people to display the energetic self-reliance and productivity we associate with the Puritan ethic in United States history.

This historical sketch illustrates John Dillenberger's comment about the "negative inherited views" of "the misery of humanity" that have characterized western Christianity. After the Reformation, despite some variations among Christian denominations, the Augustinian and Lutheran doctrines of the Fall, the nature of man, and the atonement and grace of Christ continued as a permanent inheritance in both the Catholic and the Protestant traditions. By 1820, these ideas had painted Christianity into an impossible corner, because neither the intellectual developments of recent centuries nor popular common sense in the United States took seriously the notion of man's uncontrollable evil nature. As Dillenberger put it, Protestantism had thus developed "an untenable problem," namely, how to reconcile the "new power of humanity" and the "self-reliance" of Christian religious groups with the Augustinian heritage, without nullifying the meaning of grace.

For example, a leading authority on Puritanism writes that within a century after the Puritans came to America in 1620, "the theory of the utter dependence of man on . . . God ceased to have any relevance to the facts of the Puritan experience. . . . [Still,] the preachers continued to preach [the doctrine of man's inherited evil nature] and the laymen continued to hear it; not because either of them believed it, but because they cherished it. . . . Thus the sense of sin became a genteel tradition, cherished in the imagination long after it had been surrendered in practice. The Puritan insistence on human depravity became the . . . justification of Yankee moral complacency."[20] In other words, one might say with a wink, we might as well be sinful—that's just human nature.

One reason people stopped believing in man's fallen nature was that European and American history between Luther's time and Joseph Smith's time demonstrated such irresistible evidence for the wonder of humankind's abilities. Drawing on classic Greek optimism about man's rational powers, the Renaissance and the Enlightenment fueled true revolutions in the sciences, the arts, the commercial-industrial world, and in the political sphere—as witnessed by the French and American revolutions. The turmoil of the French Revolution and its aftermath tempered many Europeans' enthusiasm for some of these ideas, but the independent and robust America of Joseph Smith's time was fairly bursting with confidence in the ability of men and women to subdue the earth and take charge of their lives through their own creative energy.

From the hundreds of possible examples of this optimistic spirit in Western history, consider only one—Goethe's *Faust,* which was published, during Joseph Smith's lifetime, in two parts, in 1808 and 1832. *Faust* is a literary masterpiece in which the central character has a consuming desire to comprehend life's meaning. He agrees to yield his eternal soul to the devil, if the devil can give him such complete access to the depths of human experience and understanding that Faust feels content enough to cease his quest for further knowledge. Mephistopheles thus leads Faust through a lifetime of complicated experiences with love, sin, disappointment, guilt, beauty, intellectual comprehension, economic power, and finally a taste of service to others. After years of ceaseless striving, it is only when Faust finally contemplates the joy of offering his knowledge and power to benefit other people that he would utter the phrase of ultimate satisfaction, "Linger awhile, thou art so fair." Faust then collapses into death, and Mephistopheles comes for his soul. But in that moment, to the devil's tormented astonishment, angels sweep down to bear off Faust's soul to heaven. The angels later explain that "whoever strives in ceaseless toil, him we may grant redemption. And when on high, transfigured love has added intercession, the blest will throng to him above with welcoming compassion."

Both Faust and his author, Goethe, embody the indomitable human confidence of the pre-Restoration era. The Enlightenment's "light" regarding human possibilities was in utter contrast to the "dark" of Augustine's Dark Ages. One intellectual historian described this optimistic spirit with words Augustine and Luther could never have accepted: "We are agents as well as observers; we are not just objects in the world, but we can change it."[21] Thus, writes a noted Faust scholar, Faust "assumes symbolic significance as the extreme exemplar of the deepest drives of western civilization. Self-realization . . . is a program without inner or outer limits."[22]

Faust also carries religious overtones. For one thing, Faust's stirring quest for knowledge in an imperfect world suggests a positive view of Adam's fall that was articulated by Goethe's friend, Schiller: He [Schiller] conceded the tragedy of the Fall, but he argued that "the fall was also an absolutely necessary first step in the higher development of mankind. . . . Without [the Fall], man would forever have remained a child of Nature, innocent but ignorant, unable to develop the faculties of distinguishing between good and evil."[23] This positive understanding of the Fall is far closer to the truth as taught by the Restoration than it is to the traditional Christian heritage.

Moreover, I read the speech by the angels to mean that heaven's mercy allowed Faust to rob Satan's claim to justice only because Faust had demonstrated honest repentance and growth in the relentless and self-initiated striving of his whole life. At the same time, neither his effort nor God's mercy alone would have sufficed by itself: he was finally rescued by mercy but only because he worked hard enough to prove worthy of it. Goethe intuitively recognized each person's innate capacity to improve himself by learning from experience, but he also saw a need for higher powers. And although he still needed to know the place of Christ's atonement and its attendant commandments and ordinances, Goethe did sense generally the relationship among justice, mercy, and repentance as taught by the Restoration. But, significantly, traditional Christian theology offered him virtually no support for that understanding, because its Augustinian premises were so limiting and so inconsistent with obvious human experience.

In that sense, Goethe and the Western thought he represented at Joseph Smith's time illustrate what Dillenberger meant in describing

Christian theology's "untenable problem": "how to reconcile the new power of humanity with the negative inherited views of humanity, without abandoning the necessity of grace." In other words, the great danger of the optimistic view of human nature and mankind's striving was that, taken to its logical extreme, that optimism finally had no need for the grace of Christ. Because "self-realization" was thought to be "without inner or outer limits," the limitless Faustian journey by itself—wherever it led, with or without grace—could serve life's limitless purpose. And that is exactly what happened, as humanistic self-confidence gained the upper hand over self-deprecating theology in the nineteenth and twentieth centuries.

Actually, Goethe had not yet fallen into that natural trap. By showing that Faust still needed angelic forces, he acknowledged human dependency on a higher power—but only after Faust did all he could. Like the large proportion of the American people whose instincts tell them more than does their theology about the reality of a meaningful heaven, Goethe's instincts told him more than did his theology about the relationship between God's grace and mankind's striving. But all of that simply underscores the theological bankruptcy of traditional Christianity on the foundation subject of Christ's atonement.

The Protestant Christianity that dominated nineteenth-century America was increasingly unable to reconcile its pessimistic heritage with the nation's new frontier optimism. The widely recognized power of human accomplishment contradicted traditional beliefs in mankind's evil nature to the point that many people not only saw little practical need for God's grace but adopted the humanistic assumption that mankind is good by nature. Having believed for centuries that people need grace primarily to overcome their evil nature, once they assumed that man is inherently good, they eliminated the need for Christ's grace altogether. Individuals still occasionally violated divine laws, but poverty and other collective failures within society's urban environment were more persuasive explanations for these failings than was any idea of inborn depravity. Thus the abstractions of Christian theology seemed ever less relevant to actual daily experience.

This gradual reduction of theological influence continued through the twentieth century until traditional Christianity was pronounced totally irrelevant to modern society in 1964 by Harvey Cox, a prominent Protestant theologian, in a book called *The Secular City*. This title was a deliberate and symbolic rejection of Augustine's preoccupation with the other world in his famous book from the fourth century, *The City of God*. Cox urged that unless the Christian churches gave up their dreaming of heavenly cities and focused on the social problems of earthly cities, Christianity would play no meaningful role in American life. Despite the continuing belief in Augustinian assumptions among a few theologically conservative Protestant groups today, experience demonstrates that most theologians among the nation's churches have clearly taken Cox's advice.

For instance, in a talk to new divinity school students earlier this year, Dean Philip Turner of the Yale Divinity School acknowledged that Augustine's thought "now appears unsatisfactory and in certain ways rather destructive." One of Augustine's errors, he said, was to place so much emphasis on the first commandment, to love God, that he ignored the second commandment, to love one's neighbor. Yet "many theologians in the modern period, partly in reaction [against this Augustinian heritage], have executed a reverse maneuver," and they emphasize love of neighbor so much that they now exclude the love and worship of God.[24] Dean Turner urged his students to put the study of divinity—God—back into divinity school. His concern is of course consistent with the absence of modern theological interest in heaven that we noted earlier.

As we survey the modern wreckage of a once elaborate Christian theological structure, Dillenberger's observation about Mormon doctrine seems even more compelling. "In stressing human possibilities," he wrote, "Mormonism brought things into line, not by abandoning the centrality of grace but by insisting that the powers of humanity were real and that they reflected the actual state of humanity as such." "Perhaps Mormonism . . . is the authentic American theology."[25]

What is this authentic American theology? This is not the place for an extended treatise on the Restoration's unique and powerful theology of grace and atonement, but, because the weakness and impracticality of traditional Christian teaching is now clearly unmasked, it is appropriate at least to introduce the general relationship among human nature, the Atonement, and the way in which belonging to Christ can sustain us in times of personal need. I am drawn toward this personal dimension because I am saddened by the thought that so many decent people outside (and inside) the Church can see no theological support for embracing and belonging to the authentic Christ—not only in heaven but on earth. For the Restoration, like the Atonement, is not only a historical and abstract message but also an intensely present and personal one.

We deal here with a restoration of truths previously taught. Because the need for a restoration depends on the existence of an apostasy, I am grateful for the recent scholarship we noted earlier that further documents the reality of the Great Apostasy during the early Christian era, especially in explaining the origins of Augustine's thought. We Latter-day Saints have not focused as much as we could on the way the apostasy changed the underlying premises of the Atonement.

According to the Savior's original doctrines, as restored through Joseph Smith, the fall of Adam made Christ's redemption necessary but not because the Fall by itself rendered all humankind inherently evil. Neither, however, is human nature inherently good. Because of transgression, Adam and Eve were expelled from Eden into a world that was subject to death and evil influences, but the Lord soon taught Adam that "the Son of God hath atoned for original guilt"; therefore, Adam's children were not evil but were "*whole* from the foundation of the world" (Moses 6:54; emphasis added). Thus, "every spirit of man was *innocent* in the beginning; and God having redeemed man from the fall, men became again, in their infant state, *innocent* before God" (D&C 93:38; emphasis added).

As the descendants of Adam and Eve then become accountable for their own sins at the age of eight, all of them taste sin to one degree or another as the result of their own curiosity and experiences in a free environment. Those whose cumulative experience leads them to love "Satan more than God" (Moses 5:28) will to that degree become "carnal, sensual, and devilish" (Moses 5:13; 6:49) by nature — "natural men." On the other hand, one who consciously accepts Christ's grace through the Atonement by faith, repentance, and baptism will yield to the "enticings of the Holy Spirit," and put off "the natural man" and become "a saint through the atonement of Christ the Lord" (Mosiah 3:19). Thus, after taking the initiative to accept the grace made available by the Atonement, one may then nourish this desire by obedience that interacts with grace until one "becomes a saint" by nature, thereby enjoying eternal, or godlike, life.

In LDS theology, therefore, grace is the absolutely indispensable source of three categories of blessings. First are the unconditional blessings — free and unmerited gifts requiring no individual action on our part. God's grace in this sense includes the very Creation as well as making gospel teachings and the plan of salvation available to us. It also includes redemption from physical death and forgiveness for Adam's and Eve's original sin.

Second, the Savior has atoned for individual sins on the condition of our repentance. Personal repentance is thus a *necessary* condition of salvation but is not by itself *sufficient* to assure salvation. Without the Atonement, our repentance availeth nothing. We must also accept the ordinances of baptism and the receipt of the Holy Ghost, by which we are born again as spirit children of Christ.

Third is the bestowal of grace after baptism along the path toward a Christlike nature. Once we have repented and are baptized unto forgiveness of sin, we have only "entered in by the gate" to the "strait and narrow path which leads to eternal life" (2 Nephi 31:18). This postbaptism stage of spiritual development does not expect perfection, but it does require our good faith effort to "endure to the end" (2 Ne. 31:20). This effort includes receiving the higher ordinances of the temple and an ongoing repentance process as needed "for the sake of retaining a remission of your sins from day to day" (Mosiah 4:26).

In Martin Luther's teachings, a Christian who performs righteous acts after receiving Christ's grace is not acting from personal initiative but is only reflecting the spontaneous fruit of internal grace. For Luther, man's fallen nature made self-generated righteousness impossible. In LDS doctrine, by contrast, "men should . . . do many things of their own free will, and bring to pass much righteousness: for the power is in them, wherein they are agents unto themselves" (D&C 58:27–28). At the same time, we lack the capacity to develop a fully Christlike nature by our own effort alone. Thus the perfecting attributes, which include hope, charity, and finally eternal life itself, are—as Mormon put it so eloquently—ultimately "*bestowed* upon all who are true followers of . . . Jesus Christ" (Moroni 7:48) by grace made possible by the Atonement. This interactive relationship between human and divine powers in LDS theology derives both from the significance that theology attaches to free will and from its optimism about the "fruit of the spirit" (Galatians 5:22) among "those who love me and keep all my commandments, *and him that seeketh so to do*" (D&C 46:9; emphasis added).

God bestows these additional, perfecting expressions of grace conditionally, as he does the grace that allows forgiveness of sin. They are given "after all we can do" (2 Nephi 25:23)—that is, as a supplement to our best efforts. In general this condition is related less to obeying particular commandments than it is to one's fundamental spiritual character, such as "meekness and lowliness of heart" (Moroni 8:26) and developing "a broken heart and a contrite spirit" (3 Nephi 9:20).

In addition, those who enter into the covenants of the Atonement with Christ through their faith, repentance, and baptism are blessed with a precious and ongoing relationship of personal and spiritual sustenance. That is the relationship of belonging to—or being children of—Christ. We celebrate and renew this relationship each time we partake of the sacrament. Through this covenant relationship, the Savior grants not only a continuing remission of our sins but he will also help compensate for our inadequacies, heal the bruises caused by

our unintentional errors, and strengthen us far beyond our natural
capacity in times of acute need. Both we and our friends outside the
Church need this Atonement-based relationship more than we need
any other form of therapy or support: "O Israel, Fear not: for I have
redeemed thee, I have called thee by thy name; thou art mine. When
thou passest through the waters, I will be with thee; and through the
rivers, they shall not overflow thee: when thou walkest through the fire,
thou shalt not be burned; neither shall the flame kindle upon thee. For
I am the Lord thy God, the Holy One of Israel, thy Savior" (Isaiah
43:1–3).

Brothers and sisters, sometimes I think we have no idea of the
strength of the Church's position. Our strength derives not just from
family values and healthy living, as important as those are; it derives
from the "authentic theology" of the restored gospel, which is the last,
best, and only hope of Christianity, and of all mankind. The Restoration not only resolves Christianity's doctrinal dilemmas but it also
offers the most complete solution to our greatest problems, whether
social or personal.

Yet the gospel's insights remain relatively hidden from a society
that has been consciously and cleverly persuaded by Mephistopheles
himself that the Church of the Restoration knows least — when in fact
it knows most — about making Jesus Christ our personal Savior. Satan
has known exactly what he is doing. What frightens him and his allies
is not that the Restoration teaches so little about the atonement and
grace of Christ but that it teaches so much. To conceal that reality,
he has been engaged in one of history's greatest cover-ups. But as recent
scholarship shows, not only the LDS life-style but now the far more
fundamental contribution of LDS doctrine is beginning to come forth
from obscurity. The new *Encyclopedia of Mormonism* is also a wonderful
step in that direction. How I hope that our LDS scholars will continue
this process. After all, the Lord told Joseph Smith that "every man
shall hear the fulness of the gospel in his own tongue" (D&C 90:11),
and that should include the language of scholarship, that fertile seedbed
of ideas and opinion from which so much future fruit can come.

Today many, many people feel a longing for heaven, where, they
want to believe, they will be welcomed into the arms of their families
and into the arms of God. The Restoration offers a complete fulfillment
of that longing, not just as momentary emotion but as the fully developed doctrine of the gospel of Jesus Christ. I can hear him saying
to all those, inside and outside the Church, who hunger and thirst to
find him in these times of trauma and famine: "Behold, . . . ye must
grow in grace and in the knowledge of the truth. Fear not, little

children, for you are mine, and I have overcome the world, and you are of them that my Father hath given me; and none of them that my Father hath given me shall be lost. . . . And inasmuch as ye have received me, ye are in me and I in you" (D&C 50:40–43). "Be faithful and diligent in keeping the commandments of God, and I will encircle thee in the arms of my love" (D&C 6:20).

NOTES

1. In *Newsweek,* 1 Sept. 1980, p. 68.

2. Colleen McDannell and Bernhard Lang, *Heaven: A History* (New Haven: Yale University Press, 1988), p. xiii.

3. Ibid., p. 307.

4. Ibid., p. 312.

5. As quoted in ibid., p. 311.

6. Ibid., p. 309.

7. Ibid., p. 308.

8. Ibid.

9. Ibid.

10. Ibid., p. 320.

11. John Dillenberger, "Grace and Works in Martin Luther and Joseph Smith," in *Reflections on Mormonism: Judaeo-Christian Parallels,* ed. Truman G. Madsen (Provo, Utah: Religious Studies Center, Brigham Young University, 1978), p. 179.

12. Stephen E. Robinson, *Are Mormons Christians?* (Salt Lake City: Bookcraft, 1991), p. 38.

13. David Paulsen, "Early Christian Belief in a Corporeal Deity: Origen and Augustine as Reluctant Witnesses," *Harvard Theological Review,* vol. 83, no. 2 (April 1990): 105.

14. Elaine Pagels, *Adam, Eve, and the Serpent* (New York: Vintage Books, 1988), pp. 99–100.

15. Ibid., p. 117.

16. Ibid., p. 99.

17. Ibid., p. 126.

18. Ibid., pp. 125–26.

19. Ibid., p. 106. See also Heinrich Boehmer, *Martin Luther: Road to Reformation* (New York: Meridian Books, 1957), p. 139.

20. Herbert W. Schneider, *The Puritan Mind* (Ann Arbor: University of Michigan Press, 1958), p. 98.

21. Robert C. Solomon, *Continental Philosophy since 1750: The Rise and Fall of the Self,* vol. 7 of *A History of Western Philosophy* (Oxford: Oxford University Press, 1988), pp. 36–37.

22. Hermann Weigand, "Goethe's *Faust:* An Introduction for Students and Teachers of General Literature," in Johann Wolfgang von Goethe, *Faust,* trans.

Walter Arndt, ed. Cyrus Hamlin (New York: W. W. Norton and Co., 1976), p. 448.

23. Ibid., p. 447.

24. Philip Turner, "To Students of Divinity: A Convocation Address," *First Things,* no. 26 (October 1992): 26.

25. Dillenberger, "Grace and Works in Martin Luther and Joseph Smith," p. 179.

2

THE REVELATIONS OF THE RESTORATION: WINDOW TO THE PAST, OPEN DOOR TO THE FUTURE

Robert L. Millet

Brigham Young University

Jesus and the apostles spoke of the coming of the end of an age, the end of the dispensation of the meridian of time. There would come a day, they warned, when men and women would "not endure sound doctrine" (2 Timothy 4:3), a day when malicious persons would seek to interject "damnable heresies" (2 Peter 2:1) into the faith. The seeds of the apostasy were in fact planted centuries before the coming of Jesus of Nazareth. The empire of Alexander the Great, as a political entity, did not survive his death in 323 B.C., but the cultural empire he founded lasted for nearly one thousand years, until the rise of Islam and the Arab conquests in the seventh century after Christ. Greek, or Hellenistic, influence was profound — upon the Roman empire, upon the world of Judaism, and, unfortunately, upon the early Christian Church. As Zenos had foreseen, for a time the grafting of branches from the "wild olive tree" (Gentile influence) would result in a season of strength for the Church (see Jacob 5:17). But it was only a matter of time before the teaching of the prophets and ideas of the philosophers would come in conflict; those with eyes to see were aware that attempts to merge the doctrines of the temple of God with the doctrines of Plato would be abortive to the Christian faith. Ecumenism would lead to shared impotence. And so it did. Philosophical error, mixed with truth, resulted in a heretical hybrid, a conceptual concoction foreign to the spiritually sensitive and certainly offensive to that God who delights in revealing himself to his children.

When the gospel sun went down almost two millennia ago, darkness reigned. Darkness filled the earth; and gross darkness, the minds of men and women. Certainly there were good and noble souls who enjoyed and hearkened to that influence we know as the Light of Christ; they strove to live according to the best light and knowledge they possessed. Nevertheless, that glorious luminary we know as revelation,

17

which always comes institutionally through the ministry of apostles and prophets and individually through the manifestations of the Spirit, was no longer enjoyed among the people of earth. The loss of the holy priesthood as well as the covenants and ordinances that lead to life eternal; the true doctrine of God, the Godhead, and man's relationship to Deity; and sacred insights into the means whereby mortals can have divine experience — these and a myriad of other treasures became mysteries to the masses and slipped into the realm of the unknowable and the unavailable. Error and falsehood crept into society and thus made their way into the hearts and minds of earth's pilgrims. The apostasy, which we call the Great Apostasy, was long and deep and broad. Its influence was extensive, and its effects reached into all facets of human endeavor — intellectual, moral, and spiritual.

THE DAWNING OF A BRIGHTER DAY

The spring of 1820 heralded the dawn of a new day. The Sacred Grove in upstate New York was not to be the location of a complete restoration, a place and a time wherein God would make all things known and correct all the flaws of a faltering world. Rather, the First Vision began the era of restitution, the times of refreshing, the season of cleansing and purification and endowment that would reach a zenith in a millennial dispensation. Unable to walk fully in the light of the Lord, the people of earth had chosen their own paths and sought to direct their own destinies. In detailing and describing the apostate condition of things in the morn of restoration, the Lord declared: "They have strayed from mine ordinances, and have broken mine everlasting covenant; they seek not the Lord to establish his righteousness, but every man walketh in his own way, and after the image of his own god, whose image is in the likeness of the world, and whose substance is that of an idol, which waxeth old and shall perish in Babylon, even Babylon the great, which shall fall" (D&C 1:15–16). The pressing problem was idolatry — devotion and dedication to anything other than the true and living God. The problem was one we observe frequently in our day — distraction from those things of greatest worth. The problem was that man had fashioned unto himself a god, an unknown god, the unreachable and the unknowable Essence, that Wholly Other. Whether Catholic or Protestant, Jew or Muslim, the religious leaders of the nineteenth century, with their congregants — even the most sincere among them, and surely there were many — had lost their way.

The prescription for earth's ills, the medication for the malady, the Lord set forth: "Wherefore, I the Lord, knowing the calamity which should come upon the inhabitants of the earth" — the spiritual calamity should the people of earth continue in apostasy, as well as the perilous times which lay ahead even for those whose faith was fully centered in their Redeemer — "called upon my servant Joseph Smith, Jun., and spake unto him from heaven, and gave him commandments; and also gave commandments to others, that they should proclaim these things" — the glad tidings of the Restoration — "unto the world; and all this that it might be fulfilled, which was written by the prophets — the weak things of the world shall come forth and break down the mighty and strong ones, that man should not counsel his fellow man" (D&C 1:17–19). That is, the children of God need no longer place their trust in or rely upon the limited wisdom of the unillumined, upon those who are not truly men and women of God (see Mosiah 23:14). Indeed, God would call upon the weak and the simple to bring forth his great and marvelous work, "those who are unlearned and despised" (D&C 35:13), those who are teachable, who are willing to unlearn falsehood and strip themselves of pride and duplicity, whose minds and hearts are open to the will of the Almighty. The Restoration heralded a day wherein men and women could come unto God, press forward through the mists of darkness, and then fall down and worship the true and living God, in the name of the Son, by the power of the Holy Ghost. The days in which only the chosen few could come unto God, those times when only a priestly hierarchy could perform the sacraments and commune with Deity, were no more. The gospel of God, the new and everlasting covenant, was restored to earth "that every man might speak in the name of God the Lord, even the Savior of the world; that faith also might increase in the earth" (D&C 1:20–21).

The Restoration would begin by a revelation, a re-revelation of doctrine and principles and precepts. It would of necessity start with the First Vision, the beginning of the revelation of God to man. It would be followed by the coming forth of the Book of Mormon, Another Testament of Jesus Christ. Through the truths contained in this sacred volume — including the verities long lost on such vital matters as the Creation, the Fall, and the Atonement — the fulness of the gospel could be had again. Revelation upon revelation would come to and through Joseph Smith, including the restoration of plain and precious truths once taken away or kept back from the Bible.

But there was more, more to come by way of truth, more than theology. The Restoration was destined to be a significant revolution. It must have been a mighty vision that filled the mind of Joseph Smith the Seer when he announced: "I calculate to be one of the instruments of setting up the kingdom [of God envisioned by] Daniel by the word of the Lord, and I intend to lay a foundation that will revolutionize the whole world." And how was this to be realized? "It will not be by sword or gun that this kingdom will roll on," the Prophet said. "*The power of truth is such that all nations will be under the necessity of obeying the gospel.*"[1]

Joseph Smith's vision of the kingdom of God—and of the power and ultimate reach of the Restoration—was cosmic. It consisted of more than preaching and study and Sabbath services; it entailed the entire renovation of the order of things on earth, the transformation of mankind and the elevation of society. The Restoration was to be as broad and as deep as the Great Apostasy. Eventually the people of Zion would know and acknowledge the truth, discern and dispel error, and teach and live the truth in all they said and did, in all facets of human endeavor—intellectual, moral, and spiritual. "Behold, I, the Lord, have made my church in these last days like unto a judge sitting on a hill, or in a high place, to judge the nations. For it shall come to pass that the inhabitants of Zion shall judge all things pertaining to Zion" (D&C 64:37–38).

" 'Mormonism' is destined to revolutionize the world," President George Q. Cannon observed. "But how many are there who realize the truth of this saying? Some, no doubt, but not nearly all who have heard it, and yet that very revolution is going on, and they are helping to promote it; it commenced many years ago—the very moment the first revelation was given to the Prophet Joseph Smith.

"But to revolutionize a world, with religions, political and social systems, the outgrowth of nearly six thousand years' experience is a slow process. . . .

"For this reason the Kingdom of God upon the earth will not be characterized by a wonderfully rapid growth, . . . but, grappling ever with, and never ceasing the strife until it is victor over, error and evil of every kind, its foundations will be securely laid in the hearts and affections of those who love and live by truth and righteousness only."[2]

A WINDOW TO THE PAST

Of Joseph Smith and all those who are called as president of the Church, the Savior said: "And again, the duty of the president of the office of the High Priesthood is to preside over the whole church, and to be like unto Moses—behold, here is wisdom; yea, to be a seer, a revelator, a translator, and a prophet, having all the gifts of God which he bestows upon the head of the church" (D&C 107:91–92; see also D&C 21:1; 124:125). Joseph Smith would not only stand as the head of this final dispensation but preside as the "choice seer" among the fruit of the loins of Joseph (2 Nephi 3:7). A seer, Ammon explained to King Limhi, is a prophet and a revelator also (Mosiah 8:16). "A *gift which is greater can no man have,*" he went on to say, "except he should possess the power of God, which no man can; yet a man may have great power given him from God. But *a seer can know of things which are past, and also of things which are to come, and by them shall all things be revealed, or, rather, shall secret things be made manifest, and hidden things shall come to light, and things which are not known shall be made known by them. . . .* Thus God has provided a means that man, through faith, might work mighty miracles; therefore he becometh a great benefit to his fellow beings" (Mosiah 8:16–18; emphasis added).

I am particularly interested in the seer's role of making known things past. Ponder for a moment on what we have come to know about the past as a result of the ministry of seers in these last days. Through what has been revealed by means of the Book of Mormon, the revelations in the Doctrine and Covenants, the Prophet's translation of the King James Bible (Joseph Smith Translation), the book of Abraham, and other inspired prophetic commentary, we sit as it were with a great Urim and Thummim before us, gazing upon the scenes of days gone by. It just may be that the Lord revealed to Joseph Smith as much or more pertaining to the past as he did in regard to the future.

Surely there could be no truth of greater worth, no insight from the Restoration of more precious value, no matter so well known and so frequently taught by the Latter-day Saints — and yet so mysterious and strange to others in the religious world — than the idea of an eternal gospel. That is to say, because of the supplementary scriptures of the Restoration, we know that Christian prophets have declared Christian doctrine and administered Christian ordinances since the dawn of time. Adam and Eve were taught the gospel. They prayed to the Father in the name of the Son, repented of their sins, were baptized by immersion, received the gift of the Holy Ghost, were married for eternity, and entered into the order of the Son of God. They knew and they taught their children and their grandchildren the plan of salvation and the eternal fact that redemption would be wrought through the shedding of the blood of the Son of Man (see Moses 5:1–9; 6:51–68). And what was true of our first parents was true of Abel and Seth and Enoch and Melchizedek and Abraham. They had the gospel. They knew the Lord, taught his doctrine, and officiated as legal administrators in his earthly kingdom. Isaac, Israel, Joseph, Ephraim, and all the patriarchs enjoyed personal revelation and communion with their Maker. Samuel, Nathan, and those from Isaiah to Malachi in the Old World and from

Nephi to Moroni in the New—all these prophets held the Melchizedek Priesthood.[3]

"We cannot believe," Joseph Smith stated, "that the ancients in all ages were so ignorant of the system of heaven as many suppose, since all that were ever saved, were saved through the power of this great plan of redemption, as much before the coming of Christ as since; if not, God has had different plans in operation (if we may so express it), to bring men back to dwell with Himself; and this we cannot believe, since there has been no change in the constitution of man since he fell."[4] Further, "Now taking it for granted that the scriptures say what they mean, and mean what they say, we have sufficient grounds to go on and prove from the Bible that *the gospel has always been the same; the ordinances to fulfill its requirements, the same; and the officers to officiate, the same;* and the signs and fruits resulting from the promises, the same."[5]

In one of the most informative statements in our literature on this principle—that the gospel message and ordinances are forever the same—Elder Bruce R. McConkie declared: "The everlasting gospel; the eternal priesthood; the identical ordinances of salvation and exaltation; the never-varying doctrines of salvation; the same Church and kingdom; the keys of the kingdom, which alone can seal men up unto eternal life—all these have always been the same in all ages; and it shall be so everlastingly on this earth and all earths to all eternity. These things we know by latter-day revelation.

"Once we know these things, the door is open to an understanding of the fragmentary slivers of information in the Bible. By combining the Book of Mormon, the Doctrine and Covenants, and the Pearl of Great Price, we have at least a thousand passages that let us know what prevailed among the Lord's people in the Old World.

"Did they have the fulness of the everlasting gospel at all times? Yes. There was not a period of ten minutes from the days of Adam to the appearing of the Lord Jesus in the land Bountiful when the gospel—as we have it in its eternal fulness—was not on earth.

"Do not let the fact that the performances of the Mosaic law were administered by the Aaronic Priesthood confuse you on this matter. Where the Melchizedek Priesthood is, there is the fulness of the gospel, and all the prophets held the Melchizedek Priesthood. . . .

"Was there baptism in the days of ancient Israel? The answer is in the Joseph Smith Translation of the Bible . . . and in the Book of Mormon. The first six hundred years of Nephite history is simply a true and plain account of how things were in ancient Israel from the days of Moses downward.

"Was there a Church anciently, and, if so, how was it organized and regulated? There was not so much as the twinkling of an eye during the whole so-called pre-Christian Era when the Church of Jesus Christ was not on earth, organized basically in the same way it now is. Melchizedek belonged to the Church . . . Laban was a member . . . so also was Lehi, long before he left Jerusalem.

"There was always apostolic power. . . . The Melchizedek Priesthood always directed the course of the Aaronic Priesthood. All of the prophets held a position in the hierarchy of the day. Celestial marriage has always existed. Indeed, such is the heart and core of the Abrahamic covenant. . . . Elias and Elijah came to restore this ancient order and to give the sealing power which gives it eternal efficacy. . . .

"People ask, Did they have the gift of the Holy Ghost before the day of Pentecost? As the Lord lives they were so endowed; such is part of the gospel; and those so gifted wrought miracles and sought and obtained a city whose builder and maker is God. . . .

"I have often wished the history of ancient Israel could have passed through the editing and prophetic hands of Mormon. If so, it would read like the Book of Mormon; but I suppose that was the way it read in the first instance anyway."[6]

BEING LOYAL TO THE RESTORATION

Largely because of the repeated emphasis by President Ezra Taft Benson in recent years, we have become very much aware of the condemnation, scourge, and judgment that rest upon the members of The Church of Jesus Christ of Latter-day Saints because of our near neglect of the Book of Mormon and modern revelation. The Lord's censure has come because we have "treated lightly the things [we] have received." The solution for ridding ourselves of this curse — extricating ourselves and subsequent generations of Saints — is simple: "They shall remain under this condemnation until they repent and remember the new covenant" — or the new testament — "even the Book of Mormon and the former commandments which I have given them, not only to say" — that is, not only to teach or discuss or declare — "but to do" — to incorporate, to inculcate, to live — "according to that which I have written." The Master also explains: "I will forgive you of your sins with this commandment — that you remain steadfast in your minds in solemnity and the spirit of prayer, in bearing testimony to all the world of those things which are communicated unto you" (D&C 84:54, 57, 61).

Some six centuries before the coming of Jesus in the flesh, Nephi offered a haunting warning. Speaking of those in the last days, he prophesied: "They wear stiff necks and high heads; yea, and because of pride, and wickedness, and abominations, and whoredoms, they have all gone astray save it be a few, who are the humble followers of Christ; nevertheless, they are led" — many of the humble followers of Christ — "that *in many instances they do err because they are taught by the precepts of men*" (2 Nephi 28:14; emphasis added). In a modern revelation a similar warning is sounded: "And when the times of the Gentiles is come in" — our time, the day when the gospel is delivered to the Gentile nations — "a light shall break forth among them that sit in darkness, and it shall be the fulness of my gospel; but *they receive it not; for they perceive not the light, and they turn their hearts from me because of the precepts of men*" (D&C 45:28–29; emphasis added). It should be clear to most of us that this prophecy will not be fulfilled solely through the rejection of Mormonism by non-Mormons. Sadly, it will find its fulfillment also in the lives of those baptized members who choose to live beneath their privileges, who exist in twilight when they could bask in the glorious light of noonday sun (see D&C 95:5–6). The doctrines of the Restoration assist us immeasurably in sifting and sorting through the views and philosophies of men and staying ourselves to that which is true and enduring.

Being loyal to the Restoration entails being ready and willing to bear witness of the truths made known to us in this latter day. We love the Bible. We cherish its truths, treasure its marvelous stories of faith, and seek to live according to its precepts. But the scriptures of the Restoration carry a spirit all their own, particularly the Book of Mormon. There is a light and an endowment of spiritual power that come into our lives through searching modern revelation that can come in no other way. Being loyal to the Restoration entails teaching from and giving preferential treatment to the things that have been delivered to Joseph Smith and his successors. Thomas B. Marsh was instructed in a modern revelation: "Lift up your heart and rejoice, for the hour of your mission is come; and your tongue shall be loosed, and *you shall declare glad tidings of great joy unto this generation.*" And what were those glad tidings? What, specifically, was Brother Marsh to declare? Was he to go forth and restate the truths of the New Testament? Was he to bear witness in the words of Peter, Paul, or John the Beloved? Was he to teach the Sermon on the Mount or repeat the words of the Master concerning the bread of life? No, he was to "declare *the things which have been revealed to my servant, Joseph Smith, Jun.*" (D&C 31:3–4; emphasis added). Likewise, Leman Copley was specifically instructed how to teach the gospel to those of his former faith, the Shakers. He was to "reason with them, not according to that which he has received of them" — the Shakers — "but according to that which shall be taught him by you my servants." And note this important detail: "By so doing I will bless him, otherwise he shall not prosper" (D&C 49:4).

Modern revelation provides, as it were, an interpretive lens, a hermeneutical key to the Bible. Much of what we understand about the Testaments is clear to us because of the Book of Mormon, the Joseph Smith Translation, the Doctrine and Covenants, and the Pearl of Great Price. There are those, however, who hesitate to "read into" the biblical record what we know from modern revelation, those who feel that to do so is to "compromise the integrity" or unique contribution of the Bible itself. In response to this posture, let me suggest an analogy. If one were eager to locate a valuable site, should one use a map that is deficient in detail or inaccurate in layout, simply because the map had been in the family for generations and was highly prized? Should one choose to ignore the precious information to be had on a more reliable or complete map, if such were available? Of course the whole matter is inextricably tied to the question of whether the traveler sincerely desires to reach his destination: maps have real value only to the degree that they guide us to a desired location. In fact, would a scholar in any discipline choose to maintain a position or defend a point of view when subsequent and available research has shed further (and perhaps clarifying) light on the subject? To do so would represent, at best, naiveté, and at worst, shoddy and irresponsible scholarship.

In that spirit, and knowing what we do about the everlasting nature of the gospel, the Church and kingdom, and the principles and or-dinances pertaining thereto, I suggest that it is perfectly appropriate and perhaps even incumbent upon us to make doctrinal inferences about personalities in scripture when recorded details may be lacking. For example, I know that Eve and Sarah and Rebekah were baptized, that Jacob received the temple endowment, and that Micah and Ma-lachi stood in the prophetic office by divine call, not because they assumed that role on their own. I know that Nephi, son of Lehi, was baptized by water and received the gift of the Holy Ghost, as well as the High Priesthood, although an account of the same is not stated directly in the Nephite record. These are valid inferences, based upon principles of doctrine and priesthood government. Because of what has been made known through Joseph Smith, we know what it takes to operate the kingdom of God and what things the people of God must do to comply.

At the same time, it may not be as safe (or sound doctrinally) to make indiscriminate historical inferences about the Book of Mormon, based upon what some feel they know about the contemporary Old

World. For example, biblical scholars might suggest that the doctrine of resurrection is not to be found in preexilic Israelite thought. But the Book of Mormon demonstrates otherwise: there were people living some five to six centuries before Christ who had a certain conviction that "our flesh must waste away and die; nevertheless, in our bodies we shall see God" (2 Nephi 9:4).

Reading modern revelation into the ancient revelations is one thing; reading what non-LDS scholars think into the Book of Mormon story is something else entirely. The former is essential; we are expected to do so, and we remain under condemnation unless we do. The latter may in some cases be helpful, but we must use caution and discernment. We always do well to consider carefully the source and thus the doctrinal reliability of whatever interpretive keys we choose to employ in understanding scripture.

There is a final matter that deserves our attention, something that is not, unfortunately, understood by some today. As members of the Church at the close of the twentieth century, we can be loyal to Joseph Smith only to the degree that we are loyal to the leaders of the Church in our own day. Those who criticize or find fault with the present Church or its constituted authorities in the name of being true to Brother Joseph know not what they do. The spirit of Joseph is with the leaders of this Church. Of that I have no question. President Joseph F. Smith testified: "I feel quite confident that the eyes of Joseph the Prophet, and of the martyrs of this dispensation, and of Brigham and John and Wilford, and those faithful men who were associated with them in their ministry upon the earth, are carefully guarding the interests of the Kingdom of God in which they labored and for which they strove during their mortal lives. I believe they are as deeply interested in our welfare today, if not with greater capacity, with far more interest, behind the veil, than they were in the flesh. I believe they know more; I believe their minds have expanded beyond their comprehension in mortal life, and their interests are enlarged in the work of the Lord to which they gave their lives and their best service. . . . I have a feeling in my heart that I stand in the presence not only of the Father and of the Son, but in the presence of those whom God commissioned, raised up, and inspired, to lay the foundations of the work in which we are engaged."[7]

Again, the spirit of Joseph is with the leaders of the Church today. This I know. It is vital that members of the Church pay heed to the words and counsel of the living oracles. Just as Noah's revelation to build an ark was not sufficient to instruct Abraham in his duties, so what the God of heaven made known to Joseph Smith is not sufficient to lead this Church today. We do well to follow the inspired counsel directed to the early missionaries of this dispensation to declare "none other things than that which the prophets and apostles have written" (D&C 52:9; see also v. 36). If the leaders of the Church do not feel the need to stress a given point that seems to be an obsession with some — to warn of coming economic crises or the eminent overthrow by foreign nations or the need to leave our present culture and re-establish an agrarian society — then we would be wise to ask ourselves why such things are not being spoken of by our leaders. Are they unaware? Are they aware but unwilling to reveal these things to us?

Though as a people we have miles to go before we rest and much spiritual development ahead of us, I bear witness that the Church is in excellent hands, is in the line of its duty, and is preparing a people for the Second Coming of the Son of Man. What is spoken by the General Authorities of the Church is what we need to hear, what the Lord would have his Saints know; those messages should become, as President Harold B. Lee once said, "the guide to [our] walk and talk" (in Conference Report, Apr. 1946, p. 68). If the Lord desires to warn his people, to provide appropriate interpretation of difficult prophetic passages, then that warning will surely come, but it will come through the channels he has established.

In March 1844 the Prophet Joseph Smith gave an unusual assignment to a group of Church leaders: they were asked to amend the Constitution of the United States, so as to make it "the voice of Jehovah."[8] Later in the week, Elder John Taylor, as a representative of a special committee of three, responded that no progress had been made toward the preparation of a constitution for the kingdom of God. The Prophet acknowledged their failure, indicating that he knew "they could not draft a constitution worthy of guiding the Kingdom of God."[9] The Prophet himself had gone before the Lord, seeking that such a constitution be made known by revelation. The answer came: "Ye are my Constitution and I am your God and ye are my spokesmen, therefore from henceforth keep my commandments."[10] In a revelation given to President John Taylor on 27 June 1882, the Savior said: "Verily, thus saith the Lord, I have instituted my Kingdom and my laws, with the keys and power thereof, and have appointed you as a spokesman and my Constitution, with President John Taylor at your head, whom I have appointed to my Church and my Kingdom as Prophet, Seer and Revelator." Later in the same revelation the Lord affirmed: "Ye are my Constitution, and I am your God."[11]

In short, this Church is to be governed by revelation — current, daily, modern revelation — and not by written documents alone. All of God's purposes for his children cannot be codified. Nothing is more fixed, set, and established than the fact that among the people of God the canon of scripture is open, flexible, and expanding.

The early Brethren of this dispensation adopted a slogan which might well serve as a rallying cry: "The Kingdom of God or nothing!" A religious leader of a former day reminds us that if we have not chosen the kingdom of God first, it will in the end make no difference what we may have chosen instead. Assessing our own loyalty to Joseph Smith and the Restoration, and, possibly more important, to the Church and its leaders today, may be difficult. Perhaps a bit of introspection would be helpful. For example:

1. Do I put first in my life the things of God's kingdom?

2. Do I accept Church assignments to which I am called, despite my feelings that I would be better suited elsewhere?

3. Am I more concerned with the visibility of my Church labors than with the sincerity and diligence of my discipleship?

4. Do I find myself becoming more and more concerned with income, social status, possessions, than is befitting a follower of the meek Nazarene?

5. Do I take of my surplus to support missionaries, care for the poor, and otherwise perform acts of Christian service?

6. Am I prone to place bounds and limitations upon the Lord's spokesmen — to accept their counsel on some matters and reject it on others?

7. Do I ever take positions or espouse causes that are at variance with the united voice of the Lord's Anointed?

8. Is my involvement with this latter-day work more than an intellectual experience? Am I grounded in simple faith and rooted in a witness of the Spirit?

9. If there are unanswered doctrinal difficulties or events from our Church history that puzzle me, am I willing to withhold judgment for the time being? Am I willing to trust Joseph Smith and his successors, who shall one day help to fill in the gaps and thereby complete the beautiful mosaic of the Restoration? Am I willing to deal with my doubts with dignity and humility?

10. Is all I say or write or do of such a nature that it builds testimony, strengthens faith, and thus contributes to the growth and spread of the gospel and Church of Jesus Christ in all the earth?

Again, with us it must be the kingdom of God or nothing!

READING THE SIGNS OF THE TIMES

On one occasion the Pharisees came to Jesus demanding a sign — physical proof of his messiahship. The Lord took that opportunity to contrast their ability to read the face of the sky (and thus to discern "signs" associated with weather patterns) with their marked inability to read the "signs of the times" (and thus discern the true meanings of messianic prophecies and testimonies). The greatest evidence that the leaders of the Jews in Jesus' day could not read the vital signs of eternity is the simple fact that they missed the Messiah when he came among them. The Hope of Ages had arrived and was ignored or rejected, and those who thus spurned the Lord of Life were left hopeless (see Matthew 16:1–6). We face a future that is, like the Second Coming, both great and terrible. There are, of course, those things that lie in futurity that frighten us, that cause us to quake and tremble. And yet there are remarkably wonderful things that lie ahead for those who prove true and faithful. How we fare in days to come will be determined largely by how well we are able to read the signs of the times.

Reading the signs of the times not only enables one to recognize and adjust to the events of the present but also to foresee and prepare for coming events. Those outside the Church who reject its teachings and doctrines are not in a position to perceive and properly adapt to the present and future social, economic, and spiritual challenges. Even those within the Church who have not been wise and thus have not taken the Holy Spirit for their guide (see D&C 45:57) lack that discernment necessary to sense the urgency of the messages of the Lord's servants.

To read the signs of the times is to perceive the unfolding of God's divine drama in these last days—it is to have the broad perspective of the plan of life and salvation and a special appreciation for the scenes incident to its consummation. It is to understand that this is the day long awaited by the prophets of old, when God would pour out knowledge and power from on high "by the unspeakable gift of the Holy Ghost," knowledge "that has not been revealed since the world was until now" (D&C 121:26).

On the other hand, to read the signs of the times in our day is to read the signs of wear and tear in the faces of those who have chosen to love and give devoted service to either questionable or diabolical causes. Error and wickedness take their terrible tolls upon the hearts and countenances of those who pursue divergent paths; the wheels of waywardness grind away slowly but inexorably to produce a character that is devoid of spirituality. To read the signs of the times is in part to recognize that Alma spoke a profound truth when he declared that "wickedness never was happiness" (Alma 41:10).

To read the signs of the times in our day does not mean seeking signs in our day. The Savior taught that a wicked and adulterous generation may be recognized by its tendency to demand physical proof as evidence of the verity of the Lord's work (see Matthew 12:39; 16:4). Interestingly enough, those who are not spiritually mature enough to read the signs of the times are so often those who demand signs. "Show us the golden plates," they cry out. "Call down the angel Moroni. Furnish the text for the Book of Abraham." Those who truly seek to be in tune with the divine will, on the other hand, become witnesses and recipients of those wonders and miracles that a gracious Lord always bestows upon his faithful flock. "Faith cometh not by signs," the holy word declares, "but signs follow those that believe" (D&C 63:9).

Finally, to read the signs of the times is to make a decision in favor of the society of Zion and the Church of the Lamb of God (see 1 Nephi 14:10) — this in contrast to a decision to enter or perpetuate Babylon. Each city — Zion and Babylon — makes definite requirements of its citizens, and as the Millennium approaches, each of these communities will insist upon the total devotion of its citizenry. To read the signs of the times is to recognize that in the future there will be fewer and fewer "lukewarm" Latter-day Saints; that the myopic and the misguided of the religious world will grow in cynicism and confusion; that the ungodly will, as time goes by, sink ever deeper into despair; that wickedness will widen and malevolence multiply until the congregants in Babylon seal themselves to him who is the father of lies.

To read the signs of the times is also to know that "Zion must arise and put on her beautiful garments" (D&C 82:14); that the Church of the Lamb shall continue to require the time, talents, and means of its members as an integral part of their growth toward perfect faith; and that through consecrating all they have and are to the Lord through his Church, the Saints of the Most High shall establish a heaven on earth and receive the glorious assurance of exaltation in the highest kingdom of heaven.

As to the destiny of the Church, as well as the specific directions to be taken by it, these matters are the responsibility of apostles and prophets. Thank heaven that at the head of this Church are men of vision, true seers, those who, like Enoch, discern and behold "things which [are] not visible to the natural eye" (Moses 6:36). The Lord be praised that the Church and kingdom set up in this final dispensation is led by those who can see "afar off" (D&C 101:54), can discern and expose the enemies of Christ, and thus prepare the Latter-day Saints and the world for what lies ahead. Speaking to the leaders of the Church in 1831—to those who later became members of the first Quorum of the Twelve Apostles—the Lord promised: "And he that believeth shall be blest with signs following, even as it is written. And unto you" — meaning, in this instance, the leaders of the Church — "it shall be given to know the signs of the times, and the signs of the coming of the Son of Man" (D&C 68:10–11). While each member of the Church has the sobering responsibility to cultivate the gifts of the Spirit and thereby come to see things as they really are and as they really will be, the Almighty has his own way of directing and preparing and readying the Saints as a body. In a revelation given to President John Taylor on 14 April 1883 concerning the organization of the priesthood and the Church, the word of the Lord came as follows: "Thus saith the Lord unto the First Presidency, unto the Twelve, unto the Seventies, and unto all my holy Priesthood, let not your hearts be troubled, neither be ye concerned about the management and organization of my Church and Priesthood and the accomplishment of my work. Fear me and observe my laws and *I will reveal unto you, from time to time, through the channels that I have appointed, everything that shall be necessary* for the further development and perfection of my Church, for the adjustment and rolling forth of my Kingdom, and for the building up and establishment of my Zion. For ye are my Priesthood, and I am your God. Even so, Amen."[12]

CONCLUSION

There are few things about which the membership of the Church need be anxious. We need to learn the gospel. We need to live the gospel, to put on Christ and put off the works of the flesh; we need to become Christian. We need to be anxiously engaged in publishing the message of the Restoration to all the world. We need to be worthy to receive the ordinances of salvation and then make the same available to our kindred dead. We need to rivet ourselves, our children, and our children's children to the redemption that is in Christ, that we and they might know to what source we must look for a remission of our sins (see 2 Nephi 25:26). Further, and this is vital, we need to look to the presidency of this Church, heed the counsel of those called and appointed to direct its destiny, and follow the Brethren as they point the way to eternal life. Though there will be individual casualties from the faith as we move toward the end, we need not be anxious about the future of the Church and kingdom of God. We need not be anxious about the leadership of the Church; we need only cultivate the little plot of ground assigned to us and leave the government of the kingdom to the King. The Lord does not ask us to magnify other people's callings.

Salvation will come to men and women who live in this final age of the earth's history because of the knowledge, keys, and powers associated with latter-day revelation, or it will come not at all. Most of what we know about God's dealings with humanity in the past, about his work and purposes in this day, and about the end times, the scenes incident to his coming in glory, we know because the heavens have been opened, because the Lord Jehovah has restored ancient records to a modern time, and because he has spoken again through prophets and apostles, has given vision to seers, has brought light and inspiration and holiness to a world that had been travelling in darkness for almost two millennia. Where once darkness reigned, love and light and pure religion are found. Where ignorance and doubt and super-stition were the order of the day, now hope and knowledge and the quiet rest of spiritual certitude prevail among the faithful. Joseph Smith the Prophet laid the foundation. By revelation he set in motion a revolution whose foreordained effects shall not be fully realized until that day when the Lord reigns in the midst of his Saints, when evil and wickedness are done away, and when the knowledge of God covers the earth as the waters cover the sea. President Spencer W. Kimball said: "Never again will the sun go down; never again will all men prove totally unworthy of communication with their Maker; never again will God be totally hidden from his children on earth. Revelation is here to remain. Prophets will follow each other in a never-ending succession, and the secrets of the Lord will be revealed without measure."[13]

NOTES

1. Joseph Smith, *Teachings of the Prophet Joseph Smith*, sel. Joseph Fielding Smith (Salt Lake City: Deseret Book Co., 1974), p. 366; emphasis added.

2. George Q. Cannon, *Gospel Truth*, ed. Jerreld L. Newquist (Salt Lake City: Deseret Book Co., 1987), pp. 322–23.

3. See Smith, *Teachings of the Prophet Joseph Smith*, pp. 180–81.

4. Ibid., pp. 59–60.

5. Ibid., p. 264; emphasis added; see also pp. 168, 308.

6. Bruce R. McConkie, *Doctrines of the Restoration: Sermons and Writings of Bruce R. McConkie*, ed. Mark L. McConkie (Salt Lake City: Bookcraft, 1989), pp. 292–93.

7. *Messages of the First Presidency*, ed. James R. Clark (Salt Lake City: Bookcraft, 1971), 5:6.

8. Joseph Smith Diary, 10 Mar. 1844, Archives, The Church of Jesus Christ of Latter-day Saints, Salt Lake City, Utah, as quoted in Andrew F. Ehat, "It Seems Like Heaven Began on Earth," in *Brigham Young University Studies*, vol. 20, no. 3 (Spring 1980): 259.

9. Ehat, "It Seems Like Heaven Began on Earth," p. 259.

10. Joseph F. Smith Minutes of the Council of Fifty, 21 Apr. 1880, as quoted in Ehat, "It Seems Like Heaven Began on Earth," p. 259.

11. Fred C. Collier, *Unpublished Revelations of the Prophets and Presidents of The Church of Jesus Christ of Latter Day Saints* (Salt Lake City: Collier's Publishing Co., 1979), pp. 132, 134; emphasis added.

12. Collier, *Unpublished Revelations,* p. 140; emphasis added.

13. Spencer W. Kimball, *The Teachings of Spencer W. Kimball,* ed. Edward L. Kimball (Salt Lake City: Bookcraft, 1982), p. 433.

3

BEING VALIANT BY FOLLOWING
THE LORD'S ANOINTED

A. Gary Anderson
Brigham Young University

The Lord declared in Doctrine and Covenants 76:79 that those who were not valiant in the testimony of Jesus were those who would inherit the terrestrial kingdom rather than the celestial kingdom. Our living prophet, Ezra Taft Benson, has said on this matter:

"Not to be valiant in one's testimony is a tragedy of eternal consequence. . . .

"One who rationalizes that he or she has a testimony of Jesus Christ but cannot accept direction and counsel from the leadership of His church is in a fundamentally unsound position and is in jeopardy of losing exaltation.

"There are some who want to expose the weaknesses of Church leaders in an effort to show that they, too, are subject to human frailties and error like unto themselves."[1]

This seems to be a very popular pursuit, one followed not only by individuals who are not members of the Church but also by Church members who hold temple recommends. That is why President Harold B. Lee declared, "That person is not truly converted until he sees the power of God resting upon the leaders of this church, and until it goes down into his heart like fire."[2]

One of the individuals living on this earth who has been as close to the prophets and presidents of the Church as any other man is Gordon B. Hinckley. You may recall his words from the October 1992 general conference of the Church: "I have worked with seven Presidents of this Church. I have recognized that all have been human. But I have never been concerned over this. They may have had some weaknesses. But this has never troubled me. I know that the God of heaven has used mortal men throughout history to accomplish His divine purposes. They were the very best available to Him, and they were wonderful."[3]

President Spencer W. Kimball counseled us in these matters when he said: "I would not say that those leaders whom the Lord chooses

34

are necessarily the most brilliant, nor the most highly trained, but they are the chosen, and when chosen of the Lord they are his recognized authority, and the people who stay close to them have safety."[4]

If we want to be among the faithful and stay close to the Lord and be counted among those who are valiant, it will be because we have a testimony of these things, as these great brethren have testified.

President George Q. Cannon said: "I have noticed . . . that where the people of God pay attention to the written word, and cherish and observe the written word, they are always better prepared to hear the oral instructions of the servants of God; . . . they have greater interest in seeking to obtain instructions, than they have when they are careless about the written word of God."[5]

Now, knowing that understanding and obeying this principle are crucial to our exaltation, let's look at the instructions of the Lord to us in the Doctrine and Covenants with the hope that understanding the doctrine may help us to be more loyal and faithful to his servants and be more concerned about hearing and following their instructions. The Doctrine and Covenants is an unusual book in that it has a preface that was dictated by the Lord to his prophet, Joseph Smith.

Notice how powerfully this preface teaches the importance of the Lord's servants: "the day cometh that they who will not hear the voice of the Lord, neither the voice of his servants, neither give heed to the words of the prophets and apostles, shall be cut off from among the people" (D&C 1:14). Members of the Church can be on the rolls of the Church and be spiritually dead to the words of the Lord to them through his servants. We need not be formally disfellowshipped or excommunicated to be cut off from among his people, although that is sometimes necessary to protect the Church from perverse actions and false doctrines taught by its members. Certainly our complacency and indifference to the Lord's servants separate us spiritually from the Lord and his leaders, and such separation is our own doing.

In that same revelation, the preface, the Lord says, "My word shall not pass away, but shall all be fulfilled, whether by mine own voice or by the voice of my servants, it is the same" (D&C 1:38). Thus the Lord clearly outlines the importance of his servants.

The Lord also dictated the concluding revelation to the Doctrine and Covenants, which was called the appendix (now Section 133). This great revelation deals with the second coming of the Lord and the Millennium and charges the Saints to prepare for that day. One of the final verses in that revelation says, "Behold, and lo, there are none to deliver you; for ye obeyed not my voice when I called to you out of the heavens; ye believed not my servants, and when they were sent unto you ye received them not" (D&C 133:71).

It seems obvious to me that we cannot expect to be prepared for the coming of the Lord while refusing to pay heed and abide the counsel of the Lord's prophets. Harold B. Lee, while president of the Church, quoted extensively from Matthew 24 as Joseph Smith revised it, emphasizing that "safety can't be won by tanks and guns and the airplanes and atomic bombs. There is only one place of safety and that is within the realm of the power of Almighty God that he gives to those who keep his commandments and listen to his voice, as he speaks through the channels that he has ordained for that purpose."[6]

Then President Lee, after quoting the Lord on the signs of the times, said: "Brothers and sisters, this is the day the Lord is speaking of. You see the signs are here. Be ye therefore ready. The Brethren have told you in this conference how to prepare to be ready. We have never had a conference where there has been so much direct instruction, so much admonition; when the problems have been defined and also the solution to the problem has been suggested.

"Let us not turn a deaf ear now, but listen to these as the words that have come from the Lord, inspired of him, and we will be safe on Zion's hill, until all that the Lord has for his children shall have been accomplished."[7]

Brothers and sisters, can you see how critical it is in these troubled times to do as the Lord has instructed us in the scriptures?

Another revelation given at the same time as the Lord's Preface and the Appendix is Doctrine and Covenants 68, in which the Lord defines *scripture* for the Latter-day Saints more clearly and powerfully than in the Bible. He says, speaking to those ordained to the priesthood: "And this is the ensample unto them, that they shall speak as they are moved upon by the Holy Ghost. And whatsoever they shall speak when moved upon by the Holy Ghost shall be scripture, shall be the will of the Lord, shall be the mind of the Lord, shall be the word of the Lord, shall be the voice of the Lord, and the power of God unto salvation" (D&C 68:3–4).

Notice that the Lord's anointed leaders when moved upon by the Spirit speak the will, mind, word, and voice of the Lord, and this is the key to salvation and exaltation with our Father in Heaven. President Spencer W. Kimball made these remarks at the conclusion of a general conference: "Let us hearken to those we sustain as prophets and seers, as well as the other brethren, as if our eternal life depended upon it, because it does!"[8]

Latter-day Saint theology teaches that the living prophet is more important to us than a dead prophet. We believe in living scripture and an open canon of scripture. President Ezra Taft Benson said it this way:

"God's revelations to Adam did not instruct Noah how to build the ark. Noah needed his own revelation. Therefore the most important prophet, so far as you and I are concerned, is the one living in our day and age to whom the Lord is currently revealing His will for us. Therefore, the most important reading we can do is any of the words of the prophet contained each week in the Church Section of the *Deseret News* and any words of the prophet contained each month in our Church magazines. Our marching orders for each six months are found in the general conference addresses which are printed in the *Ensign* magazine. . . . Beware of those who would pit the dead prophets against the living prophets, for the living prophets always take precedence."[9]

Another important revelation was given to Joseph Smith on the very day the Church was organized, 6 April 1830:

"Wherefore, meaning the church, thou shalt give heed unto all his words and commandments which he shall give unto you as he receiveth them, walking in all holiness before me; for his word ye shall receive, as if from mine own mouth, in all patience and faith. For by doing these things the gates of hell shall not prevail against you; yea, and the Lord God will disperse the powers of darkness from before you, and cause the heavens to shake for your good, and his name's glory" (D&C 21:4–6).

This revelation seems to point out very clearly the special role of the prophet and the responsibility of Church members to look to that prophet; this, however, was a difficult lesson for Church members to learn and a test of their faith. The Lord warned in a later revelation that enemies would prevail against the Church as long as the members did not give heed unto his commandments through his prophet (D&C 103:4–8). The power that Satan can have within the Church and in our individual lives will be in direct proportion to our obedience to the counsel of the Lord's prophets, especially the living prophet.

In even more modern times President Harold B. Lee brought this matter to the attention of the Church:

"We have some tight places to go before the Lord is through with this church and the world in this dispensation, which is the last dispensation, which shall usher in the coming of the Lord. . . .

"Now the only safety we have as members of this church is to do exactly what the Lord said to the Church in that day when the Church was organized. We must learn to give heed to the words and commandments that the Lord shall give through his prophet, 'as he receiveth them, walking in all holiness before me; . . . as if from mine own mouth, in all patience and faith.' (D&C 21:4–5.) . . . You may not like what comes from the authority of the Church. It may contradict your political views. It may contradict your social views. It may interfere with some of your social life. But if you listen to these things, as if from the mouth of the Lord himself, with patience and faith, the promise is that 'the gates of hell shall not prevail against you; yea, and the Lord God will disperse the powers of darkness from before you, and cause the heavens to shake for your good, and his name's glory.' (D&C 21:6.) . . .

"Your safety and ours depends upon whether or not we follow the ones whom the Lord has placed to preside over his church. He knows whom he wants to preside over this church, and he will make no mistake. . . .

"Let's keep our eye on the President of the Church."[10]

One message of our prophet Ezra Taft Benson, "To the Mothers in Zion," was received in some circles of the Church with murmuring, some even saying that it was not relevant to our day, that it was outmoded, and that President Benson did not know what he was talking about. In that message President Benson said: "Our beloved prophet Spencer W. Kimball had much to say about the role of mothers in the home and their callings and responsibilities. I am impressed tonight to share with you some of his inspired pronouncements. I fear that much of his counsel has gone unheeded, and families have suffered because of it. But I stand this evening as a second witness to the truthfulness of what President Spencer W. Kimball said. He spoke as a true prophet of God."[11]

President Benson said very little in that address that had not already been said by earlier presidents of the Church from Brigham Young to Spencer W. Kimball. President Lee was right when he said we might not like what comes from the authority of the Church. President Kimball said that "even in the Church many are prone to garnish the sepulchres of yesterday's prophets and mentally stone the living ones."[12] The reaction to President Benson's address seems to be an excellent modern-day example of mentally stoning the prophets.

Two examples in the history of the Church demonstrate the difficulty early members had in understanding the role of the prophet in receiving revelation for the Church. Even though Oliver Cowdery was present at the organization of the Church in April 1830 and was aware of what the Lord had said in naming Joseph Smith the prophet, seer, and revelator of the Church, Oliver Cowdery wrote Joseph Smith a letter that gave him both "sorrow and uneasiness." The contents of the letter are recorded in the *History of the Church*, as follows:

"He wrote to inform me that he had discovered an error in one of the commandments — Book of Doctrine and Covenants [D&C 20:37]: 'And truly manifest by their works that they have received of the Spirit of Christ unto a remission of their sins.'

"The above quotation, he said, was erroneous, and added: 'I command you in the name of God to erase those words, that no priestcraft be amongst us!'

"I immediately wrote to him in reply, in which I asked him by what authority he took upon him to command me to alter or erase, to add to or diminish from, a revelation or commandment from Almighty God.

"A few days afterwards I visited him and Mr. Whitmer's family, when I found the family in general of his opinion concerning the words above quoted, and it was not without both labor and perseverance that I could prevail with any of them to reason calmly on the subject. However, Christian Whitmer at length became convinced that the sentence was reasonable, and according to Scripture; and finally, with his assistance, I succeeded in bringing, not only the Whitmer family, but also Oliver Cowdery to acknowledge that they had been in error, and that the sentence in dispute was in accordance with the rest of the commandment."[13]

This dispute was finally resolved in July 1830, but when Joseph returned to Fayette the last of August after having spent some time in Harmony, Pennsylvania, Oliver Cowdery and the Whitmers were again deceived. Newel Knight described the events connected with this matter in his personal journal:

"[Hiram Page] had managed to get up some discussions of feeling among the brethren by giving revelations concerning the government of the Church and other matters, which he claimed to have received through the medium of a stone he possessed. . . . Even Oliver Cowdery and the Whitmer family had given heed to them. . . . Joseph was perplexed and scarcely knew how to meet this new exigency. That night I occupied the same room that he did and the greater part of the night was spent in prayer and supplication. After much labor with these brethren they were convinced of their error, and confessed the same, renouncing [Page's] revelations as not being of God."[14]

Section 28 of the Doctrine and Covenants was then given to the Church to remind the members that "no one shall be appointed to receive commandments and revelations in this church excepting my servant Joseph Smith, Jun., for he receiveth them even as Moses"

(v. 2). Joseph Smith was then recognized as the man like unto Moses, which is affirmed in later revelations (D&C 103:15–16; 107:92). The Lord pointed out that Satan had been at work to deceive the Church. The conference of the Church in September 1830 sustained this revelation as coming from the Lord to his prophet.

David Whitmer was subsequently cautioned: "You have not given heed unto my Spirit, and to those who were set over you, but have been persuaded by those whom I have not commanded" (D&C 30:2). And to the missionaries who were sent out to preach the gospel to the Lamanites, the Lord said: "And they shall give heed to that which is written, and pretend to no other revelation; and they shall pray always that I may unfold the same to their understanding" (D&C 32:4).

These were all reminders to look to the Lord and his prophet for guidance and direction in order to avoid confusion and deception. Later missionaries were cautioned to preach "none other things than that which the prophets and apostles have written" (D&C 52:9, 36). Can you imagine how the Lord could bless this Church and the lives of its members if we could follow that counsel?

The Church was slow to learn this lesson concerning revelation for the Church coming only to the Prophet. Less than six months after Hiram Page and his seer stone revelation, the following events occurred in Kirtland, as recorded by Ezra Booth: "A female [Mrs. Hubble], professing to be a prophetess, made her appearance in Kirtland, and so ingratiated herself into the esteem and favor of some of the Elders that they received her as a person commissioned to act a conspicuous part in Mormonizing the world. Rigdon, and some others, gave her the right hand of fellowship, and literally saluted her with what they called the 'kiss' of charity. But [Joseph] Smith . . . declared her an imposter, and she returned to the place from whence she came. Her visit, however, made a deep impression on the minds of many, and the barbed arrow which she left in the hearts of some, is not as yet eradicated."[15]

Joseph Smith received Section 43 of the Doctrine and Covenants in response to that incident: "There is none other appointed unto you to receive commandments and revelations. . . . And this shall be a law unto you, that ye receive not the teachings of any that shall come before you as revelations or commandments; and this I give unto you that you may not be deceived, that you may know that they are not of me" (D&C 43:3, 5–6).

Oliver Cowdery, who was close to the Prophet during this period, was the associate president of the Church, holding jointly, as it were, the keys with Joseph Smith. He was warned in an early revelation:

"Beware of pride, lest thou shouldst enter into temptation" (D&C 23:1). George A. Smith recorded that "Oliver Cowdery, previous to his apostasy, said to President Joseph Smith: 'If I should leave the Church, it would break up.' Joseph said to Oliver — 'What, who are you? The Lord is not dependent upon you, the work will roll forth do what you will.' "[16] As you know, when Oliver Cowdery left the Church, one of the charges leveled against him was denying the faith by declaring that he would not be governed by the Church in his temporal affairs. He said: " 'I will not be influenced, governed, or controlled, in my temporal interests by any ecclesiastical authority or pretended revelation whatever, contrary to my own judgment.' . . . This attempt to control me in my temporal interests, I conceive to be a disposition to take from me a portion of my Constitutional privileges and inherent right."[17]

President Benson said in his great talk on pride: "The proud cannot accept the authority of God giving direction to their lives (see Helaman 12:6). They pit their perceptions of truth against God's great knowledge, their abilities versus God's priesthood power, their accomplishments against His mighty works. . . .

"The proud wish God would agree with them. They aren't interested in changing their opinions to agree with God's."[18]

He also declared that the prophet can receive revelation on any matter — temporal or spiritual — and quoted Brigham Young, who had said: " 'I defy any man on earth to point out the path a Prophet of God should walk in, or point out his duty, and just how far he must go, in dictating temporal or spiritual things. Temporal and spiritual things are inseparably connected, and ever will be.' "[19]

Oliver Cowdery returned to the Church after ten years, but only after humbling himself and realizing that he had made a mistake.

Another early member of the Church who also learned the hard way about the path of apostasy was Thomas B. Marsh, the first president of the Quorum of the Twelve. Church members are generally conversant with the story of the conflict between the Marshes and the Harrises over the cream shared from the common cow. That may have been the incident that led Marsh to leave the Church, but there were other underlying reasons. President Marsh apparently disregarded counsel given to him in two revelations. Heber C. Kimball related:

"About the time he [Thomas B. Marsh] was preparing to leave this Church, he received a revelation in the Printing Office. He retired to himself, and prayed, and was humble, and God gave him a revelation, and he wrote it. There were from three to five pages of it; and when he came out, he read it to brother Brigham and me. In it God told him what to do, and that was to sustain brother Joseph and to believe that what brother Joseph had said was true. But no; he took a course to sustain his wife and oppose the Prophet of God, and she led him away."[20]

Orson Hyde, who was with Brother Marsh at the time of his apostasy and who also signed the affidavit that led to the Extermination Order in Missouri, described this second incident:

"During our temptation, David W. Patten was shot by the enemy, and several days afterward while Thos. B. and myself were sitting in a log cabin together in silent meditation, some being smote him on the shoulder, and said, with a countenance full of the deepest anxiety and solicitude, "Thomas! Thomas! why have you so soon forgotten?" Thomas told me it was David W. Patten, with whom, he not long before, had made a covenant to remain true and faithful until the end."[21]

This incident was related by Orson Hyde in a letter written after he had been reconciled to the Prophet and the Church in 1844. So, it appears that Marsh persisted in his apostasy even though he had been warned and the Lord had attempted to deter him on these two occasions. Marsh was subsequently excommunicated from the Church at a conference at Quincy, Illinois, 17 March 1839. An interesting statement with regard to the seriousness of Marsh's apostasy is the following given by the Prophet Joseph on 2 June 1839. The Prophet's statement is especially interesting when we remember that the Prophet spent five months in jail as a result of the betrayal of Marsh and others:

"O ye Twelve, and all Saints, profit by this important key, that in all your trials, troubles, and temptations, afflictions, bonds, imprisonment and death, see to it that you do not betray heaven, that you do not betray Jesus Christ, that you do not betray your brethren, and that you do not betray the revelations of God. . . . Yes, in all your kicking and floundering, see to it that you do not this thing, lest innocent blood be found on your skirts, and you go down to hell. We may ever know by this sign that there is danger of our being led to a fall and apostasy, when we give way to the devil so as to neglect the first known duty. But, whatever you do, do not betray your friends."[22]

Thomas B. Marsh returned to the Church in 1857, after eighteen years. He recognized his folly and warned some apostates in these words: "You don't know what you are about; if you want to see the fruits of apostasy, look on me."[23]

In a letter to Heber C. Kimball, he said further: "I have sined against Heaven and in thy sight. . . . I deserve no place . . . in the church even as the lowest member; but I cannot live long . . . without a reconciliation with the 12 and the Church whom I have injured O Bretheren once Bretheren!! How can I leave this world without your forgiveness Can I have it Can I have it?"[24]

At the time he was pleading for membership in the Church, Marsh was ill with a paralytic stroke: "I want you to get some elders to help you and take me to the river and baptize me, if you have to baptize me in a sheet. For I want to die in the Church. Oh, if I could see Joseph, and talk with him and acknowledge my faults to him, and get his forgiveness from him as I have to Brother Harris, then I would die happy."[25]

After he came to Utah, he admitted his mistake to the Church there in these words:

"If you will take my advice, you will stand by the authorities; but if you go away and the Lord loves you as much as he did me, he will whip you back again. . . .

" . . . I have frequently wanted to know how my apostasy began, and I have come to the conclusion that I must have lost the Spirit of the Lord out of my heart.

"The next question is, 'How and when did you lose the Spirit?' I became jealous of the Prophet, and then I saw double, and overlooked everything that was right, and spent all my time in looking for the evil; and then, when the Devil began to lead me, it was easy for the carnal mind to rise up, which is anger, jealousy, and wrath. I could feel it within me; I felt angry and wrathful; and the Spirit of the Lord being gone, as the Scriptures say, I was blinded, and I thought I saw a beam in brother Joseph's eye, but it was nothing but a mote, and my own eye was filled with the beam; but I thought I saw a beam in his, and I wanted to get it out; and as brother Heber says, I got mad, and I wanted everybody else to be mad."[26]

Certainly the words of the Lord in the Doctrine and Covenants are relevant to remember in our discussion of apostasy:

"Cursed are all those that shall lift up the heel against mine anointed, saith the Lord. . . .

"And those who swear falsely against my servants, that they might bring them into bondage and death —

"Wo unto them; because they have offended my little ones they shall be severed from the ordinances of mine house.

"Their basket shall not be full, their houses and their barns shall perish, and they themselves shall be despised by those that flattered them.

"They shall not have right to the priesthood, nor their posterity after them from generation to generation" (D&C 121:16, 18–21).

What a hard lesson to learn. Brother Marsh had six children, and many of his posterity are on the earth today but without the gospel. We hope that they will be reclaimed and find the truth, but we need to pay attention to the revelations in the Doctrine and Covenants, for the Lord declared: "The prophecies and promises which are in them shall all be fulfilled" (D&C 1:37).

I will share one other example of failure to support and follow the Brethren. The teachings of the Lord on this matter were given in Doctrine and Covenants 90:5 when Frederick G. Williams was sustained as a counselor in the First Presidency: "And all they who receive the oracles of God, let them beware how they hold them lest they are accounted as a light thing, and are brought under condemnation thereby, and stumble and fall when the storms descend, and the winds blow, and the rains descend, and beat upon their house."

Are the storms here? I expect they are, and there will be more. How can we believe in this book and take statements of the prophet lightly? Elder Marvin J. Ashton warned: "Any Church member not obedient to the leaders of this Church will not have the opportunity to be obedient to the promptings of the Lord."[27] We cannot afford to try to live our lives without the help and influence of the Lord if we expect to survive the temptations that surely will come.

Again, in Doctrine and Covenants 112:20—which, incidentally, was given to Thomas B. Marsh—we read: "Whosoever receiveth my word receiveth me, and whosoever receiveth me, receiveth those, the First Presidency, whom I have sent, whom I have made counselors for my name's sake unto you." Marion G. Romney said this about the importance of the First Presidency, "What they say as a presidency is what the Lord would say if he were here in person."[28]

An important admonition was given to Almon Babbitt in a revelation dated 19 January 1841:

"And with my servant Almon Babbitt, there are many things with which I am not pleased; behold, he aspireth to establish his counsel instead of the counsel which I have ordained, even that of the Presidency of my Church; and he setteth up a golden calf for the worship of my people" (D&C 124:84).

This sounds like serious business, that we in our day could be accused by the Lord of setting up a golden calf to worship instead of the true and living God. Most of us probably think that was possible in Moses' day, but certainly not in ours. Let me share some information that may help us to see what Almon Babbit did that was so displeasing to the Lord.

Almon Babbitt joined the Church in 1833, served a mission to

Canada, participated as a member of Zion's Camp, and was given leadership responsibilities in Kirtland and Nauvoo. He apparently had some training in the law. In examining the history of the Church, I found that Brother Babbitt had come into conflict with Church leaders on five different occasions from 1833 to 1841, when this revelation was given. Each time a reconciliation was made, and each time he was given another chance. I wondered what effect, if any, this revelation might have had on Brother Babbitt. I found that he continued to go against the counsel of the Brethren. He opposed John Smith when Brother Smith was sent to Ramus, Illinois, to solicit help for the Nauvoo Legion when Joseph Smith was being harrassed. Babbitt later opposed Orson Hyde in Kanesville, Iowa, after the death of the Prophet. After Babbitt was appointed secretary of the Territory of Utah by Brigham Young and was sent to Washington, D.C., to seek for statehood for Utah, Brigham's friend Thomas L. Kane wrote on several occasions to warn him of Babbitt's behavior in Washington.

When Babbitt was returning to Utah from the East in 1856, he stopped at Council Bluffs, Iowa. There he was warned by Church leaders that he should wait for a large wagon train before proceeding west because of Indian hostilities. A couple of his wagons left the next day and were attacked by Indians, the drivers killed and goods destroyed. Babbitt and Frank Rowland followed and were encouraged to wait for a military escort at Fort Kearney, but they rejected that counsel and were attacked by Cheyenne Indians near Ash Hollow and were killed. There were very few remains, and the twelve attacking Indians said that Colonel Babbitt had fought like a grizzly bear to his death.[29] How much wiser to have learned to listen to counsel.

From the day of the organization of the Church in 1830, the Lord has taught and emphasized the importance of his servants; he has carefully defined the special role of the prophet and the president of the Church in receiving guidance and revelation for the entire Church. That theme has been echoed and reechoed throughout the revelations in the Doctrine and Covenants. The Lord even said that all that his Father promised to him could be shared by the Saints if they were true to the covenant of the priesthood. Notice, however, that this promise is predicated upon these words: "And also all they who receive this priesthood receive me, saith the Lord; for he that receiveth my servants receiveth me; and he that receiveth me receiveth my Father" (D&C 84:35–37). Certainly our happiness and exaltation depend on following the Lord by following his prophets.

NOTES

1. Ezra Taft Benson, in Conference Report, Apr. 1982, pp. 89–90.

2. Harold B. Lee, in Conference Report, Apr. 1972, p. 118.

3. Gordon B. Hinckley, in Conference Report, Apr. 1992, p. 77.

4. Spencer W. Kimball, in Conference Report, Apr. 1951, p. 104, as quoted in Spencer W. Kimball, *The Teachings of Spencer W. Kimball*, ed. Edward L. Kimball (Salt Lake City: Bookcraft, 1982), p. 459.

5. George Q. Cannon, in Conference Report, Oct. 1897, p. 38.

6. Harold B. Lee, in Conference Report, Oct. 1973, p. 169.

7. Ibid., p. 170.

8. Spencer W. Kimball, in Conference Report, Apr. 1978, p. 117.

9. Ezra Taft Benson, "Fourteen Fundamentals in Following the Prophet," in *Brigham Young University Speeches of the Year, 1980* (Provo, Utah: Brigham Young University Press, 1981), p. 27.

10. Harold B. Lee, in Conference Report, Oct. 1970, pp. 152–53.

11. Ezra Taft Benson, *To the Mothers in Zion* (Salt Lake City: The Church of Jesus Christ of Latter-day Saints, 1987), p. 6.

12. *Instructor*, Aug. 1960, p. 257, as quoted in *Teachings of the Living Prophets* (Salt Lake City: The Church of Jesus Christ of Latter-day Saints, 1982), p. 11.

13. Joseph Smith, *History of The Church of Jesus Christ of Latter-day Saints*, 2d ed. rev., edited by B. H. Roberts (Salt Lake City: The Church of Jesus Christ of Latter-day Saints, 1932–51), 1:104–5.

14. As quoted in Lyndon W. Cook, *The Revelations of the Prophet Joseph Smith* (Provo, Utah: Seventy's Mission Bookstore, 1981), pp. 39–40.

15. As quoted in Cook, *Revelations*, pp. 61–62; see also Smith, *History of the Church*, 1:154.

16. George A. Smith, in *Journal of Discourses* (London: Latter-day Saints' Book Depot, 1854–86), 17:199–200.

17. Smith, *History of the Church*, 3:18 n.

18. Ezra Taft Benson, in Conference Report, Apr. 1989, p. 4.

19. As quoted in Benson, "Fourteen Fundamentals," p. 29; see also *Journal of Discourses*, 10:363–64; D&C 29:34–35.

20. Heber C. Kimball, in *Journal of Discourses*, 5:28.

21. Orson Hyde, in *The Prophet*, vol. 1, no. 4 (8 June 1844): 3.

22. *History of Joseph Smith*, 2 June 1839, as quoted in John Taylor, *The Gospel Kingdom* (Salt Lake City: Bookcraft, 1964), p. 188.

23. Thomas B. Marsh, in *Journal of Discourses*, 5:115.

24. Thomas B. Marsh to Heber C. Kimball, 5 May 1857, Archives of The Church of Jesus Christ of Latter-day Saints, Salt Lake City, Utah, as quoted in the proceedings of the 1984 Sidney B. Sperry Symposium, *Hearken O Ye People: Discourses on the Doctrine and Covenants* (Sandy, Utah: Randall Book Co, 1984), p. 185.

25. "Journal of Wandle Mace," original manuscript account of his life in Nebraska and Utah, including 1857, LDS Church Archives, as quoted in Walter C. Lichfield, "Thomas B. Marsh, Physician to the Church," master's thesis, Brigham Young University, 1956, pp. 118–19.

26. Marsh, in *Journal of Discourses*, 5:206–7.

27. In Munich Area Conference Report, Aug. 1973, p. 24, as quoted in Neal A. Maxwell, *"All These Things Shall Give Thee Experience"* (Salt Lake City: Deseret Book Co., 1979), p. 104.

28. Marion G. Romney, in Conference Report, Apr. 1945, p. 90.

29. Kate B. Carter, "Almon Whiting Babbitt," in *Our Pioneer Heritage* (Salt Lake City: Daughters of Utah Pioneers, 1968), 2:549–59.

4

THE IMPORTANCE OF THE INDIVIDUAL IN THE LORD'S REVELATIONS

Susan Easton Black
Brigham Young University

On 30 August 1992 a survey was conducted in which 250 returned missionaries were asked to respond to questions regarding Doctrine and Covenants 4.[1] It was decided to survey returned missionaries because many mission presidents and teachers at the Missionary Training Center encourage elders and sisters to memorize Section 4 because of its missionary emphasis. Of the 219 respondents, 210 claimed a content recognition, 192 claimed a memorized familiarity with the section, 69 knew that the revelation was given through the Prophet Joseph to his father,[2] and 80 correctly identified the main occupation of Joseph Smith, Sr.[3] The compiled results of this survey suggest an impressive familiarity of the respondents with the contents of Section 4 but also a relative lack of awareness of the individual in the Lord's revelation.[4] If the Lord had set aside or had forgotten the individual, as had most of the respondents, would there have been a revelation? I believe not.

The returned missionaries are perhaps typical, in this case, of other Latter-day Saints. All of us can benefit from knowing that Joseph Smith, Sr., was fifty-eight years old at the time of the revelation and was a wheat farmer. He had labored for decades with his hands, using a sickle to lay up in store a harvest that had physically sustained his family. He was now being asked by the Lord to work in a different field, to lay up in store with all his heart, might, mind, and strength the truths of the gospel. Because his eye was single to the glory of God, he was qualified for the urgency of the work that lay before him. For the next eleven years he would labor as a father, a missionary, and as a patriarch to the Church, exhorting all to faith, hope, and charity.

This additional information places Section 4 in a larger spiritual context, and its personal nature gives us insight into the life of our first patriarch. I have wondered why the surveyed missionaries had forgotten the recipient, Joseph Smith, Sr., and why many other Latter-day Saints might fail to recall other specific names mentioned by the Lord in the Doctrine and Covenants. One reason for our forgetfulness may be in the titles given to each section. The numerical titles in the Doctrine and Covenants differ from names given to segments of scripture in our other standard works.[5] For example, the Book of Mormon is named after its compiler, and each book within the text is named for an individual. Similarly, the Old Testament, much of the New Testament, and the Pearl of Great Price contain named sections. This approach helps the reader recall the individuals, whereas it appears from the respondents' answers that the numerical system does not. And yet the Doctrine and Covenants is the only book of scripture that has contemporary headings to the chapters that identify the individuals and circumstances involved. It could thus be concluded that the individuals are better identified in the Doctrine and Covenants than in other scriptural texts.

Another reason for the lack of attention we give to individuals mentioned in the Doctrine and Covenants might be our remembrance of 1 Nephi 19:23: "I did liken all scriptures unto us, that it might be for our profit and learning." This teaching is important, for all scriptures can be used for our benefit and we can liken them to our own circumstances, but it should not limit us from gaining further insights by knowing more about the individuals mentioned and their contributions to the new and everlasting gospel. Even greater truths, analogies, and "likenings" can be gained by knowing details of the people identified in the revelations of the Lord.

I believe the Lord had a purpose in including the names of individuals who made solemn covenants and associated with the Prophet Joseph Smith. One purpose might have been to provide us with additional insights as we search individual lives to determine why one was called on a mission to the south and another to the north, to discover why one would be assigned to be a recorder while another was designated a printer, and why some men were worthy to receive the Melchizedek priesthood in the early 1830s while others needed to wait.

Searching for these details begins with a careful perusal of the Doctrine and Covenants. This canonized scripture consists of the Lord's revelations received by his prophets from 1823 to 1978. Most of the revelations identified an individual. For example, of the fourteen revelations received by the Prophet Joseph Smith in 1829 and canonized in the Doctrine and Covenants, all fourteen were directed to or mentioned a contemporary of the Prophet. That correspondence may at first suggest that all of the revelations are directed to specific individuals. Closer examination shows that assumption to be incorrect, because much of the content of the revelations is revealed doctrine that applies universally. One hundred and one revelations named at least one individual other than Joseph Smith either in the text, the heading, or the italicized captions. Altogether, in the revelations recorded from 1823 to 1844, the Lord identified by name a total of 130 contemporaries of the Prophet: 128 males and 2 females, Emma Smith and Vienna Jacques.

Biographical research has given us information on all 130 individuals. Some of the information is sketchy and does not exceed one page in length, but a substantial article could be written on the lives and contributions of 80 of these early Saints. Fifty portrait photographs reveal physical characteristics of the identified individuals. Vital statistics, including birth and birthplace, are available for 126 people. Birth statistics calculated with the revelatory year reveal that the average age of the individual named by the Lord was 37.92 years.

We can also identify the oldest and the youngest men mentioned by name in the Doctrine and Covenants. The oldest was Daniel Sanborn Miles, age sixty-nine.[6] He was called on 6 April 1837 to be a president in the First Quorum of Seventy. President Joseph Young, who was also called to preside over the Seventy, later wrote that Daniel was "a man of good faith, constant in his attendance at the meetings of the council, until the time of his death, which occurred at quite an advanced stage of his life."[7] He died on 12 October 1845 at Hancock County, Illinois.

The youngest men named in the Doctrine and Covenants were Joseph Smith and Heman Basset, both seventeen years old when first mentioned. The Prophet's name appeared in connection with the visitation of the angel Moroni, and Heman's name appeared with his missionary call (D&C 2; 52:37).[8] Heman did not serve that mission, however, despite his being ordained an elder in the spring of 1831. Unfortunately, by June of that year he had become an active participant in the abnormal spiritual activities in Kirtland, Ohio. His failure to discern false spirits and to recognize his transgression led him to be one of the first to withdraw from the Church in Ohio and to reject a directive of the Lord. Heman Basset's rejection is not typical of those individuals mentioned in the Doctrine and Covenants; however, his call to missionary service is typical of the divine purpose of the Lord in naming an individual. By focusing on the individuals mentioned, we discover that the messages of the Lord primarily emphasize priesthood callings. In fact, it is possible to say that the Doctrine and Covenants was the first priesthood manual given in this dispensation.

The priesthood calling most often announced by the Lord was an invitation to serve a mission, with the phraseology being "take a journey." For example, in Doctrine and Covenants 52:23, Ezra Booth and Isaac Morley were called to "take their journey, also preaching the word by the way." In obedience they journeyed through Ohio, Indiana, Illinois, and Missouri, preaching the gospel.[9]

The second emphasis of the revelations was an invitation to preside in the Melchizedek Priesthood quorums of the Church. For example, in Doctrine and Covenants 124:137, John A. Hicks was called on 19 January 1841 to preside with Samuel Williams and Jesse Baker in the quorum of the elders. This call came just nine months after he was charged, on 19 April 1840, with slandering John P. Greene and lying. After promising to make restitution, he was extended the hand of fellowship by the Nauvoo High Council. Four months later he failed to receive a sustaining vote by a general conference of the various priesthood quorums. He was tried by the elders quorum in Nauvoo in 1841 for falsehood, engaging in schismatical conversation, and breaching the Nauvoo City ordinances. He appealed his case but was excommunicated on 5 October 1841.

The third emphasis was to identify individuals who were worthy to be ordained to the priesthood. Jared Carter was one of them.[10] He was baptized on 20 February 1831 by Hyrum Smith. Invited in Doctrine and Covenants 52:38 to be ordained a priest, Jared Carter accepted this ordination and a subsequent ordination to the Melchizedek Priesthood.

The fourth emphasis in the Doctrine and Covenants was to reprimand priesthood leaders who failed to magnify their calling, whether in the home or in the Church. For example, Almon W. Babbitt was rebuked for aspiring "to establish his counsel instead of the counsel which I have ordained . . . ; and he setteth up a golden calf for the worship of my people" (D&C 124:84).[11]

As I have searched for information on the lives of the contemporaries of Joseph Smith mentioned in the Doctrine and Covenants, I have discovered that the Lord chose to identify individuals who varied in their eventual faithfulness. That is typical of other scriptural text. For example, the Lord addressed Nephi, Laman, Lemuel, Cain, Abel, Moses, Pharaoh, and others. By their good or bad examples we can learn many lessons regarding the Lord's love for each of his children as well as their devotion or lack of it.[12] Of the 130 individuals mentioned, the information we have at present shows that 72 died as faithful members of the Church, or 55.38 percent.[13] Names of the faithful that quickly come to mind include Joseph Smith, who declared, "I knew it, and I knew that God knew it, and I could not deny it, neither dared I do it; at least I knew that by so doing I would offend God, and come under condemnation" (JS–H 1:25). Other names are Brigham Young, John Taylor, Heber C. Kimball, Edward Partridge, and Joseph Smith, Sr.

THE ALMOST FORGOTTEN FAITHFUL

Almost forgotten by the modern Saint are the names of David Fullmer, Oliver Granger, William Huntington, and Algernon Sidney Gilbert. I will illustrate this forgetfulness by focusing on the faithfulness of Algernon Sidney Gilbert and by taking one verse out of the eight sections in which his name appears in the Doctrine and Covenants.[14]

From the night in 1830 that his niece, Mary Elizabeth Rollins, brought home a copy of the Book of Mormon, Algernon showed interest in the book.[15] After staying up most of the night reading this sacred scripture, he was prepared for the missionaries, who baptized him in November 1830. He was privileged to have Joseph Smith in his home on the day of the Prophet's arrival in Kirtland, Ohio.[16]

Soon Algernon was blessed by the Prophet with added responsibilities because of his faithfulness. Those responsibilities included purchasing land, acting as a scribe for revelations, and working closely with his partner, Newel K. Whitney, in providing materially for the Saints. He accepted gratefully the opportunity to live the law of Zion and to be one of the first to live in Jackson County, Missouri. There he continued to bless the lives of the Saints temporally and spiritually.

The Lord remembered his servant Algernon and helped him and Newel resolve their concerns regarding their store in Kirtland, Ohio:

"And it is not meet that my servants, Newel K. Whitney and Sidney Gilbert, should sell their store and their possessions here; for this is not wisdom until the residue of the church, which remaineth in this place, shall go up unto the land of Zion" (D&C 64:26).

This verse provides an opportunity to illustrate the lack of remembrance of Algernon by the modern Latter-day Saint. The store mentioned by the Lord in this revelation passed through many owners until it was purchased by The Church of Jesus Christ of Latter-day Saints in 1979.[17] The Church authorized the beginning of research and restoration on the building in 1983. Historical documents and diaries were used to provide authentic detail for the reconstruction. Upon completion of the construction, the store was dedicated on 25 August 1984 by President Ezra Taft Benson.[18] The purchase, restoration, dedication, and United States Presidential citation presented to the Church for its historic preservation of the store are commendable.[19] Nonetheless, an omission exists. No mention was made of Algernon Sidney Gilbert as the co-owner with Whitney in the store's reconstruction, dedication, or citation. The title of their store was N. K. Whitney and Company. The "and Company" was Gilbert.

Historic land purchase agreements clearly identify the partnership.[20] This brief illustration of Gilbert's obscurity helps us recognize an early Saint who was faithful but is now almost forgotten.

LOST THEIR DIRECTION

Of the 36 individuals (27.7 percent) who died outside Church fellowship, very few left significant biographical information.[21] After searching journals, family group sheets, and writing to their descendants, I discovered it was almost as if they were mentioned by the Lord and then wandered off into comparative obscurity. Only a few maintained a visible presence. This they did by continuing to adhere to partial truth. One such man was Wheeler Baldwin.[22]

On 7 June 1831 the Lord, through his prophet, Joseph Smith, stated, "Let my servants Wheeler Baldwin and William Carter also take their journey" (D&C 52:31). Wheeler accepted this mission call, and at the 25 October 1831 general conference at Orange, Cuyahoga, Ohio, he bore testimony that he "felt to do the will of the Lord in all things."[23] His actions seemed to match his desires from the 1830s through the early 1840s. In March 1840 he served on a committee "to obtain affidavits and other documents to be forwarded to the city of Washington" regarding the grievances and needs of the Saints.[24] His faithfulness was short-lived, however. By the late 1840s he had joined Alpheus Cutler's congregation in Mills County, Iowa. According to his speech at the October 1862 general conference of the Reorganized Church of Jesus Christ of Latter Day Saints, he stated that Cutler "was ordained President of the High Priesthood." He had sustained him in that position and had been a missionary for the Cutlerites, baptizing more than forty individuals. He claimed that the foundation upon which they had built their church was the "Bible, Book of Mormon, and Doctrine, and Covenants."[25] Despite his initial adherence to the teachings of Cutler, when Wheeler learned of Joseph Smith III becoming president of the Reorganized Church of Jesus Christ of Latter Day Saints, he left the Cutlerites and was baptized into the Reorganization in 1863. He presided over the RLDS branches at Mills, Fremont, and Page, Iowa. He died outside the fellowship of the Saints, a leader among those who accepted only partial truth.

THE BELLIGERENT APOSTATES

Eight of the individuals mentioned in the Doctrine and Covenants, 6.15 percent, actively sought to destroy the teachings of the Prophet

Joseph Smith and to take his life.[26] John C. Bennett, William Law, Symonds Ryder, and William McLellin were such vengeful apostates. Because of new discoveries about Symonds Ryder's apostasy, I will speak of him.[27]

Symonds was mentioned only once in the Doctrine and Covenants: "In consequence of transgression, let that which was bestowed upon Heman Basset be taken from him, and placed upon the head of Simonds Ryder" (D&C 52:37). He was thirty-nine years old when he was called to serve a mission and had been a member of the Church for only two days. Instead of experiencing joy at this opportunity, it has been theorized, he found in this call the seeds of his apostasy:

"When he received communication of his ministerial call signed by the Prophet Joseph Smith and Sidney Rigdon, both in the letter he received and in the official commission to preach, however, his name was spelled R-i-d-e-r, instead of R-y-d-e-r. . . . He thought if the 'Spirit' through which he had been called to preach could err in the matter of spelling his name, it might have erred in calling him to the ministry as well."[28] The spelling of his name varies on land deeds in Hiram, Ohio. And, as illustrated by his signature on his portrait, his name may still be misspelled in the Doctrine and Covenants.

This theory of Symond's apostasy may be correct, but further research extends the hypothesis to his belief that Joseph advocated communism of goods. One historian claimed: "After a time something leaked out in regard to the Saints having an eye on their neighbor's property, that it was their design to get into their possession all the lands of those whom they converted."[29] Symonds himself wrote in his memoirs: "When they went to Missouri to lay the foundation of the splendid city of Zion, and also of the temple, they left their papers behind. This gave their new converts an opportunity to become acquainted with the internal arrangement of their church, which revealed to them the horrid fact that a plot was laid to take their property from them and place it under the control of Joseph Smith the prophet."[30]

Another theory regarding Symond's apostasy was his concern over the adjacent Hinckley property becoming the site of a planned Latter-day Saint temple.[31]

Whatever the reason, whether it was one of these theories or a combination of all, Symonds did leave the Church and took it upon himself to eradicate from all residents in the Hiram community what he saw as the seducing error of Mormonism. He joined with fellow apostate Ezra Booth in the summer of 1831, planting the seeds of hatred toward Joseph and Mormonism in Hiram. The climax of his actions was the tar-and-feathering of the Prophet on 24 March 1832. His involvement in the event was made apparent that very night to Joseph, who heard, "Simonds, Simonds, where's the tar bucket?"[32] Despite his obvious connection with the mob, Symonds was never prosecuted. An alibi was provided by his son, Hartwell Ryder, who stated that his father was "ill in bed at the time."[33]

CONCLUSION

Attempting to find information on the individuals mentioned in the Doctrine and Covenants has been like searching for the pieces of a lost puzzle whose importance is clear but whose detailed description is destroyed. The frustration of reaching an impasse on the life of one person has been compensated for by the joy of discovering new insights on another. The realization of the faithfulness of one and the disappointment of the faltering steps of another has brought to my awareness the centrality of endurance. This research has heightened my appreciation for the early Saints and the Lord's concern for each individual.

The Doctrine and Covenants teaches us that the Lord knows his children—both the faithful and the unfaithful—by name. He knows of their talents and gifts as well as their weaknesses and imperfections. He extended an invitation to greater service to the faithful, but not all chose to listen and accept his directions. Some served with great joy, and others disregarded counsel and lost direction.

The analogies and "likenings" to be gleaned from knowing more about the individuals in the Doctrine and Covenants are almost boundless. It is my hope that the readers of this book of scripture will take note of the names and begin to wonder more about who they were, where they came from, and whether they fulfilled their divine commission. Such research will lead to a greater understanding of why the Lord has preserved their names in scripture from generation to generation. It will also reveal with profound assurance a knowledge of the important role of the individual in the Lord's revelations.

NOTES

1. Following is the text of the questions asked of the 250 returned missionaries surveyed 30 August 1992 about Doctrine and Covenants 4:

    1. Are you familiar with the contents of Section 4 of the Doctrine and Covenants?

    2. Can you recite any passage(s) from Section 4?

    3. Section 4 of the Doctrine and Covenants was given by the Lord through the Prophet Joseph Smith to whom?

    4. What was the occupation of the individual to whom Section 4 was directed?

2. Other write-in answers given were Hyrum Smith (17), Oliver Cowdery (15), Samuel Smith (9), Martin Harris (4), Sidney Rigdon (4), and David Whitmer (4). The names of the following individuals were written in fewer than four times: Thomas B. Marsh, Joseph Knight, Parley P. Pratt, Peter Whitmer, Newel K. Whitney, and Hiram Page.

3. Other occupations listed were missionary (15), schoolteacher (8), and store owner (4). Answers received fewer than four times each were newspaper reporter, bishop, plumber, carpenter, lawyer, printer, and blacksmith.

4. The survey results indicate that the person addressed in the revelation is of secondary importance to the respondents. Rationale in support of the re-spondents is found in Doctrine and Covenants 4: "Therefore, O ye that em-bark . . . " The pronoun ye in the King James Bible is consistently plural, meaning "You all." In the Book of Mormon and the Doctrine and Covenants, it varies from a singular, regional colloquial usage to the plural usage.

5. Orson Pratt, a noted scientist and mathematician, put these sections in their present numerical order in 1876.

6. Daniel Sanborn Miles, son of Josiah Miles and Sarah Sanborn, was born on 23 July 1772 at Sanbornton, Belknap, New Hampshire. He was married to Electa Chamberlin on 30 September 1813. He was baptized into the Church in April 1832 at Bath, New Hampshire, and was ordained a seventy on 20 December 1836 by Hazen Aldrich.

7. Andrew Jenson, *Latter-day Saint Biographical Encyclopedia* (Salt Lake City: Western Epics, 1971), 1:192.

8. Heman A. Basset was born in 1814 at Guildhall, Essex, Vermont. He was baptized a member of the Church in the spring of 1831. After withdrawing from the Church in Ohio, he moved to California, where he managed a hotel in Petaluma for many years. He then migrated across the country to Philadelphia, Pennsylvania, where he died in 1876.

9. Because of this proselyting journey, biographers have written that they served missions together in four different states. This phraseology is often mis-interpreted by modern missionaries to mean that they served an eight-year mission together in the Midwest.

10. Son of Gideon Carter and Johannah Sims, Jared was born on 14 January 1801 at Benson, Rutland, Vermont. He married Lydia Ames and became the father of nine children.

11. Son of Ira Babbitt and Nancy Crosier, Almon Whiting Babbitt was born on 9 October 1812 at Cheshire, Massachusetts. He married Julia Ann Johnson on 23 November 1833 at Kirtland, Geauga, Ohio, and they became the parents of six children. He died on 24 October 1855 in Nebraska.

12. To date information about the enduring faithfulness of the following eleven individuals is unknown: Major Noble Ashley, Stephen Burnett, Philip Burroughs, Jared Carter, Asa Dodds, Ruggles Eames, Selah J. Griffin, Jacob Scott, Micah Welton, Calves Wilson, and Dunbar Wilson. Three were not members of the Church: Lilburn Boggs, James Covill, and Alvin Smith.

13. Seventy-two died in full fellowship with the Saints: Jesse Baker, Ezra Taft Benson, Samuel Bent, Titus Billings, Seymour Brunson, Reynolds Cahoon, Gideon Carter, John Sims Carter, Simeon Doget Carter, William Carter, Zebedee

Coltrin, Oliver Cowdery, David Dort, James Foster, David Fullmer, Algernon Sidney Gilbert, John Gould, Oliver Granger, Thomas Grover, Levi Hancock, Solomon Hancock, Emer Harris, Martin Harris, Henry Herriman, Elias Higbee, Solomon Humphrey, William Huntington, Orson Hyde, Vienna Jacques, Aaron Johnson, Luke Johnson, Heber C. Kimball, Joseph Knight, Newel Knight, Vinson Knight, Thomas B. Marsh, Daniel Miles, Isaac Morley, John Murdock, Noah Packard, Edward Partridge, David Patten, William W. Phelps, Orson Pratt, Parley P. Pratt, Zera Pulsipher, Charles C. Rich, Willard Richards, Samuel J. Rolfe, Shadrach Roundy, Lyman Sherman, Henry Sherwood, Don Carlos Smith, Eden Smith, George A. Smith, Hyrum Smith, John Smith, Joseph Smith, Jr., Joseph Smith, Sr., Samuel H. Smith, John Snider, Erastus Snow, Daniel Stanton, John Taylor, Robert Thompson, Peter Whitmer, Jr., Newel K. Whitney, Frederick G. Williams, Samuel Williams, Wilford Woodruff, Brigham Young, and Joseph Young.

14. Algernon Sidney Gilbert, son of Eli Gilbert and Lydia Hemingway, was born on 28 December 1789 at New Haven, New Haven, Connecticut. He married Elizabeth Van Benthusen on 30 September 1823, and they became the parents of one son. Algernon died on 29 June 1834 and was buried in a common grave with thirteen other Saints near Fishing River, Missouri.

15. "Mary Elizabeth Rollins Lightner," *The Utah Genealogical and Historical Magazine* 17 (July 1926): 194.

16. Autobiography of James Henry Rollins, n.p., n.d., p. 2.

17. "Store at Core of Area, Church Histories," special edition: Kirtland Heritage Days–1984, *The Kirtland Enterprise,* 22 Aug. 1984, p. 1.

18. Dedicatory prayer given by President Ezra Taft Benson at the Newel K. Whitney and Company Store on 25 Aug. 1984.

19. "Whitney Store Given Prestigious Award," *Church News,* 19 Nov. 1988, p. 3.

20. For the complete document, see Geraldine Hamblin Bangerter and Susan Easton Black, *My Servant Algernon Sidney Gilbert: Provide for My Saints (D&C 57:10)* (Salt Lake City: Rollins, Hamblin and Bangerter Families, 1989), pp. 88–90.

21. The thirty-six who died outside of Church fellowship were Almon W. Babbitt, Wheeler Baldwin, Heman Basset, Josiah Butterfield, Joseph Coe, Leman Copley, Warren Cowdery, Alpheus Cutler, Amos Davies, Edson Fuller, Isaac Galland, Jesse Gause, George Washington Harris, Peter Haws, George Fitch James, John Johnson, Lyman Johnson, Amasa Lyman, William Marks, George Miller, Hiram Page, John E. Page, Ziba Peterson, Sidney Rigdon, Burr Riggs, Emma Hale Smith, Sylvester Smith, William Smith, Northrup Sweet, Ezra Thayre, Joseph Wakefield, Harvey G. Whitlock, David Whitmer, John Whitmer, Peter Whitmer, Sr., and Lyman Wight.

22. Wheeler Baldwin was born on 7 March 1793 at Albany County, New York. He was a known resident of Strongsville, Cuyahoga, Ohio, in 1830. He was baptized into the Church on 8 January 1831 at Cuyahoga County, Ohio, by Solomon Hancock. He was ordained an elder in 1831 in Ohio and a high priest on 3 June 1831 at Kirtland, Ohio, by Lyman Wight. He died on 11 May 1887 near Stewartsville, DeKalb, Missouri.

23. Donald Q. Cannon and Lyndon W. Cook, eds., *Far West Record: Minutes of The Church of Jesus Christ of Latter-day Saints, 1830–1844* (Salt Lake City: Deseret Book Co., 1983), p. 22.

24. Joseph Smith, *History of The Church of Jesus Christ of Latter-day Saints,* 2d ed. rev., edited by B. H. Roberts (Salt Lake City: The Church of Jesus Christ of Latter-day Saints, 1932–51), 4:94.

25. *The True Latter Day Saints' Herald,* vol. 3, no. 6 (December 1862): 132.

26. The eight apostates were John C. Bennett, Ezra Booth, John Corrill, John A. Hicks, William Law, William McLellin, Robert D. Foster, and Symonds Ryder.

27. Symonds was baptized in June 1831 and was ordained an elder on 6 June 1831 by Joseph Smith, Sr.

28. Another historian claimed that when Joseph Smith "misspelled" Ryder's first name S-i-m-o-n instead of Symonds, Ryder lost faith in him, feeling that if the Lord really did speak to Smith, he would spell his name "correctly." James B. Holm, ed., *Portage Heritage* (Portage, Ohio: The Portage County Historical Society, 1957), p. 171; see also Smith, *History of the Church,* 1:261.

29. Holm, *Portage Heritage,* p. 171; see also *History of Portage County, Ohio* (Chicago: Warner, Beers, and Co., 1885), p. 474.

30. Symonds Ryder to A. S. Hayden, 1 Feb. 1868, as cited in Max H. Parkin, *Conflict at Kirtland: A Study of the Nature and Causes of External and Internal Conflict of the Mormons in Ohio between 1830 and 1838* (Salt Lake City: Max Parkin, 1966), p. 254.

31. Ibid.

32. Smith, *History of the Church,* 1:263.

33. Doris Messenger Ryder, "A History of Symonds Ryder," *The Report* (Ohio Genealogical Society), vol. 9, no. 2 (April 1969): 1–2.

ZION'S CAMP: A STUDY IN OBEDIENCE, THEN AND NOW

David F. Boone

Brigham Young University

The first Latter-day Saints to arrive in Independence, Jackson County, Missouri, were the missionaries to the Lamanites, arriving probably in late January 1831. In July 1831 Church leaders visited Jackson County, Missouri, and the Lord identified Independence as the center place of Zion (see D&C 57), suggesting a spot of great historical significance and one of future Church importance. Within weeks, several groups were called to Independence to settle the region, including the Colesville Branch of Latter-day Saints from New York, who arrived the latter part of July 1831, and other converts from New York and Kirtland, Ohio. Within the next two years, hundreds of Latter-day Saints likewise settled in Independence, Missouri, eager, it seems, to harvest blessings by virtue of being in an area rich in spiritual heritage.

All did not go well for the settlers, however. As time passed, boastful and overzealous colonizers tended to anger the old settlers with unnecessary claims that the land had been given to Latter-day Saints through divine favor and that others would be removed by force, if necessary, to fulfill the Lord's promises for the region. The old settlers resisted and resorted to a show of force in an unsuccessful effort to intimidate the Mormons. When they did not respond to the satisfaction of the Jackson County, Missourians, mob violence erupted in 1833, and by November the Latter-day Saints were forcibly removed from their homes and lands.

THE NEED FOR ZION'S CAMP

The violent expulsion of Latter-day Saints from their homes and lands in Jackson County, Missouri, precipitated the need for specific action. The action that ultimately came was a force of Saints organized militarily but for the most part without formal experience; that group is referred to in Church history as Zion's Camp. Mobs, bent on brutality and destruction despite the organization of Zion's Camp, publicized their intent to drive all Latter-day Saints beyond the Missouri borders.

Church leaders in Kirtland, Ohio, specifically the Prophet Joseph Smith, sought assistance from the courts, from the Missouri governor, from the president of the United States, and from other parties whose sympathies may have favored the Mormon position. By mid-December, the Prophet Joseph had received a revelation (D&C 101) that outlined the reasons why the Lord had allowed the Saints to be expelled from their homes and lands, a timetable for what must be done before they could redeem their personal property, and specific instructions for the Saints to rectify the situation. An important part of this revelation was a parable depicting the plight of the Missouri Saints. Referred to since as the parable of the nobleman (see vv. 43–64), the parable described specifically the literal and ultimate redemption of the Latter-day Saints to their rightful place.

Dr. Sidney B. Sperry's insights into the meaning of the parable are valuable. In his *Compendium,* he noted: "It would seem that the parable is to be interpreted in this way: the nobleman is the Lord, whose choice land in His vineyard is Zion in Missouri. The places where the Saints live in Zion are the olive trees. The servants are the Latter-day Saint settlers, and the watchmen are their officers in the Church. While yet building in Zion, they become at variance with each other and do not build the tower or Temple whose site had been dedicated as early as 3 August 1831. Had they built it as directed, it would have been a spiritual refuge for them, for from it the Lord's watchmen could have seen by revelation the movements of the enemy from afar. This foreknowledge would have saved them and their hard work when the enemy made his assault.

"But the Saints in Missouri were slothful, lax, and asleep. The enemy came, and the Missouri persecutions were the result. The Lord's people were scattered and much of their labors wasted. The Almighty rebuked His people, as we have already seen, but He commanded one of His servants (vs. 55), Joseph Smith (103:21), to gather the 'strength of Mine house' and rescue His lands and possessions gathered against them.

"Subsequently, the Prophet and his brethren in the famous Zion's Camp did go to Missouri in 1834 in an attempt to carry out the terms of the parable. Before they went, additional revelation was received (see 103:21–28) concerning the redemption of Zion. The brethren were instructed to try to buy land in Missouri, not to use force; and if the enemy came against them, they were to bring a curse upon them. Zion was not redeemed at that time, but we may look for it in the not-too-distant future. Verily, it will be redeemed when the Lord wills it."[1]

Although given as instruction to the Church, the revelation was published and distributed to others, including Missouri governor Daniel Dunklin. A part of the parable (vs. 55–57) carried a promise of armed redemption from Church leaders and members in Kirtland, Ohio, to the exiled Jackson County Saints:

"And the lord of the vineyard said unto one of his servants: Go and gather together the residue of my servants, and take all the strength of mine house, which are my warriors, my young men, and they that are of middle age also among all my servants, who are the strength of mine house, save those only whom I have appointed to tarry;

"And go ye straightway unto the land of my vineyard, and redeem my vineyard; for it is mine; I have bought it with money.

"Therefore, get ye straightway unto my land; break down the walls of mine enemies; throw down their tower, and scatter their watchmen" (D&C 101:55–57).

By mid-December, the Prophet Joseph responded to Church members' concerns by saying that "he was going to Zion, to assist in redeeming it." He called for a sustaining vote of the council in Kirtland to support his decision, which was given; and in response to his request for volunteers to assist him, thirty or forty of the men of the council agreed to go.[2]

Later that same day, the Lord revealed to the Prophet Joseph specific instructions relating to the formation and execution of the march to be taken by Zion's Camp (see D&C 103). This revelation provided the Prophet and the Church with such detailed information as the number of participants the Lord expected (vv. 30–34), the demographic makeup of the expedition (vv. 21–22), how the group was to be financed (vv. 23), how the force was to be organized (vv. 30–31), and who its principal leaders were to be (vv. 35–40).

Initially, Zion's Camp was intended to protect the rights of the Latter-day Saints after the state militia made possible the return of the exiles to their confiscated homes and other property. Before the Saints could complete their recruiting, financing, and purchasing of supplies for the camp, however, the Missouri governor reconsidered involving the state militia in the operation. Governor Dunklin, who in November 1833 had suggested such a military organization on the part of the Church, waffled because of public outcry. Dunklin ultimately withdrew his support for involving any state military force.

Meanwhile, the Saints' preparations continued, and Mormon recruits departed from Kirtland, Ohio, in the main body of Zion's Camp

on 5 May 1834. The leaders of Zion's Camp did not learn that Governor
Dunklin had reversed his position until the expedition was underway.
Upon his arrival at the Mississippi River, Elder Parley P. Pratt recalled:
"We had an interview with the Governor, who readily acknowledged
the justice of the demand, but frankly told us he dare not attempt the
execution of the laws in that respect, for fear of deluging the whole
country in civil war and bloodshed. He advised us to relinquish our
rights, for the sake of peace, and to sell our lands from which we had
been driven."[3]

As well intentioned as the governor may have been in this affair,
it is apparent that he did not understand the position of the Latter-
day Saints. Had Jackson County not been designated as the center
place of Zion and the gathering place for the Saints, it would have
been less of a sacrifice for the Saints to leave; in fact, the Saints would
likely not have settled there to start with. But the Lord had so declared
and the Saints had been obedient to settle the region in 1831 and to
buy the land, which gave them legal right to their property. That was
all according to instruction from the Lord to the earliest Saints who
settled in the area of Independence, Jackson County, Missouri: "But
unto him that keepeth my commandments I will give the mysteries of
my kingdom, and the same shall be in him a well of living water,
springing up unto everlasting life. And now, behold, this is the will
of the Lord your God concerning his saints, that they should assemble
themselves together unto the land of Zion, not in haste, lest there
should be confusion, which bringeth pestilence" (D&C 63:23–24).

The protection of the state militia was necessary to enforce the
return of the exiled Saints to their homes in Missouri; without it, the
Church paramilitary force could not ensure their safety. The politically
expedient change in the governor's position had to do with the Missourians' intense feelings against the Saints. Their united bitterness
exacerbated the situation, for many in the state's militia were also
antagonists in the Mormon relocation question. Without the support
of the state's chief executive or the militia he commanded, there was
little left for the Church leaders and Zion's Camp participants to do
except disband and return to their homes. They did not do so, however,
until the Prophet received a revelation (D&C 105) on 22 June 1834
that the Lord accepted the sacrifice of the Saints and deferred the
redemption of Zion to a later date. The disbanding of the camp came
on 25 June, less than six months after hostilities necessitated its creation
and after a march of eight hundred to a thousand miles from Kirtland,
Ohio, to Clay County, Missouri. The camp members' hardships were

severe. Hunger, thirst, unseasonable cold, disease, milk sickness, and inadequate dress combined to create suffering.

CONTRIBUTIONS OF ZION'S CAMP

Because Zion's Camp was dissolved before achieving its expressed objectives, the whole mission has been labeled a failure by many authors from 1834 to the present. Nonetheless, the expedition made numerous lasting contributions to the Church. The following are but some of those contributions.

Doctrines and Teachings

A great deal of official Church doctrine came as a result of the instructions the Lord gave for the organization of Zion's Camp. Doctrine and Covenants 101, 103, and 105 are replete with insights on such doctrinal themes as obedience, patience, testing, trust in the Lord, sacrifice, mankind's dependence upon the Lord, God's intervention in mankind's dealings, signs of the Second Coming of the Lord, millennial conditions on the earth, the judgments of God upon the earth, continuing instructions concerning the establishment of Zion, characteristics of a Zion people, the divine involvement in the establishment of the United States Constitution, and many more. Numerous other instructions were also given, including revelation to assist with the challenges facing the Latter-day Saints in Missouri. All of this comforted, encouraged, and brought hope to the hearts of Latter-day Saints who desired to learn from their experiences.

Obedience and Sacrifice

Although perhaps not fully recognized as such by its participants, one purpose of Zion's Camp was to determine who would be obedient to the Lord's counsel. Obedience often includes sacrifice, and sacrifice is not divinely recognized without obedience to eternal laws. (Saul learned from the Lord that obedience is far better than sacrifice; see 1 Samuel 15:22). The experience of traveling to Missouri was a test for each of the camp's participants. Many failed a part of the test through willful disobedience; in other words, they did not realize all that was potentially theirs if they had been obedient. Although some failed because of their attitude and unwillingness to be taught, the only real losers were those who refused to go when called to serve. If there was failure in Zion's Camp, it was attributable in part to lack of support from Church members. Elder B. H. Roberts wrote: "Had the Saints in the eastern branches had more faith—faith to send up to Zion more

men and more money with which to strengthen the hands of the
Saints . . . the history of Zion's Camp might have been different."[4]

Additional Church members were needed, but some had good
reasons to stay behind. Dennis Lake and A. Miner drew straws to
determine who would go to Missouri and who would stay home to care
for both of their families. Lake went with Zion's Camp. When he
returned, disenchanted with the experience, he apostatized. Apparently he was so bitter that he later sued the Prophet for sixty dollars,
the value of the three months' work that he had missed. Elder Brigham
Young was unable to pacify Lake, but as a part of his official assignment,
he told Brother Miner, "he would receive his blessings" as a result of
his staying home and doing his part. That greatly satisfied Brother
Miner.[5]

It appears that from the outset some participants understood the
higher principles that brought them together. Others went simply
because they were asked to go. Nonetheless, those individuals went,
whereas others elected not to.

Brother Nathan Bennett Baldwin's journal entry revealed a higher
law for participation. He spoke of consecrating that which he owned
to the service of the Lord,[6] as did others (see also Elijah Fordham's
Journal, Tuesday, 10 June 1834), and others said, "Our money was
then thrown together."[7] The law of consecration was first revealed to
the Church in February 1831 (D&C 42:30–34), only three years before
the calling of Zion's Camp. Furthermore, some areas of the Church
in Kirtland, Ohio, and in Missouri, practiced this law. It is interesting,
therefore, to note the references to individual participation as a result
of obedience to that particular law.

Various reasons were given by other men for their failure to go.
But when the Prophet chided one man, " 'Now that you have a wife,
don't say you can't go,' " the man responded: "I said my wife shan't
hinder me and went and bought me a rifle and sword. I armed myself
for battle." His wife's support continued during his absence. He wrote
later: "My wife had managed to get along with the baby without running
me in debt. Some had to pay many dollars for their wives debts. I felt
thankful for this and loved her dearly."[8]

A more significant contribution is a principle usually overlooked
about these individuals who accompanied the Prophet: all the individuals went with the realization that their lives could be forfeited for
the gospel cause, yet they were obedient to the call.

On 4 May 1834, the Prophet spoke in Kirtland to the assembled
Saints, many of whom would shortly become members of Zion's Camp.
"He impressed upon them the necessity of being humble, exercising

faith and patience and living in obedience to the commands of the Almighty, and not murmur at the dispensations of Providence. He bore testimony of the truth of the work which God had revealed through him and promised the brethren that if they all would live as they should, before the Lord, keeping his commandments, and not, like the children of Israel murmur against the Lord and His servants, they should all safely return and not one of them should fall upon the mission they were about to undertake, for if they were united and exercised faith, God would deliver them out of the hands of their enemies, but should they, like the children of Israel, forget God and His promises and treat lightly His commandments, He would visit them in His wrath, and vex them in his sore displeasure."[9]

True to the Prophet's promise to the Saints, the Lord did protect them, usually in ways that they could not comprehend. One of the best examples of divine intervention came in mid-June on the banks of the Big and Little Fishing Rivers. The camp had been under constant threat of attack from Missourians who had assembled to destroy the Mormon marchers. On the morning of Thursday, 19 June, an agitated black woman warned Luke Johnson that a large company was planning to destroy the Mormon Camp. A farmer confirmed the report later that day. The camp hastily moved forward, believing that they could receive assistance from Latter-day Saints in Clay County, Missouri, but several incidents hindered their progress: a wagon broke down and had to be repaired before the camp could proceed, and the wheels ran off at least two others. None of the delays was particularly significant in itself, but combined, they hampered progress significantly.

Zion's Camp was forced to stop "on an elevated piece of land between the forks of the Big and Little Fishing Rivers." While the main group pitched their tents, five members of the mob rode across the river and threatened the Saints that they would "see hell before morning."[10] Shortly thereafter it began raining. It rained in torrents throughout the night, "the thunder and lightning exceeded all description."[11] Heber C. Kimball related that there was continual lightning throughout the night, bright enough to see to pick up a pin. Another account suggests that small hail fell in the camp;[12] many others indicate that hail the size of eggs fell only outside camp. Many of the brethren took refuge in a local church house, but others remained in their tents. Their enemies hid under wagons. One of the mob was reportedly killed by lightning, and another's hand was torn off by a fractious horse frightened by the storm.[13] Tree limbs as large as four inches in diameter were torn from trees. The storm disorganized the

Missourians, which curtailed their achieving their destructive objectives. They left, having failed in their intent to destroy Zion's Camp.

Many of the camp members perceived the terrible storm to be providential intervention. Nathan B. Baldwin recorded: "The Lord had previously said He would fight the battles of His Saints; and it seemed as though the mandate of heaven had gone forth from his presence to apply the artillery of heaven in defense of his servants. Some small hail fell in the camp but from a half mile to one mile around, we were told by inhabitants that the hail stones were as big as tumblers; and the appearance of their destructiveness showed that their size was not overestimated. Limbs of trees were broken off, fence rails were marred and splintered, and the growing corn was cut down into shreds. But the casualties were all on the side of our enemies."[14]

George A. Smith further declared: "I have ever felt thankful to my Heavenly Father that He by this storm and sudden rise of the streams prevented our having a bloody conflict with our enemies, who were thereby prevented from attacking us." The stream rose to a depth of between thirty and forty feet. After leaving camp and seeing the destruction caused by the severe hailstorm, the brethren once again prayerfully expressed gratitude for their divine preservation.[15]

Like the children of Israel, members of Zion's Camp were sobered by the experience and repentant, and they did better for a time. But, like the Nephites, they regressed from sincere repentance and the blessing of improved conditions to murmuring and complaining, again to be rebuked and chastened by the Lord until they returned to a more humble, teachable condition. Neither was the value of their experience lost on those who intended to destroy the Saints after the rise of the river. Wilford Woodruff reported that the captain of the mob noted how strange it was that nothing could be done against the Mormons but that some calamity prevented them from being successful. Elder Woodruff editorialized, "But they did not feel disposed to acknowledge that God was fighting our battles."[16]

Others, however, did make such an acknowledgment: "They [the mob] declared that if that was the way God fought for the Mormons, they [themselves] might as well go about their business."[17] A Colonel Sconce also remarked, "I see that there is an Almighty power that protects this people, for I started from Richmond, Ray county, with a company of armed men, having a fixed determination to destroy you, but was kept back by the storm."[18]

The Saints learned again that the chastening hand of God is a great blessing to his people. With the numbers of the assembled mob and the comparative weakness of the camp, little but divine intervention could have kept them from destroying the Saints.

Despite these warnings, many participants failed to follow the Prophet's advice. Repeatedly through the Zion's Camp march, the Prophet had to warn, exhort, encourage, and reprimand the participants to greater faithfulness. He reminded them of their duty; he encouraged their obedience; and he chastised them for their laxness in keeping the commandments. Through it all, many listened and as a result believed, and their view of spiritual things expanded. Others picked up a few truths and were better for their effort but did not live up to their potential. And still others, like Brother Dennis Lake, felt their time was wasted and even heaped future indignation upon themselves by creating dissension within the Church and apostatizing.

Some Church members apostatized because the Prophet instructed the Camp of Israel to take up arms. "They did not believe it right to arm themselves, or fight in self defense."[19] Luke Johnson, on the other hand, though he believed it wrong to take up arms, nevertheless was obedient and followed the Prophet. He recorded: "May 1st 1834 I started with some of the brethren for Missouri for the 1st time [in my life] that I had consented to take firearms to go into the field of battle."[20]

Some camp members complained because of lack of bread at mealtime,[21] about the butter, the meat, the horses or the lack of them, about the company they were forced to keep, and about almost every other imaginable problem. Others endured every privation, every setback, every challenge and opportunity with self-respect and fortitude.

Through it all, the Prophet was reassuring, correcting, and pacifying many of the men. On Saturday, 17 May, the Prophet warned that "they would meet with misfortunes, difficulties and hindrances as the certain result of giving way to such a [rebellious and contentious] spirit and said, 'you will know it before you leave this place.' He exhorted them to humble themselves before the Lord and become united, that they might not be scourged."[22]

When the camp awakened the next morning, they discovered that almost every horse in the camp was foundered, a debilitating condition often caused by overfeeding. The condition hindered movement by the animal, but movement was essential to the animal's survival. When the Prophet Joseph realized the condition of their horses, he said to the men "that for a witness that God overruled and had His eye upon them, all those who would humble themselves before the Lord, should know that the hand of God was in this misfortune, and their horses should be restored to health immediately."[23] Most of the men complied, and "by noon the same day, the horses were as nimble as ever." One man who had a "rebellious spirit" and would not be humbled found his horse dead soon afterwards. Such experiences for the camp were numerous and poignant, teaching the brethren their duty and responsibility to the Lord.[24]

Within days of the experience on the Fishing rivers, another example of divine protection unfolded but once again neither its severity nor its final result could have been anticipated. Partially as a result of disobedience, contention, and murmurings within the camp and partially because of the further need for protection from the mobs, the Camp of Israel was smitten with the dreaded cholera. Cholera is a gastrointestinal disorder that causes severe cramping, vomiting, and a weakening of the victim because of the inability to keep down or process nutrients. Hyrum Smith indicated that "it seized [us] like the talons of a hawk."[25]

Joseph Bates Noble was stricken but lived to share the following description of his painful ordeal: "I there was violently seized with the Cholera, vomiting and purging powerfully, then cramping from head to foot in the most powerful manner, with a burning fever in my bowels. In this situation I lay forty hours, my voice and my hearing had nearly left me. While in this situation, Bros. Brigham Young, [and others] . . . prayed for me. . . . While praying in this situation the veil became very thin between me and my God and I noticed things that I never before thought of. Such was the blessing of God upon me that I nearly had an open vision. Through the faith of my brethren that was exercised for me, I got up and with their assistance put on my clothes. . . . Never had I experienced such manifestations of the blessings of God as at this time."[26]

Cholera struck quickly. George A. Smith recorded that "many of the brethren were violently attacked . . . some falling to the ground while they were on guard."[27] The disease spread quickly in the unsanitary conditions and, not uncommonly, by and to those who cared for those already infected. The numbers of casualties from the disease in Zion's Camp vary. Most sources suggest thirteen or fourteen; one indicates that as many as twenty died from the disease. Burial was quick because of the rapid decomposition of the bodies. Many wrote of this incident, regretting that they couldn't do more for their fallen comrades. Joseph Bates Noble, who had been caring for his dear friend, Elbur Wilcox, lamented: "Never in my life did I feel to mourn like as on this occasion. I was sensible that a strong chord of friendship bound us together, but I did not know that our hearts were so completely knit together as they were."[28] Heber C. Kimball wrote, "We felt to sit and weep over our brethren, and so great was our sorrow that we could have washed them with our tears."[29]

Three weeks earlier, the Prophet had warned the camp of repercussions from their disobedience: "The Lord had revealed to me that a scourge would come upon the camp in consequence of the fractious and unruly spirits that appeared among them, and they should die like sheep with the rot."[30] He further said that "the scourge must come; repentance and humility may mitigate the chastisement, but cannot altogether arrest it."[31]

One bright spot in an otherwise dismal situation was that the mob's fear of the sickness kept them at bay. Elder Heber C. Kimball noted: "This was our situation, the enemies around us, and the destroyer in our midst."[32] Six months later, in conversation with some of the veterans of the march, the Prophet Joseph indicated he had received a vision of those who had given their lives as a part of Zion's Camp. "I have seen those men who died of the cholera in our camp; and the Lord knows, if I get a mansion as bright as theirs, I ask no more." As the Prophet shared this experience, he wept and was unable to speak for some time.[33]

MISSIONARY LABORS

Another aspect of Zion's Camp has long been neglected and usually completely omitted: the missionary efforts of Zion's Camp participants. Missionary work has been characterized as the lifeblood of the Church. Rarely will you find assembled Latter-day Saints who are not affecting the lives of others, either as examples of Christlike living or in active proselyting efforts. Zion's Camp was no exception. Three brief examples will suffice, although others are available.

The old wagon road that Zion's Camp was to travel through Missouri passed immediately by the three hundred twenty acres of William Adams Hickman, approximately eleven miles east of Huntsville, Missouri, near present-day Missouri State Highway 24. Hickman was a prosperous young farmer, only about twenty years old. He and his wife, Bernetta, noted the approach of Zion's Camp with interest. Although there was an air of secrecy surrounding the advancing company, it was extremely difficult to hide the identity of such a large contingent of fighting men. Hickman and his wife knew the camp's identity and were hospitable to the weary marchers when they arrived.

Bernetta's brother, Greenlief Burchardt, also knew who they were, but he was antagonistic and even hostile toward the camp. Apparently the differences of opinion between the two men were expressed, and in the passion of the moment, William Hickman challenged his

brother-in-law Greenlief to a fistfight in defense of his right to entertain
the Mormons on his farm. There is no evidence that the fight ever
took place, but there is reason to believe that William and Bernetta
treated the Mormon marchers kindly. Sources suggest that the Hickmans invited some of the marchers into their home for dinner, and
evidence shows that the Mormons received fresh water, a scarce com-
modity, from their benefactor's well.

Undoubtedly as a result of this early introduction and apparently
strengthened by the defense of the members of Zion's Camp, William
Adams Hickman, Bernetta Burchardt Hickman, and their young family
threw in their lot with the Latter-day Saints by being baptized members
of the Church. During the expulsion of the Mormons from Missouri
in 1838, the Hickmans sold their spacious farm and joined the Saints
in Commerce, Illinois.[34]

Nathan and John Joshua Tanner traveled with Zion's Camp. They
heard the Prophet Joseph prophesy, teach, and exhort the Saints to
faithfulness. They saw him act in his prophetic role and recognized
the significance of his teaching. Their father, the venerable John Tanner, a recent convert himself, "put in very near half the money that
paid the expenses of Zion's Camp."[35]

Upon their arrival in Missouri and the ultimate disbanding of Zion's
Camp, the two younger Tanners remained for a time in the land of
Zion before attempting to return to Kirtland. Even though there was
plenty of money at home, the two ran into financial trouble on the
return journey. Fiscally embarrassed, they relied on the kindness of the
local citizenry. Nathan and John attempted to find work, but wet
weather prevented their consistent employment. They continued toward home until they were literally down to their last dime. A local
farmer named Eldredge inquired where they were from and where they
were going. Upon their reply the inquisitor said, "Then I take it you
are Mormons" and invited them to dinner. At the end of the meal
Eldredge presented them with a sizable contribution to help them home.
They refused it and instead offered to borrow the money if their benefactor would trust them to send it back upon their arrival home. Eldredge
indicated he would be in their region during the coming fall and would
collect his money then.

The young men continued their journey, and within a few weeks,
the farmer visited the John Tanner home and stayed two weeks. In
addition to receiving his money, Eldredge and his son John were baptized members of the restored Church. But the story does not end there.
As a result of contact with returning members of Zion's Camp, the
gospel was taken to the rest of the widowed farmer's family: at least

one other son embraced the faith of the Latter-day Saints, Horace S. Eldredge. Horace became a general authority in 1854, as well as a successful Utah merchant, marshall, brigadier general in the Utah militia, a legislator, banker, and twice a financial agent and emigration representative for the Church in the East.[36]

William Taylor was also a farmer by trade. He moved his large family from Bowling Green, Kentucky, to Clay County, Missouri. Taylor purchased six hundred forty acres of rich farmland between the forks of the Big and Little Fishing rivers. This was the area of Clay County where the camp stopped to repair the wagons during the horrific storm that protected the Saints.

The raised levels of the Little and Big Fishing rivers that protected the Saints likewise prevented them from continuing their journey. Throughout Saturday and Sunday, the Zion's Camp marchers were obliged to remain there. Many of the marchers were forced to seek shelter in the local Baptist meeting house. Later, they also learned that it was the house of worship for William Taylor, his family, and many of his neighbors. On Sunday morning, 21 June, the worshippers assembled and, finding Camp members already there, encouraged them to preach. The gospel was taught. "Having heard one sermon, William Taylor was converted." Before the camp moved on the following Tuesday (22 June), William Taylor, his wife, Elizabeth, eight of their fourteen children, and some eighteen others were baptized in the same river that four days earlier had held the persecutors at bay. "Two days after meeting Joseph Smith, William Taylor manifested his confidence in the Prophet by fitting up his own son and his son in law with provisions, munitions, and equipment to [themselves] become members of Zion's camp."[37] He was ordained an elder and soon thereafter proselyted for the Church.

Descendants of the Taylor family, like those of the Eldredge and Hickman families, are still in the Church. John Taylor of Snowflake, Arizona, is a great-grandson of William. John, like many other family members, continues the legacy of faith and devotion begun by William and Elizabeth in 1834. John has been a bishop, stake president, and mission president, and currently serves as a patriarch. His civic career is no less distinguished. Yet, who could know in 1834 that the example and teachings of faithful Latter-day Saint marchers could create a legacy of adherence to the saving principles of the gospel. As a result of the Prophet's teachings then, Saints today are likewise benefited and blessed by that experience.

THE SANCTITY OF LIFE

On numerous occasions the Prophet Joseph was compelled to rebuke the members of Zion's Camp for their carelessness of the value
of life. In Elder George A. Smith's reminiscence, for example, at least
seven incidents were noted between men and rattlesnakes. Apparently
the natural tendency of the men was to destroy the reptile and be done
with the threat. The Prophet repeatedly upbraided the brethren: "How
will the serpent ever lose his venom, while the servants of God possess
the same disposition, and continue to make war on it? Men must
become harmless, before the brute creation; and when men lose their
vicious dispositions and cease to destroy the animal race, the lion and
the lamb can dwell together."[38]

The teaching of the Prophet Joseph apparently had some effect,
because in several future episodes the men carefully relocated unwanted
serpents from their immediate campsites. Solomon Humphrey, being
older than many of the camp members, became fatigued by the exertion
of the march and the heat of the day. Humphrey lay down and napped
but upon his awakening found a large rattlesnake coiled just a short
distance from his head. Some of the men hurried to his rescue, bent
on killing the snake, but Humphrey, undoubtedly remembering the
earlier counsel of the Prophet, rebuffed his protectors, exclaiming,
"No, I'll protect him [the snake]; you shan't hurt him, for he and I
had a good nap together."[39] In addition to the comic relief that the
experience provided in a tense situation, it further suggests that some
were "hearing" and taking seriously the counsel of their prophet-leader.

Others did not learn so quickly or so well. These individuals continued in their old ways despite what the Prophet had taught them.
Those who maintained their independence and their disposition to
ignore prophetic counsel had cause to regret their decision, some of
them immediately. On Wednesday, 4 June, as a result of the scarcity
of food, the men went searching for almost anything edible. That
created a dangerous situation because enemies of the Church lingered
close to the camp. With the men scattered, the whole camp was more
vulnerable to attack, not to mention the individuals who were out
searching for food.

Some men found on a sandbar some eggs they believed to be turtle
eggs and highly edible. The Prophet Joseph, however, said that they
were not turtle eggs but snake eggs, which, if consumed, would make
the men ill. The men preferred their own reasoning to the Prophet's
counsel. Again the Prophet warned the men against eating the eggs,
but they persisted, probably driven to disobedience because of hunger

as well as an unwillingness to hearken to prophetic counsel. The men who ate the eggs provided again substantial evidences of the prophetic role of Joseph Smith, because they became violently ill upon consuming the eggs.[40]

The Prophet protected forms of life other than snakes. Men were sometimes required to walk rather than continually overburden the horses. Sylvester Smith, the "chronic complainer" of the camp, was enraged when a dog in the camp snarled at him. His emotions out of control, he threatened to kill the dog if it bit him. The Prophet, having already dealt with Sylvester's insolence on several previous occasions, promised him that if he killed the dog, he, the Prophet, would whip him.[41] Further, the Prophet warned Smith that he had a wicked spirit, which if continued unchecked, would lead to the literal as well as the spiritual destruction of Sylvester Smith. Although Sylvester continued to be the camp's self-appointed critic, complainer, and gadfly, finally, after the camp was disbanded, he did repent, made himself available, and was useful in Church service.

Although these examples are in some respects simple and perhaps largely insignificant to the outcome of Zion's Camp as a whole, they demonstrate that the Prophet was attempting to teach lessons with far greater value and significance to the individuals than it might seem at first. The lessons he was teaching included valuable information that his followers could use the rest of their lives.

The Prophet was determined to teach the marchers the sin and senselessness of unnecessary and wasteful killing of harmless animals. He recorded: "I came up to the brethren who were watching a squirrel on a tree, and to prove them and to know if they would heed my counsel, I took one of their guns, shot the squirrel and passed on, leaving the squirrel on the ground. Brother Orson Hyde, who was just behind, picked up the squirrel, and said, 'We will cook this, that nothing may be lost.' I perceived that the brethren understood what I did it for, and in their practice gave more heed to my precept than to my example, which was right."[42]

The Prophet's teachings were important to those who were willing to learn; however, not all had ears to hear. Upon the arrival of the camp in Missouri and the declaration by the Lord through the Prophet that the time had not yet come for the redemption of Zion (see D&C 105:9), some of the men expressed great anger and resentment at the prospect of not being allowed to destroy the life of another human being. "Soon after this revelation was given several of the brethren apostatized because they were not going to have the privilege of fighting."[43] They had not heard the Lord's counsel; neither had they

learned the important lesson of the sanctity of life. Instead, as Nathan
Tanner recorded, they felt that "they would rather die than return
without a fight." Instead of making necessary preparations to return
to Kirtland, Ohio, to family, friends, and additional service to the
Church, some of the unhappy participants "became angry . . . drew
their swords and went a short distance from the camp and gave vent
to their wrath on a patch of Pawpaw brush, and mowed them down
like grass."[44]

JOSEPH SMITH AS A LATTER-DAY MOSES

Zion's Camp, often called the Camp of Israel, has been compared
to the camp of the former-day children of Israel, so it seems fair to
compare the latter-day Prophet Joseph Smith to the great prophet
Moses. The Lord does just that in citing the call and affirming the
work of the latter-day Joseph (see D&C 28:2; 1 Nephi 22:20; D&C
103:16).

In reading journals and other materials on Zion's Camp, I am
impressed, as were the journalists, with the great spiritual prowess of
the Prophet Joseph, whose spiritual magnanimity was evidenced in his
travels with Zion's Camp. A few insights into his spiritual attributes
will benefit us all either by way of hearing them for the first time or
in reviewing the experiences again.

Already recounted are the experiences of protection and intervention by the Lord to protect his covenant people. The Prophet was
likewise protected, generally along with the others, but more specifically
as the Lord's anointed. During the outbreak of cholera, the Prophet's
sympathies were with those who were afflicted. Already recounted are
the grief and tender feelings he had for those who succumbed to the
disease—he loved them in spite of their having brought down upon
themselves the judgments of God. The Prophet's sympathies were such
that he seems to have interfered with the directed course of Deity, and
as a result he suffered severe consequences.

"June 24. This night the cholera burst forth among us, and about
midnight it was manifested in its most virulent form. Our ears were
saluted with cries and moanings, and lamentations on every hand. . . .
At the commencement, I attempted to lay on hands for their recovery,
but I quickly learned by painful experience, that when the great Jehovah
decrees destruction upon any people, and makes known His determination, man must not attempt to stay His hand. The moment I
attempted to rebuke the disease I was attacked, and had I not desisted
in my attempt to save the life of a brother, I would have sacrificed my
own. The disease seized upon me like the talons of a hawk, and I said

to the brethren: 'If my work were done, you would have to put me in the ground without a coffin.' "[45]

The same reasoning could also be used to explain the preservation of the Saints by means of the terrific storms while they were camped between the Fishing rivers. The Prophet Joseph had a promise of life until his work was finished, and his allusion to his life being spared because his work was not yet finished is significant.

MIRACLES

Holy writ and modern prophets alike testify that miracles will attend the administration of a true prophet. Several participants referred in their journals to examples of the miracles that attended the camp. From the *Juvenile Instructor* in 1883 come the reminiscences of marcher Hiram Winters. Brother Winters recorded: "About four days before we were disbanded, our company ran short of provisions. We ate the last bite for breakfast. I applied at the commissary wagon for something for dinner, but received nothing, for the very good reason that it was empty. During the day, however, Joseph Hancock, while hunting, killed a deer, and, just after coming into camp at night, sent us about two pounds of venison. This, together with a two-pound loaf of bread . . . had to serve as supper for twelve men.

"The meat and bread were divided into equal parts [about 2.6 oz. each] and passed to the company. By the blessing of the Lord we all ate till we were satisfied, and there was some left."[46]

WARNINGS

Frequently the Prophet was warned about the precarious position of the camp. At times he would wake up his fellow marchers and insist that they move to a better location. On other occasions, he would go to the woods or other natural covering and beseech the Lord for safety, returning to the camp with the prophetic assurance that all would be well through the night, even though the enemies of the Saints lurked about them.[47] Luke Johnson recounted, "Our enemies oft tried to come upon us and destroy us, but the Lord by his providence as oft defeated them."[48]

PROPHECY

The gift of prophecy likewise played an important role in the survival of the camp of Israel and in their success. On numerous occasions the Prophet would prophesy. "At dinner time some of the brethren expressed considerable fear on account of milk sickness, with which the people were troubled along our route. Many were afraid to use milk or butter, and appealed to me to know if it was not dangerous. I told them to use all they could get, unless they were told it was 'sick.' Some expressed fears that it might be sold to us by our enemies for the purpose of doing us injury. I told them not to fear; that if they would follow my counsel, and use all they could get from friend or enemy, it should do them good, and none be sick in consequence of it."[49]

With this promise and others that he gave the camp, the Prophet warned the men not to trifle with the principle or to tempt the Lord. The Prophet recorded: "Although we passed through neighborhoods where many of the people and cattle were infected with the sickness, yet my words were fulfilled."[50]

HEALING

Except for when the Prophet was seized with sickness while trying to heal another, he manifested a great ability to heal and be healed. Brother Burr Riggs was taken ill while standing guard over the camp. His military supervisor recounted: "I was sergeant of the night-guards, with instructions to see each guard every fifteen minutes, and speak to him in a whisper and receive a reply.

"The last night, about twelve o'clock, in going the third round, Burr Riggs was missing from his post. I found his body behind a log that lay about a rod away, as stiff as the log itself. Calling to Alexander Whiteside, I asked him to carry the body to his tent while I went for Joseph. We lifted the body to his shoulder and it still remained perfectly straight. I soon found Joseph and Hyrum and F. G. Williams, who administered to him; and it was not over fifteen minutes from the time I found him till he was back at his post."[51]

VISIONS

"Where there is no vision the people perish" (Proverbs 29:18). Several visions of the Prophet are recounted during the march toward Missouri. One example was related by Nathan Tanner: "I had the pleasure of seeing him in a vision when he saw the country over which we had traveled in a high state of cultivation. This was while he was riding, and when he camped, he had a wagon run out in the middle of the corral of wagons, and got up into it, and told the camp what he had seen while in the Spirit. It was glorious and grand to hear."[52]

There may have been many other such events that were not recorded or even known by most in the camp.

PROPHETIC INSIGHTS

Other instances represent the spiritual and prophetic powers of Joseph Smith. Young George A. Smith remembered: "I got into the wagon to ride a short distance with Presidents Joseph and Hyrum Smith and Brother Ezra Thayer. We were traveling through a thicket of small timber of recent growth. Brother Joseph said, 'I feel very much depressed in spirits; there has been a great deal of bloodshed here at some time. When a man of God passes through a place where much blood has been shed he will feel depressed in spirits and feel lonesome and uncomfortable.' "[53]

The cause of the Prophet's depression later was determined by the finding of a large hill covered with holes exposing human bones. Brother Hyrum Smith suggested that "he believed that a great army had some time been slain and piled up and covered with earth, an ancient manner of burying the dead from a battlefield. The country around for miles was level."[54]

EXAMPLE

A final illustration of Joseph Smith's prophetic stature and standing within the camp of Israel was his example to the other members of the camp. Despite discouragement, disobedience, grumbling, sickness, and low morale the Prophet never seemed to lose perspective. "In addition to the care of providing for the camp and presiding over it, he [Joseph] walked most of the time and had a full proportion of blistered bloody and sore feet, which was the natural result of walking from 25 to 40 miles a day in a hot season of the year."[55] On one occasion, the Prophet gave a pair of shoes to his cousin George A. Smith, who was ill-prepared for the march.

"During the entire trip he [Joseph] never uttered a murmur or complaint, while most of the men in the Camp complained to him of sore toes, blistered feet, long drives, scanty supply of provisions, poor quality of bread, bad corn dodger, frouzy butter, strong honey, maggoty bacon and cheese, &c., even a dog could not bark at some men without their murmuring at Joseph. If they had to camp with bad water it would nearly cause rebellion, yet we were the Camp of Zion, and many of us were prayerless, thoughtless, careless, heedless, foolish or devilish and yet we did not know it. Joseph had to bear with us and tutor us, like children. There were many, however, in the Camp who never murmured and who were always ready and willing to do as our leaders desired."[56]

Like King David or Alexander the Great, the Prophet Joseph would not allow himself special privileges that were not also available to his men. He ate the same food they ate, he walked the same distances they walked, he slept in the same tents they used and refused special treatment for himself or others unless through empathy he attempted to make another's burden lighter. "At noon, the Prophet discovered that a part of [the] mess had been served with sour bread, while he had received good sweet bread from the same cook, whom he reproved for this partiality, saying, 'He wanted his brethren to fare as well as he did, and preferred to eat his portion of sour bread with them.' "[57] Further, we have accounts of the Prophet eating meat that others believed to be spoiled and taking his turn at difficult tasks, in addition to his rigorous responsibilities of leadership.

The Lord through the Prophet promised the Saints protection and preservation *if* certain things were accomplished. Most of the marchers adhered to some of the conditions, and a few of the marchers met most of the conditions, but as a camp, they were not obedient to all of the particulars.

A few of the participants apostatized after Zion's Camp. They had various reasons, including not getting to fight, personal disgruntlements, disillusionment, and so forth, but the great majority of the camp members remained faithful and many of them became very productive leaders in the Church. Approximately seven months later, in February 1835, the Prophet, having returned to Kirtland with most of the marchers, asked Brigham and Joseph Young to assemble the veterans of Zion's Camp for a mission reunion of sorts. Incidentally, this practice, although interrupted for a time, was reinstituted after the Saints arrived in the West, and the reunions were held for several years while there was a sizable group of its participants still living. From the assembled veterans in February 1835, the Prophet laid his hands on the heads of the Three Witnesses to the Book of Mormon, whose responsibility it was to select the Twelve Apostles.[58] After the blessing, the witnesses retired from the group for about an hour and then returned with the names of those chosen. Nine of the original Twelve Apostles in this dispensation had served faithfully during the trek of Zion's Camp.

CONCLUSION

The success of Zion's Camp cannot be determined solely by whether or not their initial objectives were met. Other important factors must be considered. We believe that Zion will yet be redeemed in the Lord's wisdom and on his timetable. During the weeks that Zion's Camp marched toward Missouri, the Lord convincingly manifested sufficient power through the elements and through his servants to show that he could redeem Zion at any time if the redemption of Zion alone meant returning the Saints to their lands. The timetable was his, the means of fulfillment were known to him, and he showed that neither the mobs nor anyone else was a match for his power. Independence, Missouri, was the desired destination, but the creation of a Zion society was the ultimate objective. According to Elder Neal A. Maxwell, "God is more concerned with growth than with geography. Thus, those who marched in Zion's Camp were not exploring the Missouri countryside but their own possibilities."[59] Looked at in this light, then, we may conclude that Zion's Camp was ideally named because—

1. The camp was made up of a group of Latter-day Saints who were individually committed to creating Zion by establishing the kingdom of God on earth. Furthermore, they willingly consecrated all that they had, including their lives if necessary, to see the Lord's ideal realized.

2. Participants were obedient in agreeing to go to the revealed center place of Zion to fulfill the will of the Master as revealed by his servant, the Prophet Joseph Smith.

3. Camp members were taught and tested on such principles as unity, obedience to counsel, consecration, brotherly love, sacredness of life, and so forth. These characteristics were necessary prerequisites to living together in peace, whether or not the ultimate objectives were realized at that time. These principles are likewise necessary wherever the Lord's people live.

4. The participants in Zion's Camp were being tried, stretched, refined, tutored, and tested like Abraham of old to determine their obedience to the Lord in all things. Abraham was obedient to the Lord's command, and likewise, the participants in Zion's Camp were generally obedient.

Furthermore, the march of Zion's Camp was a veritable "School of the Prophets," for many of the marchers later became leaders. They received virtually the same instruction, manifestations, and spiritual outpouring as did the members of the School of the Prophets held in the Whitney Store in Kirtland, Ohio.

Zion's Camp was to the dispensation of the fulness of times as the camp of the children of Israel was to the dispensation of the days of Moses. Both experiences showed the extent of God's patience and his love to bring a covenant people from where they were to where they needed to be. Both experiences exemplify that "unto whom much is given much is required" (D&C 82:3).

The expedition of Zion's Camp illustrated that God will fight the battles of his chosen people and intervene for their welfare.

The march of Zion's Camp was a preparatory phase, in which

future Church leaders were tutored against a day when specific skills and personalities were needed to—

1. Lead the Saints from Kirtland, Ohio, to Missouri in a group known as Kirtland Camp.

2. Lead the Saints from Nauvoo, Illinois, to settlements in Iowa and Nebraska called the Camp of Israel.

3. Lead the Saints from Winter Quarters, Nebraska, to the Great Basin.

4. Provide a pattern for leadership for many thousands of emigrant Saints to follow in subsequent years as they came from all parts of the earth.

Zion's Camp was a means of identifying, teaching, and testing future leaders of the Church. Of the first twenty-five apostles of this dispensation, including four future Church presidents, fourteen (56 percent) were members of Zion's Camp; seven of that number were not yet members of the Church, and two others were already in Missouri. Of those available to serve, fourteen of sixteen (88 percent) participated in Zion's Camp. The leadership skills gained from Zion's Camp spanned the Church's history from 1834, when they marched, until after the dawning of the twentieth century.

When asked what they had gained by their extended absence from family, business, and personal concerns, Brigham Young responded that they had accomplished everything in Zion's Camp that they had set out to do. "I would not exchange the knowledge I have received this season for the whole of Geauga County [Ohio]."[60]

Similarly, Wilford Woodruff observed on 12 December 1869: "When the members of Zion's Camp were called, many of us had never beheld each other's faces; we were strangers to each other and many had never seen the prophet. . . . We were young men, and were called upon in that early day to go up and redeem Zion, and what we had to do we had to do by faith. . . . God accepted our works as he did the works of Abraham. We accomplished a great deal. . . . We gained an experience that we never could have gained in any other way. We had the privilege of beholding the face of the prophet, and we had the privilege of travelling a thousand miles with him, and seeing the workings of the spirit of God with him, and the revelations of Jesus Christ unto him and the fulfilment of those revelations. . . . Had I not gone up with Zion's Camp I should not have been here today, and I presume that would have been the case with many others in this Territory."[61]

A great blessing to the Church from these experiences is that the descendants of these two individuals are still members of the Church and are still providing support and strength for the kingdom. Those individuals were obedient then and their descendants are still being obedient to the Lord's anointed today.

Zion's Camp was the composite of some two hundred individuals' personal experiences, and, as such, the experience as a whole was greater than the sum of all of their individual experiences. In addition to the redemption of Zion, an important objective of the march was to focus the Saints involved on still higher purposes of building the kingdom of God on earth. They fought their good fight, and they have their reward. The value of Zion's Camp today as a legacy of obedient adherence to the commandments of God is determined by what we can learn from their faithfulness and the efforts we will expend in further building the kingdom in our day.

NOTES

1. Sidney B. Sperry, *Doctrine and Covenants Compendium* (Salt Lake City: Bookcraft, 1960), pp. 521–22.

2. Joseph Smith, *History of The Church of Jesus Christ of Latter-day Saints,* 2d ed. rev., edited by B. H. Roberts (Salt Lake City: The Church of Jesus Christ of Latter-day Saints, 1932–51), 2:39.

3. Parley P. Pratt, *Autobiography of Parley P. Pratt,* ed. Parley P. Pratt, Jr. (Salt Lake City: Deseret Book Co., 1985), p. 94.

4. Smith, *History of the Church,* 2:123 n.

5. Typescript of Tamma Durfee Miner Autobiography, Special Collections, Harold B. Lee Library, Brigham Young University, Provo, Utah, p. 2; hereafter cited as BYU Library.

6. Typescript of Nathan B. Baldwin Journal, Special Collections, BYU Library, p. 9.

7. Levi Hancock Journal, Special Collections, BYU Library, p. 53.

8. Ibid., pp. 53, 57.

9. "George Albert Smith's History of Zion's Camp," 4 May 1834, p. 1.

10. Ibid., 19 June 1834, p. 21.

11. Ibid., p. 22.

12. Nathan B. Baldwin Journal, p. 12.

13. "George Albert Smith's History of Zion's Camp," 19 June 1834, p. 22.

14. Nathan B. Baldwin Journal, p. 12.

15. "George Albert Smith's History of Zion's Camp," 19 June 1834, p. 22.

16. Smith, *History of the Church,* 2:104 n.

17. Ibid., p. 105.

18. Ibid., p. 106.

19. "George Albert Smith's History of Zion's Camp," p. 1.

20. Raymond P. Draper, "The Early Life of Luke S. Johnson: From the

Absolute Beginning to Oct. 11, 1836," entry for 1 May 1834, p. 3. Typescript in possession of the author.

21. "George Albert Smith's History of Zion's Camp," 14 May 1834, p. 3.

22. Ibid., p. 5.

23. Ibid.

24. Ibid., 18 May 1834, pp. 5–6.

25. Smith, *History of the Church*, 2:114.

26. As quoted in Michael Jay Noble, "Joseph Bates Noble," p. 4.

27. "George Albert Smith's History of Zion's Camp," 25 June 1834, p. 23.

28. As quoted in Noble, "Joseph Bates Noble," p. 4.

29. Heber C. Kimball, in *Times and Seasons*, vol. 6, no. 5 (15 March 1845): 839.

30. Smith, *History of the Church*, 2:80.

31. Ibid., p. 107.

32. Kimball, in *Times and Seasons*, vol. 6, no. 5 (15 March 1845): 839.

33. Smith, *History of the Church*, 2:181 n.

34. In *Church News*, 7 Oct. 1984, p. 7.

35. George S. Tanner, *John Tanner and His Family* (Salt Lake City: John Tanner Family Association, 1974), p. 382.

36. Lawrence R. Flake, *Mighty Men of Zion: General Authorities of the Last Dispensation* (Salt Lake City: Karl D. Butter, 1974), pp. 410–11.

37. Lella Marler Hogan, "William Taylor," p. 1; see also Family Group Record for William and Elizabeth Patrick Taylor.

38. Smith, *History of the Church*, 2:71.

39. Ibid., pp. 73–74.

40. Ibid., p. 82 n.

41. "George Albert Smith's History of Zion's Camp," 6 June 1834, p. 16.

42. Smith, *History of the Church*, 2:72.

43. "George Albert Smith's History of Zion's Camp," 22 June 1834, p. 23.

44. Tanner, *John Tanner and His Family*, p. 382.

45. Smith, *History of the Church*, 2:114.

46. Hiram Winters, in *Juvenile Instructor*, vol. 18, no. 6 (15 March 1883): 86.

47. Smith, *History of the Church*, 2:101–2.

48. Draper, "Luke S. Johnson," 1 May 1834, p. 3.

49. Smith, *History of the Church*, 2:66.

50. Ibid., pp. 66–67.

51. Winters, in *Juvenile Instructor*, vol. 18, no. 6 (15 March 1883): 86.

52. Tanner, *John Tanner and His Family*, pp. 382–83.

53. "George Albert Smith's History of Zion's Camp," 16 May 1834, p. 3.

54. Ibid., pp. 3–4.

55. Ibid., 25 June 1834, p. 23.

56. Ibid., pp. 23–24.

57. Ibid., 29 May 1834, p. 9.

58. Smith, *History of the Church*, 2:186–87; see also D&C 18:37–39.

59. Neal A. Maxwell, in Conference Report, Oct. 1976, p. 16.

60. Brigham Young, in *Journal of Discourses* (London: Latter-day Saints' Book Depot, 1854–86), 2:10.

61. Wilford Woodruff, in *Journal of Discourses*, 13:158.

6

STRENGTHENING MARRIAGE AND FAMILY RELATIONSHIPS – THE LORD'S WAY

Douglas E. Brinley

Brigham Young University

The Doctrine and Covenants and the prophets of the Restoration have had much to say about marriage and family, for celestial marriage is a doctrine of major significance. The Creator ordained the family as the basic unit of his kingdom, both in this life and beyond. He has an interest in how families function, for the plan of salvation was designed to exalt his family. Jesus Christ made it possible for us to live forever as male and female beings; therefore it is only natural that after years in marriage and parenting roles, our greatest interest would be the continuation of these relationships when we are resurrected beings in the hereafter. In truth, that is the plan God ordained for his children. Exaltation, the highest of eternal opportunities, is the continuation of marriage and family relationships beyond this brief span of mortality (D&C 131:1–4). We came to this earth to qualify for eternal life, and marriage is one of the requirements. The highest degree of glory is a family kingdom (D&C 131:4). The apostle Paul said, "Neither is the man without the woman, neither the woman without the man, in the Lord" (1 Corinthians 11:11). Such a lofty ideal is of little value, however, if our family relationships are not strong and healthy in this life. Does it not seem inconsistent to think that our dislike for each other in this life will suddenly change at death, and we then will be forever deeply committed to each other?

The Lord's way of strengthening marriage and family relationships is to reveal to his children the doctrine of their origin and potential. Doctrine is the basis for ethical or Christlike behavior, because what we believe determines how we behave. When people comprehend their relationship to Deity and understand their potential for exaltation, they tend to use their agency to make choices that lead to eternal life. Therefore, it is doctrine that provides a theory or framework to keep marriage and family relationships "on course." Elder Boyd K. Packer explains the link between doctrine and personal actions:

"True doctrine, understood, changes attitudes and behavior.

"The study of the doctrines of the gospel will improve behavior quicker than a study of behavior will improve behavior. . . . That is why we stress so forcefully the study of the doctrines of the gospel."[1]

Knowing that marriage is eternal influences us not only to exercise care in our mate selection but also to do all in our power to ensure the success of this newly formed partnership. How we feel about each other, how we treat each other, and how we meet each other's needs are factors that contribute to marital satisfaction; how willingly and how well we function in our marital roles is grounded in our doctrinal framework.

We also need to understand the importance of marriage and family in the eternal plan. In a general conference address, Elder Bruce R. McConkie explained:

"From the moment of birth into mortality to the time we are married in the temple, everything we have in the whole gospel system is to prepare and qualify us to enter that holy order of matrimony which makes us husband and wife in this life and in the world to come.

"Then from the moment we are sealed together . . . everything connected with revealed religion is designed to help us keep the terms and conditions of our marriage covenant, so that this covenant will have efficacy, virtue, and force in the life to come. . . .

"There is nothing in this world as important as the creation and perfection of family units of the kind contemplated in the gospel of Jesus Christ."[2]

From this perspective, it is clear why prophet-leaders have made statements that give such a high priority to family life. President David O. McKay: "No other success can compensate for failure in the home."[3] President Harold B. Lee: "The most important work you will ever do will be within the walls of your own home."[4] President Spencer W. Kimball: "Our success [as a people, as a Church] will largely be determined by how faithfully we focus on living the gospel in the home."[5] President Ezra Taft Benson: "No other institution can take the place of the home or fulfill its essential function."[6]

DOCTRINES THAT INFLUENCE OUR ACTIONS IN MARRIAGE AND FAMILY RELATIONSHIPS

Doctrines that can generate in our hearts a desire to be effective marriage partners and parents include the doctrines of—

1. The premortal life and the purpose of mortality.

2. Eternal marriage.
3. The three degrees of glory.
4. The damnation and curse of Lucifer.
5. Rearing the children of God.

These doctrines provide meaning and perspective to marriage. Covenants strengthen commitment, and Christlike behavior (patience, meekness, charity, kindness, and forgiveness, for example) prepares us for exaltation. It is a dynamic process to move from understanding doctrinal principles to gaining exaltation, and the atonement of Christ makes the plan operational.

The Premortal Life and the Purpose of Mortality

The doctrine of the premortal life proclaims us to be the literal offspring of heavenly parents. We lived before this life, in their presence, as their male and female spirit children. Our spirit bodies were similar in appearance to our mortal bodies (Ether 3:16–17); however, these bodies in the premortal state were not capable, at least to our knowledge, of reproduction, and therefore marriage was not possible. In fact, one of the primary purposes in our coming to this "second estate" was to obtain a body of element—flesh and blood—to begin, for the first time, our stewardship in marriage and parenthood. The Lord explains that marriage was ordained of him, and that the earth was created so that his children could fulfill their destiny:

"I say unto you, that whoso forbiddeth to marry is not ordained of God, for marriage is ordained of God unto man. Wherefore . . . they twain shall be one flesh, and all this [marriage] that the earth might answer the end of its creation; and that [the earth] might be filled with the measure of man, *according to his creation before the world was made*" (D&C 49:15–17; emphasis added).

This earth, then, becomes the residence for our spirit bodies, which are united with a body of element in a probationary state. Here we are born as infants and grow to be adult men and women. Ideally, we marry and exercise our divine powers to create and bear offspring. For the first time in our existence, we are privileged to marry and participate in a functional sex role whereby we can reproduce "after our kind."

In the premortal life, each of us was a single adult, a spirit son or daughter of God, and we lived in his presence for some time. Brigham Young explained our relationship: "You are well acquainted with God our Heavenly Father, or the great Elohim. You are all well acquainted with him, for there is not a soul of you but what has lived in his house and dwelt with him year after year. . . .

"There is not a person here to-day but what is a son or a daughter of that Being. In the spirit world their spirits were first begotten and brought forth, and they lived there with their parents for ages before they came here."[7]

In the premortal realm, the only family relationships we experienced were those of sons or daughters of God and brothers or sisters to each other. There we were never intimately involved with one of the opposite sex in a marriage relationship, possessing the ability to create children.

Consider how long each of us anticipated this opportunity to come to earth to marry and become parents. It has been almost six thousand years since Adam and Eve brought about the Fall; at least seven thousand years were required to create the earth (using the most conservative estimates from Abraham 3:4, 9); there was a period from the beginning of the earth's creation backward to the Council in Heaven; and even further back was our birth as spirit children and a maturing period to become an adult male or female spirit before the Council in Heaven. Even a conservative estimate of these earlier periods (and perhaps it was really eons of time) makes it evident that we waited a substantial period of time as "single adults" to come to this earth to experience marriage and the privilege of beginning our own family life.

In comparison to this lengthy premortal period of time as single adults, we are married for only a brief period here in this probation — fifty to perhaps eighty years at most. Yet the staggering reality is that the quality of our marriage and family relationships in this life greatly influences whether these privileges will be extended into eternity. Here we have the privilege to form an eternal partnership, if we are faithful to the laws and covenants upon which this relationship is based. How important it is that we build an eternal foundation under marriage and family relationships.

Eternal Marriage

In the Doctrine and Covenants, we learn that "the spirit and the body are the soul of man. And the resurrection from the dead is the redemption of the soul" (D&C 88:15–16). The soul is two separate "bodies," born of two different sets of parents — one mortal, the other immortal. Our flesh-and-blood bodies were created by parents who transmitted to us the effects of the Fall. Neither our bodies, nor those of our children, will escape death and dissolution. But the parents of our spirit body are immortal, resurrected parents, and therefore our spirit bodies are not subject to death.[8] Sexual relations, conception, and birth are important elements in the creation of a soul, for these processes bring together our two bodies for an earthly probation. Through the power of procreation, we assist our Heavenly Father in bringing his children to their mortal state. At death the mortal body and eternal spirit separate. Mortal remains are committed to the earth, while our spirit, the "real" us, inhabits the "spirit world."[9] When resurrected, there is no further separation of the body and spirit, for a resurrected person cannot die.

Concerning the spirits who were awaiting the resurrection, the Lord explained, "Their sleeping dust was to be restored unto its perfect frame, bone to his bone, and the sinews and the flesh upon them, the spirit and the body to be united never again to be divided, that they might receive a fulness of joy" (D&C 138:17).

Clearly we are in a very important phase of our eternal existence. The Savior's atonement makes possible our resurrection with "a body of flesh and bones as tangible as man's" (D&C 130:22). Our resurrection enables our eternal spirit to be restored to its former body of "dust" (now refined and purified) with male or female attributes. Exalted beings have bodies capable of generating life.[10] Our association as husband and wife in that sphere will be "coupled with eternal glory, which glory we do not now enjoy" (D&C 130:2). Priesthood keys restored by Elijah to Joseph Smith allow the organization of eternal families through sealings for time and eternity (see D&C 110:13).

If a couple in mortality are married by priesthood authority (the authority of an eternal being), are faithful to their covenants, and become Christlike in nature, they will come forth in the resurrection clothed with immortality and eternal lives, meaning that they shall continue to bear children. "Then shall they be gods, because they have no end; therefore shall they be from everlasting to everlasting, because they continue" (D&C 132:20). As resurrected beings, husband and wife will have the power to beget spirit children. On 30 June 1916 the First Presidency and the Council of the Twelve Apostles explained the principle of "eternal lives":

"So far as the stages of eternal progression and attainment have been made known through divine revelation, we are to understand that only resurrected and glorified beings can become parents of spirit offspring. Only such exalted souls have reached maturity in the appointed course of eternal life; and these spirits born to them in the eternal worlds will pass in due sequence through the several stages or estates by which the glorified parents have attained exaltation."[11]

The Three Degrees of Glory

Another tenet intertwined with the doctrine of eternal marriage is that of the assignment of souls to degrees of glory. In eternity, the power to beget children is limited to those who reach the highest degree of glory (D&C 131:4). Elder Melvin J. Ballard explained the meaning of "eternal increase":

"What do we mean by endless or eternal increase? We mean that through the righteousness and faithfulness of men and women who keep the commandments of God they will come forth with celestial bodies, fitted and prepared to enter into their great, high and eternal glory in the celestial kingdom of God; and unto them, through their preparation, there will come spirit children. I don't think that is very difficult to comprehend. The nature of the offspring is determined by the nature of the substance that flows in the veins of the being. When blood flows in the veins of the being the offspring will be what blood produces, which is tangible flesh and bone; but when that which flows in the veins is spirit matter, a substance which is more refined and pure and glorious than blood, the offspring of such beings will be "spirit children."[12]

The Doctrine and Covenants explicitly states that only those who attain to the highest degree of glory remain married and possess the power of increase or "eternal lives": "In the celestial glory there are three heavens or degrees; and in order to obtain the highest [degree], a man must enter into this order of the priesthood (meaning the new and everlasting covenant of marriage); and if he does not [enter this order of marriage], he cannot obtain it [the highest degree of glory]; he may enter into the other [degrees], but that is the end of his kingdom; he cannot have an increase" (D&C 131:1–4).

This scripture confirms that those who retain the powers of increase in the next life are those who inherit the highest degree of glory. A temple sealing confers keys to allow a man and woman to come forth in the resurrection and retain these life-giving powers. At the time of marriage, they enter into the same covenant as did Abraham, in which he was promised innumerable seed (Abraham 2:9–11). Elder Bruce R. McConkie says: "Those portions of [the Abrahamic Covenant] which pertain to personal exaltation and eternal increase are renewed with each member of the house of Israel who enters the order of celestial marriage."[13] Those keys were restored by Elias, who appeared to Joseph Smith in the Kirtland Temple on 3 April 1836. He restored the "dispensation of the gospel of Abraham, saying that in us and our seed all generations after us should be blessed [with the gospel and the priesthood]" (D&C 110:12). In the resurrection, with death no longer a factor, our seed shall be as innumerable as the "sand upon the seashore" (D&C 132:30).

The Damnation and Curse of Lucifer

Another doctrine that adds to our perspective of marriage and parenthood is that of the limitations placed upon Lucifer for his rebellion in the premortal world. His damnation consists of his never being allowed to marry or have posterity. He is single and impotent forever, and he wants all of mankind to be as he is. He does not want any who kept their first estate, who now are in their "second estate," to retain the powers of procreation beyond this life. He realizes that we have these powers in mortality, but he knows that if he can prevent us from using these powers within the bounds God has set, or if we fail to build marriages worthy of exaltation, we will lose these powers when we die. Elder Orson Pratt wrote of Satan's limitations and of those who attain to lower degrees of glory:

"God . . . has ordained that the highest order and class of beings that should exist in the eternal worlds should exist in the capacity of husbands and wives, and that they alone should have the privilege of propagating their species. . . . Now it is wise, no doubt, in the Great Creator to thus limit this great and heavenly principle to those who have arrived or come to the highest state of exaltation . . . to dwell in His presence, that they by this means shall be prepared to bring up their spirit offspring in all pure and holy principles in the eternal worlds, in order that they may be made happy. Consequently, He does not entrust this privilege of multiplying spirits with the terrestrial or telestial, or the lower order of beings there, nor with angels. But why not? Because they have not proved themselves worthy of this great privilege."[14]

Individuals who suffer "deaths" (D&C 132:25) are those who no longer are able to propagate their own kind after resurrection. On another occasion Elder Orson Pratt wrote on a similar theme:

"Could wicked and malicious beings, who have irradicated every feeling of love from their bosoms, be permitted to propagate their species, the offspring would partake of all the evil, wicked, and malicious nature of their parents. . . .

" . . . *It is for this reason that God will not permit the fallen angels to multiply:* it is for this reason that God has ordained marriages for the righteous only [in eternity]: it is for this reason that God will put a final stop to the multiplication of the wicked after this life: it is for this reason that none but those who have kept the celestial law will be permitted to multiply after the resurrection: . . . for they alone are prepared to beget and bring forth [such] offspring."[15]

From these statements we understand what a great privilege it is to come to earth to obtain a physical body, to learn self-discipline, to be valiant sons and daughters (faithful to eternal principles), to marry, and to rear a posterity. Satan will do his best to destroy the plan of God by destroying families. He can destroy us if we are careless or fail to keep our covenants.

Rearing the Children of God

When we speak of "our children," we mean the spirit children of our Heavenly Father. He places a great trust in us when he assigns his children to our custody. We are honored by the stewardship we are given to create bodies for his spirit children. Because women conceive, carry to term, and bear his offspring, their importance to God's plan is critical. The Lord explains:

"For [a wife is] given unto [her husband] to multiply and replenish the earth, according to my commandment, and to fulfill the promise which was given by my Father before the foundation of the world, and for [her] exaltation in the eternal worlds, that [she] may bear the souls of men; for herein is the work of my Father continued, that he may be glorified" (D&C 132:63).

If couples were to decide not to have children (and many in our society are making that decision), the Father's plan would cease to function. We are privileged to assist God in his great work to "bring to pass the immortality and eternal life" of his children (Moses 1:39). We bring them to this earth to fulfill their eternal destiny, the same as our parents have done for us.

Could there be a greater trust given to two people than to have the children of God assigned to them with the responsibility to prepare them for exaltation? Certainly our heavenly parents have a great interest in how their children are reared during their probationary state. An understanding of this doctrine would surely prevent the physical, verbal, and mental abuse of many of these children in our day.

DOCTRINE LEADS TO THE DEVELOPMENT
OF CHRISTLIKE ATTRIBUTES

The five doctrines discussed above can create in us a broader vision of the purpose of life, of marriage, and of our purpose in mortality. We realize that to succeed in these stewardships, our example, our model, must be Christ, for he taught the qualities that are essential to succeed in family relationships. Not only did Christ make the Father's plan operational through his atonement, but he also came to the earth to teach us the character traits that are necessary if we are to be part of a celestial society. Gospel doctrine and our faithful observance of covenants make it more probable that we will develop Christlike traits in our character. The Doctrine and Covenants lists a number of these traits that would undoubtedly make a remarkable difference in our marriage and family behavior if were we to incorporate them into our nature: repentance, charity, humility, kindness, temperance, diligence, faith, hope, love, a spirit of meekness, an eye single to the glory of God, virtue, knowledge, patience, brotherly kindness, godliness, be one with God and man, ask, knock, keep the commandments, seek to bring forth and establish the cause of Zion, seek not for riches but for wisdom, assist in bringing forth God's work, do good, hold out faithful to the end, inquire of God, be sober, doubt not, fear not, be faithful, murmur not, resist temptation, study it out in our mind, pray always, harden not our hearts, read the scriptures, seek counsel from church leaders, guard against hypocrisy or guile, allow virtue to garnish our thoughts unceasingly, possess a broken heart and a contrite spirit, love our husband or wife with all our heart, live together in love, practice virtue and holiness before the Lord, have the Holy Ghost as a constant companion, and endure to the end.

How could a marriage fail if each spouse made these traits his or her creed to live by? Such attributes would make us more attractive, lovable, and competent marriage partners. On the other hand, when we emulate Satan's traits (temper, anger, contention, bickering), we become repulsive, and relationships suffer. Our goal must be to strive to be like the Savior in every way—emotionally, spiritually, mentally, and physically. If we follow His example, our marriages will be stronger and our children may be more likely to choose to adopt our values and follow our example.

Understanding his atonement and resurrection brings an appreciation for Christ, not only for what he did to remit sins but also for how, in overcoming both physical and spiritual death, he made it possible for marriage and family life to be eternal. The resurrection restores our bodies of element and spirit, male and female attributes in those bodies, and relationships organized by the sealing power to be forever. In the resurrection we retain all of the deep affections of the heart we have come to prize in this life. Elder Parley P. Pratt marveled at this doctrine:

"It was at this time that I received from him [Joseph Smith] the first idea of eternal family organization, and the eternal union of the sexes in those inexpressibly endearing relationships which none but the highly intellectual, the refined and pure in heart, know how to prize, and which are at the very foundation of everything worthy to be called happiness. . . .

"It was from [Joseph] that I learned that the wife of my bosom might be secured to me for time and all eternity; and that the refined sympathies and affections which endeared us to each other emanated from the fountain of divine eternal love. It was from him that I learned that we might cultivate these affections, and grow and increase in the same to all eternity. . . .

"I had loved before, but I knew not why. But now I loved — with a pureness — an intensity of elevated, exalted feeling, which would lift my soul from the transitory things of this groveling sphere and expand it as the ocean."[16]

Marriage and Family Life — Practical Implications

These five doctrines should influence in a practical way how well our families function. Knowing the importance of marriage in this life and that we anticipated this experience; knowing that Christ's atonement and resurrection restore bodies and sexuality; knowing that the Judgment assigns individuals to kingdoms of no marriage and family if they do not function well in marital roles; realizing that Lucifer's damnation was the denial of marriage and the impossibility of his ever becoming a father, thus explaining his relentless efforts to destroy us and prevent us from having these blessings beyond this life; and realizing that our children are lent to us by eternal parents who expect us to rear them in righteousness — all these should provide us with powerful reasons and incentives to build strong families.

Practically speaking, how could a person who understands these principles abuse a spouse or child? How could a person with an eternal perspective of family life, who has made sacred covenants with the Author of the plan, use anger to control or manipulate or intimidate a spouse or child when it is obvious he is using Satan's techniques? Could an unrepentant person who had violated a position of trust as spouse or parent ever, in all eternity, be allowed those roles again, especially if that person was no longer subject to death so that his evil influence would never end? It is not reasonable that God would allow a being with that temperament to remain married or continue in a parenting role. A degree of glory with no marriage or children would best satisfy justice. The powers of increase for such a person would be removed at the time of death.

These doctrines should have another effect — that of humbling us. We know so little about marriage or parenting during our brief experience here. Why do we think we are experts on marriage matters or parenting practices when we have been in these roles for such a short period of time? As we look back on a lifetime of parenting, we all realize that we could have done some things better. Marriage is a commitment to learn and work together if we are to succeed in this adventure. We must be good students of marriage and family life as we learn from our spouse and children their perceptions, feelings, and responses, which often vary from ours. Parents must teach, be firm, and insist on obedience to commonsense rules, because they are responsible for the direction of the family and they have been down the road a little farther; but even then, our teaching should be charitable and kind to those we are helping along the path. If we choose to be angry or careless through our own spiritual immaturity and offend others, when we regain our senses (perspective), surely we would seek forgiveness as we realize the destructive nature of our actions. We would want to restore our relationships through apologies and repentance. We would make things right with the most important people in our lives. How relieved we would be to know that an atonement had been made that allows us to repent and seek forgiveness of God and others for our mistakes and misjudgments; for when we offend members of our family, we offend God. Anger causes a withdrawal of the Spirit, and that departure should serve as a further reminder to us of our need to repent and repair damaged relationships in seeking a return of the Spirit.

Furthermore, a Christlike attitude would cause us, if others were thoughtless towards us, to quickly forgive, for we realize how shallow it would be to take offense when none was intended and we realize that we too have offended. The Golden Rule would apply. How easily we would forgive little children or an eternal companion for any "offense." In fact, how could a man or woman take offense at the words or actions of any other family member when he or she understands the nature of relationships in the plan of salvation?

It sounds simple, doesn't it? But why shouldn't this be the outcome? Perhaps we fail to follow this model because we do not review these doctrines of marriage and family periodically, or we have lost our eternal perspective. If we have never had the vision, or if we lose the ideal of marriage, then we allow the carnal side of our natures to prevail. When our vision is clouded, we act more like the "natural man," and if we are not careful, we will follow Lucifer more than the Savior. When we "lose our temper," or say hurtful things, or make statements that devastate others, we need to stop that behavior and begin using skills that will bless and strengthen others. The gospel is repentance-oriented; perhaps that is why the Lord has us renew our covenants with him each week through the sacrament. A time for rethinking, or renewal, serves to remind us of our origins and our dependence on him if we expect to gain eternal life. When we do not take the sacrament or renew our eternal perspective and make needed changes (repent), we lose the spirit of the Lord, turn inward, and become insensitive to the needs and feelings of others, and our family relationships suffer.

We complicate repentance by justifying and defending our behavior or resorting to blaming others for our failures. An arrogant attitude, personal pride and selfishness may prevent us from humbly reviewing our family relationships to help us make needed changes.

When doctrine guides our minds and hearts, we will never allow anger or negative feelings to generate in the first place. We *are* free agents. We *can* choose how we respond to events. We *can* prevent our interpretation of external events from being used to devastate family members. We surely had that ability to choose responses when we were in our dating years. If a date misses a golf or tennis ball, we laugh; in contrast, when a family member misses the ball, we may be sarcastic and critical. Who does not remember being angry and upset with a family member about some matter, only to have a friend call and we answer with a different voice and demeanor. Somehow, it seems, we have the ability to act more civilized with strangers who have no eternal connections to us than we do with those of our own household whom we have invited to join our eternal family! When people date, seek affection or intimacy, try to impress customers in business, or visit close friends, they go out of their way not to offend or take offense because they realize that to act on negative emotions brings undesirable consequences. At such times we are able to exercise self-discipline — clear evidence that these responses are within our control.

It was this ability to choose how he would respond that made the Savior perfect. Though he was "in all points tempted like as we are" (Hebrews 4:15), he chose not to respond destructively or in ways that hurt others. (Occasionally the hypocrisy of his enemies made it necessary for him to confront them, in which case they chose to take offense rather than repent.) His understanding of doctrine and his role as the Son of God in the plan of salvation gave him a perspective and love for his brothers and sisters that made it possible for him not to sin against people.

Modern prophets have emphasized selfishness and pride as common reasons we take offense, delay repentance, or remain unforgiving — traits never part of Christ's nature. Our sins are a result of our carelessness in losing our eternal perspective and becoming entangled in worldliness. At times we act as if we enjoy being offended, so that we have an excuse to retaliate. Or we hold grudges against others to justify our position, not evaluating righteously the circumstances. It seems, at times, as if we prefer being cantankerous rather than exercising charity and forgiveness. When we choose to behave in this manner, we act more like Satan than like Christ.

The Lord told his disciples, "Ye ought to forgive one another; for he that forgiveth not his brother his trespasses standeth condemned before the Lord; *for there remaineth in him the greater sin.* I, the Lord, will forgive whom I will forgive, but of you it is required to forgive all men. And ye ought to say in your hearts — let God judge between me and thee, and reward thee according to thy deeds" (D&C 64:9–11). How could disciples who knew gospel principles and had the vision of eternity do otherwise? No wonder repentance is at the heart of the gospel, and the Atonement is so critical to our spiritual progress.

When individuals understand how the doctrines of the gospel apply to their family life and have a vision of eternity, they are able to establish a Zion society — a place not only where people are physically cared for but also where they love each other as they understand their relationships to one another and help each other to obtain eternal life. This condition existed for some time after the visit of the resurrected Lord to the American continent:

"There were no envyings, nor strifes, nor tumults, nor whoredoms, nor lyings, nor murders, nor any manner of lasciviousness; and surely there could not be a happier people among all the people who had been created by the hand of God. There were no robbers, nor murderers, . . . And how blessed were they! For the Lord did bless them in all their doings; yea, even they were blessed and prospered . . . and there was no contention in all the land" (4 Nephi 16–18).

This condition results when people possess a doctrinal perspective on the purposes of mortality, their hearts are softened, and they are under covenant to honor God and to bless their fellow beings. Applying Christlike principles in family relationships is natural under these conditions, thanks to the knowledge and commitment of the participants to the plan of salvation and the place of marriage and family in their lives.

MARRIAGE AND FAMILY – A PERSONAL EXPERIENCE

When we talk of marriage and family, we touch on the things of eternity, for we are eternal beings. We touch on the true source of happiness, on the fountain of life, on feelings and emotions. God established that man and woman should not be alone. It is through marriage that we develop companionship and intimate relationships that are sacred and divine.

To share my own feelings on this matter, the longer I am married to my wife, the more I love her and cherish our association. The more we share our feelings and experiences, the stronger my love and appreciation for her grows. The more intertwined our lives become through our children, finances, intimacy, and a host of things we must do in life to live together, as we learn to meet each other's needs and deal with mortal limitations (including aging factors), the more I care about her.

Given our intimate association, would I want to worship a God who designed a plan of salvation that has me come to earth, gain a mortal body, marry and have children, spend all of my mortal years in a family, and then, after all the cherished experiences and emotional affiliations gained through such associations, allow me to die and lose my family connections and ties in the grave? Without any hesitation my answer would be no. If that were the result of this mortal experience, I would want nothing to do with so-called religion. What an uninspired ending! If the atonement of Jesus Christ had not the power to restore to me a resurrected body and my family associations (knowing that I must be worthy), I could not worship the God who implemented it. Such a theology would cause us to live in constant fear that we might lose our life and cut our family associations short. The death of a loved one would be tragic. Every honest soul would ask himself, under such assumptions, "Why would God perpetrate such a hoax? Why would a Being who knows all things and who has all power instigate such a useless and wasteful plan?" Surely one would be compelled to ask, "What was the purpose of it all?" "Why marry?" "Why bear and rear children?" As the song says, "If love never lasts forever, tell me, what's forever for?"[17]

I feel the same about my children. I find myself deeply involved in their lives, wanting to know how to help and assist them without interfering. Each child is important to me and contributes to my happiness. It must be my work (and perhaps my glory) to bring to pass their eternal life in any way that I can. I know in some small degree from my own limited experience with my little kingdom how my Heavenly Father must feel about each of his children. And would not these feelings about marriage and parenting cause any husband or wife, mother or father, to control his own reactions and responses?

President George Q. Cannon summarized the potential of this noble adventure of marriage and family: "We believe that when a man and woman are united as husband and wife and they love each other, their hearts and feelings are one, that that love is as enduring as eternity itself, and that when death overtakes them it will *neither extinguish nor cool that love, but that it will brighten and kindle it to a purer flame,* and that it will endure through eternity; and that if we have offspring they will be with us and our mutual associations will be one of the chief joys of the heaven to which we are hastening. . . . God has restored the everlasting priesthood, by which ties can be formed, consecrated and consummated, which shall be as enduring as we ourselves are enduring, that is, as our spiritual nature; and husbands and wives will be united together, and they and their children will dwell and associate together eternally, and this, as I have said, will constitute one of the chief joys of heaven; and we look forward to it with delightful anticipations."[18]

That is one of the "plain and precious" truths restored in the present dispensation (1 Nephi 13:34). The Lord told Joseph Smith: "And verily I say unto you, let this house be built unto my name, that I may reveal mine ordinances therein unto my people; for I deign to reveal unto my church things which have been kept hid from before the foundation of the world, things that pertain to the dispensation of the fulness of times" (D&C 124:40–41).

One of the "things" that have been revealed in our day is the eternal nature of the family, information apparently lost during the Great Apostasy. Marriage and family life was meant to be eternal, for we ourselves are eternal.

Adam and Eve made mortality possible in order for us to experience marriage and have children, and Jesus Christ made it possible for marriage to never end. No wonder we shouted for joy in the premortal existence at the prospect of earth life. This is our opportunity to marry, and it provides us the privilege to plumb the depths of another soul in an outpouring and sharing of feelings and passion while participating in the miracle of conception and birth. What a profound experience for a husband to watch his wife bring forth their offspring—to bring into mortality another being, a kindred spirit, with similar desires to accept this mortal stewardship to fashion his or her own eternal family unit. Marriage connects our past eternity of singleness to a never-ending future of marriage and family life. Never again will we be without the companionship of our spouse. Our theology blesses married lovers.

CONCLUSION

When we understand clearly the doctrines associated with marriage and family and the priority of marriage and family in the plan of salvation, we are struck with the desire to live in harmony with doctrines that will exalt. Doctrines place in perspective the purpose and meaning of marriage and family; priorities keep us on the path to our potential, which is eternal life. With a vision of eternity, we are more likely to monitor prayerfully and carefully each relationship in our family because we know our potential. We are more interested and sensitive to the needs of our spouse and children because of our long-range commitment. We are eager to develop bonds of affection and caring when we understand the "big picture." We are more willing to communicate and share information, our lives, and our feelings to strengthen our relationships with each other when we know we are building for eternity.

When we comprehend the doctrine of eternal families, we gain the power to discipline ourselves (repent) to be the kind of husbands and wives, fathers and mothers, who will develop Christlike traits and characteristics essential to qualify to live together in love and happiness in this life as a prelude to eternal life.

The Lord's solution to marriage and family problems is for each of us to understand the doctrines of the gospel as they apply to marriage and family life. These doctrines place in perspective mortality and the Atonement. We come to know how God would have us live and act if we are to achieve eternal life—the kind of life that he lives. What would be more natural than for two married people to desire to be as their heavenly parents? As God's children we have that right, if we will abide the laws, covenants, and principles of the gospel. If we will repent, the Atonement clears the way for us to be an eternal family. With an eternal perspective we can fulfill our destiny of gaining immortality and "eternal lives."

NOTES

1. Boyd K. Packer, in Conference Report, Oct. 1986, p. 20.

2. Bruce R. McConkie, "Salvation Is a Family Affair," *Improvement Era*, June 1970, pp. 43–44.

3. David O. McKay, in *Improvement Era*, June 1964, p. 445.

4. Harold B. Lee, *Stand Ye in Holy Places* (Salt Lake City: Deseret Book Co., 1974), p. 255.

5. Spencer W. Kimball, *Ensign*, May 1979, p. 83.

6. Ezra Taft Benson, "The Values by Which to Live," *Leaders Magazine*, Oct.-Nov. 1984, p. 154.

7. Brigham Young, *Discourses of Brigham Young*, comp. John A. Widtsoe (Salt Lake City: Deseret Book Co., 1951), p. 50.

8. When we speak of a spirit body, it is, nevertheless, a body of matter. "There is no such thing as immaterial matter. All spirit is matter, but it is more fine or pure, and can only be discerned by purer eyes; we cannot see it [in our finite, mortal state]; but when our bodies are purified [resurrected] we shall see

that it is all matter" (D&C 131:7–8). Thus bodies formed in the premortal life were bodies of celestial matter.

9. The "spirit world" is here on this earth. "The earth and other planets of a like sphere, have their inward or spiritual spheres, as well as their outward, or temporal [spheres]. The one is peopled by temporal tabernacles, and the other by spirits. A veil is drawn between the one sphere and the other, whereby all the objects in the spiritual sphere are rendered invisible to those in the temporal." Parley P. Pratt, *Key to the Science of Theology*, 9th ed. (Salt Lake City: Deseret Book Co., 1965), pp. 126–27.

10. In mortal life we create bodies that are subject to death and dissolution. In the resurrection, however, since we will no longer be subject to death, we will have the power to organize bodies that will never die—an endowment greater than that given us in mortal life.

11. *Messages of the First Presidency*, comp. James R. Clark (Salt Lake City: Bookcraft, 1971), 5:34.

12. *Melvin J. Ballard—Crusader for Righteousness* (Salt Lake City: Bookcraft, 1966), p. 211.

13. Bruce R. McConkie, *Mormon Doctrine*, 2d ed. (Salt Lake City: Bookcraft, 1966), p. 13.

14. Orson Pratt, in *Journal of Discourses* (London: Latter-day Saints' Book Depot, 1854–86), 13:186.

15. Orson Pratt, in *The Seer*, Jan. 1853, pp. 156–57; emphasis added.

16. Parley P. Pratt, *Autobiography of Parley Parker Pratt*, 3d ed., edited by Parley P. Pratt, Jr. (Salt Lake City: Deseret Book Co., 1970), pp. 297–98.

17. "What's Forever For," by Rafe Vanhoy (Nashville: Hal Leonard Publishing, 1978).

18. George Q. Cannon, in *Journal of Discourses*, 14:320–21; emphasis added.

7

"I WILL GO BEFORE YOUR FACE": EVIDENCE OF DIVINE GUIDANCE DURING THE TWENTIETH CENTURY

Richard O. Cowan

Brigham Young University

Some Latter-day Saints wonder why there are not as many examples of miraculous spiritual manifestations now as in the days of Joseph Smith or the pioneers. Are there really fewer instances of divine power or guidance today, or is the supposed difference merely one of perception? After years of researching the Church in the twentieth century, I am convinced that the Lord is blessing and leading his Church as much today as in any previous time.

The Doctrine and Covenants promised that the Lord would strengthen and direct those in his service. To Thomas B. Marsh he promised: "It shall be given you by the Comforter what you shall do and whither you shall go" (D&C 31:11). While Joseph Smith and Sidney Rigdon were on a short mission in western New York, they were assured: "I, the Lord, have suffered you to come unto this place; for thus it was expedient in me for the salvation of souls. . . . Speak the thoughts that I shall put into your hearts, and you shall not be confounded before men; for it shall be given you in the very hour, yea, in the very moment, what ye shall say. . . . And I give unto you this promise, that inasmuch as ye do this the Holy Ghost shall be shed forth in bearing record unto all things whatsoever ye shall say" (D&C 100:4–6, 8; compare 84:85). The Lord promised a particularly close working relationship with those in his service: "And whoso receiveth you, there I will be also, for I will go before your face. I will be on your right hand and on your left, and my Spirit shall be in your hearts, and mine angels round about you, to bear you up" (D&C 84:88). Speaking again to Thomas B. Marsh, who by this time had become president of the Twelve, Jesus Christ counseled: "Be thou humble; and the Lord thy God shall lead thee by the hand, and give thee answer to thy prayers" (D&C 112:10).

Concerning the reality of continuing revelation, Elder Spencer

W. Kimball testified: "Since that momentous day in 1820, additional
scripture has continued to come, and numerous pertinent and vital
revelations have been flowing in a never-failing stream from God to his
prophets on the earth. These scriptures are called the Doctrine and
Covenants. We declare them to be divine and official and authentic
communications from the Lord to men through divinely appointed
prophets and that there never has been and never shall be an end to
the prophets so long as men have faith and believe and live righteously.

"There are those who would assume that with the printing and
binding of these sacred scripture records, that would be 'the end of the
prophets.' But again, we testify to the world that revelation continues
and that the vaults and files of the Church are full.

"Revelations come from month to month and from day to day,
and since 1830, they have continued. As long as time shall last, a
prophet, recognized of God, will continue to interpret the mind and
will of God. . . .

"Revelation does not always mean 'walking with God,' nor 'face-
to-face,' nor 'lips-to-ear.' There are many kinds of revelation — some
more and some less spectacular. . . .

"Most recorded revelations in the Doctrine and Covenants and in
the Bible were from deep feelings and an impressive consciousness of
direction from above. But some were more direct . . .

"Brigham Young received a vision before building this beautiful
[Salt Lake] temple. . . . Here are his own words:

" ' . . . five years ago last July, I was here and saw in the Spirit
the Temple not ten feet from where we have laid the Chief Corner
Stone. I have not inquired what kind of a Temple we should build.
Why? Because it was represented before me.' . . .

"If all the spectacular manifestations and visions and pertinent
dreams and healings and other miracles were written in books, it would
take a great library to hold them.

"Comparable to the numerous revelations of the past would be the
one of Wilford Woodruff, President of the Church in the last century:

" 'I had some remarks last Sunday upon . . . revelation. Read the
life of Brigham Young and you can hardly find a revelation that he
had wherein he said, "Thus saith the Lord." But the Holy Ghost was
with him; he taught by inspiration and revelation. . . . Joseph said,
"Thus saith the Lord" almost every day of his life, in laying the foundation of this work. But those who followed him have not deemed it
always necessary to say, "Thus saith the Lord." Yet they have led the
people by the power of the Holy Ghost. . . .

" ' . . . He is giving us revelation, and will give us revelation until the scene is wound up.

" 'I have had some revelations of late and very important ones to me and I will tell you what the Lord has said to me. . . .

" ' . . . The Lord . . . has told me exactly what to do . . . I went before the Lord, and I wrote what the Lord told me to write [referring to the "Manifesto," or Official Declaration 1]. . . .'

"Revelations have continued: Brother Merrill, president of the Logan Temple, received a comforting manifestation; Elder Melvin J. Ballard's call, as told by President Grant, was remarkable. President Joseph F. Smith's vision in 1918 on the redemption of the dead [D&C 138] was most comprehensive; the temple work for the signers of the Declaration of Independence is illuminating; President Grant's Arizona experience is remarkable; Heber C. Kimball's experience of unusual discernment in the Endowment House — these and numerous experiences of latter-day authorities all are testimony that, as George Q. Cannon said, *there has never been a single minute since 1830 when the people were left without the revealed guidance of the Lord.* . . .

"The Almighty is with this people. We shall have all the revelations that we shall need if we will do our duty and keep the commandments of God."[1]

One must be cautious in compiling and sharing accounts of divine manifestations. Because events tend to be embellished when recounted in second- or third-hand sources, it is important to seek witnesses as close to the actual event as possible. The credibility and reliability of those who report them is especially important. Particularly fantastic stories often cannot be substantiated. Finally, good taste suggests that particularly sensitive or sacred events, especially those of a very personal nature, should not be discussed too publicly.

An abundance of material exists that meets these criteria. Almost all the examples Elder Kimball cited came from the nineteenth century, but what about the twentieth? Some of the most impressive twentieth-century manifestations have been linked to calls into Church service and to the selection of temple sites.

INSPIRED CALLS TO CHURCH SERVICE

The fifth article of faith declares: "We believe that a man must be called of God, by prophecy." Here, the word *prophecy* means that inspired calls come by revelation. The following examples illustrate how revelation may anticipate calls to be given later, may come at the moment the call is made, or may confirm the inspiration of the call after it has been received.

In 1899, David O. McKay was a young elder serving as a missionary in Scotland. At a special priesthood conference, James L. McMurrin, a counselor in the European mission presidency, turned to Elder McKay and promised, "If you will keep the faith, you will yet sit in the leading councils of the Church."[2] David O. McKay was called to the Quorum of the Twelve Apostles in 1906, became a counselor in the First Presidency in 1934, and served as president of the Church from 1951 to 1970.

President Heber J. Grant was guided by inspiration as he appointed General Authorities. In 1919, one of his first duties as president of the Church was to fill the vacancy created in the Twelve by his own call. "As he reviewed in his mind the men he considered to be worthy and able to fill that position, he returned again and again to his lifelong friend, Richard W. Young." In a meeting of the Twelve, he fully intended "to present him to the council for approval. But for a reason he could never fully explain, he was unable to do so; instead, he presented the name of Melvin J. Ballard, president of the Northwestern States Mission, a man with whom he had had very little personal contact."[3] Elder Ballard served as a highly respected member of the Twelve for the next two decades.

Elder Harold B. Lee was sustained as a member of the Twelve at the April conference in 1941. Elder Lee later recalled: "It was on the day or so following conference that President Stephen L Richards, who was then chairman of the Church radio and publicity committee, approached me and said, 'Brother Lee, next Sunday is Easter, and we have decided to ask you to give the Sunday night radio talk, the Easter talk, on the resurrection of the Lord.' And then he added, 'You understand now, of course, that as a member of the Council of the Twelve, you are to be one of the special witness[es] of the life and mission of the Savior and of that great event.' The most overwhelming of all the things that have happened to me was to begin to realize what a call into the Council of the Twelve meant.

"During the days which followed, I locked myself in one of the rooms over in the Church Office building, and there I read the story of the life of the Savior. As I read the events of his life, and particularly the events leading up to and of the crucifixion, and then of the resurrection, I discovered that something was happening to me. I was not just reading a story; it seemed actually as though I was living the events; and I was reading them with a reality the like of which I had never before experienced. And when, on the Sunday night following, after I had delivered my brief talk and then declared, simply, 'As one of the humblest among you, I, too, know that these things are true, that Jesus died and was resurrected for the sins of the world,' I was speaking from a full heart, because I had come to know that week, with a certainty which I never before had known."[4]

Inspiration has not been limited only to calling General Authorities. Several Church leaders have borne testimony that mission calls are inspired. Elder Robert E. Wells tells of a young man from Sweden who was called to serve his mission in Chile and was assigned to work with a native companion. The Swedish elder was surprised to discover that his companion's parents were then living in his own hometown in Sweden. The Chilean elder's parents, not members of the Church, were political exiles who had gone to Sweden to work. The Swedish elder's parents made contact with them and taught them the gospel. Imagine the inspiration it required for the prophet to send a Swedish elder to Chile and the mission president's inspiration to assign those particular companions to work together.[5]

INSPIRED SELECTION OF TEMPLE SITES

The Lord has also guided the Church in the selection of sites for Latter-day Saint temples. Once again, revelation has anticipated future site selections, been part of the actual site selection process, or has confirmed the correctness of selections already made.

In the summer of 1924, Elder George Albert Smith was in San Francisco attending regional Boy Scout meetings. On that occasion he met with the presidents of the small branches in San Francisco and Oakland, the only Church units in the area at that time. They met at the Fairmont Hotel high atop San Francisco's Nob Hill. From the hotel terrace, they had a panoramic view of the San Francisco Bay. W. Aird Macdonald, president of the Oakland Branch, later recalled: "As we admired the beauty and majesty of the scene, President Smith suddenly grew silent, ceased talking, and for several minutes gazed intently toward the East Bay hills.

" 'Brother Macdonald, I can almost see in vision a white temple of the Lord high upon those hills,' he exclaimed rapturously, 'an ensign to all the world travelers as they sail through the Golden Gate into this wonderful harbor.' Then he studied the vista for a few moments as if to make sure of the scene before him. 'Yes, sir, a great white temple of the Lord,' he confided with calm assurance, 'will grace those hills, a glorious ensign to the nations, to welcome our Father's children as they visit this great city.' "[6] Reports of Elder Smith's comments led the northern California Saints to anticipate the time when the Oakland Temple would be built. The site was purchased in 1943 and the temple dedicated in 1964.

In 1954 President McKay appointed Wendell B. Mendenhall, who was then directing the Church's building program in the Pacific, to confidentially investigate possible temple sites. Brother Mendenhall looked over various properties in New Zealand but felt that he had not yet seen the temple site. One day he felt impressed to go to Hamilton, where the Church college was then under construction. "While in the car on the way, the whole thing came to me in an instant," he recalled. "The temple should be there by the college. The Church facilities for construction were already there, and that was the center of the population of the mission. Then, in my mind, I could see the area even before I arrived, and I could envision the hill where the temple should stand. As soon as I arrived at the college and drove over the top of the hill, my whole vision was confirmed." This hill commanded a spectacular view not only of the Church college but also of the fertile Waikato River valley.

About ten days later President McKay arrived in Hamilton. Brother Mendenhall first met him in the presence of others, so nothing could be said about a temple site. Brother Mendenhall described their first visit to the hill: "After we stepped from the car and were looking around, President McKay called me to one side. By the way he was looking at the hill, I could tell immediately what was on his mind. I had not said a word to him. He asked, 'What do you think?' I knew what his question implied, and I simply asked in return, 'What do you think, President McKay?' And then in an almost prophetic tone he pronounced, 'This is the place to build the temple.' "[7] Brother Mendenhall was convinced that he had divine help in overcoming obstacles and purchasing the site.

In the light of such examples of revelation guiding the selection of temple sites, some people wondered what went wrong when the Church experienced opposition in obtaining a site for the Denver Temple. Nevertheless, those involved in the difficult process of finding the site were convinced that they had witnessed the hand of the Lord guiding them. When the preferred location proved not to be available, they turned to two other sites. In each case, citizens concerned that an increase in traffic would alter the character of their neighborhood blocked approval. By this time the originally preferred site had become available. Church officials, having benefited from experience in dealing with opposition, were able to gain the support of the temple's neighbors.[8] The beautiful Denver Temple was completed in 1985.

REVELATION GUIDES MEMBERS IN CHURCH SERVICE

On assignment from President Heber J. Grant, Elder David O. McKay spent the year 1921 visiting the Church's missions around the world. At several points he was convinced that divine guidance spared his life or helped him fulfill his assignments. While touring the Hawaiian Mission, Elder McKay's party visited the Kilauea volcano. Elder McKay and others climbed down onto a ledge to get a better view of the smoldering and ever-shifting lava. After some time on the volcanic platform, Elder McKay suddenly exclaimed, "Brethren, I feel impressed that we should get out of here." No sooner had they moved to safety than the "balcony crumbled and fell with a roar into the molten lava a hundred feet or so below." Everyone was silent as they pondered what could have happened. "Some might say it was merely inspiration," a sister missionary in the group reflected, "but to us, it was a direct revelation given to a worthy man."[9]

While visiting Palestine, Elder David O. McKay received instructions from the First Presidency to meet J. Wilford Booth and with him tour the Armenian Mission. The problem was that Elder McKay had no idea where to find Brother Booth, and without his knowledge of the language the mission tour would be almost impossible. Before leaving Jerusalem, Elder McKay ascended the Mount of Olives and, kneeling in a secluded spot, prayed earnestly "that we should be led by inspiration on our trip to the Armenian Mission." Afterwards he felt impressed to take the train to Haifa rather than touring other parts of the Holy Land by automobile as they had previously planned. "If you feel that way," responded Hugh J. Cannon, Elder McKay's traveling companion, "we had better take the train." After they had boarded the train, they both realized that neither had remembered to get the name of a good hotel at Haifa. "The delay caused by seeking information about hotels brought us to the station office door just at the same moment that another traveler reached it. He touched me on the shoulder saying, 'Isn't this Brother McKay?'

"Astonished beyond expression to be thus addressed in so strange a town, I turned, and recognized Elder Wilford Booth, the one man above all others whom we were most desirous of meeting." Elder McKay was convinced that he could not have met Brother Booth at a better time or place. "As we recounted to each other our experiences, we had no doubt that our coming together was the result of divine interposition. . . .

"Indeed, had it not been for our having met at Haifa, our trip to the Armenian Mission would have been, so far as human wisdom can tell, a total failure."[10]

President Heber J. Grant described the process by which the principles of the Church's Welfare Plan were hammered out during the 1930s: "We have been meeting morning after morning for months. . . .

After we had evolved a plan I went especially in prayer to the Lord and prayed with all earnestness to know whether or not this plan met with his approval. In response there came over me, from the crown of my head to the soles of my feet such a sweet spirit and a burning within, that I knew God approved."[11] In 1935, Harold B. Lee, then a stake president, received the assignment to put the plan into operation. "I prayed most earnestly," President Lee recalled. "I had started out with the thought that there would have to be some new kind of organization set up to carry forward the Welfare Program. . . . My spiritual understanding was opened, and I was given a comprehension of the grandeur of the organization of the Church and the Kingdom of God, the likes of which I had never contemplated before. The significant truth which was impressed upon me was that there was no need for any new organization to do what the Presidency had counseled us to do. It was as though the Lord was saying: 'All in the world that you have to do is to put to work the organization which I have already given.' "[12]

With the approach of World War II, missionaries needed to be evacuated from Germany with some urgency. Mission president M. Douglas Wood assigned Norman G. Seibold, a missionary, to locate thirty-one missionaries who might need funds to buy railway tickets to Denmark. President Wood didn't know exactly where they might be found, so instructed Elder Seibold "to follow his impressions entirely." Elder Seibold commenced his search by train. In some towns he remained on board, but at others he was impressed to get off. In one small town, he felt inspired to walk out in the community. "It seemed silly to me at the time," Elder Seibold recalled, "but we had a short wait and so I went." He found two elders in a restaurant who were very glad to see him. "As surely as if someone had taken me by the hand, I was guided there."[13]

Several years later, at the conclusion of the war, Elder Ezra Taft Benson of the Quorum of the Twelve received the assignment to go to Europe, supervise the distribution of welfare supplies and arrange for the resumption of missionary work. During his ten months there in 1946, he experienced one miracle after another. When President Benson's companion, Frederick W. Babbel, was unable to obtain visas for their visit to Poland, Elder Benson said, "Let me pray about it." Brother Babbel recalled: "Some two or three hours after President Benson had retired to his room to pray, he stood in my doorway and said with a smile on his face, 'Pack your bags. We are leaving for Poland in the morning!' . . .

" . . . He stood there enveloped in a beautiful glow of radiant light. His countenance shone as I imagine the Prophet Joseph's countenance shone when he was filled with the Spirit of the Lord."[14] Providentially, the needed doors were opened, and within a few days Elder Benson had completed his visit to the destitute Polish Saints.

Stories of how Matthew Cowley, as mission president in New Zealand, was guided by the Spirit are legendary. "The Maori people used to pray for President Cowley to come to them. One day he drove up to the front of a post office in a rather distant city in New Zealand. There were two sisters standing by the post office waiting. When he got out of the car, one said to the other, 'See, I told you he would be here soon.' President Cowley said, 'Hey, what's going on here?' One of the sisters said, 'We needed you and we've been praying. We knew you would be coming, and you always go directly to the post office, so we decided to wait here until you arrived.' It was just that simple. People would tell the Lord what they wanted, and somehow or other President Cowley was led by the Spirit to go where they were."[15]

Missionaries who served under President Cowley were undoubtedly influenced by his spirituality. Two examples will illustrate. After being in New Zealand for several weeks, Robert L. Simpson had a vivid dream that impressed him with the need to put forth an effort to learn the Maori language. He was left with the impression that "you are going to need this language when you get through with your mission. You are going to need it." Elder Simpson heeded the warning, learned the language, and served a successful mission. Shortly afterwards, World War II broke out and Robert joined the Air Force. While awaiting orders he thought, "Here I go right back to New Zealand." Much to his surprise, just before his group of hundreds of men were to sail out into the Pacific, he and four others were reassigned to a small American air base near Cairo, Egypt. "I don't know what the Lord has in mind," Brother Simpson reflected, "but I'll just do the best I can, and I am sure that everything will work out all right." Within forty-eight hours he discovered that an entire Maori battalion was stationed "within the very shadows" of the American air base. "For nearly two years I had the privilege of being there and meeting each Sunday with these Maori boys, bearing testimony with them in their own tongue, organizing them into small groups as they went up into the front lines in order that they might have their sacrament meetings and do the things that they needed to do. . . . I want to tell you," Elder Simpson concluded, "that the Lord had a hand in writing military orders because of all of the places in this world that Air Force men were being sent, very few were sent to Cairo, Egypt."[16] Robert L. Simpson's need for the language did not end there. In later years he became president of the New

Zealand mission and, as a General Authority, supervisor of the Pacific Area with headquarters at Auckland, New Zealand.

Glen L. Rudd, another of Matthew Cowley's missionaries, later became president of the Florida Mission. In this capacity, he was responsible for Church members throughout the Caribbean. He received a request from Flavia Salazar Gomez, a convert from Mexico then living in the Dominican Republic, to give her a blessing because she was critically ill with cancer. A few weeks later as President Rudd and a local Church member drove towards the city where Flavia lived, they suddenly realized that they did not have her address. As they entered the large, congested city, President Rudd was blessed to know which streets to take. When they found a parking place, they asked a man standing nearby if he knew Flavia Salazar Gomez. The man with surprise responded, "Yes, she's my wife. She's just inside that door." They had parked right in front of her home. The desired blessing was given and, a few months later, President Rudd was grateful to learn that Flavia had been healed of her cancer.

In 1946 Elder Spencer W. Kimball of the Twelve received the assignment to give leadership to the Church's Lamanite program. While touring the Mexican Mission the following year, he received a vision or dream in which he saw the future destiny of the Lamanites:

"Maybe the Lord was showing to me what great things this people would accomplish. . . .

" . . . I no longer saw you [as] the servant of other people, but I saw you as the employer, the owner of banks and businesses. . . .

"I saw you in legislative positions where as good legislators and good Latter-day Saints you were able to make the best laws for your brothers and sisters.

"I saw many of your sons become attorneys. I saw doctors, as well as lawyers, looking after the health of the people. . . .

"I saw the Church growing in rapid strides and I saw wards and stakes organized. I saw stakes by the hundreds.

"I saw a temple."[17] This vision sustained and motivated Elder Kimball as he directed the Church's efforts among these people.

Expansion of the Church during the second half of the twentieth century brought into contact an increasing number of ethnic groups and cultures worldwide. This became the setting for one of the most remarkable revelations of all. Church leaders pondered the policy by which blacks were not permitted to receive the priesthood. President Kimball recalled, "I went to the temple alone, and especially on Sundays and Saturdays when there were not organizations in the temple, when I could have it alone. It went on for some time as I was searching for this, because I wanted to be sure. We held a meeting of the Council of the Twelve in the temple on the regular day [1 June 1978]. We considered this very seriously and thoughtfully and prayerfully.

"I asked the Twelve not to go home when the time came. I said, 'Now would you be willing to remain in the temple with us?' And they were. I offered the final prayer and I told the Lord if it wasn't right, if He didn't want this change to come in the Church that I would be true to it all the rest of my life and I'd fight the world against it if that's what He wanted.

"We had this special prayer circle, then I knew that the time had come. I had a great deal to fight, of course, myself largely, because I had grown up with this thought that Negroes should not have the priesthood and I was prepared to go all the rest of my life till my death and fight for it and defend it as it was. But this revelation and assurance came to me so clearly that there was no question about it."[18]

Of this sacred occasion, Elder Bruce R. McConkie wrote: "It was during this prayer that the revelation came. The Spirit of the Lord rested mightily upon us all; we felt something akin to what happened on the day of Pentecost and at the dedication of the Kirtland Temple. From the midst of eternity, the voice of God, conveyed by the power of the Spirit, spoke to his prophet. The message was that the time had now come to offer the fulness of the everlasting gospel, including celestial marriage, and the priesthood, and the blessings of the temple, to all men, without reference to race or color, solely on the basis of personal worthiness. And we all heard the same voice, received the same message, and became personal witnesses that the word received was the mind and will and voice of the Lord. . . .

"In the days that followed the receipt of the new revelation, President Kimball and President Ezra Taft Benson—the senior and most spiritually experienced ones among us—both said, expressing the feelings of us all, that neither of them had ever experienced anything of such spiritual magnitude and power as was poured out upon the Presidency and the Twelve that day in the upper room in the house of the Lord."[19]

What conclusions can be drawn from the evidence presented here? Numerous revelations given to the Lord's servants in the modern era can be documented. Although most of the examples cited in this study have involved General Authorities, there have been instances of divine guidance to individuals in other callings as well. These revelations have blessed a variety of Church activities—calls to office, temple service, missionary work, the Welfare and Lamanite programs, and many more. Most of these revelations came by inspiration rather than through such spectacular means as personal visitations or visions. Interestingly and significantly, inspiration is likewise the source of most revelations recorded in the Doctrine and Covenants. Some might argue that the examples of divine guidance cited in this paper are not that unique — that many other similar manifestations have been experienced by any number of Church members. Such a contention simply confirms that the Lord guides and strengthens his Church today as much as in any former time.

NOTES

1. Spencer W. Kimball, in Conference Report, Oct. 1966, pp. 23, 25–26; see also *Ensign*, May 1977, pp. 76–78; *Journal of Discourses* (London: Latter-day Saints' Book Depot, 1854–86), 1:133; *Deseret News*, Nov. 7, 1891; Doctrine and Covenants, p. 292; *Journal of Discourses*, 26:64.

2. David O. McKay, *Cherished Experiences from the Writings of President David O. McKay*, comp. Clare Middlemiss (Salt Lake City: Deseret Book Co., 1955), p. 14.

3. Francis M. Gibbons, *Heber J. Grant: Man of Steel, Prophet of God* (Salt Lake City: Deseret Book Co., 1979), p. 175.

4. Harold B. Lee, in Conference Report, Apr. 1952, pp. 126–27.

5. See Robert E. Wells, in *Brigham Young University Speeches of the Year, 1982* (Provo, Utah: Brigham Young University Press, 1983), pp. 173–74.

6. Harold W. Burton and W. Aird Macdonald, "The Oakland Temple," *Improvement Era*, 67 (May 1964): 380.

7. Allie Howe, "A Temple in the South Pacific," *Improvement Era*, 58 (November 1955): 811–13; see also Wendell B. Mendenhall, in Conference Report, Apr. 1955, p. 5.

8. *[BYU] Daily Universe*, 28 Oct. 1986, p. 7, and 10 Nov. 1986, p. 6.

9. McKay, *Cherished Experiences*, p. 56.

10. Ibid., pp. 80–83.

11. William E. Berrett, "A General History of Weekday Religious Education," CES Archives, Salt Lake City, pp. 103–9.

12. In *Church News*, 26 Aug. 1961, p. 8.

13. Norman G. Seibold, interviewed by David F. Boone, as quoted in Richard O. Cowan, *The Church in the Twentieth Century* (Salt Lake City: Bookcraft, 1985), p. 179.

14. Frederick W. Babbel, *On Wings of Faith* (Salt Lake City: Bookcraft, 1972), p. 132.

15. Glen L. Rudd, in *Brigham Young University Speeches of the Year, 1987–88* (Provo, Utah: Brigham Young University Press, 1988), p. 99.

16. Robert L. Simpson, *The Lord Is Mindful of His Own*, Brigham Young University Speeches of the Year (Provo, 4 Apr. 1962), pp. 9–10.

17. In *Church News*, 19 Feb. 1977, p. 3.

18. In *Church News*, 6 Jan. 1979, p. 4.

19. Bruce R. McConkie, "The New Revelation," *Priesthood* (Salt Lake City: Deseret Book Co., 1981), p. 128.

8

"EXALT NOT YOURSELVES": THE REVELATIONS AND THOMAS MARSH, AN OBJECT LESSON FOR OUR DAY

Ronald K. Esplin

Brigham Young University

Our purpose here is to understand the historical setting for several revelations related to the Quorum of the Twelve Apostles in 1837 and 1838, most notably Doctrine and Covenants 112, but also 114, 118, and the very short 126 (dated July 1841); and, aided by that understanding, better understand the revelations. At the same time, in the spirit of Nephi, who "did liken all scriptures unto us, that it might be for our profit and learning" (1 Nephi 19:23), we will see the relevance for today of inspired counsel from the 1830s. Reviewing how Thomas Marsh responded to challenges and adversity provides profitable reminders for the conduct of our own lives.

What follows is a chapter in the early history of the Quorum of the Twelve Apostles that transpired before Joseph Smith, in 1841, formally invited them to take their place next to the First Presidency in governing the whole Church. Before that, especially in Kirtland, the Twelve had neither prominence nor precedence (over, for example, the Kirtland High Council), though revelation and inspired counsel from the beginning made clear that this was their potential. This lack of status or formal authority within organized stakes rankled some and contributed to misunderstandings and disharmony, but in retrospect we can see it as an important period of testing and preparation before greater responsibility was given to the Twelve. In Doctrine and Covenants 112, which we will examine in detail, the Lord says of the Twelve specifically that "after their temptations and much tribulation, behold, I, the Lord, will feel after them," *if* they harden not their hearts (D&C 112:13). Their history provides a specific example of the general principle that "after much tribulation come the blessings" (D&C 58:4; see also 103:12; Ether 12:6).

On Sunday, 6 September 1857, in Salt Lake City, Thomas B. Marsh, who had been called in 1835 as an apostle and as president of the first Quorum of the Twelve Apostles, stood before the Saints for the first time in nearly two decades. A broken man, a shadow of his former self, he felt acutely the pain of opportunities and blessings irretrievably lost. Among lost blessings was his health. A once vigorous man, Marsh now referred to himself as old and infirm, and so he appeared—a dramatic illustration of the toll of apostasy and disobedience. Standing comparatively young and robust, President Young cheerfully pointed out that Thomas was his senior by less than two years. For his part Marsh acknowledged faults that led him first to jealousy and anger and finally to apostasy, which brought only misery and affliction.[1] Four months earlier he had confessed to Heber C. Kimball:

"I have sined against Heaven and in thy sight. . . . I deserve no place . . . in the church even as the lowest member; but I cannot live long . . . without a reconciliation with the 12 and the Church whom I have injured O Bretheren once Bretheren!! How can I leave this world without your forgiveness Can I have it Can I have it? Something seems to say within yes. . . . can you speak one word of comfort to me. . . . Can I find peace among you?"[2]

What he sought now, and what the audience voted unanimously to extend, was not office or position but simply fellowship with the Saints. In the 1830s, he had aspired to much more.

When the Quorum of the Twelve Apostles was organized in February 1835, Thomas B. Marsh became president because he was the eldest of those selected, though seniority thereafter would be determined by date of ordination, not age. A member since 1830, when the Church was still in New York, and an effective missionary, Marsh appeared to be a reasonable choice to head the new quorum. David Whitmer had baptized him, Oliver Cowdery had ordained him an elder, he was one of the first to receive the high priesthood in 1831, and in 1834 he became a member of the first high council organized in Zion, or Missouri. An 1831 revelation declared that he would be "a physician unto the church" (D&C 31:10).

But there were also warning signs, or at least foreshadowings, of possible trouble. The Quorum of the Twelve was uniquely charged to carry the gospel to all the world, and from the Church's beginning, members looked toward the day they could begin that work abroad by preaching in England, yet the same 1831 revelation that named Marsh a "physician unto the church" warned that he could not be a physician "unto the world, for they will not receive you" (v. 10). Furthermore, an impressive charge to the new apostles in February 1835, delivered by Oliver Cowdery in Kirtland before Marsh had arrived from Missouri, stressed the need for brotherhood and unity within the Twelve and warned the apostles to cultivate humility, beware of pride, and give all credit to God. Rather than playing to natural strengths, these requirements challenged Marsh where he was weakest, for he tended toward an overblown concern about appearances and position and toward officiousness. The 1831 revelation concerning him had ended with a warning and a promise. "Pray always, lest you enter into temptation and lose your reward," Marsh was told, but "be faithful unto the end, and lo, I am with you" (D&C 31:12–13).

Members of a new quorum with scriptural precedents but without institutional memory or living example to rely on, the apostles at first struggled to understand their proper role and to develop effective ways of working together as a quorum and in harmony with other leaders. In preparation for their first mission—again even before Marsh had arrived from Missouri—Joseph instructed them by counsel and by revelation. In March 1835, feeling unprepared and unworthy, they had petitioned the Prophet to "inquire of God for us, and obtain a revelation, (if consistent) that our hearts may be comforted."[3] The significant revelation "On Priesthood" (D&C 107) was the result. Among its instructions was the declaration that the Quorum of the Twelve Apostles "form a quorum equal in authority and power" to the presidency of the Church—but only when they are united and in harmony as a quorum—along with a reminder, accompanied with a promise, that relationships within the quorum must be characterized by "lowliness of heart, meekness and long suffering, and . . . temperance, patience, godliness, brotherly kindness and charity" (D&C 107:4, 30). Despite such guidelines, only with time and experience could these men learn in detail what it meant to be apostles. In the meantime, understandably, they would occasionally grope and stumble.

As it turned out, both inexperience and personality made it difficult for Thomas Marsh to lead the new quorum effectively. In terms later used by Joseph Smith in writing about priesthood leadership, too easily do pride, vain ambition, even compulsion enter into relationships that should be based only on persuasion, long-suffering, gentleness, meekness, and love unfeigned (see D&C 121:37, 41). For Thomas Marsh and others like him—young men in a young church, uneducated, inexperienced as leaders—the style demanded by such principles remained a distant ideal. Faced with opportunities for growth and improvement, for the moment Marsh was part of the committed but struggling generation in Missouri whose "jarrings, and contentions, and envyings, and strifes, and lustful and covetous desires," in the words of revelation, brought them into difficulties (D&C 101:6). Here, clearly, was a man of ability. But it was less clear that he would learn to govern his feelings enough to reach his potential or learn to meet challenges and snubs with patience and love rather than "jarrings and strife."

The new apostles spent that summer of 1835 traveling together in the East on their first (and only) missionary undertaking under President Marsh as a full quorum. With pointed counsel and revelation vividly in mind, they conscientiously labored to carry out their commission, and the result was a successful mission. But that fall they returned home not to accolades but to accusations, and these they handled much less well. What should have been minor difficulties arising from affronts or simple miscommunication aroused intense feelings, and soon the new Quorum of the Twelve found itself immersed in charges and countercharges with the First Presidency, concerns about position and precedence with the High Council, and divisive complaints among its own members.[4]

President Marsh generally met these challenges in a manner that stressed rights, justice, and his (or his quorum's) prerogatives more than brotherhood or humble submission to counsel. The difficulties cannot all be attributed to Marsh, of course. All were inexperienced, none yet fully understood their calling, and some others shared Marsh's unfortunate focus on potential authority and prestige greater than the actual. Moreover, Joseph Smith ruffled the feelings of his sensitive apostles as often as he soothed them. Whether this was a conscious ploy to teach that humility and service must precede authority, as Brigham Young came to believe, or simply a consequence of his own style, the results were the same. Anxious to be powerful men in the kingdom, some of the apostles bristled and complained at every slight.

For the apostles and other Church leaders in Kirtland, the fall of 1835 should have been a joyful season devoted to preparing hearts and spirits for long-awaited blessings in the nearly completed Kirtland Temple. Instead, hurt feelings required that council after council be dedicated to airing complaints, soothing feelings, and generally working to reestablish brotherhood.[5] These efforts did bear fruit, however, and as far as records reveal, by November comparative harmony seemed to prevail. Then, without clarifying explanation, on 3 November the Prophet recorded in his diary the following: "Thus came the word of the Lord unto me concerning the Twelve [saying] behold they are under condemnation, because they have not been sufficiently humble in my sight, and in consequence of their covetous desires, in that they have not dealt equally with each other." The revelation named several of the apostles as offenders and then concluded that "all must humble themselves before me, before they will be accounted worthy to receive an endowment."[6]

Understandably this caused a stir among the apostles. The only other revelation addressing them specifically had been the great revelation "On Priesthood," and now, only months later, this. Records do not preserve President Marsh's response to this chastisement, though we can surmise that he took it personally and was not pleased, but Joseph did record that Elders Hyde and McLellin, two of those named, stopped by to express "some little dissatisfaction." Brigham Young, on the other hand, "appeared perfectly satisfied" with the chastisement.[7] Perhaps he felt no need to take it personally or, if he did, remembered the inspired counsel of the June 1833 revelation that became Doctrine and Covenants 95: "Whom I love I also chasten that their sins may be forgiven, for with the chastisement I prepare a way for their deliverance in all things out of temptation" (D&C 95:1).

No doubt Brigham Young also recognized the justice of the rebuke. Not only had the apostles clashed with other church officials but they had also experienced disunity, jealousy, and pettiness within their own quorum. Years later Young characterized the Kirtland Twelve as "continually sparring at each other." To illustrate, he told of once being summoned to answer for having accepted an invitation to preach. By what authority, demanded his fellow apostles, had he "presumed to appoint a meeting and preach" without consulting them? Under Thomas Marsh the Twelve met very often, Young continued, "and if no one of them needed cleaning, they had to 'clean' some one any how."[8] On another occasion President Young contrasted his own style as president, trying to be a father to all, with President Marsh's: "like a toad's hair comb[ing] up and down."[9]

There is no doubt that the personality of Thomas Marsh contributed to the pettiness and self-concern that plagued his quorum. Concerned about prerogatives, his leadership could be intrusive and officious. He was also impatient with criticism and tended to view a difference of opinion or even initiative by others as a challenge to his leadership. And he was impatient about the status of the Twelve in Kirtland. According to Brigham Young, he was among those who, when Joseph "snubbed" the apostles, exclaimed, "We are apostles[!] it's an insult for us to be so treated."[10] Brigham, on the other hand, came to see the snubbing, the trials, in a way Thomas never did: as a testing, a necessary preparation, before they were ready for power. This he once explained to his president when Marsh complained of their treatment. "If we are faithful," insisted Brigham Young, "we shall

see the day . . . that we will have all the power we shall know how
to wield before God."[11]

Although it took until January 1836, the apostles eventually settled
important differences and came to enjoy both increased unity within
their quorum and general harmony with other leaders. Thus prepared,
they shared with other Kirtland Saints the extraordinary blessings and
manifestations associated with the Kirtland Temple in early 1836.

But for the Quorum of the Twelve, unity, harmony, and new
spiritual strength did not last. Instead of moving as a quorum to Missouri, as earlier contemplated once the temple was finished, Joseph
Smith announced that they were now free to move or not, as they
chose; and instead of another quorum mission, he suggested that each
was free to preach where he would—though each understood his duty
to take the gospel abroad as soon as possible. Thomas Marsh and David
Patten, the two senior apostles, returned to Missouri, whereas most of
the others continued to call Kirtland home. Within a year the Twelve
would be as divided spiritually as they were geographically.

In 1837 dissension and rebellion swept the Church, especially
among the leaders. Although most retained faith in the Book of Mormon and believed in the necessity of restored authority, not everyone
shared the Prophet's enthusiasm for the "ancient order of things." To
some a society modeled after ancient Israel, where prophetic authority
directed all aspects of life (not just the religious), portended a reduction
in cherished social and economic freedoms. Too "Papist," they declared, too "un-American." Those concerns underlay the discontent
of many who ostensibly blamed Joseph for "meddling" in the Kirtland
Bank, which ultimately failed, or who had other complaints against
his conduct of economic or civic affairs.[12] While most members trusted
the Prophet and continued to remain loyal even if they did not yet
fully understand his vision, a rift developed between Joseph and many
leaders, including some in the presidency and in the Twelve, who were
certain they understood more, or at least better, than he did. Of the
apostles in Kirtland, only Brigham Young and Heber Kimball expressed
unwavering support for Joseph Smith and his program.

When news of the rebellion reached President Marsh in Missouri,
he was appalled. Word that several of his own quorum members were
prominent among dissenters especially humiliated him. He had envisioned leading a united quorum abroad to introduce the gospel to
Great Britain, and now this. He was also distressed to learn that an
impatient Parley Pratt (and perhaps others) intended to leave on a
foreign mission without him. Hurt, angry, and determined, Marsh
hoped to "right-up" the Twelve and reestablish himself as an effective

leader by holding a dramatic meeting with his quorum in Kirtland in which he would interject himself vigorously into the fray on the side of the Prophet. On 10 May he and Elder Patten dispatched an urgent letter to Parley Pratt, advising him not to depart for England:

"The 12 must get together difficulties must be removed & love restored, we must have peace within before we can wage a successful war without. . . . shall the 12 apostles of the Lambe be a disorganised body pulling different ways, Shall one [go] to his plough another to his merchandise, another to England &c. No! I even I Thomas will step in (if their is none other for it is my right in this case) and give council to you."[13]

The letter appointed 24 July for an extraordinary council "to break through every obstacle" and prepare for their mission abroad.

Since at least February 1837, Kirtland apostles had spoken of a summer mission to England; Parley Pratt was not alone in this. But amid dissension and the continuing absence of President Marsh, the mission appeared doubtful. Heber Kimball was thus shocked when the Prophet told him in early June that "for the salvation of His church" the mission must go forth without delay and that he must head it.[14] Joseph needed Brigham Young in Kirtland, he insisted, Parley had joined the others in rebellion, and they could not wait for Marsh and Patten. Begging forgiveness, Orson Hyde sought reconciliation the very day Kimball was set apart for his mission and requested permission to accompany him. Thus it was that Elders Kimball and Hyde, not Marsh and Patten, left Kirtland 13 June to open the work abroad.[15]

A few days later, after Brigham Young tried but failed to reconcile him with Joseph, Parley Pratt suddenly departed for Missouri. Providentially, Parley encountered Marsh and Patten en route and they succeeded (where Brigham had not) in turning him around.

As soon as they reached Kirtland, Brigham Young briefed Elders Marsh and Patten on the perplexing problems. Marsh then went directly to Joseph's home — his headquarters during his Kirtland stay — and set to work reconciling the disaffected. (David Patten, meanwhile, visited first the dissenters and, according to Brigham, "got his mind prejudiced," and insulted Joseph. The Prophet reacted strongly to the affront, which, in Young's view, "done David good," and quickly returned him to his senses.)[16] The Prophet arranged a special meeting at his home for several of the prominent malcontents, no doubt including apostles. Marsh "moderated" and, he reported later, "a reconciliation was effected between all parties."[17] Without question President Marsh contributed to the healing and reconciliation in Kirtland that summer. He labored with the "merchant apostles," Lyman Johnson and John

Boynton, and with Constable Luke Johnson. Following his arrival, Elders Orson Pratt and Parley Pratt, among others, made public confessions and expressions of support for Joseph. Although neither Marsh nor the Prophet swept away the basic differences in outlook that had brought dissent, as president of the Twelve Marsh was able to return a modicum of civility and unity to his quorum. An early departure for England seemed out of the question, however, and there is no evidence that Marsh convened the "extraordinary meeting" he had earlier proposed for 24 July.

Despite modest success, President Marsh was still troubled— troubled that members of his quorum had rebelled and troubled also that missionary work abroad was proceeding without him. Concerned about his own status and wondering if the Lord could still accept the Twelve, he went to Joseph on 23 July, the day before his extraordinary council would have been held, to discuss his concerns. That evening the Prophet dictated as Thomas wrote "the word of the Lord unto Thomas B. Marsh, concerning the Twelve Apostles of the Lamb" (headnote to D&C 112).

The revelation acknowledged Marsh's prayerful concern for his quorum and counseled him to continue to pray for them and, as needed, to admonish them sharply, for "after their temptations, and much tribulation . . . I will feel after them, and if they harden not their hearts . . . they shall be converted, and I will heal them" (v. 13). It admonished the Twelve—"Exalt not yourselves; rebel not against my servant Joseph" (v. 15)—and counseled Marsh to be more faithful and humble, at the same time reaffirming his position as president of the Twelve. The revelation also approved Marsh's residence in Missouri where he worked with the printing office, "for I, the Lord, have a great work for thee to do, in publishing my name among the children of men" (v. 6).

With that background, we are now ready to closely examine Doctrine and Covenants 112, given on 23 July 1837 for Thomas Marsh and the Twelve, noting how it applied to them and how it might apply to us.

"I have heard thy prayers," says verse 1, " . . . in behalf of those, thy brethren, . . . chosen to bear testimony . . . abroad," men who were "ordained through the instrumentality of my servants." Though we are not of their quorum, this passage describes a duty common to many priesthood holders, especially missionaries.

In verse 2 President Marsh is told that "there have been some few things in thine heart and with thee" with which the Lord is not pleased. Again, this is something that applies to us all.

Verse 3 tells Marsh that "inasmuch as thou hast abased thyself," he can still be exalted and that his sins are forgiven. (*Abase* means to humble, a universal requirement for forgiveness and reconciliation.)

So, in verse 4, President Marsh is told to let his heart be of good cheer and — now this was what he was *really* concerned about — "thou shalt [yet or still, despite all the problems] bear record of my name" and "send forth my word unto the ends of the earth." Even though Elders Kimball and Hyde had departed, Thomas Marsh might yet have his day.

Therefore, says verse 5, "Contend thou, therefore, morning by morning; and day after day let thy warning voice go forth." A good description of what we all should be about.

More specifically, verse 6 says that President Marsh is not to move his household from Missouri, for from there, as printer, he is to publish the word abroad.

Verse 7 warns Marsh to engage himself in the work, to gird up his loins and to "*let thy feet be shod also,* for thou art chosen" to do this work. Where? "Among the mountains" (a hint of the Rocky Mountains?[18]) and "many nations" (which because of apostasy he failed to fulfill).

Verses 8 and 9 indicate that Marsh's word will bring down the exalted and exalt the lowly and that he will rebuke the transgressor. Priesthood leaders generally share this responsibility to rebuke when so inspired. Given the history of his quorum, one might conclude that these two verses apply to counseling his brethren, but because a reminder about that specific responsibility begins with verse 12, this reference appears to be more general.

Verse 10 preserves one of the great promises in scripture, one that surely can be adopted as a general principle and applied to all: "Be thou humble, and the Lord thy God shall lead thee by the hand, and give thee answer to thy prayers." This and related scriptural promises (see, for example, Romans 8:28 and D&C 90:24) all include qualifications. To claim the promised blessings, we must be humble, faithful, love God, and honor his commandments. Ultimately with us, as with President Marsh, worthiness determines whether we can claim the promise.

Verses 11 through 14 contain pleadings and admonitions for the Twelve. Here the Lord tells President Marsh that he knows his heart and has heard his prayers for his brethren. As president it is his right and duty to be concerned, of course, and to express and extend love, but the Lord reminds him that he should equally love "all men," especially "all who love my name" (v. 11). Again, though we may each have specific responsibilities, beyond that, we must learn to love all men.

Marsh should, of course, continue to "pray for thy brethren of the Twelve" and "admonish them sharply" for their sins. But likewise (harking back to verse 2, where he is reproved), he is told: "Be ye faithful before me" (v. 12; emphasis added).

Reprove them as required, Marsh is told, for "after their temptations, and much tribulation," there is still a promise: "I, the Lord, will feel after them, and if they harden not their hearts, and stiffen not their necks against me, they shall be converted, and I will heal them" (v. 13). Note that even though they were apostles, these men— young, inexperienced, in transgression—needed anew to be converted. Similarly, we should search our own hearts about where we stand. When we find ourselves stumbling or kicking against the pricks, this verse reminds us of the way back.

The passage concludes with this counsel to President Marsh, counsel that "I say unto all the Twelve" (and to us): "Gird up your loins, take up your cross, follow me, and feed my sheep" (v. 14). For the Twelve in 1837, this charge specifically meant that they should prepare to take the gospel abroad to His sheep in other lands.

Then follows, in verses 15 through 22, counsel clarifying the roles and duties of the First Presidency and the Twelve. After President Marsh specifically had been warned in verse 10 to be humble, here all the members of the Twelve are told: "Exalt not yourselves." The warning was not against "general" pride alone but against a tendency to place themselves above their leaders: "Rebel not against my servant Joseph; for verily I say unto you, I am with him." We can now understand why that was essential counsel to them at that time—as well as a reminder for us. Verse 15 goes on to clarify, as do earlier revelations, that while both the First Presidency and the Twelve have keys, the Prophet Joseph is the head: "My hand shall be over him," and his keys "shall not be taken from him till I come" (v. 15).

Verses 16 and 17 are at the heart of what weighed heavily on President Marsh's mind when he approached the Prophet seeking the word of the Lord: "Verily I say unto you, my servant Thomas, thou art the man whom I have chosen to hold the keys of my kingdom, as pertaining to the Twelve [still, despite the difficulties], abroad among all nations" (even in England!) and "to unlock the door of the kingdom in all places."

Unfortunately, instead of humbly accepting this assurance as a renewed opportunity, Thomas immediately visited Vilate Kimball and, backed by this affirmation, told her that Heber could not open an "effectual door" in England because *he*, Thomas, had not sent him! The Prophet had assured him, Marsh explained, that since proclaiming the gospel abroad was his special responsibility, the door could not be "effectually" opened until *he* sent someone or went himself.

In pressing this point, Thomas Marsh once again missed the mark, as the revelation itself makes clear. That very verse continued: Marsh held the keys "to unlock the door of the kingdom in all places *where my servant Joseph*" and his counselors, i.e., the First Presidency, "cannot come"; and, said verse 18, "*On them* have I laid the burden of *all* the churches for a little season." "Wherefore, whithersoever they shall send you [or Heber Kimball and Orson Hyde or *whomever*], go ye, and I will be with you; and in whatsoever place ye shall proclaim my name an effectual door shall be opened unto you, that they may receive my word" (v. 19; emphasis added). Stated again: the Prophet's keys held precedence even over those of the president of the Quorum of the Twelve.

Heber understood that principle. When he learned in England of Marsh's claim, he was philosophical, allowing that "Brother Joseph sed it was all right to prepare the way . . . so we have come to prepare the way before Brother Thomas. And we have baptised a good lot of them."[19] Even so, he added, Brother Marsh would have to do some of the work himself if he intended to claim some of the credit.

As if that were not clear enough, and apparently it was not for Marsh, verse 20 tries still again to clarify: who receives my word receives me, who receives me receives the First Presidency, "whom I have sent, whom I have made counselors . . . unto you." Others also have power—especially the Twelve with their special calling and responsibility to take the gospel abroad—but it is all under the Presidency.

Verses 21 and 22 add: "And again, I say unto you, that whosoever ye shall send in my name *by the voice of your brethren*, the Twelve" (that is, Quorum President Marsh was not to act alone; compare to the principle of unity and unanimity in D&C 107:27ff), "shall have power to open the door . . . unto any nation whithersoever ye shall send them" (v. 21; emphasis added). Any nation? Always? "Inasmuch as they shall humble themselves . . . , and abide in my word, and hearken to the voice of my Spirit" (v. 22).

Verses 23 through 26 shift the focus. These verses warning of a day of weeping, desolation, and mourning that "cometh speedily" (v. 26) may speak of things yet to occur; certainly the principles are more broadly applicable than merely Kirtland in 1837. But they also had a specific application to Kirtland, and it is that connection that we will examine.

Why will there be troubles? Because, says verse 23, "darkness covereth the earth, and gross darkness the minds of the people, and all flesh has become corrupt." (That sounds like a description of today.) *Where* will there be troubles? "Upon my house shall it begin, and from my house shall it go forth" (v. 25). *Who* will suffer? Those who "have professed to know my name and have not known me, and have blasphemed against me in the midst of my house" (v. 26). Surely some of the wayward apostles, soon to be cut off, could be among that number. Why "my house?" Already there had been difficulties and soon there would be riots, disorder, and blasphemy *in the temple* in Kirtland, and perpetrators would include John Boynton, apostle, and Warren Parrish, recently Joseph Smith's private secretary.

"Therefore" — therefore what? Therefore the Twelve should labor at home where the problems are and try to straighten things up? No! Verses 27 and 28 tell the apostles: "Therefore, see to it that ye trouble not yourselves concerning the affairs of my church in this place, saith the Lord" but rather purify *your hearts* and then go about *your* labor, which is, of course, to take the gospel to all the world.

The message seems to be that the Lord himself can care for his house and, moreover, as verses 28 through 33 suggest, what can be more important for the Twelve than to preach divine truth with power and authority? They are to preach to every creature who has not received the gospel, either to their damnation or to their salvation, for "unto you, the Twelve, and those, the First Presidency, who are appointed with you to be your counselors and your leaders [again the emphasis on order, everyone under the First Presidency], is the power of this priesthood given, for the last days and for the last time" (v. 30). These are the same keys which "have come down from the fathers" (v. 32), and "Verily . . . behold how great is your calling" (v. 33).

So great is the calling that they — and we — must cleanse themselves and do their duty "lest the blood of this generation be required at your hands" (v. 33). But, and the revelation closes with this in verse 34, for the faithful, the Lord says, the "reward is with me to recompense every man according as his work shall be."

Despite the best efforts of Joseph, Sidney, Thomas, David, and Brigham, the Church could not be saved in Kirtland. Up to this point, the Prophet had patiently worked with dissenters, bringing back many, but when open rebellion broke out again in the fall of 1837, patience was no longer a virtue and backsliders were cut off. Anger mounted, division deepened, apostates grew more bold, and by year's end Brigham Young, the most vigorous and outspoken among the Prophet's defenders, was forced to flee for his life. In early January Joseph Smith and Sidney Rigdon followed, their families close behind, and by spring most of the faithful were on their way to Missouri.

Joseph Smith arrived in Far West, Missouri, in March 1838. After firming up local organization and leadership, he then set about the business begun in Kirtland of removing apostates. At the 7 April conference David Patten reviewed the status of each of the Twelve, including concerns about William Smith and his inability to recommend at all Elders McLellin, Boynton, Johnson, and Johnson. At proceedings that commenced 12 April, the four apostles, along with Oliver Cowdery and David Whitmer, were each formally tried and cut off. After months of concern and labor with his quorum, Thomas's twelve were now eight, and one of those could not be relied upon. Feeling deep concern for their quorum, no doubt Marsh and the remaining apostles were cheered by a revelation for David Patten received 7 April.

In Doctrine and Covenants 114, given 7 April 1838, verse 1 advised Patten to prepare himself to "perform a mission unto me next spring, in company with others, even twelve including himself, to testify of my name and bear glad tidings unto all the world." What twelve, including himself? There were no longer twelve apostles in his quorum, nor had any ever been added since its organization more than three years before. Verse 2 supplied the answer: "For verily . . . inasmuch as there are those among you who deny my name, others shall be planted in their stead" and receive their reward. By noting that fallen brethren would be replaced and commanding Elder Patten to prepare, after all, for a mission "with others, even twelve," this short revelation foreshadows several of the key points made more explicitly three months later.

On 8 July, in answer to the query "Show us thy will, O Lord, concerning the Twelve" (headnote), another revelation, now Doctrine and Covenants 118, imparted firm direction and new life to the Quorum of the Twelve. "Let men be appointed to supply the place of those who are fallen," declared the revelation (v. 1), which concluded by naming John Taylor, John E. Page, Wilford Woodruff, and Willard Richards to the Twelve. Thomas Marsh was to "remain for a season in the land of Zion," where he was now coeditor with Joseph of the *Elder's Journal*, "to publish my word" (v. 2). The others were to resume preaching and, as a quorum, prepare for a spring 1839 mission abroad. They would depart, continued the revelation, from the Far West temple site on 26 April, the very day an earlier revelation (see D&C 115) had named for laying the temple cornerstone.

Verse 1 of Doctrine and Covenants 118, given 8 July 1838,

announced: "Let a conference be held immediately; let the Twelve be organized; and let men be appointed to supply the place of those who have fallen."

Verse 2 then authorized President Marsh to remain in Far West, Missouri, "for a season." This was not a choice between Kirtland and Missouri, as before in Doctrine and Covenants 112, but between staying for a time in Far West and going abroad immediately. Verse 3 instructed "the residue," the other apostles who had remained faithful or who had returned to full fellowship, to "continue to preach from that hour." It promised that if they would do this "in all lowliness of heart, in meekness and humility, and long-suffering," they could still fulfill their divine mission (that is, despite disaster and division they had not yet lost the possibility of fulfilling their destiny) "and an *effectual door* shall be opened for them, from henceforth" (emphasis added; compare D&C 112:19).

Moreover, if they were thus faithful they had another promise, that while they were serving abroad, "I will provide for their families" (v. 3).

Verses 4 and 5 instructed that "next spring let them [the residue and the new] depart to go over the great waters, and there promulgate my gospel [in Britain]. . . . Let them take leave of my saints in the city of Far West, on the twenty-sixth day of April next, on the building-spot of my house, saith the Lord."

The revelation closed, with verse 6, by naming those "appointed to fill the places of those who have fallen": John Taylor, John E. Page, Wilford Woodruff, and Willard Richards.

The following day, the apostles, for the first time in months, held a formal quorum meeting. They agreed to notify immediately the four new apostles, none of whom were in Far West, and to prepare for their mission abroad. The anticipated ordination of new apostles, the return from England later in the month of Elders Kimball and Hyde, and this renewal of their commission to carry the gospel to the nations seemed to portend a new day for Marsh's shattered quorum. The command had been given, the date was known: finally President Marsh would have the opportunity to lead his colleagues abroad.

But it was not to be. Before the spring mission, indeed even before existing vacancies could be filled, there would be two more, one when David Patten was killed during the violence that soon erupted in northern Missouri, and the other caused by the disaffection of President Marsh himself, also in some ways a by-product of that same Missouri conflict.

Marsh's disillusionment and decision to leave the Church were the result of many factors, having to do with pride, misunderstanding, hurt feelings, suspicion, and, in Marsh's own later words, stubbornness and a loss of the Spirit.[20] Troubled of mind and spirit, feeling himself wavering, he humbled himself before the Lord in his printing shop long enough to receive a revelation about what course he should take. After sharing it with Heber Kimball and Brigham Young, he promptly went out and did the opposite. Once his face was set, the stubborn, inflexible Thomas was not a man who could be turned. By removing himself from the Saints he escaped the violence that soon decimated Far West and drove his coreligionists from Missouri, but at what cost? As he eventually came to acknowledge, his loss was the greater.

From Liberty Jail, the Prophet named George A. Smith to fill the vacancy created by the death of Elder Patten, but Marsh's position remained vacant for nearly three years. In the meantime, under the direction of President Brigham Young, now senior apostle, the available apostles—William Smith was not to be found, Parley Pratt was in prison, Willard Richards was in England—boldly returned to Missouri, whence they had so recently escaped, to fulfill the July 1838 revelation (D&C 118) requiring them to depart 26 April 1839 from "the building-spot of my house" in Far West.

Enemies had boasted that the revelation proved Joseph Smith a false prophet because it could not be fulfilled. So certain were they that no one would attempt it that they did not even bother to post a guard. Perhaps, under the circumstances, the Lord would "take the will for the deed," some Latter-day Saints urged, but Brigham Young and his associates would not allow even supposed failure to stand as a witness against Joseph. In the predawn hours they and a small group of Saints sang hymns, ordained two apostles, laid a symbolic corner-stone, excommunicated dissidents, and departed before the first sur-prised anti-Mormon reached the site.

From Far West the apostles returned to the new city abuilding in Illinois on the banks of the Mississippi to complete their preparations and to situate their families as well as possible before departing. Instead of keeping them at arm's length as had often been the case in Kirtland, Joseph Smith embraced them, instructed them, blessed them, and participated fully in their preparations. No one, however, had means to help their families. Destitute after the Missouri tragedy, without adequate shelter or provisions, everyone suffered—the more so when summer diseases befell them in the damp, sickly hollows along the river. Consequently, it was a great test of faith to leave their families in such circumstances in order to fulfill their mission. Because they understood that the Church could provide little help, essentially they left their families in the hands of God to embark on a mission that could not be postponed and which would eventually transform the Church. The apostles did not forget that the revelation commanding their departure also declared: "I . . . give unto them a promise that I will provide for their families" (D&C 118:3). As Brigham Young wrote to his wife from England, though he longed to be able to administer to their needs, he had faith enough not to be unduly concerned, "for the Lord said by the mouth of Brother Joseph, that they should be provided for, and I believed it."[21]

The result of this sacrifice, of obedience in difficult circumstances, and of diligent efforts to labor together with unity and harmony was perhaps the most successful single mission in the history of the Church. As Elder Jeffrey R. Holland noted after reading a recent book on the subject, after this mission, "neither this group of men, the British Isles, nor the Church would ever be the same again."[22] Finally the Twelve had fulfilled the promise inherent in their calling that had so eluded them during the years under President Marsh.

The rewards for service are many and often individualized. No doubt each of the apostles received assurances and blessings fitted to his needs, as suggested by Doctrine and Covenants 82:10: "I, the Lord, am bound when ye do what I say; but when ye do not what I say, ye have no promise." Doctrine and Covenants 126, the last section in our story, simply preserves one example: the knowledge that service is acceptable to the Lord: "My servant Brigham," began the revelation, given 9 July 1841, "it is no more required at your hand to leave your family as in times past, for your offering is acceptable to me." Verse 2 affirmed that "I have seen your labor and toil . . . for my name" and, verse 3: "I therefore command you to send my word abroad [from now on send, rather than take it], and take especial care of your family."

Under Brigham Young, the "new" Quorum of the Twelve proved competent and fiercely loyal to Joseph and his principles and rendered extraordinary service at great sacrifice. After shared experiences in Britain molded this new quorum into an effective, united body of power, they returned home at a time when the Prophet's needs for loyal assistance had multiplied. The result, announced by Joseph Smith on 16 August 1841, was a significant realignment of assignment and au-thority, with the Twelve taking their place next to the First Presidency in managing all Church affairs. The ambiguity between the high coun-cils and the Twelve that had so vexed Thomas Marsh and the apostles in Kirtland was over. The apostles had completed their preparation and the Prophet judged them, to use Brigham Young's phrase, "fit for power." What Thomas Marsh had dreamed of was now reality.

Throughout his service as president of the Twelve, Thomas Marsh had thought it his special mission to lead his quorum in taking the gospel abroad, and the July 1838 revelation (D&C 118), a few months before his apostasy, reaffirmed that mission. His 1857 letter to Heber Kimball pleading for readmission revealed that nineteen years later he still remembered: "I know what I have done a mision was laid upon me & I have never filled it and now I fear it is too late but it is filled by another, I see, the Lord could get along very well without me and He has lost nothing by my falling out of the ranks; But O what have I lost?"[23]

Had Thomas B. Marsh remained faithful in 1838, he would have led the Quorum of the Twelve to England instead of Brigham Young and he would have presided over the "new quorum" and the "new role"—the one he had so impatiently longed for—that resulted from that mission. All this occurred, instead, without him.

NOTES

1. Brigham Young and Thomas B. Marsh, in *Journal of Discourses* (London: Latter-day Saints' Book Depot, 1854–86), 5:206–10.

2. Thomas B. Marsh to Heber C. Kimball, 5 May 1857, Heber C. Kimball Papers, Archives, The Church of Jesus Christ of Latter-day Saints, Salt Lake City, Utah; hereafter cited as LDS Church Archives.

3. Minutes, 28 Mar. 1835, Kirtland Record Book, p. 198, LDS Church Archives.

4. See Ronald K. Esplin, "The Emergence of Brigham Young and the Twelve to Mormon Leadership, 1830–1841," Ph.D. diss., Brigham Young University, 1981, pp. 166ff.

5. For details, see Esplin, "Emergence of Brigham Young," chap. 4.

6. Joseph Smith Diary, 3 Nov. 1835, in Dean C. Jessee, ed., *The Papers of Joseph Smith* (Salt Lake City: Deseret Book Co., 1992), 2:63–64.

7. Joseph Smith Diary, 5 Nov. 1835, in Jessee, *Papers of Joseph Smith*, 2:65–66.

8. Historian's Office Journal, 16 Feb. 1859, LDS Church Archives.

9. Minutes, 12 Feb. 1849, LDS Church Archives.

10. Minutes, 30 Nov. 1847, Brigham Young Papers, LDS Church Archives.

11. Brigham Young, in *Journal of Discourses*, 8:197.

12. For details of the Kirtland crisis, see Esplin, "Emergence of Brigham Young," chaps. 5–7, and Milton V. Backman, Jr., *The Heavens Resound: A History of the Latter-day Saints in Ohio, 1830–1838* (Salt Lake City: Deseret Book Co., 1983), chaps. 17–18; details not otherwise documented are from Esplin, "Emergence of Brigham Young."

13. Thomas B. Marsh and David Patten to Parley P. Pratt, 10 May 1837, Joseph Smith letterbook, Joseph Smith Papers, LDS Church Archives.

14. Joseph Smith, *History of The Church of Jesus Christ of Latter-day Saints*,

2d ed. rev., edited by B. H. Roberts (Salt Lake City: The Church of Jesus Christ of Latter-day Saints, 1932–51), 2:489.

15. The story of Kimball's call and of the Kimball-Hyde mission is told in James B. Allen, Ronald K. Esplin, and David J. Whittaker, *Men with a Mission: The Quorum of the Twelve Apostles in the British Isles, 1837–1841* (Salt Lake City: Deseret Book Co., 1992), pp. 23–53.

16. Wilford Woodruff Diary, 25 June 1857, LDS Church Archives.

17. Marsh autobiography published in *Deseret News*, 24 Mar. 1858.

18. If this is the allusion, it would not necessarily be an anachronism. Discussion of and prophecies about a destiny in the Rocky Mountains can now be demonstrated long before Nauvoo.

19. Esplin, "Emergence of Brigham Young," p. 313, n. 44.

20. Ibid., pp. 339ff.

21. Brigham Young to Mary Ann Young, 16 Oct. 1840, in Allen, Esplin, and Whittaker, *Men with a Mission*, p. 399.

22. Jeffrey R. Holland to Allen, Esplin, and Whittaker, 31 July 1992.

23. Thomas B. Marsh to Heber C. Kimball, 5 May 1857, Heber C. Kimball Papers, LDS Church Archives.

9

MISSIONARY WORK: A VIEW FROM THE DOCTRINE & COVENANTS

H. Dean Garrett

Brigham Young University

The Lord declared that the message of the Restoration must be preached to every nation, kindred, tongue and people (see D&C 133:37). Every person shall hear "the fulness of the gospel in his own tongue, and in his own language, through those who are ordained unto this power" (D&C 90:11). Early Church members inquired of the Lord how they were to fulfill this commandment. Through the Prophet Joseph Smith the Lord revealed how that was to be accomplished: the Lord issued a call to preach, defined the qualifications necessary for those who preach, revealed the message to be delivered, and declared the blessings promised to those who go forth. An understanding and application of these revelations relating to missionary work can greatly aid all Church members in personally fulfilling this great responsibility.

THE CALL TO PREACH

A primary obligation of Church members is to spread the gospel message throughout the world. In one of the first revelations given in this dispensation, the Lord declared, "The field is white already to harvest" (D&C 4:4). This important declaration was repeated several times (see D&C 6; 11–12; 14–16; 33) with the decree that it is "the eleventh hour, and the last time that I shall call laborers into my vineyard" (D&C 33:3). The laborers are to "gather mine elect from the four quarters of the earth, even as many as will believe in me, and hearken unto my voice" (D&C 33:6). Thus, the laborers are called by the Lord to thrust in their sickles and "reap with all [their] might, mind, and strength" (D&C 33:7).

Although opportunities for missionary work are available to all members of the Church, Melchizedek Priesthood holders in particular are called to serve as missionaries. The Lord declared: "As many as shall come before my servants . . . shall be ordained and sent forth to preach the everlasting gospel among the nations. . . . And this commandment shall be given unto the elders of my church that every man which will embrace it with singleness of heart may be ordained and sent forth even as I have spoken" (D&C 36:5, 7). To others he commanded: "Take upon you mine ordination, even that of an elder, to preach faith and repentance and remission of sins, according to my word, and the reception of the Holy Spirit by the laying on of hands" (D&C 53:3; see also 55:2). It is evident from these scriptures that when a man receives the Melchizedek Priesthood, he accepts the responsibility to preach the restored gospel to the children of God.

The servants of God will declare the message of the Restoration "unto the Gentiles first, and then, behold, and lo, they shall turn unto the Jews" (D&C 90:9). Then eventually the gospel will be preached unto "the heathen nations" (D&C 90:10). It is under these circumstances that "every man shall hear the fulness of the gospel in his own tongue, and in his own language, through those who are ordained unto this power" (D&C 90:11).

When the first missionaries were sent forth, the means of transportation and communication were the same as in Moses' time when he dealt with Pharaoh. Transportation was on foot or by animal, and communication was by word of mouth or mail delivered on foot or by animal. At the time these revelations were received, it probably seemed almost impossible that all individuals could be taught in their own tongue or language. Now, however, we live in a day when modern transportation, satellite and television communication, and computer translation and printing capabilities make it possible for every individual in the world to hear the gospel in his own tongue. Today missionaries are trained in languages and sent to every part of the world in fulfillment of this command to spread the gospel "unto every nation, and kindred, and tongue, and people" (D&C 133:37).

One cannot be self-appointed to preach in God's kingdom. In the early stages of the Restoration, while the Book of Mormon was still being translated, Hyrum Smith wanted to go forth immediately and issue the warning voice. He was told by the Lord: "You need not suppose that you are called to preach until you are called" (D&C 11:15). In giving his law to the Church, the Lord declared: "It shall not be given to anyone to go forth to preach my gospel, or to build up my church, except he be ordained by some one who has authority" (D&C 42:11).

QUALIFICATIONS TO PREACH

The response given by the Lord when Joseph Smith, Sr., asked how He wanted him to serve in the kingdom is commonly called "the qualification for the ministry." He was told that to serve in the kingdom, the Lord's servants must have the commitment to serve God "with all [their] heart, might, mind and strength" (D&C 4:2). The Lord requires total commitment. That is the basic building block for service in the kingdom. Our allegiance to whom we serve will greatly determine how we serve. The Lord does not allow for divided allegiance. We cannot "serve two masters: for . . . [we] will hate the one, and love the other" (Matthew 6:24).

The Lord does not require total commitment because of arrogance but because he knows what is necessary to build his kingdom and to save souls. Therefore, he requires total commitment of the heart (emotional), might (spiritual), mind (intellectual), and strength (physical) of the individual. The whole soul of the individual is required if success is to be obtained.

With a commitment to serve the Lord, the objective is to "seek to bring forth and establish the cause of Zion" (D&C 11:6). We are to "seek not for riches" (D&C 6:7) but rather to build God's kingdom. Elder John A. Widtsoe observed: "From one point of view it is selfish enough, perhaps, to keep the commandments that I may be blessed, but it is something even greater to keep the commandments that Zion may be established. . . . Unless we give of ourselves we cannot build Zion, or anything else worthy of the great cause that the Lord has given us."[1]

The Lord revealed other qualifications that he desires in those who would preach his gospel to the nations of the earth. To be effective, missionaries should strive to obtain these qualities:

1. *Desire.* To qualify to serve in the kingdom of God, we must desire to serve. The Lord informed the Prophet's father, Joseph Smith, Sr., "If ye have desires to serve God ye are called to the work" (D&C 4:3). To Hyrum Smith and others the injunction was "Whoso desireth to reap let him thrust in his sickle with his might, and reap while the day lasts" (D&C 11:3; see also D&C 6; 12; 14). Desire is the beginning of our behavior. Elder Neal A. Maxwell stated: "Desire both initiates our actions and sustains us—for good or evil. If we desire wealth or power, these will tend to be the moving causes of our actions. If instead we desire spiritual things and are obedient, the promised blessings will come to us. Just as it is not possible to save an individual against his will, so blessings do not come against our wills.

"True discipleship is for volunteers only."[2] This sense of volunteerism is the heart of the kingdom of God—to serve in his kingdom, one must have the desire. God will never force. That is especially evident in missionary work.

When accepting a call to preach, we need to analyze the reason we desire to serve. Our motivation for serving is very critical. Elder Dallin H. Oaks observed six reasons that motivate service: earthly reward, good companionship, fear of punishment, duty or loyalty, hope of reward, and charity. He suggested that charity, the pure love of Christ (Moroni 7:47), should be the true reason for serving: "It must be unconcerned with self and heedless of personal advantage. It must be accomplished for the love of God and the love of his children."[3] This type of service does not come automatically. Even though we may serve for various reasons at different times, as we continue to grow spiritually and develop Christlike qualities, the time will come when we will serve not for self but for God and his sons and daughters. It is then that we will serve God with "all [our] heart, might, mind and strength" (D&C 4:2).

When we have the desire to serve, we should not postpone that service. Hyrum Smith was told to thrust in his sickle "while the day lasts" (D&C 11:3). We, too, must thrust in our sickle and serve while the day lasts. Opportunities to serve come, but they also pass. The key is to serve when God wants us to serve. That ability does not come easily. Circumstances or demands on time or talents can dampen our desire. Desire can be lost. The decision to wait until it is more convenient or comfortable might not be wise. We should serve when the desire is strong.

BECOME GODLIKE

A desire to serve comes by knowing God and emulating him (see D&C 93). A love for God and the desire to be like him motivate an individual to develop a godlike character, and developing a godlike character is essential to qualify to serve in the kingdom. The Lord instructed Joseph Smith, Sr., that "faith, hope, charity and love, with an eye single to the glory of God, qualify him for the work" (D&C 4:5). The Lord further advised him to "remember faith, virtue, knowledge, temperance, patience, brotherly kindness, godliness, charity, humility, diligence" (D&C 4:6). In our mortal condition, these godlike characteristics do not manifest themselves automatically in a person; they must be developed and cultivated. The Lord counseled: "Ask, and ye shall receive; knock, and it shall be opened unto you" (D&C 4:7). This counsel applies directly to the qualifications to be missionaries in his kingdom. If we earnestly seek these qualities and ask God for them, they will be given to us. In other words, each member of the Church can be qualified to serve in the kingdom. We must have the desire to serve and then do whatever is necessary to develop the qualities essential for service. To an early believer, Joseph Knight, the Lord summarized the godlike qualities necessary: "No one can assist in this work except he shall be humble and full of love, having faith, hope, and charity, being temperate in all things, whatsoever shall be entrusted to his care" (D&C 12:8).

OBTAIN HIS WORD

To be effective missionaries, we must have a strong spiritual base on which to build. As we study the scriptures, our spirituality increases and our love of God and of his children intensifies. Hyrum Smith was instructed: "Seek not to declare my word, but first seek to obtain my word, and then shall your tongue be loosed; then, if you desire, you shall have my Spirit and my word, yea, the power of God unto the convincing of men" (D&C 11:21). If we are to teach, we must know the subject to be taught. Hyrum was told to "study my word" (D&C 11:22). The members of the Church are also instructed to "search these commandments [the Doctrine and Covenants] for they are true and faithful and the prophecies and promises which are in them shall all be fulfilled" (D&C 1:37). Shortly after the Church was organized, Joseph Smith and his companions were commanded: "Let your time be devoted to the studying of the scriptures, and to preaching" (D&C 26:1). The Lord was emphatic when he declared to a group of early missionaries: "Ye are not sent forth to be taught, but to teach the children of men the things which I have put into your hands by the power of my Spirit" (D&C 43:15). That statement has explicit reference to the Book of Mormon and the Doctrine and Covenants.

Obtaining God's word through scripture study not only produces knowledge but also develops spirituality. Elder Bruce R. McConkie said: "I think that people who study the scriptures get a dimension to their life that nobody else gets and that can't be gained in any way except by studying the scriptures.

"There's an increase in faith and a desire to do what's right and a feeling of inspiration and understanding that come to people who study the gospel — meaning particularly the Standard Works — and who ponder the principles, that can't come in any other way."[4]

A special relationship can develop between the Lord and his sons and daughters when they study his revealed word. President Spencer W. Kimball declared: "I find that when I get casual in my relationships with divinity and when it seems that no divine ear is listening and no divine voice is speaking, that I am far, far away. If I immerse myself in the scriptures the distance narrows and the spirituality returns. I find myself loving more intensely those whom I must love with all my heart and mind and strength, and loving them more, I find it easier to abide their counsel."[5]

OBTAIN HIS SPIRIT

The key to successful missionary work is obtaining the companionship of the Holy Ghost. Once we have obtained godlike characteristics, we are prepared to receive the companionship of the Holy Ghost. It is through the Holy Ghost that teaching takes place. The Lord taught the elders in the law of the Church that they were to teach the principles of the gospel as found in the scriptures "as they shall be directed by the Spirit. And the Spirit shall be given unto you by the prayer of faith; and if ye receive not the Spirit ye shall not teach" (D&C 42:13–14). It is the Holy Ghost that converts an individual to the truth. The Lord warned the elders that if they did not have the Spirit attendant with their teaching, they would only go through the motions of teaching because true conversion and understanding will not take place without the Holy Ghost. Having the Spirit is so critical to the teaching process that, said the Lord, "He that is ordained of me and sent forth to preach the word of truth by the Comforter, in the Spirit of truth, doth he preach it by the Spirit of truth or some other way? And if it be by some other way it is not of God" (D&C 50:17–18). Even if truth is taught, it is not of God unless it is taught by the Spirit of truth.

The Lord revealed that the learner of truth must also learn by the Spirit of truth. "And again, he that receiveth the word of truth, doth he receive it by the Spirit of truth or some other way? If it be some other way it is not of God" (D&C 50:19–20). The process of learning by the Spirit is important because it is the only way that the change called rebirth can take place. "Whosoever believeth on my words, them will I visit with the manifestation of my Spirit; and they shall be born of me, even of water and of the Spirit" (D&C 5:16).

On the other hand, the Spirit does not attend the works of unrighteous servants. In responding to the sinful behavior of a group of early elders, the Lord declared that because of the evil in their hearts, "I, the Lord, withheld my Spirit" (D&C 64:16). Sidney Rigdon "exalted himself in his heart, and received not counsel, but grieved the Spirit" (D&C 63:55). At another time the Lord warned that when "the Spirit of the Lord is grieved" (D&C 121:37), it withdraws.

So important is the Spirit in the building of the kingdom of God that very early in the Restoration, the Lord instructed Oliver Cowdery on the workings of the Spirit. When Oliver traveled to Harmony, Pennsylvania, to determine the truthfulness of the claims of Joseph

Smith, the Lord said to him: "As often as thou hast inquired thou hast received instruction of my Spirit. If it had not been so, thou wouldst not have come to the place where thou art at this time. Behold, thou knowest that thou hast inquired of me and I did enlighten thy mind; and now I tell thee these things that thou mayest know that thou hast been enlightened by the Spirit of truth" (D&C 6:14–15).

As further evidence of the influence of the Holy Ghost in the decisions of Oliver Cowdery, the Lord reminded him of a further witness when he prayed in his heart to know the truths that he had heard. "Did I not speak peace to your mind concerning the matter? What greater witness can you have than from God?" (D&C 6:23). Later, when Oliver wanted to translate the Book of Mormon, the Lord taught him that the translation was done by the Spirit of revelation: "I will tell you in your mind and in your heart, by the Holy Ghost, which shall come upon you and which shall dwell in your heart. Now, behold, this is the spirit of revelation; behold, this is the spirit by which Moses brought the children of Israel through the Red Sea on dry ground" (D&C 8:2–3).

It is evident from these instructions to Oliver Cowdery that the Lord speaks to our mind and heart via his Spirit. Thus, it is critical that a preacher of the gospel have a pure mind and heart. God will bestow his Spirit "on those who love him and purify themselves before him" (D&C 76:116). That is why the Lord has said that the basic qualification to serve in the kingdom is to "love the Lord thy God with all thy heart, with all thy might, mind, and strength" (D&C 59:5) and "to keep my commandments, yea, with all your might, mind and strength" (D&C 11:20). That prepares us to be in tune with the Holy Ghost.

The Spirit is given to us "by the prayer of faith" (D&C 42:14). Martin Harris, for example, was commanded to "pray always, and I will pour out my Spirit upon you" (D&C 19:38). The members of the Church are also promised that if they partake of the sacrament with the proper attitude, they will "always have his Spirit to be with them" (D&C 20:77). Therefore we who engage in the preaching of the gospel can, if we desire, have the Holy Ghost as our companion. We can "go forth in the power of my Spirit, preaching my gospel, two by two, in my name, lifting up your voices as with the sound of a trump, declaring my word like unto angels of God" (D&C 42:6).

THE MESSAGE

The Lord revealed what should be taught to the world by those qualified to preach. When the early brethren who had already accepted the gospel inquired of the Lord what would be the most important thing for them to do, the answer was "Declare repentance unto this people, that you may bring souls unto me" (D&C 15:6; see also 16:6). The Lord commanded Ezra Thayre and Northrop Sweet: "Open your mouths and they shall be filled, saying: Repent, repent, and prepare ye the way of the Lord, and make his paths straight; for the kingdom of heaven is at hand" (D&C 33:10). To cry nothing but repentance is more than merely standing on a soapbox and decrying sin. "When the Lord calls upon his servants to cry nothing but repentance, he does not mean that they may not cry baptism, and call upon the people to obey the commandments of the Lord, but he wishes that all that they say and do be in the spirit of bringing the people to repentance. Any missionary who fails to do this in his ministry is derelict in his duty."[6]

The message of the Restoration must be sent to the world. The Lord has assessed the world as being "corrupted every whit; and there is none which doeth good save it be a few; and they err in many instances because of priestcrafts, all having corrupt minds" (D&C 33:4). Thus priestcraft has distracted many from the truth. So corrupt has the world become that for many the truth is hard to recognize or find. "For there are many yet on the earth among all sects, parties, and denominations, who are blinded by the subtle craftiness of men, whereby they lie in wait to deceive, and who are only kept from the truth because they know not where to find it" (D&C 123:12). It was for this reason that the Lord called Joseph Smith and "spake unto him from heaven, and gave him commandments" (D&C 1:17). The Lord gave Joseph Smith power to translate the Book of Mormon, which contains "the fulness of the gospel of Jesus Christ to the Gentiles and to the Jews also" (D&C 20:9). One purpose of the Book of Mormon is to prove "to the world that the holy scriptures [Bible] are true, and that God does inspire men and call them to his holy work in this age and generation, as well as in generations of old; thereby showing that he is the same God yesterday, today, and forever" (D&C 20:11–12). The messengers of the Restoration are to teach of Joseph Smith and the restored gospel, especially from the Book of Mormon and the Doctrine and Covenants. It is important that we understand that the Book of Mormon and Doctrine and Covenants were brought forth "for the salvation of a ruined world" (D&C 135:6). The gospel was not restored to benefit only the present members of the Church. The Lord declared that the gospel covenant has been confirmed upon us "not for [our] sakes only, but for the sake of the whole world. And the whole world lieth in sin and groaneth under darkness and under the bondage of sin" (D&C 84:48–49).

Thus, a main focus of the members of the Church must be on the preaching of the gospel, both as a warning voice and as an invitation to accept the truths of the revealed gospel and follow the living God. The messengers of the Restoration carry a warning voice of repentance to the world: "And the rebellious shall be pierced with much sorrow; for their iniquities shall be spoken upon the housetops, and their secret acts shall be revealed. And the voice of warning shall be unto all people, by the mouths of my disciples, whom I have chosen in these last days" (D&C 1:3–4).

The Lord's disciples are sent forth with much power and authority. The mission of the Church and the missionary effort is not just to baptize; it is to declare "repentance unto this generation" (D&C 11:9). The Lord's servants are given power to "seal both on earth and in heaven, the unbelieving and rebellious; yea, verily, to seal them up unto the day when the wrath of God shall be poured out upon the wicked without measure — unto the day when the Lord shall come to recompense unto every man according to his work, and measure to every man according to the measure which he has measured to his fellow man" (D&C 1:8–10). The invitation will be given to all to repent and come to Christ. "Wherefore the voice of the Lord is unto the ends of the earth, that all that will hear may hear" (D&C 1:11). Those who repent will be accepted into his kingdom (D&C 20:37), and those who refuse to heed the warning voice will be sealed up to the judgment of God.

PROMISED BLESSINGS

As missionaries go forth under the influence of the Holy Ghost, the Lord has given great promises to them. He told the early missionaries to "speak the thoughts that I shall put into your hearts, and you shall not be confounded before men; for it shall be given you in the very hour, yea, in the very moment, what ye shall say" (D&C 100:5–6). If the missionaries will "declare whatsoever thing ye declare in my name, in solemnity of heart, in the spirit of meekness, in all things," the Lord promised, "the Holy Ghost shall be shed forth in bearing record unto all things whatsoever ye shall say" (D&C 100:7–8). Therefore, the warning message and the call to repentance can successfully be given even if individuals do not accept them or respond positively to them.

Perhaps the greatest promise to faithful missionaries is a personal one. To a group of early missionaries who had just returned from Missouri, the Lord said: "There are those among you who have sinned; but verily I say, for this once, for mine own glory, and for the salvation of souls, I have forgiven you your sins" (D&C 64:3). To another group of missionaries traveling to Jackson County, the Lord declared this great promise: "Nevertheless, ye are blessed, for the testimony which ye have borne is recorded in heaven for the angels to look upon; and they rejoice over you, and your sins are forgiven you" (D&C 62:3). He commanded the missionaries to "lift up their voice and declare my word with loud voices, without wrath or doubting, lifting up holy hands upon them. For I am able to make you holy, and your sins are forgiven you" (D&C 60:7). A relationship appears to exist between forgiveness of sin and the bearing of testimony in missionary work.

SUMMARY

The prophets have declared that we do not need just missionaries but better-prepared missionaries. With the tremendous responsibilities placed upon the members of the Church to warn and cry repentance to a world full of sin, we must strive to develop the qualities necessary to meet these responsibilities. We must desire to serve and be prepared to deliver the message God has revealed for the world. Elder John A. Widtsoe summarized God's expectations as follows:

"So we need, in this Church and Kingdom, for our own and the world's welfare a group of men and women in their individual lives who shall be as a light to the nations, and really standards for the world to follow [D&C 45:9; 115:4–5]. Such a people must be different from the world as it now is. There is no opportunity for Latter-day Saints to say we shall be as the world is, unless the world has the same aim that we have. We are here to build Zion to Almighty God, for the blessing of all the world. In that aim we are unique and different from all other people. We must respect that obligation, and not be afraid of it. We cannot walk as other men, or talk as other men, or do as other men, for we have a different destiny, obligation, and responsibility placed upon us, and we must fit ourselves for that great destiny and obligation."[7]

NOTES

1. John A. Widtsoe, in Conference Report, Apr. 1940, p. 36.

2. Neal A. Maxwell, "Not My Will, but Thine" (Salt Lake City: Bookcraft, 1988), p. 89.

3. Dallin H. Oaks, Pure in Heart (Salt Lake City: Bookcraft, 1988), pp. 47–48.

4. In Church News, 24 Jan. 1976.

5. Spencer W. Kimball, *The Teachings of Spencer W. Kimball,* ed. Edward L. Kimball (Salt Lake City: Bookcraft, 1982), p. 135.

6. Joseph Fielding Smith, *Church History and Modern Revelation* (Salt Lake City: Deseret Book Co., 1953), 1:57.

7. Widtsoe, in Conference Report, Apr. 1940, p. 36.

10

"ETERNITY SKETCH'D IN A VISION": THE POETIC VERSION OF DOCTRINE & COVENANTS 76

Richard Neitzel Holzapfel

CES Coordinator, Irvine, California

Early 1843 was a busy season for the Prophet as he, along with his clerks William Wines Phelps and Wilford Woodruff, began reading proofs of a second edition of the Doctrine and Covenants.[1] Joseph was also involved in preparing his personal history for publication, portions of which were already appearing serially in the *Times and Seasons*. In particular he was reviewing the period of February and March 1832 for Richards and Phelps as they began to compose this portion of his history.[2] That period was, of course, the time when the Vision (D&C 76) was received in Hiram, Ohio.

The Prophet and his people also had cause at this time for great celebration. An Illinois court had advised Governor Thomas Ford that a writ issued for Joseph Smith's extradition to Missouri was illegal, and a federal district judge discharged the Prophet on 7 January 1843. While accompanying the Prophet home from Springfield, Wilson Law and Willard Richards sang *A Jubilee Song* in honor of Joseph's newfound freedom.[3] A day of fasting, prayer, and thanksgiving was held in Nauvoo on 17 January to express gratitude for the Prophet's "release and delivery."[4] Next day a group assembled at Joseph's home for "a day of conviviality and rejoicing, and [that] might properly be called a day of jubilee or release."[5] A printed handbill with several songs, including one composed by Eliza R. Snow, was distributed, and the songs were sung to the Prophet. At the end of the festivities, Wilford Woodruff noted, "We returned to our homes rejoicing that [we] could again have the privilege of enjoying the society of our prophet seer."[6] Two days later, W. W. Phelps presented Joseph a poem entitled *Vade Mecum*, or *Go with Me*, as part of the jubilee celebration.[7]

It was in this setting in February 1843 that a poetic version of the Vision entitled *The Answer* was first published, under Joseph's name, in the *Times and Seasons* as a rejoinder to Phelps's jubilee poem, *Vade*

Mecum.[8] The *History of the Church* states: "In reply to W. W. Phelps's *Vade Mecum*, or "Go with me," of 20th of January last [1843], I [Joseph] dictated an answer: [It consisted of the "Revelation known as the Vision of the Three Glories," Doctrine and Covenants, section lxxvi, made into verse]."[9]

Naturally, the question of authorship of this poem arises.[10] Did Joseph write it himself, or did someone else write it? Can we be sure the ideas communicated represent the Prophet's own expression?

It is certain that Joseph often depended upon others to produce material under his direction. At one time, he may have simply asked someone to compose an item for him; at another time he may have given someone the main ideas; in other instances, he was involved heavily in the final literary creation. Although Joseph's ideas are present in these documents, the particular literary structure (grammar, punctuation, spelling, and other aspects of style) often depended upon who was writing for him at the time.

Many of the editorials in the *Times and Seasons* were not Joseph's own words, although he took over as editor of the newspaper in March 1842. The Prophet indicated that only those editorials "having my signature" were those for which he was personally responsible.[11] It is therefore highly significant that the 1843 poem ends, "Joseph Smith, Nauvoo, Feb. 1843." The first-person singular "I, Joseph, the prophet" in stanza 11 of the poem itself also seems to confirm his acceptance of the material, even if it had been drafted by someone else.

John Taylor, a close associate with Joseph at the time and the new editor of the *Times and Seasons*, indicated that in his most recent legal contest Joseph's defense attorney had made some comments about biblical poetry. For Taylor, the poetic rendition of the Vision was ample proof that "modern Prophets can prophecy in poetry, as well as the ancient prophets and that no difference, even of that kind any longer exists." He believed Joseph was responsible for the poem, and he emphasized "the ideas" as the most significant aspect when he stated in the published introduction to the poem: "The following very curious poetic composition, is at once both novel and interesting; for while the common landmarks of modern poetry are entirely disregarded; there is something so dignified and exalted conveyed in the ideas of this production, that it cannot fail to strike the attention of every superficial observer."[12]

Whether W. W. Phelps, Parley P. Pratt or someone else helped Joseph compose the poetic rendition may be difficult to prove. On the other hand, that Joseph accepted it as representing his own ideas seems a reasonable proposition. It therefore can be argued that the poetic rendition can give us insight into how Joseph understood the implications of the Vision, or alternatively, as he was willing to reveal it to the Saints in 1843.

THE ANSWER
to W. W. Phelps, Esq.
A VISION

1. I will go, I will go, to the home of the Saints,
   Where the virtue's the value, and life the reward;
   But before I return to my former estate
   I must fulfil the mission I had from the Lord.

2. Wherefore, hear, O ye heavens, and give ear O ye earth;
   And rejoice ye inhabitants truly again;
   For the Lord he is God, and his life never ends,
   And besides him there ne'er was a Saviour of men.

3. His ways are a wonder; his wisdom is great;
   The extent of his doings, there's none can unveil;
   His purposes fail not; from age unto age
   He still is the same, and his years never fail.

4. His throne is the heavens, his life time is all
   Of eternity *now*, and eternity *then*;
   His union is power, and none stays his hand, —
   The Alpha, Omega, for ever: Amen.

5. For thus saith the Lord, in the spirit of truth,
   I am merciful, gracious, and good unto those
   That fear me, and live for the life that's to come;
   My delight is to honor the saints with repose;

6. That serve me in righteousness true to the end;
   Eternal's their glory, and great their reward;
   I'll surely reveal all my myst'ries to them, —
   The great hidden myst'ries in my kingdom stor'd —

7. From the council in Kolob, to time on the earth.
   And for ages to come unto them I will show
   My pleasure & will, what my kingdom will do:
   Eternity's wonders they truly shall know.

8. Great things of the future I'll show unto them,
   Yea, things of the vast generations to rise;

> For their wisdom and glory shall be very great,
> And their pure understanding extend to the skies:

9. And before them the wisdom of wise men shall cease,
   And the nice understanding of prudent ones fail!
   For the light of my spirit shall light mine elect,
   And the truth is so mighty 't will ever prevail.

10. And the secrets and plans of my will I'll reveal;
    The sanctified pleasures when earth is renew'd,
    What the eye hath not seen, nor the ear hath yet
       heard;
    Nor the heart of the natural man ever hath view'd.

11. I, Joseph, the prophet, in spirit beheld,
    And the eyes of the inner man truly did see
    Eternity sketch'd in a vision from God.
    Of what was, and now is, and yet is to be.

12. Those things which the Father ordained of old,
    Before the world was, or a system had run, —
    Through Jesus the Maker and Savior of all;
    The only begotten, (Messiah) his son.

13. Of whom I bear record, as all prophets have,
    And the record I bear is the fulness, — yea even
    The truth of the gospel of Jesus — *the Christ*,
    With whom I convers'd, in the vision of heav'n.

14. For while in the act of translating his word,
    Which the Lord in his grace had appointed to me,
    I came to the gospel recorded by John,
    Chapter fifth and the twenty ninth verse, which you'll
       see.

Which was given as follows:
"Speaking of the resurrection of the dead, —
"Concerning those who shall hear the voice of the son of man —
"And shall come forth: —
"They who have done good in the resurrection of the just.
"And they who have done evil in the resurrection of the unjust.

15. I marvel'd at these resurrections, indeed!
    For it came unto me by the spirit direct: —
    And while I did meditate what it all meant,
    The Lord touch'd the eyes of my own intellect: —

16. Hosanna forever! they open'd anon,
    And the glory of God shone around where I was;
    And there was the Son, at the Father's right hand,
    In a fulness of glory, and holy applause.

17. I beheld round the throne, holy angels and hosts,
    And sanctified beings from worlds that have been,
    In holiness worshipping God and the Lamb,
    Forever and ever, amen and amen!

18. And now after all of the proofs made of him,
    By witnesses truly, by whom he was known,
    This is mine, last of all, that he lives; yea he lives!
    And sits at the right hand of God, on his throne.

19. And I heard a great voice, bearing record from heav'n,
    He's the Saviour, and only begotten of God —
    By him, of him, and through him, the worlds were all
        made,
    Even all that career in the heavens so broad,

20. Whose inhabitants, too, from the first to the last,
    Are sav'd by the very same Saviour of ours;
    And, of course, are begotten God's daughters and sons,
    By the very same truths, and the very same pow'rs.

21. And I saw and bear record of warfare in heav'n;
    For an angel of light, in authority great,
    Rebell'd against Jesus, and sought for his pow'r,
    But was thrust down to woe from his Godified state.

22. And the heavens all wept, and the tears drop'd like
        dew,
    That Lucifer, son of the morning had fell!
    Yea, is fallen! is fall'n, and become, Oh, alas!
    The son of Perdition; the devil of hell!

23. And while I was yet in the spirit of truth,
    The commandment was: write ye the vision all out;
    For Satan, old serpent, the devil's for war, —
    And yet will encompass the saints round about.

24. And I saw, too, the suff'ring and mis'ry of those,
    (Overcome by the devil, in warfare and fight,)
    In hell-fire, and vengeance, the doom of the damn'd;
    For the Lord said, the vision is further: so write.

25. For thus saith the Lord, now concerning all those
    Who know of my power and partake of the same;
    And suffer themselves, that they be overcome
    By the power of Satan; despising my name: —

26. Defying my power, and denying the truth; —
    They are they — of the world, or of men, most forlorn,
    The Sons of Perdition, of whom, ah! I say,
    'T were better for them had they never been born!

27. They're vessels of wrath, and dishonor to God,
    Doom'd to suffer his wrath, in the regions of woe,
    Through the terrific night of eternity's round,
    With the devil and all of his angels below:

28. Of whom it is said, no forgiveness is giv'n,
    In this world, alas! nor the world that's to come;
    For they have denied the spirit of God.
    After having receiv'd it: and mis'ry's their doom.

29. And denying the only begotten of God, —
    And crucify him to themselves, as they do,
    And openly put him to shame in their flesh,
    By gospel they cannot repentance renew.

30. They are they, who must go to the great lake of fire,
    Which burneth with brimstone, yet never consumes,
    And dwell with the devil, and angels of his,
    While eternity goes and eternity comes.

31. They are they, who must groan through the great
       second death,
    And are not redeemed in the time of the Lord;
    While all the rest are, through the triumph of Christ,
    Made partakers of grace, by the power of his word.

32. The myst'ry of Godliness truly is great; —
    The past, and the present, and what is to be;
    And this is the gospel — glad tidings to all,
    Which the voice from the heavens bore record to me:

33. That he came to the world in the middle of time,
    To lay down his life for his friends and his foes,
    And bear away sin as a mission of love;
    And sanctify earth for a blessed repose.

34. 'Tis decreed, that he'll save all the work of his hands,
    And sanctify them by his own precious blood;
    And purify earth for the Sabbath of rest,
    By the agent of fire, as it was by the flood.

35. The Savior will save all his Father did give,
    Even all that he gave in the regions abroad.
    Save the Sons of Perdition: They're lost; ever lost.
    And can never return to the presence of God.

36. They are they, who must reign with the devil in hell,
    In eternity now, and eternity then,
    Where the worm dieth not, and the fire is not
        quench'd; —
    And the punishment still, is eternal. Amen.

37. And which is the torment apostates receive,
    But the end, or the place where the torment began,
    Save to them who are made to partake of the same,
    Was never, nor will be, revealed unto man.

38. Yet God shows by vision a glimpse of their fate,
    And straightway he closes the scene that was shown:
    So the width, or the depth, or the misery thereof,
    Save to those that partake, is forever unknown.

39. And while I was pondering, the vision was closed;
    And the voice said to me, write the vision: for lo!
    'Tis the end of the scene of the sufferings of those,
    Who remain filthy still in their anguish and woe.

40. And again I bear record of heavenly things,
    Where virtue's the value, above all that's pric'd —
    Of the truth of the gospel concerning the just,
    That rise in the first resurrection of Christ.

41. Who receiv'd and believ'd, and repented likewise,
    And then were baptis'd, as a man always was,
    Who ask'd and receiv'd a remission of sin,
    And honored the kingdom by keeping its laws.

42. Being buried in water, as Jesus had been,
    And keeping the whole of his holy commands,
    They received the gift of the spirit of truth,
    By the ordinance truly of laying on hands.

43. For these overcome, by their faith and their works,
    Being tried in their life-time, as purified gold,
    And seal'd by the spirit of promise, to life,
    By men called of God, as was Aaron of old.

44. They are they, of the church of the first born of
       God, —
    And unto whose hands he committeth all things;
    For they hold the keys of the kingdom of heav'n,
    And reign with the Savior, as priests, and as kings.

45. They're priests of the order of Melchisedek,
    Like Jesus, (from whom is this highest reward,)
    Receiving a fulness of glory and light;
    As written: They're Gods; even sons of the Lord.

46. So all things are theirs; yea, of life, or of death;
    Yea, whether things now, or to come, all are theirs,
    And they are the Savior's, and he is the Lord's,
    Having overcome all, as eternity's heirs.

47. 'Tis wisdom that man never glory in man,
    But give God the glory for all that he hath;
    For the righteous will walk in the presence of God,
    While the wicked are trod under foot in his wrath.

48. Yea, the righteous shall dwell in the presence of God,
    And of Jesus, forever, from earth's second birth —
    For when he comes down in the splendor of heav'n,
    All these he'll bring with him, to reign on the earth.

49. These are they that arise in their bodies of flesh,
    When the trump of the first resurrection shall sound;
    These are they that come up to Mount Zion, in life,
    Where the blessings and gifts of the spirit abound.

50. These are they that have come to the heavenly place;
    To the numberless courses of angels above:
    To the city of God; e'en the holiest of all,
    And to the home of the blessed, the fountain of love:

51. To the church of old Enoch, and of the first born:
    And gen'ral assembly of ancient renown'd.
    Whose names are all kept in the archives of heav'n,
    As chosen and faithful, and fit to be crown'd.

52. These are they that are perfect through Jesus' own
     blood,
    Whose bodies celestial are mention'd by Paul,
    Where the sun is the typical glory thereof,
    And God, and his Christ, are the true judge of all.

53. Again I beheld the terrestrial world,
    In the order and glory of Jesus, go on;
    'Twas not as the church of the first born of God,
    But shone in its place, as the moon to the sun.

54. Behold, these are they that have died without law;
    The heathen of ages that never had hope,
    And those of the region and shadow of death,
    The spirits in prison, that light has brought up.

55. To spirits in prison the Savior once preach'd,
    And taught them the gospel, with powers afresh;
    And then were the living baptiz'd for their dead,
    That they might be judg'd as if men in the flesh.

56. These are they that are hon'rable men of the earth;
    Who were blinded and dup'd by the cunning of men:
    They receiv'd not the truth of the Savior at first;
    But did, when they heard it in prison, again.

57. Not valiant for truth, they obtain'd not the crown,
    But are of that glory that's typ'd by the moon:
    They are they, that come into the presence of Christ,
    But not to the fulness of God, on his throne.

58. Again I beheld the telestial, as third,
    The lesser, or starry world, next in its place,
    For the leaven must leaven three measures of meal,
    And every knee bow that is subject to grace.

59. These are they that receiv'd not the gospel of Christ,
    Or evidence, either, that he ever was;
    As the stars are all diff'rent in glory and light,
    So differs the glory of these by the laws.

60. These are they that deny not the spirit of God,
    But are thrust down to hell, with the devil, for sins,
    As hypocrites, liars, whoremongers, and thieves,
    And stay 'till the last resurrection begins.

61. 'Till the Lamb shall have finish'd the work he begun;
    Shall have trodden the wine press, in fury alone,
    And overcome all by the pow'r of his might:
    He conquers to conquer, and save all his own.

62. These are they that receive not a fulness of light,
    From Christ, in eternity's world, where they are,
    The terrestrial sends them the Comforter, though;
    And minist'ring angels, to happify there.

63. And so the telestial is minister'd to,
    By ministers from the terrestrial one,
    As terrestrial is, from the celestial throne;
    And the great, greater, greatest, seem's stars, moon,
        and sun.

64. And thus I beheld, in the vision of heav'n,
    The telestial glory, dominion and bliss,
    Surpassing the great understanding of men, —
    Unknown, save reveal'd, in a world vain as this.

65. And lo, I beheld the terrestrial, too,
    Which excels the telestial in glory and light,
    In splendor, and knowledge, and wisdom, and joy,
    In blessings, and graces, dominion and might.

66. I beheld the celestial, in glory sublime;
    Which is the most excellent kingdom that is, —
    Where God, e'en the Father, in harmony reigns;
    Almighty, supreme, and eternal, in bliss.

67. Where the church of the first born in union reside,
    And they see as they're seen, and they know as they're
        known;
    Being equal in power, dominion and might,
    With a fulness of glory and grace, round his throne.

68. The glory celestial is one like the sun;
    The glory terrestrial is one like the moon;
    The glory telestial is one like the stars,
    And all harmonize like the parts of a tune.

69. As the stars are all different in lustre and size,
    So the telestial region, is mingled in bliss;
    From least unto greatest, and greatest to least,
    The reward is exactly as promis'd in this.

70. These are they that came out for Apollos and Paul;
    For Cephas and Jesus, in all kinds of hope;
    For Enoch and Moses, and Peter, and John;
    For Luther and Calvin, and even the Pope.

71. For they never received the gospel of Christ,
    Nor the prophetic spirit that came from the Lord;
    Nor the covenant neither, which Jacob once had;
    They went their own way, and they have their reward.

72. By the order of God, last of all, these are they,
    That will not be gather'd with saints here below,
    To be caught up to Jesus, and meet in the cloud: —
    In darkness they worshipp'd; to darkness they go.

73. These are they that are sinful, the wicked at large,
    That glutted their passion by meanness or worth;
    All liars, adulterers, sorc'rers, and proud;
    And suffer, as promis'd, God's wrath on the earth.

74. These are they that must suffer the vengeance of hell,
    'Till Christ shall have trodden all enemies down,
    And perfected his work, in the fulness of times:
    And is crown'd on his throne with his glorious crown.

75. The vast multitude of the telestial world —
    As the stars of the skies, or the sands of the sea; —
    The voice of Jehovah echo'd far and wide,
    Ev'ry tongue shall confess, and they all bow the knee.

76. Ev'ry man shall be judg'd by the works of his life,
    And receive a reward in the mansion prepar'd;
    For his judgments are just, and his works never end,
    As his prophets and servants have always declar'd.

77. But the great things of God, which he show'd unto me,
    Unlawful to utter, I dare not declare;
    They surpass all the wisdom and greatness of men,
    And only are seen, as has Paul, where they are.

78. I will go, I will go, while the secret of life,
    Is blooming in heaven, and blasting in hell;
    Is leaving on earth, and a budding in space: —
    I will go, I will go, with you, brother, farewell.

JOSEPH SMITH
Nauvoo, Feb. 1843.[13]

A careful study of the poetic rendition of the Vision demonstrates that it is more than a reworking of the message of the 1832 revelation; indeed, it is a one-of-a-kind commentary. Surprisingly, few gospel scholars have explicitly used this poetic writing to help interpret the Vision itself. That the poem did not receive much attention during the last half of the nineteenth century and the first part of the twentieth century may be because the early printed sources of the poem were not easily accessible. When the *History of the Church* was published in 1909, the text of poem was not included, a significant lapse in making the document available to a wider audience in the beginning of this century. It was not until N. B. Lundwall reprinted it in 1951 that the poem generally became available.[14] Several important twentieth-century studies neglect the poem altogether.[15] A few more recent works make slight reference to it.[16] A final group reproduce the poem in its entirety as an addendum but do not specifically cite it in their commentary.[17]

The poetic version of Doctrine and Covenants 76 emphasizes several helpful points relating to the premortal experience; the Savior's mission and power; Satan and his kingdom; the telestial, terrestrial, and celestial kingdoms; and Joseph Smith's life and mission.

THE PREMORTAL EXPERIENCE

That individuals existed as premortal spirits either was not known or not understood during the first years after the Church's founding in 1830. Possibly the first hint of such a knowledge came in 1833, when Joseph received a revelation now recorded in Doctrine and Covenants 93. Privately, as early as 1839, Joseph began teaching that there was a mother in heaven—the mother of our premortal spirits. By 1841, Joseph publicly declared, "Spirits are eternal."[18] When the Book of Abraham was published in March 1842, the doctrine was further clarified (see Abraham 3:18).

The connection between a foreordained mission and the premortal life is stated positively in the poetic rendition:

I will go, I will go, to the home of the Saints,
Where the virtue's the value, and life the reward;
But before I return to my former estate
I must fulfil the mission I had from the Lord.
(Stanza 1; emphasis added)

Joseph emphasized the doctrine of the premortal existence when he stated on 12 May 1844, "Every man who has a calling to minister to the inhabitants of the world, was ordained to that very purpose in the Grand Council of Heaven before this world was—I suppose that I was ordained to this very office in that Grand Council."[19]

The Prophet expanded the Saints' understanding of the importance of Kolob (already known to the Saints as a great governing star—see Abraham 3:1–3) and the connection it had with the premortal council. A great "council in Kolob" was held before the earth was created. He wrote, "From the council in Kolob, to time on the earth" (stanza 7). The implication is, of course, that at least part of the premortal experience occurred in Kolob.

THE SAVIOR'S MISSION AND POWER

Joseph revealed to the Saints the power of Christ's atonement. In the poetic rendition of Doctrine and Covenants 76, he proclaimed:

Wherefore, hear, O ye heavens, and give ear O ye earth;
And rejoice ye inhabitants truly again;
For the Lord he is God, and *his life never ends,*
And besides him *there ne'er was a Saviour of men.*

. . . .

. . . *Jesus the Maker* and Savior of all;
The only begotten, (Messiah) his son.
Of whom I bear record, as all prophets have,
And the record I bear is the fulness,—yea even
The truth of the gospel of Jesus—*the Christ.*

. . . .

He's the Saviour, and only begotten of God—
By him, of him, and through him, the worlds were all
    made,
Even all that career in the heavens so broad,
Whose inhabitants, too, from the first to the last,
Are sav'd by the very same Saviour of ours;
And, of course, are begotten God's daughters and sons,
By the very same truths, and the very same pow'rs.
(Stanzas 2, 12–13, 19–20; emphasis added)[20]

Joseph Smith taught that the redemption of Christ was not limited to this world nor to a specific period of time. It reached backward in time and forward into the future, and just as it had crossed the oceans and continents during the first century to bless the lives not only of those at Jerusalem but also of the Nephites and Lamanites in America, the Atonement spread across the vastness of space. It was a final act that did not necessitate another sacrifice in the future.

SATAN AND HIS KINGDOM

One of the most startling passages from the poetic rendition of Doctrine and Covenants 76 is the knowledge revealed concerning Lucifer's position in the premortal life. Joseph wrote:

> And I saw and bear record of warfare in heav'n;
> For an angel of light, in authority great,
> Rebell'd against Jesus, and sought for his pow'r,
> But was thrust down to woe *from his Godified state.*
> And the heavens all wept, and the tears drop'd like dew,
> That Lucifer, son of the morning had fell!
> Yea, is fallen! is fall'n, and become, Oh, alas!
> The son of Perdition; the devil of hell!
> (Stanza 21–22; emphasis added)

The 1842 publication of the Book of Abraham apparently taught that many of the premortal "intelligences" reached a spiritual stature of "godhood" (see Abraham 3–4). That these premortal spirits would eventually take a body was stated by the Prophet just a few months after the publication of the poem. In August 1843 Joseph stated, "But the Holy Ghost is yet a spiritual body and [is] waiting to take to himself a body, as the Savior did or as God did, or the gods before them took bodies."[21]

That Lucifer held a position of prominence in the premortal life is certain, but here and only here does Joseph identify Lucifer's "godified state" before he fell to the earth to become the devil.[22] Shortly after the publication of the poem, Joseph said: "In the other world [spirit world] there is a variety of spirits — some who seek to excel — and this was the case with the devil when he fell, he sought for things which were unlawful, hence he was cast down and it is said he drew away many with him" (some punctuation added).[23]

THE KINGDOMS OF GLORY

The central facet of both the poem and the original revelation is the series of visions of the eternal kingdoms of glory. The poem compares the kingdoms in an interesting fashion:

> The glory celestial is one like the sun;
> The glory terrestrial is one like the moon;
> The glory telestial is one like the stars,
> *And all harmonize like the parts of a tune.*
>
> As the stars are all different in lustre and size,
> So the telestial region, is mingled in bliss;

From least unto greatest, and greatest to least,
The reward is exactly as promis'd in this.
(Stanzas 68–69; emphasis added)

The Telestial Kingdom

To emphasize the final results of accepting and believing in creeds of postbiblical Christianity, Joseph noted that the telestial kingdom will include:

These are they that came out for Apollos and Paul;
For Cephas and Jesus, in all kinds of hope;
For Enoch and Moses, and Peter, and John;
For Luther and Calvin, and even the Pope.
(Stanza 70; emphasis added)

The 1843 poem underscores that the acceptance of creeds instead of covenants is the real issue. Joseph added to the original revelation a significant phrase:

They never received the gospel of Christ
. . . .
Nor the covenant neither, which Jacob once had;
They went their own way, and they have their reward.
(Stanza 71; emphasis added)

In addition to those already cited as being those who will inherit telestial glory, the Prophet added "hypocrites" to the list (stanza 60). That seems to refer to those pretending to be religious or believing in a false creed but whose hearts are far away from God. While it is a "lesser, or starry world, next in its place," the telestial kingdom is a place where the Lord sends "the Comforter [Holy Spirit]. . . / And minist'ring angels, to happify there"; it is a kingdom of "glory, dominion and bliss" (stanzas 58, 62).

An often-repeated story associated with the telestial kingdom deals with something Joseph Smith was purported to have said: "The telestial kingdom is so great, if we knew what it was like we would kill ourselves to get there." Wilford Woodruff recounted a comment by the Prophet that may be the basis of that apocryphal story. According to Charles Lowell Walker, Wilford Woodruff "refered to a saying of Joseph Smith, which he heard him utter (like this) That if the People knew what was behind the vail, they would try by every means to commit suicide that they might get there, but the Lord in his wisdom had implanted the fear of death in every person that they might cling to life and thus accomplish the designs of their creator."[24] What he may have meant by this statement may never be known, but we do know that the happy state of those who inherit the telestial kingdom is emphasized in the poem.

The Terrestrial Kingdom

Those who receive a terrestrial glory seem to fit into four categories. The first are those "that have died without law"—the gospel law—and did not receive it in the spirit world. The Prophet further noted they are

> The heathen of ages that never had hope,
> And those of the region and shadow of death,
> The spirits in prison, that light has brought up.
> (Stanza 54)

Another group is represented by those

> . . . spirits in prison the Savior once preach'd,
> And taught them the gospel, with powers afresh;
> And then were the living baptiz'd for their dead,
> That they might be judg'd as if men in the flesh.
> (Stanza 55)

A third group

> . . . are they that are hon'rable men of the earth;
> Who were blinded and dup'd by the cunning of men:
> They receiv'd not the truth of the Savior at first;
> But did, when they heard it in prison, again.
> (Stanza 56)

The fourth and final category are those

> Not valiant for truth, they obtain'd not the crown,
> But are of that glory that's typ'd by the moon: They are
>   they, that come into the presence of Christ,
> But not to the fulness of God, on his throne.
> (Stanza 57)

The Celestial Kingdom

By capitalizing the word *Gods* in stanza 45 of the poetic rendition of Doctrine and Covenants 76, Joseph may have attempted to be more precise regarding the stature of those who obtain the highest degree of the celestial kingdom: "As written: They're Gods; even sons of the Lord."[25] In the original publication of the Vision in 1832, the word *gods* was not capitalized. Reorganized Latter-Day Saint apologists used the 1832 version, which uses the lowercase *gods*, during the nineteenth century and first half of the twentieth century as a means of countering the full implications of the doctrine of eternal glory.[26] Thus, in this poem, which uses the uppercase *Gods*, Joseph may have attempted to reveal in a plainer fashion his intention.

In 1844 William Law, formerly a counselor in the First Presidency, formed a new church, which accepted the Book of Mormon and the 1835 Doctrine and Covenants as standard works but rejected Joseph Smith, claiming that he was a "fallen Prophet." In their newspaper on 7 June 1844, Law and his associates accused Joseph of teaching "false and damnable doctrines . . . such as plurality of Gods above the God of this universe."[27]

Nine days later, the Prophet responded to their charges: "Oh Apostates did ye never think of this bef[ore] these are the quotations that the apostates take to the scrip[tures] — they swear that they bel[ieve] the Bible [and] the Book of Mormon [and etc.]." Joseph continued, "Go [and] read the vision [Section 76] — there is glory [and] glory — Sun, moon & Stars — & so do they differ in glory & every man who reigns is a God — [and] the text of the Do[trine] & Cov[enan]t damns themselves."[28] For Joseph, the doctrine had always been present since the 1832 revelation was first printed and if the apostates had only just discovered it, then they never truly understood the implications of the Vision.

Although the 1832 revelation used the phrase "kings and priests" to describe celestial beings, the full implications of such titles certainly were not understood by the Saints until Joseph began to reveal the ordinances of the holy endowment to the "Quorum of the Anointed" in 1842.[29] The 1832 revelation indicated that these righteous Saints "are they who are the church of the first-born: They are they into whose hands the Father has given all things: they are they who are priests and kings."[30]

The 1843 poetic rendition clarifies and expands upon several aspects of this description. Joseph indicated that the "church of the first-born" is "of God." He also indicated what is meant to have the Father place into one's hand "all things" when he said: "For they hold the *keys of the kingdom of heav'n*" (stanza 44; emphasis added).

As early as April 1842, Joseph began introducing a theme regarding the "keys of the kingdom" in his public and private discourses. During an early Relief Society meeting he "exhorted the sisters always to concentrate their faith and prayers for, and place confidence in, those who God has appointed to honor, who God has placed at the head to lead [Church leaders] — that we should arm them with our prayers — that the keys of the kingdom are about to be given them."[31] The "keys" referred to were given in the endowment, when the term took on greater meaning than before.

The poetic rendition emphasizes the stature of the celestial Saints and indicates that the spirit of promise can be sealed upon an individual by a living agent of God:

> For these overcome, by their faith and their works,
> Being tried in their life-time, as purified gold.
> And seal'd by the spirit of promise, to life,
> *By men called of God, as was Aaron of old.*
> (Stanza 43; emphasis added)

While the glorious doctrines of exaltation were being opened to them, Joseph cautioned the Saints:

> 'Tis wisdom that man never glory in man,
> But give God the glory for all that he hath.
> (Stanza 47)

JOSEPH SMITH'S LIFE AND MISSION

Just a few days before Joseph published the poem, he stated, "I know what I say; I understand my mission and business. God Almighty is my shield, and what can man do if God is my friend. I shall not be sacrificed until my time comes — then I shall be offered freely."[32] Contemporary sources confirm the Prophet's sense of mission and his knowledge regarding his death.[33] Joseph began his poetic rendition:

> I will go, I will go, to the home of the Saints,
> Where the virtue's the value, and life the reward;
> But before I return to my former estate
> I must fulfil the mission I had from the Lord.
> (Stanza 1)

A foreboding feeling is found in the words "I will go, I will go." This theme is emphasized again:

> I will go, I will go, while the secret of life,
> Is blooming in heaven, and blasting in hell;
> Is leaving on earth, and a budding in space: —
> I will go, I will go, with you, brother, farewell.
> (Stanza 78)

Early in his mission, Joseph felt confident of the protection God had promised him. In Nauvoo, he began to discover for himself and reveal to the Saints his mortal destiny—martyrdom. In two dramatic prophecies, the first dated 9 April 1842 and the second just a few weeks later, on 28 April, Joseph began to prepare the Saints for his early departure. During a funeral address, he reflected upon the sadness of parting prematurely from family and friends. He then stated:

"Some have supposed that Brother Joseph could not die, but this is a mistake. It is true there have been times when I have had the promise of my life to accomplish such and such things, but having accomplished those things I have not at present any lease of my life, and am as liable to die as other men."[34]

The minutes of an early Nauvoo Relief Society noted:

"[Joseph] did not know as he should have many opportunities of teaching them, that they were going to be left to themselves; they would not long have him to instruct them; that the Church would not have his instructions long, and the world would not be troubled with him a great while and would not have his teachings."[35]

These sources, along with many others, demonstrate the Prophet's foreknowledge of his impending death. The poetic version of Section 76 is another contemporary source that details Joseph's own sense of mission and his knowledge concerning his own mortal destiny. That a knowledge of his martyrdom made him somewhat melancholy on occasions is revealed in the emotionally charged phrase, "I will go, I will go, with you, brother, farewell."

ADDITIONAL INSIGHTS

The poem also includes a number of additional insights. For example, the Prophet clarified the phrase, "meridian of time," when it was noted "he [Christ] came to the world in the middle of time" (stanza 33). The destiny of those who had turned from the truth was emphasized in these words:

And which is the torment apostates receive,
But the end, or the place where the torment began,
Save to them who are made to partake of the same,
Was never, nor will be, revealed unto man.
(Stanza 37)

And the eternal nature of the gospel was reemphasized:

Who receiv'd and believ'd, and repented likewise,
And then were baptis'd, *as a man always was*,

Who ask'd and receiv'd a remission of sin,
And honored the kingdom by keeping its laws.
(Stanza 41; emphasis added)

CONCLUSION

Over the Prophet's signature, a commentary on the Vision was
published in Nauvoo. That poetic rendition of Doctrine and Covenants
76 adds to our understanding of the original principles communicated
in the revelation as Joseph understood it or, alternatively, as he was
willing to reveal it to the Saints in 1843. And, as the poem stated:

I, Joseph, the prophet, in spirit beheld,
And the eyes of the inner man truly did see
Eternity sketch'd in a vision from God,
Of what was, and now is, and yet is to be.
(Stanza 11)

NOTES

1. See Wilford Woodruff Journal, 1 Feb. 1843, Archives, The Church of
Jesus Christ of Latter-day Saints, Salt Lake City, Utah; hereafter cited as LDS
Church Archives.

2. On 10 February 1843 Joseph reviewed the mobbing of 24 March 1832;
see Joseph Smith Diary, 10 Feb. 1843, LDS Church Archives.

3. Joseph Smith Diary, 7 Jan. 1843; Wilson Law's poem, "All hail to our
Chief! Who has come back to us in honor" was published in *Times and Seasons*,
4 (15 February 1843): 112.

4. Woodruff Journal, 17 Jan. 1843.

5. In *Times and Seasons*, 4 (1 February 1843): 96.

6. Woodruff Journal, 18 Jan. 1843.

7. See Joseph Smith Diary, 20 Jan. 1843. Following Joseph's death in 1844,
Phelps changed the title and added several new stanzas; see Joseph Smith, *History
of The Church of Jesus Christ of Latter-day Saints*, 2d ed. rev., edited by B. H.
Roberts (Salt Lake City: The Church of Jesus Christ of Latter-day Saints, 1932–
51), 5:253–54.

8. In *Times and Seasons*, 4 (1 February 1843): 81–82.

9. Smith, *History of the Church*, 5:288; see also "Joseph Smith's History,"
Deseret News (14 May 1856): 1–2. This entry was probably composed by Willard
Richards after the Prophet's martyrdom. Exactly what is meant by "I dictated an
answer" may be impossible to determine. What is significant, however, is that this
date was chosen as the day of composition, not on or before 20 January, the same
day Phelps gave Joseph his poem. The *Deseret News* version also included the
poem, which B. H. Roberts did not include in the 1909 edition of the *History of
the Church*, probably as a result of space constraints.

10. Several individuals have argued for Phelps's authorship; see *A Believing
People: Literature of the Latter-day Saints*, ed. Richard H. Cracroft and Neal E.

Lambert (Salt Lake City: Bookcraft, 1979), p. 184; and Bruce A. Van Orden, "William W. Phelps's Service in Nauvoo as Joseph Smith's Political Clerk," *Brigham Young University Studies,* 32 (Winter and Spring 1991): 94.

11. Smith, *History of the Church,* 4:551.

12. John Taylor, "Ancient Poetry," *Times and Seasons,* 4 (1 February 1843): 81.

13. In *Times and Seasons,* 4 (1 February 1843): 82–85.

14. See N. B. Lundwall, comp., *The Vision; or, The Degrees of Glory* (Kaysville, Utah: Inland Printing Co, 1951), pp. 156–64.

15. See Hyrum M. Smith, *The Doctrine and Covenants* (Liverpool: Hyrum M. Smith, 1916), the precursor to the classic 1923 Smith and Sjodahl commentary; Sidney B. Sperry, *Doctrine and Covenants Compendium* (Salt Lake City: Bookcraft, 1960); Roy W. Doxey, *The Latter-day Prophets and the Doctrine and Covenants,* 4 vols. (Salt Lake City: Deseret Book Co., 1964); Daniel H. Ludlow, *A Companion to Your Study of the Doctrine and Covenants,* 2 vols. (Salt Lake City: Deseret Book Co., 1978); and *The Doctrine and Covenants Student Manual (Religion 324–325)* (Salt Lake City: The Church of Jesus Christ of Latter-day Saints, 1981).

16. See L. G. Otten and C. M. Caldwell, *Sacred Truth of the Doctrine and Covenants,* 2 vols. (Springville, Utah: LEMB, 1983), 2:27–28, 34; Richard Cowan, *The Doctrine and Covenants: Our Modern Scripture,* rev. and enl. (Salt Lake City: Bookcraft, 1984), p. 115; and Monte Nyman, "Six Visions of Eternity: Section 76," in the proceedings of the 1984 Sperry Symposium, *Hearken, O Ye People: Discourses on the Doctrine and Covenants* (Salt Lake City: Randall Book Co., 1984), pp. 105–18.

17. See Lyndon W. Cook, *The Revelations of the Prophet Joseph Smith* (Salt Lake City: Deseret Book Co., 1985), pp. 158–66; Michael J. Preece, *Learning to Love the Doctrine and Covenants* (Salt Lake City: MJP Publishing, 1988), pp. 152–63; and Larry E. Dahl, "The Visions of Glory (D&C 76)," in Robert L. Millet and Kent P. Jackson, eds., *The Doctrine and Covenants,* vol. 1 of *Studies in Scripture* (Salt Lake City: Randall Book, 1984), pp. 295–305.

18. William Clayton's Private Book, 5 Jan. 1841, LDS Church Archives, as cited in Andrew F. Ehat and Lyndon W. Cook, *The Words of Joseph Smith: The Contemporary Accounts of the Nauvoo Discourses of the Prophet Joseph* (Provo: Brigham Young University Religious Studies Center, 1980), p. 60.

19. Thomas Bullock Report, 12 May 1844, LDS Church Archives.

20. When the poem has been cited, it has usually been these two stanzas; see, for example, Edward Wheelock Tullidge, *Life of Joseph the Prophet* (New York: n.p., 1878), p. 361; Bruce R. McConkie, *Mormon Doctrine* (Salt Lake City: Bookcraft, 1958), p. 66; Truman G. Madsen, *Eternal Man* (Salt Lake City: Deseret Book Co., 1966), p. 34; L. G. Otten and C. M. Caldwell, *Sacred Truth of the Doctrine and Covenants,* 2:27–28, 34; and Richard Cowan, *The Doctrine and Covenants: Our Modern Scripture,* p. 115.

21. In Eugene England, ed., "George Laub's Nauvoo Journal," *Brigham Young University Studies,* 18 (Winter 1978): 176; see also George Laub Journal, 27 Aug. 1843, LDS Church Archives.

22. The phrase "godified state" has been changed to "glorified state" in several

twentieth-century versions of the poem; see, for example, Cracroft and Lambert, *A Believing People*, p. 186.

23. Woodruff Journal, 14 May 1843.

24. *Diary of Charles Lowell Walker,* ed. A. Karl Larson and Katharine Miles Larson (Logan: Utah State University Press, 1980), p. 465; see also Charles Lowell Walker Diary, 19 Aug. 1877, LDS Church Archives.

25. It is evident that the use of uppercase and lowercase for many words was not consistent in manuscript and printed sources of the period, and it would be difficult to determine with certainty whether Joseph was directly responsible for typesetting the 1843 poem for publication. That it was intentional may be argued, however, because of a participant in its publication: Wilford Woodruff. He was working at the Nauvoo printing establishment during this period and two years later used the uppercase *Gods* for this verse in the first European edition of the Doctrine and Covenants (1845); see The Book of Doctrine & Covenants (Liverpool: James and Woodburn, Printers, 1845), p. 267. This capitalization continued in the next five European editions (1849, 1852, 1854, 1866, and 1869). The 1844 American edition was reprinted in 1845 and 1846, unchanged, from the same plates. Eventually, the third American edition (1876) was prepared for publication by Orson Pratt, under the direction of Brigham Young. This edition changed the word *gods* to *Gods* following the lead of Wilford Woodruff's 1845 European edition; see The Doctrine and Covenants (Salt Lake City: Deseret News Office, 1876), p. 248. Later, Pratt prepared a new European edition in 1879, and this edition's plates were used to print an 1880 American edition in Salt Lake City. Pratt retained the capitalization of *Gods* in both editions. From 1880 to 1920, the Church produced at least twenty-eight printings of this edition. The lowercase *gods* was reintroduced in the text of the 1921 edition.

26. See Book of Doctrine and Covenants of the Church of Jesus Christ of Latter Day Saints (Cincinnati: Publishing Committee of the Reorganized Church of Jesus Christ of Latter-Day Saints, 1864), p. 213.

27. *Nauvoo Expositor,* 1 (7 June 1844): 2.

28. Bullock Report, 16 June 1844.

29. Variations of this phrase were used by these Saints to describe their group. For a fuller discussion, see Richard Neitzel Holzapfel and Jeni Broberg Holzapfel, *Women of Nauvoo* (Salt Lake City: Bookcraft, 1992), chap. 1, n. 9.

30. Section 91, Doctrine and Covenants of the Church of the Latter Day Saints (Kirtland, Ohio: F. G. Williams & Co., 1835), p. 228.

31. A Record of the Organization and Proceedings of the Female Relief Society of Nauvoo, 28 April 1842, LDS Church Archives; hereafter cited as Relief Society Minutes.

32. Woodruff Journal, 22 Jan. 1843.

33. See, for example, Ronald K. Esplin, "Joseph Smith's Mission and Timetable: 'God Will Protect Me until My Work Is Done,' " in Larry C. Porter and Susan Easton Black, eds., *The Prophet Joseph: Essays on the Life and Mission of Joseph Smith* (Salt Lake City: Deseret Book Co., 1988), pp. 280–319.

34. Woodruff Journal, 9 Apr. 1842.

35. Relief Society Minutes, 28 Apr. 1842.

11

PROPHECIES OF THE LAST DAYS IN THE DOCTRINE & COVENANTS AND THE PEARL OF GREAT PRICE

Kent P. Jackson

Brigham Young University

The topic of the last days is of considerable interest to Latter-day Saints and has been since the restoration of the gospel. But lately, as the result of current events and recent books, tapes, firesides, and lectures, this subject has taken on an interest that is even greater than usual. It thus seems timely and appropriate that we examine what the scriptures have to say about this matter, so that all of us can measure the things that we hear against the standard of what God has revealed. Frequently they are not the same.

This discussion will be restricted to the Doctrine and Covenants and the Pearl of Great Price, which, for convenience, I will call "modern revelation."[1] In order to write this paper, I first read these two books of scripture to identify every passage in them that foretells something about the dispensation of the fulness of times — the time from the restoration of the gospel to the end of the Millennium. I then took those passages, sorted them by subject matter, and arranged them into a rather extensive index. Having thus collected and categorized all the relevant data, I was then able to analyze what I had found and write this paper. Modern revelation places special emphasis on certain key topics relevant to the future. In this paper, I will examine briefly the seven topics that are emphasized most in the revelations, and I will present them roughly in chronological order. The topics are the preaching of the gospel, the gathering, the building of Zion, God's judgments on the world, the Saints, the Second Coming, and the Millennium.

THE PREACHING OF THE GOSPEL

The Lord has placed upon us the awesome responsibility to take the gospel to the world. The revelations make this responsibility clear. They are written with a sense of urgency, for this work is not only of life-and-death importance, but the time to do it is short. Our mission is to preach the gospel for the last time (D&C 33:3; 39:17; 43:28; 88:84). With the promise that nothing will hinder them in this work (D&C 1:5), our missionaries will bear testimony before kings and rulers (D&C 1:23), as well as the poor and the meek (D&C 35:15). They are to preach repentance, and to warn of coming judgments (D&C 1:4; 43:20; 63:37; 88:84–85). In doing so, they will assist in preparing the way for Christ's coming (D&C 34:6; 65:5–6).

Our missionaries are to be considered the weak and the simple of the earth (D&C 1:23). We should not look upon this designation as an insult, for even Joseph Smith, the greatest prophet save Jesus only (D&C 135:3), is described in similar terms (D&C 124:1). But how marvelous it is that the Lord has chosen his servants from among the humble and unlearned — according to the world's false standards — to preach the greatest message in the universe.

To whom shall the message be taught? The revelations are perfectly clear on this matter. The gospel is to be preached to "all people" (D&C 1:4), to "every creature" (D&C 18:28), to "the uttermost parts of the earth" (D&C 58:64), to "the ends of the earth" (D&C 65:2), and to "all the world" (D&C 84:62). The Doctrine and Covenants contains a dozen passages that teach clearly that the gospel is intended for all people and that we as a church are commanded to take it to everyone (D&C 1:4, 23; 18:28; 39:15; 42:58; 58:64; 65:2; 77:8; 84:62; 90:9; 112:1; 133:37). The New Testament (Mark 16:15) and the Pearl of Great Price (JS–M 1:31) say the same thing. In 1974, President Spencer W. Kimball promised us that the Lord would open the doors when we would be ready to enter them.[2] We have seen in the past few years how quickly and how miraculously the Lord can do his work. Many doors are still closed, and we have much to do to be prepared to enter them. But in God's due time, we will. In short, as the Lord told the prophet Joseph Smith, "This gospel *shall* be preached unto every nation, and kindred, and tongue, and people" (D&C 133:37; emphasis added).

THE GATHERING

The gathering receives considerable emphasis in the scriptures. We live in a great day of gathering, and thus its purposes and its results have been made clear in modern revelation. The keys of the gathering have been brought from the heavens to The Church of Jesus Christ of Latter-day Saints (D&C 110:11; 113:6). Thus it stands to reason that the gathering of which the scriptures speak is to be done under the auspices of the Church and under the explicit direction of its prophets, who hold those keys. We have seen this already in Church history as the prophets have directed the Saints to gather first to central gathering places, such as Missouri, Illinois, and Utah, and as they now have instructed them to remain in their homelands to gather with their countrymen there. The gathering will thus continue under prophetic guidance, whether in a center place or in many lands. And since the Lord's house is a house of order, it seems safe to say that those who choose to run ahead of Church leaders to "gather" independently of prophetic direction will reap disappointment in due time. As Elder Boyd K. Packer has said, "If there is to be any gathering, it will be announced by those who have been regularly ordained and who are known to the Church to have authority."[3]

These remarks have placed emphasis on a physical gathering—a relocation from one place to another. But it is important that we understand that physical relocation is not the primary aspect of the gathering. The gathering is first and foremost a gathering to the gospel and its covenants. One is gathered when one joins the Church through baptism and comes together with the Saints in local wards and stakes (D&C 101:21)—a gathering "out of the world [and] into the Church."[4] We gather when we come unto Christ. Still, the idea of physical relocation plays two significant roles in the scriptures:

1. From time to time, the Lord brings together a critical mass of Saints in order to build temples and to strengthen his people with regard to material things.[5] The best example of this has been the nineteenth-century gathering to Utah, which facilitated, within its first fifty years, the construction of four temples. This gathering has also enabled the Saints to achieve a level of material prosperity such that they could afford to send their daughters and sons on missions to take the gospel message elsewhere.

2. There may be places where the idea of physical gathering or returning to promised lands is used metaphorically to represent the gathering to the gospel. This seems to be more the case in the Old Testament than in modern revelation. Gathering to Christ is the key issue.

According to modern revelation, as well as the Bible, the gathering will take place both before and after the beginning of the Millennium. While some future events are clearly identified in scripture to take place before the Second Coming, and others after, the language of almost all gathering prophecies is ambiguous with regard to when. It seems to me that this ambiguity teaches us that the principles and circumstances which bring about the gathering in our own time will continue beyond the Second Coming into the Millennium. These include continued missionary work, conversion to the gospel, baptism, the acceptance of temple covenants, and the willingness to receive assignments wherever the Lord desires us to serve.

Briefly, modern revelation teaches us the following about the gathering: Christ will gather his people (D&C 10:65; 29:2; 33:6). The keys of the gathering have been restored to the Church (D&C 110:11; 113:6). We are commanded to gather ourselves (D&C 101:22, 67; 133:4, 7, 9, 12–15) and to gather others (D&C 29:7; 109:58). People of every nation will gather (D&C 33:6; 45:69–71; 64:41–42; 133:7; Moses 7:62; JS–M 1:37). Independence, Missouri, has been consecrated to be the center place of the gathering (D&C 57:1–3; 84:2–4; 105:15), and in other places, stakes will be established for the same purpose (D&C 101:21). The gathering to Zion and her stakes is to be for a defense and a refuge from the coming judgments against the wicked (D&C 115:6; 124:36), and it will prepare the Saints for those judgments (D&C 29:8; 63:36; 101:64–66; 115:6). The righteous will be gathered from among the wicked (D&C 86:7; 101:65). The New Jerusalem will be built by the gathering of the Saints (D&C 84:4), and in the Millennium, they will be assembled there (D&C 42:9, 35–36; 84:2).

THE BUILDING OF ZION

Joseph Smith wrote: "The building up of Zion is a cause that has interested the people of God in every age; it is a theme upon which prophets, priests and kings have dwelt with peculiar delight; they have looked forward with joyful anticipation to the day in which we live; and fired with heavenly and joyful anticipations they have sung and written and prophesied of this our day; but they died without the sight; we are the favored people that God has made choice of to bring about the Latter-day glory; it is left for us to see, participate in and help to roll forward the Latter-day glory."[6]

These intense feelings expressed by the Prophet reflect the emphasis that modern revelation places on Zion. There are very few topics that receive greater attention than the building of Zion and the qualities of its citizens. The establishment of Zion is one of the greatest assignments of those of us who live in the latter days (D&C 6:6; 109:58).

What is Zion? In the broadest sense, it is The Church of Jesus Christ of Latter-day Saints and its members throughout the world, who endeavor to become "of one heart and one mind, and [dwell] in righteousness" (Moses 7:18).[7] The revelations teach us that there will be a center place of Zion and that there will also be stakes of Zion in other locations. Since these stakes and those who live within them are to reflect in every way the character of Zion, we can apply to the stakes the revealed messages that deal in their original context with the center place. Thus, the word "Zion" is to be understood to refer both to the center place and to the Saints in the stakes throughout the Church. In our period of history, the character of Zion's people is more important than the geography of Zion's borders.

As with the gathering, most prophecies of Zion cannot be assigned with much certainty either to the period before the Second Coming or to the period thereafter. We learn from the scriptures that Zion will be built to some degree before Christ's coming—both among the pure in heart throughout the world and in the New Jerusalem in Missouri (D&C 49:25; Moses 7:62). But in the Millennium it will become even more glorious, as it will be the dwelling place of Jesus Christ.

The Prophet Joseph Smith learned that the center place of Zion, the New Jerusalem, will be located at Independence, in Jackson County, Missouri (D&C 57:1–3; 58:7; 84:2–4; A of F 10), which is consecrated for the gathering of the Saints (D&C 57:1; 105:15). There will be a temple there (D&C 84:4). Despite the trials that our ancestors experienced in their unsuccessful attempt to establish it, the Lord has revealed that it will one day be built, and that its location has not changed (D&C 101:17, 20). In the meantime, stakes, which we can view as the "suburbs" of Zion, will continue to be established (D&C 101:21). The Saints are to obey the command to gather to Zion (D&C 63:36; 84:2; 133:4, 9, 12; Moses 7:62), even to flee (D&C 133:12), for the gathering will be for a defense and a refuge (D&C 115:6; 124:36). Zion will be built by the gathering of the Saints (D&C 84:4), and it will be their inheritance (D&C 38:19–20; 101:18). But it can only be built on the principles of the law of the celestial kingdom (D&C 105:5, 29), for its inhabitants must be the obedient (D&C 64:34–35) and the pure in heart (D&C 97:21; 100:16; 101:18).

Revelations tell us that Zion will be established and will flourish before Christ's coming (D&C 49:25; Moses 7:62). It will prosper (D&C 64:41; 82:14; 97:18), flow with milk and honey (D&C 38:18), and be a place of peace and safety (D&C 45:66, 68–70). It will be a holy city, for God's tabernacle will be there (Moses 7:62). Those of the world who renounce bloodshed will flee to it (D&C 45:68–69). Its inhabitants will be the Lord's people, the Lord will be their God (D&C 42:9), and his glory will be upon them (D&C 45:67; 64:41; 97:19). Zion will be honored by the nations (D&C 97:19), and they will acknowledge its sovereignty (D&C 105:32). It will be an ensign to the world (D&C 64:42), and people of all nations will gather to it (D&C 45:69, 71; 64:42). Zion will cause the nations to tremble and fear (D&C 64:43). The wicked will not come to it, because the terror of the Lord will be upon it (D&C 45:67, 70). Jesus Christ will be Zion's protection (D&C 97:19–20; 105:15).

In accordance with the Lord's command, the Prophet Joseph Smith sent Church members to Jackson County to build the city of Zion at the appointed place. Filled with the heavenly vision of the New Jerusalem, he knew that the Lord's promises concerning it would be fulfilled. But perhaps the great seer, who saw the end from the beginning, was not shown the time sequence of Zion's redemption. The trials of the Saints in Missouri caused him tremendous sorrow. He lamented the fact that the Lord would not let him know why such calamities had come upon Zion and how she will finally be redeemed.[8]

When will Zion be redeemed? The revelations give us only broad hints. The Lord told his Prophet that it would be "many years" before the Saints would receive their inheritance in Zion (D&C 58:44), or "a little season" in another revelation (D&C 105:9, 13). One reason was opposition from the world. Another was the Saints' unreadiness; Zion could only be redeemed following chastening (D&C 100:13).

In God's own due time, Zion will be redeemed (D&C 136:18). The Lord's enemies will be removed (D&C 105:15), and his presence will go before the Saints to help them possess it (D&C 103:20). This redemption will come by power (D&C 103:15–18), and it will be as the deliverance of ancient Israel (D&C 103:16–18), meaning, it appears, that it will be brought about by acts of divine intervention, rather than by acts of human power. It is likely that these passages ultimately refer not only to the New Jerusalem, but also to the pure in heart throughout the world, who build Zion wherever they are called to serve.

The Saints in Zion will be blessed. If they are faithful, they will escape God's judgments on the world (D&C 97:25–26) and will not be cursed when Christ comes (D&C 38:18). Enoch's city will return and join with them (D&C 84:99–100; Moses 7:63), and resurrected Saints will be with their Savior there (D&C 133:56). He will live in Zion (Moses 7:64) and will speak from Zion in the Millennium (D&C 133:20–21). And with the ultimate glorification of the earth, Zion will be the possession of the Saints in all eternity (D&C 38:20).

GOD'S JUDGMENTS ON THE WORLD

A most striking aspect of last-days prophecy in modern scripture is the powerful vocabulary used to describe the Lord's acts of judgment against the wicked world. Before Christ can dwell on earth in glory, the wickedness of the world must be removed, because it cannot exist where he is. Wickedness will be removed from the earth, either voluntarily through repentance or by some other means. Sadly, it appears that many will reject the Lord's invitations to repent and thus will be destroyed before or at the time of his coming. The revelations testify that God's judgments will indeed come upon the world (D&C 1:36; 19:3; 39:16; 43:29; 45:47; 56:1, 16; 84:87, 96; 88:84, 92, 104; 99:5; 101:11; 109:38, 45; 133:2, 50; Moses 7:66; JS–H 1:45) and that he will recompense each individual according to his or her works (D&C 1:10; 56:19; 112:34). For the wicked, it will not be a day of rejoicing.

Christ will put all enemies under his feet (D&C 49:6; 58:22). His arm will fall upon them (D&C 45:45, 47; 56:1), as will his sword (D&C 1:13; 35:14; 101:10). The unrighteous will be cut off (D&C 1:14; 45:44; 133:63), and the proud and wicked will be as stubble (D&C 29:9; 64:24; 133:64; JS–H 1:37), reaped as tares, tied in bundles, and burned (D&C 29:9, 21; 38:12; 45:50; 63:34, 54; 64:23–24; 85:3; 86:7; 88:94; 101:65–66; 109:46; 112:24; 128:24; 133:64; JS–H 1:37). Their flesh will fall from their bones, and their eyes will fall from their sockets (D&C 29:19). They will experience calamity (D&C 1:17; 45:50; 109:46), tribulation (D&C 29:8; Moses 7:61, 65; JS–M 1:33, 36), destruction (D&C 34:9; 105:15; JS–M 1:31, 55; JS–H 1:40), desolation (D&C 29:8; 35:11; 45:33; 63:37; 84:117; 88:85; 112:24; JS–H 1:45), and woe (D&C 5:5). They will be subject to earthquakes (D&C 45:33; 87:6; 88:89; JS–M 1:29), famines (D&C 87:6; JS–M 1:29; JS–H 1:45), flies and maggots (D&C 29:18), hailstorms (D&C 29:16), the shaking of the heavens (D&C 45:48; 49:23; JS–M 1:33, 36), and the shaking of the earth (D&C 49:23; 84:118; 88:87; Moses 8:61). They will be punished by lightnings (D&C 87:6; 88:90), plagues (D&C 84:97; 87:6), pestilences (JS–M 1:29; JS–H 1:45), wars (D&C 45:26, 33, 69; 63:33; 87:2, 3, 6; JS–M 1:23, 28, 29, 45), a desolating scourge (D&C 5:19; 45:31; 97:23), vapors of smoke (D&C 45:41), tempests (D&C 88:90), and thunders (D&C 87:6; 88:90). In all of this, they will experience great sorrow, mourning, and fear (D&C 29:15; 34:8; 45:26, 49–50, 74–75; 63:6, 33; 87:6; 88:91; 97:21; 112:24; 133:42; Moses 7:66).

There should be no misunderstanding as to the seriousness of these matters. In about twenty passages, the Lord uses such terms as *indignation, wrath, anger,* and *vengeance* to describe his feelings toward the evils of the world and those who practice them (D&C 1:9, 13; 29:17; 43:26; 56:1; 63:6; 85:3; 87:6; 88:8, 85, 88, 106; 97:22–24; 101:11; 109:38; 112:24; 115:6; 124:52, 106; 133:51). While the faithful will be protected from these acts of divine judgment, unworthy Church members will not, for God's vengeance will begin upon his own house (D&C 112:25–26; see also 97:25–26).

A hopeful note in this message of sorrow and doom is the reminder that obedience and repentance can indeed avert the coming judgments (D&C 5:5, 19; 39:18; 124:8). It is no wonder, then, that in more than twenty passages, the Lord invites us to prepare for what lies ahead (D&C 1:12–13; 29:8; 38:8–9; 43:20–21; 49:23; 61:38; 63:37; 64:23; 65:3, 5; 88:84, 92; 101:23; 104:59; 106:4–5; 109:38, 45–46; 133:2–4, 10, 17, 19, 58). And he tells us how. The scriptural formula for preparing for these events does not include the stockpiling of weapons, the construction of bomb shelters, or the building of settlements in the wilderness.[9] Instead, the divine word simply states, "He that repents and does the commandments of the Lord shall be forgiven" (D&C 1:32), and "Inasmuch as they do repent and receive the fulness of my gospel, and become sanctified, I will stay mine hand in judgment" (D&C 39:18).

The Lord will not initiate these calamities without warning. The restoration of the gospel took place, among other reasons, to give the world an opportunity to repent. "Knowing the calamity which should come upon the inhabitants of the earth," the Lord said, he called Joseph Smith, revealed the gospel to him, and commanded him and others to proclaim the message "unto the world" (D&C 1:17–18). And what is that message? Again and again the Lord commands his servants to call upon the world to repent — to repent as a means of escaping what lies ahead (e.g., D&C 88:84–85). But the words of the Lord's missionaries will not be the only warnings. Before the Lord will send tribulations to punish and cleanse the world, he will send others, earlier, to encourage the world to repent — to get the world's attention. These will include thunderings, lightnings, tempests, earthquakes, hailstorms, famines, and "pestilences of every kind" (D&C 43:25). But in general the world will not heed their message, and the Lord will say, "O, ye nations of the earth, how often would I have gathered you together as a hen gathereth her chickens under her wings, but ye would not! How oft have I called upon you . . . and would have saved you with an everlasting salvation, but ye would not!" (D&C 43:24–25). Then the judgment is pronounced: "Behold, the day has come, when the cup of the wrath of mine indignation is full" (D&C 43:26).

God's warnings to the world will thus include the testimony of his servants and what we call "natural disasters." If these fail to motivate the world to repent, then the punishment will come. The Lord said: "After your testimony cometh wrath and indignation upon the people. For after your testimony cometh the testimony of earthquakes. . . . And also cometh the testimony of the voice of thunderings, and the voice of lightnings, and the voice of tempests, and the voice of the waves of the sea heaving themselves beyond their bounds. And all things shall be in commotion; and surely, men's hearts shall fail them; for fear shall come upon all people" (D&C 88:88–91). It appears that these calamities are not warnings to repent. For that, the day will already have passed.

THE SAINTS

The events leading up to Christ's coming will serve as signs, to show that the hour is nigh (D&C 45:35–38; JS–M 1:39). Will the Saints be able to recognize them and ascertain their message? According to modern revelation, they will. The righteous will watch for the signs (D&C 39:23; 45:39; 61:38), and they will know them when they take place (D&C 68:11; JS–M 1:39). But they will have an even greater advantage over the rest of the world. As ancient Amos knew and as modern Saints understand, the Lord will do nothing without revealing his will to his servants the prophets (Amos 3:7). It stands to reason, therefore, that faithful Latter-day Saints in that day, who heed the counsel of the leaders of the Church, will not be caught by surprise and will not be unprepared. If Church members understood this principle as they should, they would not be so susceptible to all the odd and unscriptural ideas regarding the last days that seem to be so popular among us. The key for us will be to live worthy lives and to follow the direction of the Brethren.

Do the Saints have cause to fear the future? Yes, but we have equal cause to fear the present. Temptation, sin, and evil will always surround us, and today's trials require our finest efforts. But as time progresses, evil will become even more abundant, and the forces of wickedness with which we will be called to contend will be even more open, more powerful, and more popular (D&C 1:35; 45:27, 33). But Church members should reject the suggestion that the Saints will not be able to rise to the occasion. We have power on our side that all the forces of evil combined cannot defeat.

This is what the modern scriptures reveal about the Saints in the last days. They are commanded to gather and stand in holy places (D&C 101:22), which President Benson has defined as the places where "holy men and holy women stand," including "our temples, our chapels, our homes, and the stakes of Zion."[10] They will gather from all the earth (Moses 7:62; JS–M 1:27, 37). Christ will reign in their midst and have power over them (D&C 1:36). They will have peace, refuge, and safety in Zion (D&C 45:66), whether we define Zion as a location or as an orientation. There they will have the power of God (D&C 35:13–14; 133:59). The faithful Saints will be wise, they will receive the truth, they will take the Holy Spirit for their guide, and they will not be deceived (D&C 45:57; JS–M 1:37). The forces of evil will not overcome them (D&C 38:9; 45:32, 56–57; 63:20; 124:45), but they will be preserved by God (D&C 35:14; 101:12; 115:6; Moses 7:61). Though in some instances they will barely escape, still the Lord will be with them (D&C 63:34), and they will be saved in Zion (D&C 115:6; 124:10, 36).

The picture painted in these verses recognizes the reality of the world's trials, but it makes clear the fact that the Lord will be with his people, and they will withstand both the evils and the calamities of the last days. Will all worthy Saints survive God's judgments? The Prophet Joseph Smith pointed out that because of the weakness of our mortal bodies, some Saints will fall prey to the diseases and tribulations that will plague the earth.[11] But the revelations of the Doctrine and Covenants lead us to believe that we can look forward to many examples of divine intervention to preserve the Lord's faithful people in safety.

When Christ comes, the Saints will be blessed (D&C 133:44–45, 52). They will abide the day of his coming (D&C 45:56–57) and will be caught up to meet him (D&C 88:96–97; 109:75). They will then inherit the earth in the Millennium (D&C 45:58; 56:19–20; 63:20; 103:7) and will be comforted from their trials (D&C 101:14). Christ will be in their midst (D&C 45:59), and they will know him (D&C 84:98). They will be God's people, and he will be their God (D&C 42:9).

THE SECOND COMING

No future event is more extensively documented in modern revelation than the fact that Jesus will come again. The Second Coming is mentioned in more than fifty passages in the Doctrine and Covenants and the Pearl of Great Price, attesting that it is a literal event that will indeed transpire (D&C 1:12; 7:3; 27:18; 29:11–12; 33:18; 34:6–8, 12; 35:15–16, 27; 38:8, 17; 39:20–21, 24; 41:4; 42:36; 43:29; 45:16, 39, 44–53; 49:6–7, 28; 51:20; 54:10; 58:65; 61:38; 63:34–35, 49–50; 64:23; 65:5; 68:11, 35; 76:63; 87:8; 88:92, 95–98, 126; 99:5; 101:23; 106:4–5; 109:74–75; 112:34; 124:10; 128:24; 130:1, 14–17; 133:17–22, 40–52, 56; Moses 7:60, 65; JS–M 1:36–37, 43). It is worth noting and emphasizing that the Second Coming will be an actual event, because much of the Christian world has abandoned the idea of a literal return of Jesus. Jesus will come again.

According to the revelations, Jesus will come in a cloud (34:7; 45:16, 44; JS–M 1:36). He will come in glory (D&C 7:3; 29:11, 12; 34:7; 45:16, 44; 56:18; 65:5; 109:74; 133:46, 49; JS–M 1:36), with power (D&C 29:11; 34:7; 45:44; 56:18; 133:46; JS–M 1:36), and with intense heat (D&C 133:40–41). The mountains will flow at his presence (D&C 109:74; 133:40, 44), and the heavens and earth will shake (D&C 45:48). These prophecies clearly foresee a dramatic, unprecedented event, which will be an unimaginable display of power. All nations will tremble and mourn at Christ's coming (D&C 34:8; 45:49; 133:42). When he comes he will come in judgment (D&C 1:36; 43:29; 99:5; 133:2; JS–M 1:44–45), and only the worthy will survive (D&C 29:11; 38:8; 45:44, 50; 63:34; 64:23; 128:24; 133:44, 50–52). Signs will be shown to prepare the world for his coming (D&C 29:14; 45:35–42; 61:38; 68:11; 88:93; JS–M 1:39). The righteous will look for them (D&C 35:15; 39:23; 45:39, 44; 61:38), and they will know them when they are shown (D&C 68:11; JS–M 1:39). There will be seen a great sign in heaven (D&C 88:93), which the scriptures do not describe, and one half hour of silence will immediately precede the Savior's appearance (D&C 88:95).

The revelations teach us that Jesus will come with the hosts of heaven (D&C 45:44; 76:63; 133:18). Other passages suggest what this means. At his coming the Saints who have died since his resurrection will be resurrected themselves (D&C 29:13; 43:18; 45:45–46; 63:49; 88:97–98; 109:75; 133:56). They will then be caught up into the clouds to meet him (D&C 45:45; 88:97–98; 109:75), as will the Saints then living on earth (D&C 27:18; 88:96). This event is clearly one that should be understood as literal. If we view it in light of the parable of the wheat and the tares (as explained in modern revelation, 86:1–7 and JS–M 13:30), we learn that the Saints will first be gathered to safety — by being brought up to meet Christ in the cloud — and then the world and the worldly will be burned.

The Lord will be dressed in red when he comes, which, according to revelation, will symbolize the blood of those whom he will slay when he comes in vengeance (D&C 133:46, 48–51). His coming will be as obvious and as universally witnessed as the light of the morning coming out of the east, shining to the west, and covering the whole earth (JS–M 1:26). Indeed, all flesh will see him together (D&C 101:23). So great will be his glory, that the sun will hide its face in shame at his presence, the moon will withhold its light, and the stars will be hurled from their places (D&C 133:49).

When will the Second Coming take place? We do not know. As the scriptures teach, no one knows the day or the hour (D&C 39:21; 49:7; 51:20; 61:38; 124:10; 130:14–17; JS–M 1:46, 48). But we know that Christ will come quickly (D&C 33:18; 34:12; 35:27; 39:24; 41:4; 49:28; 51:20; 54:10; 68:35; 87:8; 88:126; 99:5; 112:34; 124:10) and, according to more than a dozen revelations that were given over a century and a half ago, he will come soon (D&C 1:12; 34:7; 35:15–16; 38:8; 39:20–21, 24; 49:6; 63:35; 106:4–5; 124:10; 128:24; 133:17).

Most people on earth do not know Jesus, and relatively few others believe in his literal Second Coming. Thus, to the world, he will come unexpectedly (D&C 106:4; JS–M 1:41–43). But the Lord's Saints are not of the world. They will expect his coming and will not be surprised when it takes place. The signs will show them that it is near, the prophets will prepare them, and they will be ready. For them, Christ's return will not be "as a thief in the night" (D&C 106:4). "Ye, brethren, are not in darkness," Paul wrote, "that that day should overtake you as a thief. Ye are all the children of light, and the children of the day" (1 Thessalonians 5:4–5; see also D&C 106:5).

THE MILLENNIUM

Modern scripture has a great deal to say about the Millennium, which will come as prophesied (D&C 43:30). It will be the culmination of all our aspirations for Zion. Indeed, it will be in the Millennium that Zion will flourish to its fullest degree, with the center place at the New Jerusalem. It may well be said that all the earth will be Zion then, for as Isaiah foretold, in that day "the earth shall be full of the knowledge of the Lord, as the waters cover the sea" (Isaiah 11:9). According to our tenth Article of Faith, "the earth will be renewed and receive its paradisiacal glory."

This is what we learn about the Millennium. When Christ returns, Satan will be bound (D&C 43:31; 84:100; 101:28). This fact alone will make the world an entirely different place from what humankind has experienced since the Fall. Can we imagine what life will be like then, when Satan, his demons, and his works will be absent from the earth? Nephi wrote that "because of the righteousness" of those who will be living then, Satan will have "no power over the hearts of the people" (1 Nephi 22:26). Because wicked people and wicked things will have been destroyed at Christ's coming, and because the Lord will be with us, the earth will rest (Moses 7:61, 64) and be glorified (D&C 77:12; 84:101; 101:25). It will be translated and transformed to a more sublime state than that which we see around us today. Many of the principles of science that we observe now will no longer be in operation, and new realities will prevail, commensurate with the higher degree of glory that the earth will then have. Among other things, time will cease (D&C 84:100), a condition that is incomprehensible to us now, but which will hopefully make sense then.

Christ will dwell on earth a thousand years (D&C 29:11; Moses

7:65). He will be in the midst of his people (D&C 45:59; 84:101), and he will be their king and their lawgiver (D&C 38:21–22; 41:4; 43:29; 45:59; 58:22; 76:63; 84:119; 133:25; A of F 10). His people will reign with him (D&C 43:29). These revelations lead to the conclusion that the systems of human government that now prevail will be replaced by one that is greater, in which Christ at the head will make known his divine will, and his subjects will welcome his divine leadership. How glorious that will be, after all the evil that has prevailed in the world as the result of unrighteous and unwise rulers. The earth will be given to the Saints (D&C 45:58), and the poor in heart will inherit its wealth (D&C 56:18–20).

Those who have mourned will be comforted (D&C 101:14). There will be no sorrow (D&C 101:29). There will be no death (D&C 101:29). There will be no wickedness (D&C 29:9, 11).

Changes will take place in the character of all nature. For example, the animals' fear of humans will cease (D&C 101:26). Indeed, the enmity of all flesh will come to an end (D&C 101:26). Since there will be no death, then clearly there will be no carnivores, either human or animal, and Isaiah's prophecy will be fulfilled literally when the "wolf also shall dwell with the lamb, and the leopard shall lie down with the kid" (Isaiah 11:6; see also v. 7).

In that day, all people will know the Lord (D&C 84:98; 101:25), which means that all will be bound by covenant with him and will do his works. Everything that we will ask will be given us (D&C 101:27). It will be a great day of revelation, for Christ will reveal all things (D&C 101:32–34; 121:27–32). Things never before revealed will be made known (D&C 128:18).

Men and women will continue to beget and bear children, who will be raised in a world dramatically unlike our own — a world in which people will behave as they should have all along. A revelation explains that their children in the Millennium will grow up without sin unto salvation (D&C 45:58). Can they do that while Satan is bound? Certainly. They can exercise their agency, reject evil, and make decisions in harmony with God's will. Evil will not be impossible, simply because Satan is bound. In fact, however, people will choose to do what is right.

Although there will be no death, individuals will still need to undergo the process that we call resurrection, which for them will be a change from their translated state to a state of celestial glory. The scriptures teach that we will grow old, and then we will be changed in the twinkling of an eye to an exalted condition (D&C 43:32; 63:50–51; 101:30–31).

How glorious will be that millennial day! We live now in a perverse world that we sometimes wrongly think is normal. It is not. We are surrounded by aberration, corruption, degeneration, and depravity. How blessed will be the time when Christ comes and makes all things right!

SOME WORDS OF CAUTION

There is nothing wrong with having an interest in, and even a feeling of excitement about, the great events of the last days. They are important, and we rejoice to see the Lord unfold his plan. But there is danger. This topic lends itself to sensationalism, speculation, and overzealousness, things which work best when (a) we are misinformed, and (b) the Holy Ghost is not present. From time to time, individuals afflicted with an inordinate zeal about the last days are led into making unwise decisions.[12]

In a very important address at Brigham Young University in 1981, President Ezra Taft Benson showed both by precept and by example how to teach about the last days. His method, as he explained it, was to "quote liberally from the words of the Lord to our dispensation," so that we will have guidance "from the Lord himself."[13] As President Benson taught, the primary source for our study of this and every other gospel topic is the word of the Lord that was revealed to Joseph Smith. We find this in the Book of Mormon, the Doctrine and Covenants, the Pearl of Great Price, and in the Prophet's sermons and writings.

Sometimes, well-meaning Latter-day Saints try to obtain an understanding of the last days by searching ancient revelations — such as Isaiah or the book of Revelation — with a focus on interpretations that are not supported by modern scripture. Wise students of the gospel will do otherwise; they will follow President Benson's admonition and turn to modern revelation, taking seriously the Lord's proclamation to Joseph Smith: "This generation shall have my word through you" (D&C 5:10). President Marion G. Romney wrote: "In each dispensation, . . . the Lord has revealed anew the principles of the gospel. So that while the records of past dispensations, insofar as they are uncorrupted, testify to the truths of the gospel, still each dispensation has had revealed in its day sufficient truth to guide the people of the new dispensation, independent of the records of the past. . . . The gospel, as revealed to the Prophet Joseph Smith, is complete and is the word direct from heaven to this dispensation. It alone is sufficient to teach us the principles of eternal life."[14] In practical terms, this means that we love the Bible, but we get our doctrine from modern revelation. The words of ancient prophets can be used to confirm, to bear witness to, and to illustrate the truths of modern revelation, but our knowledge of the gospel comes through what was revealed to Joseph Smith. This principle is especially important with respect to revelations concerning the last days. Many of those in the Bible are written in dramatic symbolic language that is easily susceptible to misinterpretation. Modern scripture, in contrast, is generally written in a clear and understandable style. We should exercise caution concerning any understanding of the last days that has not been explicitly revealed in our own time.

In October 1972, President Harold B. Lee responded to some concerns in the Church with the following words: "There are among us many loose writings predicting the calamities which are about to overtake us. Some of these have been publicized as though they were necessary to wake up the world to the horrors about to overtake us. Many of these are from sources upon which there cannot be unquestioned reliance. Are you . . . aware of the fact that we need no such publications to be forewarned, if we were only conversant with what the scriptures have already spoken to us in plainness?"[15]

Three things stand out in President Lee's statement:

First, some of these "loose writings" (and perhaps in our generation we might include videotapes, audiotapes, firesides, and lectures) are set forth "as though they were necessary to wake up the world." I am confident that if the Lord wants to wake up the world or the Church, he will do it through his prophets, who have been called, sustained, and ordained to that purpose (see D&C 42:11). God has selected them, and he knows how to communicate with them. And they know how to make his desires known to us. We can be sure that anyone else who feels a calling or a stewardship to assume that role and to warn the Church is going beyond the bounds of his or her privileges. In some circles, some individuals have lamented the fact that the Brethren do not sound the alarm sufficiently about the coming tribulations and how to avoid them. Some have suggested that God has silenced the prophets from emphasizing such things because of our failure to listen to them. Perhaps those who hold this view do so because they are not hearing in general conference the things they want to hear. Others have gone so far as to promote the notion that the Brethren are not aware of the dangers of the world and the gravity of the doom that awaits us, thereby necessitating other interpreters who are not apostles and prophets but who have a better understanding of these things. This belief is not only false, but it constitutes, in my opinion, a denial of the faith.

Elder Boyd K. Packer addressed this issue in the October 1992 general conference: "There are some among us now who have *not* been regularly ordained by the heads of the Church who tell of impending political and economic chaos, the end of the world. . . . Those deceivers say that the Brethren do not know what is going on in the world or that the Brethren approve of their teaching but do not wish to speak of it over the pulpit. Neither is true. The Brethren, by virtue of traveling constantly everywhere on earth, certainly know what is going on, and by virtue of prophetic insight are able to read the signs of the times. Do not be deceived by them—those deceivers."[16]

Second, as President Lee taught, if we are "conversant with what the scriptures have already spoken," we will not feel a need for the information that comes from "loose writings" about the last days. My experience has been that those who know the scriptures well are generally not attracted to such things. But as usual, some who are honest in their desires to learn will become confused or misled by looking for truth in the wrong places and by trusting the judgment and interpretations of those who are not called. President Lee warned that these "strange sources" may have "political implications." He encouraged the Saints to turn to modern revelation for "the sure word" concerning the last days, "rather than commentaries that may come from those whose information may not be the most reliable and whose motives may be subject to question."[17]

At the April 1973 general conference, President Lee said: "We have a rash of writings by certain persons who claim to be of good standing in the Church, going into considerable detail as they recite their past and present Church affiliations and activities in the foreword, interlude, and advertising. There are sensational predictions and observations, and to make their writings appear to have Church sanction, they use quotations and addresses from Church leaders, past and present, taken out of context in such a way as to make it appear as though these quotations were the endorsement of the book they wish to sell to Church members, who may thereby be induced to accept their writings as from unquestioned sources. . . . Furthermore, some designing individuals have solicited opportunities to speak at church gatherings, firesides, priesthood quorums, sacrament meetings. Now, brethren, we feel it is of the utmost importance to lift a warning voice so that our people will be safeguarded against such tactics as an all too obvious self-seeking opportunity to spread their own propaganda for their own interests. We must urge that priesthood leaders use careful discretion in screening out those whose motives may be subject to serious questions."[18]

Third, as President Lee pointed out, the scriptures speak to us "in plainness." This should come as no surprise, but some in the Church have been taught to believe otherwise. It seems only reasonable that if the Lord wants us to know and understand something, he reveals it in such a way that we can know and understand it! With very rare exceptions, the Lord's revelations (ancient and modern) are presented so they can be understood. And if not, it is the prerogative of the prophets alone to interpret them in behalf of the Church. Elder Packer warned against those who "pretend to have some higher source of inspiration concerning the fulfillment of prophecies than do ward or stake leaders or the General Authorities of the Church."[19] Some individuals with interest in the last days propose to have special methods or even special wisdom or enlightenment for understanding and explaining the scriptures. Not only is such an idea out of harmony with the Lord's pattern of doing things, but it attracts attention to the interpreter rather than to the message. Whatever the motives of such individuals may be, the effect of their work is usually to do harm to the Church. As the prophets have counseled us, they should be avoided.

A PRIVILEGE TO LIVE IN THIS GENERATION

We should view it as a privilege to live in a generation that is preparing for the return of our Savior. As John was sent to prepare the way for Christ's first coming, we in the Church today are sent to assist in the preparation for his second. This preparation includes our aiding in the establishment of Zion and our spreading the good news of salvation throughout the world. As all things in God's house are to be done in order, our responsibility is to take direction from the Lord's servants and to magnify the callings that we receive from them.

There is nothing mysterious about what is required of us in the last days. Above all, our personal worthiness and devotion must be appropriate for those who are called to be Saints. As Elder M. Russell Ballard has taught, the Lord "has given us adequate instruction that, if followed, will see us safely through any crisis."[20] Those individuals who follow the prophets, read the scriptures, seek the Lord's guidance in prayer, pay their tithes and offerings, obey the commandments, and are true and faithful to their covenants, will be ready, and will be worthy to stand when Christ appears.

NOTES

1. The Book of Mormon, because it was revealed in our time, is also properly called modern revelation, but it will not be included in this study.

2. Spencer W. Kimball, "When the World Will Be Converted," *Ensign,*

Oct. 1974, p. 7: "I feel that when we have done all in our power that the Lord will find a way to open doors. That is my faith. . . . Is anything too hard for the Lord? . . . If he commands, certainly he can fulfill. . . . I believe the Lord can do anything he sets his mind to do. But I can see no good reason why the Lord would open doors that we are not prepared to enter."

3. Boyd K. Packer, "To Be Learned Is Good If . . . ," *Ensign*, Nov. 1992, p. 73.

4. Ibid., p. 71. See also Spencer W. Kimball, *The Teachings of Spencer W. Kimball*, ed. Edward L. Kimball (Salt Lake City: Bookcraft, 1982), p. 439: "The gathering of Israel consists of joining the true church and their coming to a knowledge of the true God. . . . Any person, therefore, who has accepted the restored gospel, and who now seeks to worship the Lord in his own tongue and with the Saints in the nations where he lives, has complied with the law of the gathering of Israel and is heir to all of the blessings promised the Saints in these last days."

5. See Joseph Smith's comments on this in *The Words of Joseph Smith*, ed. Andrew F. Ehat and Lyndon W. Cook (Provo, Utah: Religious Studies Center, Brigham Young University, 1980), pp. 212–13. See also Joseph Smith, *Teachings of the Prophet Joseph Smith*, sel. Joseph Fielding Smith (Salt Lake City: Deseret Book Co., 1938), p. 308.

6. Smith, *Teachings of the Prophet Joseph Smith*, p. 231.

7. See also Harold B. Lee, "Strengthen the Stakes of Zion," *Ensign*, July 1973, p. 3.

8. *The Personal Writings of Joseph Smith*, ed. Dean C. Jessee (Salt Lake City: Deseret Book Co., 1984), pp. 308–9: "I know that Zion, in the own due time of the Lord will be redeemed, but how many will be the days of her purification, tribulation and affliction, the Lord has kept hid from my eyes; and when I enquire concerning this subject the voice of the Lord is, Be still, and know that I am God! . . . Now there are two things of which I am ignorant and the Lord will not show me. . . . and they are these, Why God hath suffered so great calamity to come upon Zion; or what the great moving cause of this great affliction is. . . . And again by what means he will return her back to her inheritance." See also Smith, *Teachings of the Prophet Joseph Smith*, p. 34.

9. Elder Packer spoke of self-appointed leaders who "are misleading members to gather to colonies or cults." He called them "deceivers" and warned strongly against them. "To Be Learned Is Good If . . . ," p. 73.

10. Ezra Taft Benson, "Prepare Yourselves for the Great Day of the Lord," in *Brigham Young University Fireside and Devotional Speeches, 1981* (Provo, Utah: Brigham Young University, 1981), p. 68.

11. Smith, *Teachings of the Prophet Joseph Smith*, p. 162.

12. Including "extreme preparations," as Elder M. Russell Ballard recently reminded us in "The Joy of Hope Fulfilled," *Ensign*, Nov. 1992, p. 32.

13. Benson, "Prepare Yourselves," p. 65.

14. Marion G. Romney, "A Glorious Promise," *Ensign*, Jan. 1981, p. 2.

15. Harold B. Lee, "Admonitions for the Priesthood of God," *Ensign*, Jan. 1973, p. 106.

16. Packer, "To Be Learned Is Good If . . . ," p. 73; emphasis in the original.

17. Lee, "Admonitions for the Priesthood of God," p. 106. He recommended the following sources: JS–M; D&C 38; 45; 101; 133.

18. Harold B. Lee, "Follow the Leadership of the Church," *Ensign,* July 1973, pp. 97–98.

19. Boyd K. Packer, "Reverence Invites Revelation," *Ensign,* Nov. 1991, p. 21.

20. Ballard, "The Joy of Hope Fulfilled," p. 32.

12

"MY DISCIPLES SHALL STAND IN HOLY PLACES": JESUS CHRIST IN THE TWENTY-FIRST CENTURY

Clark V. Johnson

Brigham Young University

That the Doctrine and Covenants is a modern witness to a modern world of a living Christ makes it a unique book. It is not a modern translation of an ancient document revealing the Christ to a modern world. Rather, it contains revelations given to nineteenth- and twentieth-century prophets. In those revelations the Savior restores his Church to the earth, gives laws of conduct to his disciples, testifies of his own atonement, and reveals in vision the ultimate destiny of mankind. The book has too many divergent themes and subjects to make it a smooth, flowing narrative. It is the Author of the book, Jesus Christ, that gives the book continuity and deep meaning. The Lord speaks to us: "You can testify that you have heard my voice, and know my words" (D&C 18:36). The voice of Jesus Christ permeates the Doctrine and Covenants. In the first two verses, for example, the Lord invokes his power and authority, calling all to attention:

"Hearken, O ye people of my church, saith the voice of him who dwells on high, and whose eyes are upon all men . . . listen together. For verily the voice of the Lord is unto all men, and there is none to escape; and there is no eye that shall not see, neither ear that shall not hear, neither heart that shall not be penetrated" (D&C 1:1–2).

The Savior is clearly the center of the Doctrine and Covenants. He reveals himself to us in his own voice, telling us who he is and what he expects of us.

The revelations in the Doctrine and Covenants teach us that Jesus, or Jehovah, was the Savior of the ancients — Adam, Noah, Shem, Abraham — the Savior of those who are living today, and the Savior of those who will live in the twenty-first century. The revelations clearly point out that Jesus is our Head and that men and women who follow him become his children. The Doctrine and Covenants shows Jesus' love for all the children of God. Indeed, the Doctrine and

Covenants teaches that the Father placed his name upon his Son, which gives Jesus full authority to act for the Father; and in return, Jesus gives the credit and glory to his Father. From the beginning, Jesus identifies himself as the Creator and as the God with whom we make covenants.

The revelations clearly establish Jesus as the head of his Church and show that he is concerned about individual people. Some sections of the Doctrine and Covenants are responses to personal inquiries. In each of those sections, the person is called to repent and to serve. Through repentance and under the Savior's tutelage, individuals grow spiritually, emotionally, and physically until they are ready to meet the Father. Jesus also gives to each person time to accomplish his or her mission in mortality. And he instructs his disciples to avoid deception by following his living prophets.

THE FATHER PLACED HIS NAME UPON JESUS

When the council of Gods met before the organization of the earth, the Father presented his plan to those who were present (D&C 121:32).[1] During the meeting a conflict arose. Satan wanted to redeem all of God's children, and he demanded the credit (Moses 4:2). Jesus said, however, "Father, thy will be done, and the glory be thine forever" (Moses 4:2). In this council, "the Father placed His name upon the Son; and Jesus Christ spoke and ministered in and through the Father's name; and so far as power, authority, and Godship are concerned His words and acts were and are those of the Father."[2]

The Savior exercises his divine authority as he directs his Church and reveals the commandments and doctrines necessary to exalt those who make covenants with him. For example, Doctrine and Covenants 29 begins, "Listen to the voice of Jesus Christ, your Redeemer, the Great I AM, whose arm of mercy hath atoned for your sins" (D&C 29:1). Later in the same revelation the Savior says, "But, behold, I say unto you that I, the Lord God, gave unto Adam and unto his seed, that they should not die as to the temporal death, until I, the Lord God, should send forth angels to declare unto them repentance and redemption, through faith on the name of mine Only Begotten Son" (D&C 29:42). Jesus is still the God giving the information, but in verse 42 he is speaking as though he were the Father, which is his divine right. President Joseph Fielding Smith wrote:

"In giving revelations our Savior speaks at times for himself; at other times for the Father, and in the Father's name, as though he were the Father, and yet it is Jesus Christ, our Redeemer who gives the message."[3] Even though the Father bestowed upon his Son the divine right to speak in the Father's name, Jesus gives the honor and glory to his Father. "Nevertheless, glory be to the Father, and I partook and finished my preparations unto the children of men" (D&C 19:19).

When the Savior gave directions establishing a storehouse for the poor in Zion, he said to his prophet that it was for the benefit of mankind, "to the glory of your Father who is in heaven," and to make Church members equal in "earthly things" so that they could become equal in "obtaining heavenly things" (D&C 78:4–6).

Jesus' earthly mission was to do the will of the Father. He stated that he and the Father are one (D&C 20:28). To the Nephites he said: "I am in the Father, and the Father in me, and the Father and I are one" (3 Nephi 11:27). During his appearance to the Nephite Twelve, he said, "I am even as the Father; and the Father and I are one" (3 Nephi 28:10). This passage is often interpreted to mean that they are one in purpose. While that is true, the scriptures teach that the relationship between the Father and the Savior goes beyond being one in purpose. In a revelation from Christ to Nephi, the son of Helaman, the Savior said: "I will bless thee forever . . . for thou shalt not ask that which is contrary to my will," meaning that whatever Nephi said would be done (Helaman 10:5). The scriptures further indicate that Nephi's desire in life had been to serve God. Jesus reminded Nephi that he had not sought the will of man and that he had served God "with unwearyingness" (Helaman 10:4). Nephi had reached a oneness with God that went beyond purpose. The words, acts, and deeds of Nephi were the words, acts, and deeds of Jehovah. Thus, the oneness spoken of by the Savior when referring to his relationship with the Father extends beyond purpose and means that the actions he has taken are the actions the Father would have taken were he present in place of the Son.

JESUS CHRIST, THE CREATOR AND GIVER OF LIFE

In the Book of Mormon, King Benjamin taught his people that Jesus was "the Father of heaven and earth, the Creator of all things from the beginning" (Mosiah 3:8). The Doctrine and Covenants affirms Jesus' role in the Creation. "Worlds were made by him . . . and through him, and of him" (D&C 93:10), and "I gave unto you a commandment that you should call your solemn assembly, that your fastings and your mourning might come up into the ears of the Lord of Sabaoth, which is by interpretation, the creator of the first day, the beginning and the end" (D&C 95:7). At a conference held nine months after the organization of the Church, Jesus said to those assembled: "Thus saith the Lord your God, even Jesus Christ, the Great I AM, Alpha and

Omega, the beginning and the end, the same which looked upon the wide expanse of eternity . . . before the world was made . . . I am the same which spake, and the world was made, and all things came by me" (D&C 38:1, 3). Referring to his majesty and power, the revelations teach that "he is in the sun . . . in the moon . . . [and] the light of the stars, and the power thereof by which they were made" and shine (D&C 88:7–9). Christ did more than just organize the planets, however. He gives life to all his creations, including the children of God who live on the earth (D&C 88:13; 93:9). From him comes the "light that quickeneth" mankind's understanding and fills "the immensity of space" (D&C 88:11–12). Finally, Jesus is the person who redeems the soul, and through whom men and women may sanctify (purify) themselves from "all unrighteousness, that [they] may be prepared for the celestial glory" (D&C 88:18). Thus those who become disciples of Jesus become his "friends" after they have made covenants with him (D&C 84:77; see also 88:117; 93:45).

JESUS CHRIST IS THE HEAD OF HIS CHURCH

Because of the power invested in him by his Father, the Savior spoke with full authority when he organized his Church in this last dispensation: "Hearken, O ye people of my church, saith the voice of him who dwells on high, and whose eyes are upon all men" (D&C 1:1). Jesus identified The Church of Jesus Christ of Latter-day Saints as his Church (D&C 115:4). In a revelation to the Prophet Joseph Smith shortly after the organization of the Church, the Savior reminded Joseph that he had given him "the keys of my kingdom, and a dispensation of the gospel for the last times; and for the fulness of times" (D&C 27:13). In the dispensation of the fulness of times, there will be a unifying of all of the Savior's work since the earth's creation. After the restoration of the "keys of [the] kingdom," conferences were held during which the organization of the Church was established. Bishops, apostles, and seventies were called during various conferences, and the organization of quorums took place (D&C 41; 107). Jesus gave the officers of his Church definite responsibilities. The First Presidency presided over all the quorums. The Quorum of Twelve Apostles was second in authority to the First Presidency, and the Quorum of Seventy served under the direction of the first two quorums (D&C 107:22–30).

As these officers began to function, Jesus increased the responsibilities of his followers. On one occasion he instructed them that when they give their own "substance unto the poor, ye will do it unto me." He further instructed that the donations "shall be laid before the bishop of my church and his counselors, two of the elders, or high priests, such as he shall appoint or has appointed and set apart for that purpose" (D&C 42:31). The Savior directed that the disposition of donated properties be handled by the First Presidency, the Quorum of the Twelve, and the Presiding Bishop and his council (D&C 120:1). On another occasion he called for his disciples, or Church members, "to labor in my vineyard, and to build up my church, and to bring forth Zion" (D&C 39:13).

JESUS IS THE GOD WITH WHOM WE COVENANT

King Benjamin taught that those who make covenants "shall be called the children of Christ" (Mosiah 5:7). The Doctrine and Covenants identifies the principles and ordinances attending that covenant relationship. The Prophet Joseph was commanded: "Thou shalt declare repentance and faith on the Savior, and remission of sins by baptism, and by fire, yea, even the Holy Ghost" (D&C:19:31). Those who accept baptism, who keep his commandments, and obey his law will be redeemed (D&C 49:5, 8–14; Mosiah 5:7; 15:30).

Jesus referred to the price he paid to save mankind. His suffering in Gethsemane caused him "to tremble because of pain, and to bleed at every pore, and to suffer both body and spirit." The intense pain in Gethsemane caused the Savior to wish that he "might not drink the bitter cup" (D&C 19:18). In another revelation he says, "Even as many as have believed in my name, for I am Christ, and in mine own name, by the virtue of the blood which I have spilt, have I pleaded before the Father" for you (D&C 38:4). Clearly his suffering places him in a position to intercede in our behalf if we repent. "He redeemed us with his blood."[4] His suffering and death give life to all mankind; however, only those who obey his law, enter into covenants with him, and receive the ordinances of the priesthood become his children. For them, redemption extends beyond mere salvation to include exaltation, or eternal life.

The Doctrine and Covenants teaches that the ordinances of the priesthood reveal to men and women the nature of God. Without the ordinances men and women cannot know God nor enter into his presence. The revelations teach that "in the ordinances [of the priesthood] . . . the power of godliness is manifest. And without the ordinances thereof, and the authority of the priesthood, the power of godliness is not manifest unto men in the flesh" (D&C 84:20–21). Thus, through faithful obedience to the ordinances of baptism, the gift of the Holy Ghost, the endowment, and temple marriage or sealing, all performed by the authority of the priesthood, men and women become

Christ's sons and daughters (D&C 20:73, 77, 79; 25:1; 131:1–4; Mosiah 5:7).

The Prophet Joseph Smith understood this doctrine and taught the Saints "that baptism is a sign ordained of God, for the believer in Christ to take upon himself in order to enter into the kingdom of God. . . . Those who seek to enter [God's kingdom] in any other way will seek in vain; for God will not receive them."[5] On another occasion the Prophet said, "I feel disposed to speak a few words . . . concerning the endowment: All who are prepared, and are sufficiently pure to abide the presence of the Savior will see Him in the solemn assembly."[6] Concerning temple marriage, or sealing, Joseph taught: "If you have power to seal on earth and in heaven . . . [then] go and seal on earth your sons and daughters unto yourself, and yourself unto your fathers in eternal glory."[7]

Once individuals have received all the ordinances of the temple, then Jesus' atonement in Gethsemane and on the cross has full effect upon them, providing they keep the covenants they have made. Nephi taught that it is "by grace that we are saved, after all we can do" (2 Nephi 25:23). The price the Savior paid in Gethsemane and on the cross ransomed man from physical and spiritual death. He did that which no mortal man or woman could do. He took upon himself the sins of each person who has lived or ever will live on the earth. He provided the way wherein men and women can reenter the presence of God if they repent. To Martin Harris the Savior said, "I, God, have suffered these things for all, that they might not suffer if they would repent; but if they would not repent they must suffer even as I" (D&C 19:16–17). The revelations in the Doctrine and Covenants clearly teach "that justification [and] . . . that sanctification through the grace of our Lord and Savior Jesus Christ is just and true, to all those who love and serve God with all their mights, minds, and strength" (D&C 20:30–31). People justify themselves when they make covenants with the Savior, and they become his "sons and daughters" through obedience to the promises they have made him (D&C 76:24). As they demonstrate their determination to serve him at all costs, he sanctifies them. Hence, the cleansing power of the Atonement takes time as each individual learns to do things the Savior's way. During that period the Savior responds to their needs, which helps them draw closer to him and his father.

JESUS' CONCERN FOR INDIVIDUALS

Some of the revelations given in the Doctrine and Covenants were addressed to individual men and women. Joseph and Emma were visited

by the Prophet's parents while they were living at Harmony, Pennsylvania, in February 1829. Father Smith made personal inquiry, asking
what the Lord wanted him to do. Joseph received a revelation detailing
the qualities of faith, hope, charity, brotherly kindness, and love, that
Father Smith was required to have to serve in God's kingdom (D&C
4).

Oliver Cowdery made an inquiry similar to Father Smith's.
Through the Prophet Joseph, Oliver was admonished to trust God and
not to seek for the world's riches but to seek "wisdom" and that "the
mysteries of God" would be "unfolded" to him (D&C 6:7). Oliver
learned some lessons the hard way. In 1829 while he and Joseph worked
to translate the Book of Mormon, Oliver desired that he too might
have the gift of translation. The Lord promised Oliver that he would
bless him with the gift of revelation. The Savior said, "I will tell you
in your mind and in your heart, by the Holy Ghost, which shall come
upon you and which shall dwell in your heart" (D&C 8:2). Oliver was
also admonished to "not ask for that which you ought not" (D&C
8:10). Later in the same month Oliver tried to translate and failed.
The Lord directed a second revelation to him through Joseph in which
he told Oliver to "be patient, my son, for it is wisdom in me, and it
is not expedient that you should translate at this present time" (D&C
9:3). The Savior reminded Oliver that he had been called to write for
the Prophet and should labor in that capacity until he received further
direction (D&C 9:4, 13–14).

Even though he mildly reprimanded Oliver, the Lord revealed to
him the principles a person needs to use to receive revelation. Jesus
said: "Behold, you have not understood; you have supposed that I
would give it unto you, when you took no thought save it was to ask
me. But, behold, I say unto you, that you must study it out in your
mind; then you must ask me if it be right, and if it is right I will cause
that your bosom shall burn within you; therefore, you shall feel that
it is right. But if it be not right you shall have no such feelings, but
you shall have a stupor of thought that shall cause you to forget the
thing which is wrong" (D&C 9:7–9). Had Oliver known the principle
and been obedient to it, he could have translated part of the Book of
Mormon (D&C 9:10).

A few months after the Church was organized, the Lord directed
a revelation to Emma Smith. In it the Savior called her an elect lady
and gave her instructions regarding her conduct and a call "to make
a selection of sacred hymns" (D&C 25:11; see also 3, 5, 7, 12). He
also admonished Emma to give time "to writing and to learning much"
(D&C 25:8).

In 1833, after the First Presidency had been organized, Frederick G. Williams, Sidney Rigdon, Newel K. Whitney and Joseph Smith, Jr., were all reprimanded by the Lord for not teaching their families the gospel (D&C 93:41, 44, 47, 50). Each was told to teach their children. The Lord "rebuked" Joseph and told him, "Your family must needs repent and forsake some things, and give more earnest heed unto your sayings, or be removed out of their place" (D&C 93:47–48).

Sometimes growth under the direction of the Master is painful because the individual must learn to do the required task Jesus' way for as long as he is called. A person must be stripped of pride and personal ambition; his only desire must be to serve God (6:19; 23:1; 88:121; 121:37). Christ consoled Oliver, saying, "Do not murmur, my son, for it is wisdom in me that I have dealt with you after this manner" (D&C 9:6).

Joseph Knight, David Whitmer, Peter Whitmer, Sr., John Whitmer, Peter Whitmer, Jr., Martin Harris, Hyrum Smith, Samuel H. Smith, Ziba Peterson, Thomas B. Marsh, Ezra Thayre, and others made inquiries and received personal responses from Jesus through his prophet. The Church has increased numerically to the point that the prophet cannot receive revelation in behalf of each Church member. Still, Jesus shows his love by providing stake patriarchs, bishops, priesthood leaders, home teachers, and fathers who, through the power of the priesthood, bless those over whom they preside. These blessings provide direction, comfort, and peace to the disciples of Christ, who struggle to follow him. Just as in the days when the Church was small, revelations are available for the individual's personal growth.

THERE IS A TIME FOR EACH PERSON

In the "day of this life," defined by Alma as beginning with our birth into mortality and ending when we are resurrected, each of us is confined by time. In our society, we are acutely aware that there are sixty seconds in a minute, sixty minutes in an hour, twenty-four hours in a day, three hundred sixty-five days in a year, and seventy years in an average life. Most of us forget that our Father in Heaven doesn't view time from our mortal perspective.

The revelations in the Doctrine and Covenants refer to timing, delay, waiting, limits, events, opportunity, progress, past, present, and future. Hyrum Smith was commanded to "wait a little longer" and to "hold [his] peace" until he received more knowledge before preaching the gospel (D&C 11:16, 22). Edward Partridge was called to "spend all his time in the labors of the church" (D&C 41:9).

After Martin Harris had lost the 116-page translation of the Book of Mormon, he was admonished: "You should have been faithful; and he [Christ] would have extended his arm and supported you . . . in every time of trouble" (D&C 3:8). Later, the Lord reminded Joseph that he had "lost [his] gift at the same time, and [his] mind became darkened" (D&C 10:2). Joseph learned that it takes time to repent, to learn the lesson the Lord is teaching, and that it takes time to heal from the pain resulting from disobedience.

The Savior taught that "there is a time appointed for every man, according as his works shall be" (D&C 121:25). Jesus revealed to Joseph, who was confined in Liberty Jail in March 1839, that his enemies' "bounds are set, they cannot pass." The Savior said to Joseph: "Thy days are known, and thy years shall not be numbered less; therefore, fear not what man can do" (D&C 122:9).

Jesus taught that time in mortality is a transition in eternity. He revealed that those who are ill and call for an administration from the priesthood, "if they die they shall die unto me, and if they live they shall live unto me. . . . It shall come to pass that he that hath faith in me to be healed, and is not appointed unto death, shall be healed" (D&C 42:44, 48). Every man, woman, and child has an appointed mission. Each is given time in mortality to pursue that divine mission. No matter how long mortality may last, each person born has the opportunity to prepare for eternal life (D&C 121:25).

The Redeemer's promise of life after mortality gives peace and assurance to his disciples as they struggle to comply with the covenants they have made. The promise of eternal life confirms for each of us the mental security that even though we may not understand, God is in control. President John Taylor's statement that "we are in the hands of God" gives hope to those of us who have lost a loved one through sin or death.[8]

Frequently during early Church history mobs arose against the Saints. Referring to the violence suffered at the hands of their persecutors, the Lord promised the Saints: "I will smite them . . . in mine own due time" (D&C 24:16). The Lord told of Zion's redemption that would occur in his "own due time" (D&C 136:18). He explained that "God's time, angel's time, prophet's time, and man's time" depended upon "the planet on which they reside" (D&C 130:4). Jesus foretold of a "time to come in the which nothing shall be withheld" from his disciples (D&C 121:28).

The time referred to in these verses is apparently when the Bridegroom comes. Referring to himself as the Bridegroom and the Church as his bride, Jesus taught that "the Book of Mormon and the holy scriptures are given of me for your instruction" at this time and promised that "the power of my Spirit quickeneth all things. Wherefore, be faithful, praying always, having your lamps trimmed and burning, and oil with you, that [Church members] may be ready at the coming of the Bridegroom" (D&C 33:16–17; see also 133:19).

All references to the Bridegroom refer to the second coming of the Savior: "Prepare ye the supper of the Lamb, make ready for the Bridegroom" (D&C 65:3); "the Bridegroom cometh; go ye out to meet him. And immediately there shall appear a great sign in heaven, and all people shall see it together" (D&C 88:92–93).

With reference to the preparation necessary to meet the Bridegroom, the Prophet Joseph Smith taught that the Second Coming would not happen until "you are endowed and prepared to preach the Gospel to all nations, kindreds, and tongues, in their own languages." He counseled Church members to "faithfully warn all, and bind up the testimony, and seal up the law." He promised that "the Saints will be gathered . . . and stand in holy places ready to meet the Bridegroom when he comes."[9] The instructions revealed concerning the coming of the Bridegroom teach us how to prepare to meet the Savior.

JESUS INSTRUCTS US TO FOLLOW HIS PROPHETS

There were some who were deceived during Joseph Smith's life. Overcome by millennial fever, some declared visions and signs of the Second Coming. A Mr. Redding openly avowed that he had seen the Savior coming in the clouds of heaven. Referring to Mr. Redding's experience, the Prophet said, "I shall use my right, and declare that, notwithstanding Mr. Redding may have seen a wonderful appearance in the clouds one morning about sunrise (which is nothing very uncommon in the winter season) he has not seen the sign of the Son of Man, as foretold by Jesus; neither has any man, nor will any man, until after the sun shall have been darkened and the moon bathed in blood; for the Lord hath not shown me any such sign."[10]

The Prophet Joseph Smith reminded us of the words of the ancient prophet Amos, who said, "Surely the Lord God will do nothing, but he revealeth his secret unto his servants the prophets" (Amos 3:7). Joseph Smith taught the Saints that "the Lord will not come to reign over the righteous, in this world, in 1843, nor until everything for the Bridegroom is ready."[11]

The revelations in the Doctrine and Covenants teach us how to avoid deception by following God's prophets. Jesus gives direction through his living prophet. Early in the history of the Church, some of the brethren objected to some of the language used in the revelations. They felt that parts of the revelations were true while other parts were not true, or at least weak, because of Joseph Smith's lack of ability (D&C 67:5). The Lord challenged them to "Seek" the weakest revelation they could find in "the Book of Commandments." The Savior challenged these men to "appoint him that is the most wise among you" to write a similar revelation. Then Jesus said, "If there be any among you that shall make one like unto it, then ye are justified in saying that ye do not know that they are true; but if ye cannot make one like unto it, ye are under condemnation if ye do not bear record that they are true" (D&C 67:6–8).

William E. M'Lellin stepped forward and "endeavored to write a commandment like unto one of the least of the Lord's, but failed."[12] Joseph commented that it is "an awful responsibility to write in the name of the Lord."[13] Jesus warned these men to "strip [themselves] from jealousies and fears, and humble" themselves before him and "continue in patience until ye are perfected" (D&C 67:10, 13).

When communicating to his Church, the Savior always speaks through his prophet (D&C 28:2, 5–7). The Doctrine and Covenants teaches that when we receive the words of the prophet, we receive the words of the Christ, and when we receive the words of the Christ, we receive the words of our Father in Heaven (see D&C 84:36–37). Following this prescription prepares us to return to the presence of God.

PERSONAL REFLECTIONS

Joseph Smith said, "Knowledge through our Lord and Savior Jesus Christ is the grand key that unlocks the glories and mysteries of the kingdom of heaven."[14] The Doctrine and Covenants more than testifies of the Savior: it places him next to the Father in power and glory.

The Doctrine and Covenants reiterates that the Savior is the Creator and the representative of the Father, it shows his desire for each person's eternal welfare, and it demonstrates that God gives "time" to each individual to work out his or her divine mission. The revelations in the Doctrine and Covenants show how Jesus organized his Church and teach how he accomplishes his work through living prophets.

Taken as a whole, the Doctrine and Covenants teaches that only through covenants, repentance, obedience, sacrifice, and service can we ever come to know Christ. Obedience and repentance are not so much what we abstain from as what we hope for. These principles allow us to remember and renew our covenants, which assure us of a secure and personal relationship with the Savior. The great Jehovah who made these same principles and covenants available to the ancients has made them available to us and will make them available to those living in the twenty-first century. Jesus "is the same yesterday, today, and forever," and his covenants and laws are the same forever (D&C 20:12; 35:1). Those who follow Jesus become his children.

When individuals choose this course in mortality, their lives are changed, they are born of the Spirit, and they know peace. From time to time they are taught by the Holy Ghost, and they catch glimpses of eternity by remembering the covenants they have made. Eventually these changes sanctify them, and when they are brought into the presence of the Savior, they will "see him as he is" because they have become "like him" (Moroni 7:48).

NOTES

1. Near the end of his life, the Prophet Joseph Smith taught: "In the beginning, the head of the Gods called a council of the Gods; and they came together and concocted a plan to create the world and people it." *Teachings of the Prophet Joseph Smith*, sel. Joseph Fielding Smith (Salt Lake City: Deseret Book Co., 1974), p. 349.

2. James E. Talmage, *The Articles of Faith* (Salt Lake City: The Church of Jesus Christ of Latter-day Saints, 1977), p. 471.

3. Joseph Fielding Smith, *Doctrines of Salvation*, comp. Bruce R. McConkie (Salt Lake City: Bookcraft, 1954–56), 1:27.

4. LDS Bible Dictionary, s.v. "Redemption," p. 760.

5. Smith, *Teachings of the Prophet Joseph Smith*, p. 198; see also D&C 76:51.

6. Smith, *Teachings of the Prophet Joseph Smith*, p. 92.

7. Joseph Smith, *History of The Church of Jesus Christ of Latter-day Saints*, 2d ed. rev., edited by B. H. Roberts (Salt Lake City: The Church of Jesus Christ of Latter-day Saints, 1932–51), 6:253.

8. John Taylor, *Prophets of the Restored Church, Brigham Young to Heber J. Grant*, video (Provo, Utah: Brigham Young University Productions).

9. Smith, *Teachings of the Prophet Joseph Smith*, p. 92. The "holy places" referred to by the Prophet Joseph are temples. He concluded his discussion by saying: "I feel disposed to speak a few words more to you, my brethren, concerning the endowment: All who are prepared, and are sufficiently pure to abide the presence of the Savior, will see Him in the solemn assembly." Ibid.

10. Ibid., p. 280.

11. Ibid.

12. Smith, *History of the Church*, 1:226.

13. Ibid.

14. Smith, *Teachings of the Prophet Joseph Smith*, p. 298.

OFFICIAL DECLARATION 2: REVELATION ON THE PRIESTHOOD

E. Dale LeBaron

Brigham Young University

As a young boy in Primary memorizing the ninth article of faith, I never imagined that I would live to see the Lord reveal anything as "great and important" as the revelation of June 1978, which extended priesthood and temple blessings to all worthy male members of the Church. Elder Bruce R. McConkie, who was present when this revelation was received, stated:

"It was a revelation . . . that would reverse the whole direction of the Church, procedurally and administratively; one that would affect the living and the dead; one that would affect the total relationship that we have with the world. . . . This affects what is going on in the spirit world. . . . This is a revelation of tremendous significance."[1]

As far as we know, this was the first time since Cain and Abel that all the blessings of the gospel of Jesus Christ were made available to all people of all races living upon this earth. And it was the first time that temple ordinances could be performed for all people back to the beginning of time.

On 30 September 1978, at the 148th Semiannual General Conference of The Church of Jesus Christ of Latter-day Saints, President N. Eldon Tanner, first counselor in the First Presidency, read Official Declaration—2, which included the following:

"In early June of this year, the First Presidency announced that a revelation had been received by President Spencer W. Kimball extending priesthood and temple blessings to all worthy male members of the Church. . . . This revelation . . . came to him after extended meditation and prayer in the sacred rooms of the holy temple. . . .

"We have pleaded long and earnestly in behalf of these, our faithful brethren [from whom the priesthood has been withheld], spending many hours in the Upper Room of the Temple supplicating the Lord for divine guidance.

"He has heard our prayers, and by revelation has confirmed that the long-promised day has come when every faithful, worthy man in the Church may receive the holy priesthood, with power to exercise its divine authority, and enjoy with his loved ones every blessing that flows therefrom, including the blessings of the temple. . . .

"Recognizing Spencer W. Kimball as the prophet, seer and revelator, and president of The Church of Jesus Christ of Latter-day Saints, it is proposed that we as a constituent assembly accept this revelation as the word and will of the Lord. . . .

"The vote to sustain the foregoing motion was unanimous in the affirmative."

Of the revelations now in the Doctrine and Covenants, this is the only one received within the past seventy-four years. Because this important revelation is so relevant to us today, it should receive our careful and prayerful study. It should have a deep, spiritual influence upon our souls and lives. The manner in which the revelation on the priesthood was revealed and accepted is powerful evidence of the Church's inspired leadership, the Lord's divine direction, and the members' discipleship.

BEFORE THE REVELATION ON THE PRIESTHOOD

Clearly, the gospel is intended for all people. In the preface to the Doctrine and Covenants, the Lord declared, "For verily the voice of the Lord is unto all men. . . . And the voice of warning shall be unto all people. . . . Wherefore the voice of the Lord is unto the ends of the earth" (D&C 1:2, 4, 11). Then, in the appendix to this book of scripture, the Lord stated: "And this gospel shall be preached unto every nation, and kindred, and tongue and people" (D&C 133:37). There are seventy-eight references in the Doctrine of Covenants pertaining to the Lord's dealings with every nation or with the nations of the earth.

Modern prophets have echoed that message. For example, Elder Bruce R. McConkie taught that before the second coming of the Savior, stakes will be organized in Red China, Russia, and other nations where the gospel was not then established.[2] President Spencer W. Kimball said in a great visionary message:

" 'Go ye into all the world, and preach the gospel to every creature.' (Mark 16:15.) . . .

" . . . Surely there is significance in these words! There was a universal need and there must be universal coverage. . . .

" . . . It seems to me that the Lord chose his words when he said 'every nation,' 'every land,' 'uttermost bounds of the earth,' 'every tongue,' 'every people,' 'every soul,' 'all the world,' 'many lands.' " [3]

The gospel has not always been sent to all people, however. From the beginning, the Lord has sent the gospel to people according to his priorities, and the priesthood has been given selectively. During the fourteen centuries from Moses to Christ, only the house of Israel had the gospel. Only the tribe of Levi was permitted to hold the Aaronic priesthood, and a few others were chosen to hold the Melchizedek priesthood. Elder Bruce R. McConkie observed:

"Not only is the gospel to go, on a priority basis and harmonious to a divine timetable, to one nation after another, but the whole history of God's dealings with men on earth indicates that such has been the case in the past; it has been restricted and limited where many people are concerned."[4]

Early in this dispensation, the Lord revealed that those of the black race were not to receive the priesthood and temple blessings. In 1949 the First Presidency reaffirmed the Lord's command:

"The attitude of the Church with reference to the Negroes remains as it has always stood. It is not a matter of the declaration of a policy but of direct commandment from the Lord, on which is founded the doctrine of the Church from the days of its organization, to the effect that Negroes may become members of the Church but that they are not entitled to the priesthood at the present time."[5]

That position has not always been understood or accepted, even by some in the Church. Because it did not receive specific scriptural status in the Doctrine and Covenants, some question its origin; however, not all revelations are made public. In 1977, President Kimball said, "We testify to the world that revelation continues and that the vaults and files of the Church contain these revelations which come month to month and day to day."[6]

Statements by the prophets in this dispensation suggest that there were some unanswered questions relating to blacks and the priesthood. Fifteen years before receiving the revelation, Elder Spencer W. Kimball expressed his views about this delicate and difficult matter: "The things of God cannot be understood by the spirit of men. . . . I have wished the Lord had given us a little more clarity in the matter. But for me, it is enough. The prophets for 133 years of the existence of the Church have maintained the position of the prophet of the Restoration that the Negro could not hold the priesthood nor have the temple ordinances which are preparatory for exaltation. . . . The doctrine or policy has not varied in my memory. . . . I know the Lord could change his policy. . . . If the time comes, that he will do, I am sure."[7]

Then Elder Kimball caustically rebuked members of the Church who were pressuring Church leaders to make a change regarding blacks and the priesthood: "These smart members who would force the issue, and there are many of them, cheapen the issue and certainly bring into contempt the sacred principle of revelation and divine authority."[8]

In 1973, when President Kimball became president of the Church and was asked about the position of the Church regarding the blacks and the priesthood, he answered:

"I am not sure that there will be a change, although there could be. We are under the dictates of our Heavenly Father, and this is not my policy or the Church's policy. It is the policy of the Lord who has established it, and I know of no change, although we are subject to revelations of the Lord in case he should ever wish to make a change."[9]

A few months later President Kimball gave a powerful and visionary address. He spoke of "armies of missionaries" taking the gospel to areas of the world, even to lands where the Church had never been. But no mention was made of one continent — Africa. The revelation on the priesthood had to precede the gospel message being spread throughout Africa. David M. Kennedy, who served as a special representative of the First Presidency to help move the gospel to foreign nations, told of a large atlas that President Kimball kept in his office. When they studied it together, Brother Kennedy would place his hand over sub-Saharan Africa, saying, "We can't go there unless they have the priesthood." Returning from the temple after receiving the revelation of June 1978, President Kimball stopped at David Kennedy's office and said, "You can take your hand off that map, David. We can now go to Africa!"[10]

In this dispensation some Church leaders believed the blacks would not receive the priesthood before the Millennium. Similarly, the prophets and apostles at Jesus' time did not fully comprehend some of the basic principles of the gospel or the Lord's timetable. It wasn't until after glorious revelations were received that they completely understood the doctrines of the Atonement, resurrection, or of taking the gospel to all nations. Elder McConkie said that because the gospel had been only for the house of Israel, the earliest apostles were not able to envision that after the resurrection the gospel should then go to all the world.[11] But Peter was still a prophet, even though he had to receive a vision before he fully understood that the gospel was to be taken to the gentiles at that time.

In this dispensation, some Church leaders spoke from limited understanding regarding when the priesthood would be given to the blacks. Elder McConkie spoke of that matter: "There are statements in our literature by the early brethren that we have interpreted to mean that the Negroes would not receive the priesthood in mortality. I have said the same things. . . . We spoke with a limited understanding and without the light and knowledge that now has come into the world.

"We get our truth and our light line upon line and precept upon precept. We have now had added a new flood of intelligence and light on this particular subject, and it erases all the darkness and all the views and all the thoughts of the past. They don't matter any more."[12]

REVELATION BY THE POWER OF GOD

Typically, before a large worldly organization makes a significant change in direction, philosophy, or practice, the leaders carefully ensure that their constituency will continue to support them. That is true of political, business, and religious organizations. They first participate in studies, surveys, conferences, pilot testing, debates, Vatican councils, or bishops synods to determine whether change is advisable. When changes are made, they are usually implemented carefully and gradually.

For example, a Canadian newspaper reported on challenges facing the newly appointed moderator of the United Church of Canada (Canada's largest Protestant denomination):

"The church was just concluding what could arguably be termed the most difficult four months in its 60-year history because of the outcry over a report which recommended the church sanction the ordination of homosexual clergy.

"Smith's first duty as moderator was to chair the fractious debate on what to do about the issue."[13]

Similarly, under the heading, "Episcopal Church report asks sanction of non-marital sex," an American newspaper reported:

"The Episcopal Church should recognize and bless committed non-marital sexual relationships between homosexuals, young adults, the divorced and widowed, a report from the church's Newark diocese urges. . . .

"The report by the diocese's Task Force On Changing Patterns of Sexuality and Family Life aims to ignite a new debate on sexual ethics among leaders of the nation's 3 million Episcopalians in hopes they will amend church doctrine to embrace all believers."[14]

The Church of Jesus Christ of Latter-day Saints is subject to the Lord, not to popular opinion. The Church has used some research methods before implementing such programs as family home evening and the consolidated meeting schedule; however, when it comes to doctrines, principles, or ordinances of the gospel, change is a matter of revelation from the Lord to his prophet.

At the time of the revelation on the priesthood, my wife and I were presiding over the South Africa Johannesburg Mission, then the only mission on the continent of Africa. About six months before the revelation came, I received a copy of a letter from the First Presidency that was sent to all priesthood leaders. The letter restated the Lord's position with regard to the blacks' being denied the priesthood and temple blessings. I heard no more about this matter until the announcement of the revelation. The brethren did not survey the feelings of the Church membership or do studies to determine the effects that such a change might have. To observe the Church make such a sudden and major change of course so smoothly is a miracle of incredible proportions.

President N. Eldon Tanner observed that President Kimball had defended the position of the Church for some thirty years as a member of the Twelve, yet when the revelation came, he immediately reversed himself.[15] As an apostle and then as the prophet, President Kimball traveled throughout the Church. His sensitive spirit reached out in love to all people, especially to those deprived of priesthood and temple blessings because of lineage. He noted: "This matter had been on my mind all these years. We have always considered it."[16] President Kimball described his sacred struggle:

"Day after day I went alone and with great solemnity and seriousness in the upper rooms of the temple, and there I offered my soul and offered my efforts to go forward with the program. I wanted to do what he wanted. I talked about it to him and said, 'Lord, I want only what is right. We are not making any plans to be spectacularly moving. We want only the thing that thou dost want, and we want it when you want it and not until.' "[17]

Unknown to anyone except the First Presidency and the Twelve, President Kimball had asked each of them to carefully research the scriptures and statements of the earlier brethren, to make an exhaustive study of all that had been recorded concerning this issue. For months before the revelation, the First Presidency and the Quorum of the Twelve discussed these sacred matters at length in their temple meetings. He also met privately with each of the brethren to learn their feelings on the matter.[18]

On Thursday, 1 June 1978, the general authorities held their regular monthly fast and testimony meeting. The members of the Seventy and the Presiding Bishopric were then excused, and President Kimball, his two counselors, and ten of the apostles remained (Elder Mark E. Peterson was in South America, and Elder Delbert L. Stapley was in the hospital).

Before offering the prayer that brought the revelation, President Kimball asked each of the brethren to express their feelings and views on this important issue. For more than two hours they talked freely and openly. Elder David B. Haight, the newest member of the Twelve, observed: "As each responded, we witnessed an outpouring of the Spirit which bonded our souls together in perfect unity—a glorious experience. In that bond of unity we felt our total dependence upon heavenly direction if we were to more effectively accomplish the Lord's charge to carry the message of hope and salvation to *all* the world.

"President Kimball then suggested that we have our prayer at the altar. Usually he asked one of us to lead in prayer; however, on this day he asked, 'Would you mind if I be voice at the altar today?' This was the Lord's prophet asking us. Such humility! Such meekness! So typical of this special servant of all.

" . . . The prophet of God pour[ed] out his heart, pleading eloquently for the Lord to make his mind and will known to his servant, Spencer W. Kimball. The prophet pleaded that he would be given the necessary direction which could expand the Church throughout the world by offering the fullness of the everlasting gospel to all men, based solely upon their personal worthiness without reference to race or color."[19]

In response to a prophet's humble prayer of faith, united with those of twelve other prophets, seers, and revelators, the Lord poured out his Spirit—and his answer—in a most powerful way. Elder McConkie testified:

"It was during this prayer that the revelation came. The Spirit of the Lord rested mightily upon us all; we felt something akin to what happened on the day of Pentecost and at the dedication of the Kirtland Temple. From the midst of eternity, the voice of God, conveyed by the power of the Spirit, spoke to his prophet. . . . And we all heard the same voice, received the same message, and became personal witnesses that the word received was the mind and will and voice of the Lord.

" . . . On this occasion, because of the importuning and the faith, and because the hour and the time had arrived, the Lord in his providences poured out the Holy Ghost upon the First Presidency and the Twelve in a miraculous and marvelous manner, beyond anything that any then present had ever experienced."[20]

In an attempt to stifle speculation, Elder McConkie also explained what did *not* happen:

"The Lord could have sent messengers from the other side to deliver it, but he did not. He gave the revelation by the power of the Holy Ghost. . . . And maybe some . . . would like to believe that the Lord himself was there, or that the Prophet Joseph Smith came to deliver the revelation. . . . Well, these things did not happen. The stories that go around to the contrary are not factual or realistic or true."[21]

Elder Gordon B. Hinckley described his impressions as follows: "There was a hallowed and sanctified atmosphere in the room. For me, it felt as if a conduit opened between the heavenly throne and the kneeling, pleading prophet of God who was joined by his Brethren. . . .

"It was a quiet and sublime occasion. . . .

" . . . There was a Pentecostal spirit, for the Holy Ghost was there. . . .

" . . . Not one of us who was present on that occasion was ever quite the same after that. Nor has the Church been quite the same. . . .

" . . . There was perfect unity among us in our experience and in our understanding."[22]

Elder Haight related the events immediately following the historic revelation:

"President Kimball arose from the altar. (We surrounded it according to seniority, I being number twelve.) . . . He turned to his right, and I was the first member of the circle he encountered. He put his arms around me, and as I embraced him I felt the beating of his heart and the intense emotion that filled him. He then continued around the circle, embracing each of the Brethren. No one spoke. Overcome with emotion, we simply shook hands and quietly went to our dressing rooms."[23]

The manner in which this revelation came is unique in our Church history because of the power with which it came, the numbers who received it, and the powerful effects it would have upon so many. Both President Kimball and President Benson said that they had never "experienced anything of such spiritual magnitude and power" as this revelation.[24] The reason the Lord chose to reveal this to the First Presidency and the Twelve, rather than only to his prophet, is due to the tremendous import and eternal significance of what was revealed, according to Elder McConkie. Hence, "the Lord wanted independent witnesses who could bear record that the thing had happened."[25]

Some have questioned why this revelation came when it did. Some critics of the Church suggest that it came in response to pressures upon the Church. External pressures on Church leaders regarding the blacks and the priesthood immediately before the revelation were minor compared to the 1960s when civil rights were a major issue. As to why the revelation came when it did, Elder McConkie stated that it "was a matter of faith and righteousness and seeking on one hand, and it was a matter of the divine timetable on the other hand."[26] President Kimball further stated: "There are members of the Church who had brought to President David O. McKay their reasons why it should be changed. Others had gone to Joseph Fielding Smith and Harold B. Lee and to all the former presidents and it had not been accepted because the time had not come for it."[27]

AFTER THE REVELATION ON THE PRIESTHOOD

Could there be any news ever revealed by God to this earth which has caused so many of his children to immediately respond with such exquisite gladness and gratitude, as did this marvelous revelation? I will never forget the overwhelming feelings I experienced after hearing of the revelation. Although we did not have any black male members of the Church in southern Africa at that time — until 1978 the Church had little involvement with blacks — it was powerfully evident that the revelation had a great and immediate effect upon that continent and its people. After June 1978 blacks began contacting us about the Church, although they knew nothing about the revelation. I will cite two examples.

First, I received a letter, dated 8 June 1979, from a non-LDS black man in Zimbabwe. He asked if he could translate the Book of Mormon into the Shona and Ndebele languages, the two African dialects of Zimbabwe. He said he had been called of God to take the gospel message to his people. He ended his letter with: "I wish you [to] confirm this with the prophets."[28]

Second, about the same time, I received a packet of materials from the Church missionary department. It contained a letter from a group of Africans in an isolated part of South Africa who had founded their own church and called it "The Church of Jesus Christ of Latter-day Saints." Missionary work soon commenced among them.

I will also share three experiences which brought tears of gratitude to some faithful brethren in Africa. Soon after I arrived in South Africa as a mission president in 1976, I met a black African by the name of Moses Mahlangu. As he shook my hand he said, "So you are the new mission president." I told him I was and asked if he had known any others. He named each mission president who had served during the previous twelve years. When I asked him how he knew them, he told me his conversion story.

While serving as a lay minister in a Protestant church, Moses found a copy of the Book of Mormon in their church library. He began to read it. He soon knew it was true. He searched until he found the Church and was taught by the missionaries. The mission president was so impressed with Moses' knowledge and testimony of the gospel and his sincerity and honesty that he wrote to the First Presidency asking permission to baptize Moses. Because of the strict apartheid laws at that time, it was illegal for Moses to attend any religious meeting where whites were present. That would prevent him from receiving the sacrament. The First Presidency advised Moses to wait for baptism. And so Moses waited—for fourteen years. During that time he came by the mission office every few months and got a supply of pamphlets and copies of the Book of Mormon, which he distributed among his people. He held meetings in his home regularly and taught his people about the Book of Mormon and the restoration of the gospel. He is fluent in nine languages and a most articulate gospel teacher.

Soon after the revelation of 1978, I was privileged to conduct a baptismal interview for Moses. It was one of my most sacred and humbling experiences. To every question I asked, I received the same answer: "I have been keeping that commandment for fourteen years." For fourteen long years, this great soul had been faithfully living the gospel and sharing it with his family and friends.

Another experience involved Joseph W. B. Johnson of Cape Coast, Ghana. In 1968 he was given a copy of the Book of Mormon, which he prayerfully read. He received a witness of its truth and a vision directing him to preach the message of the Restoration to his people. Brother Johnson wrote often to Church headquarters requesting literature and missionaries to teach and baptize them. Church literature was sent, but he was told, "The time is not yet; you must wait." For ten years he devoted his time and energies to teaching the gospel, gathering believers, and organizing and strengthening twelve church congregations in Ghana. Brother Johnson was sustained by frequent spiritual experiences, but he and his people became discouraged when their pleadings and prayers to be sent missionaries were not answered. Then, on the night of 9 June 1978, because of despair and discouragement, he could not sleep. He felt impressed to listen to the BBC short-wave news broadcast, which he had not done for several years. After struggling with the old radio for more than an hour, he finally tuned in to the BBC at midnight. He related: "I heard the message of President Kimball's prophecy concerning the priesthood, that all worthy males in all of the world could receive the priesthood. I burst into tears of joy, because I knew the priesthood would come to Africa, and if we did the right things, we would all receive the priesthood."[29]

A third experience involved a faithful member of the Church in South Africa. He was a convert of twelve years and a counselor in a branch presidency. About six months before the revelation, this good brother shared a deep concern with me. His wife was not a member of the Church and was quite bitter about his involvement in the Church. That put a strain on their marriage, but he tried his best to work things out. They had two sons, whom he had raised in the Church. One boy was thirteen years of age and the other almost twelve. Although it was not apparent, his wife came from a negroid lineage. His sons were not aware that they could not hold the priesthood. Deacons were needed in their branch and the boys were wondering why the oldest one had not already been ordained. Both were talking about serving missions. He did not know what to do or how to approach this matter. He was afraid his sons might either resent their mother or resent the Church.

I told him that he would need to speak to them and urged him to fast, pray, and study the scriptures in preparation. He said he would. Four months later he had not yet talked with his sons about the matter, but he assured me that he would soon.

After I heard about the revelation on the priesthood, I thought of this good man and his sons. Not having his phone number, I called his branch president and asked him to go immediately to his counselor's home and inform him of the revelation. Upon hearing the news, this great soul collapsed into a chair, put his head in his hands, and began to sob uncontrollably. Over and over he said, "Thank God! Thank God!" He had been fasting for two days in preparation for the difficult task. He was planning to speak to his sons within minutes. An enormous burden had been removed. I felt that the infinite wisdom and goodness of a loving Heavenly Father considers the welfare of the Church but also the heavy burden of one faithful father.

I was inspired by the way members of the Church generally responded to this revelation. The key to accepting revelation faithfully is found in the following statement by President George Q. Cannon: "The Latter-day Saint who lives near to God, and has the Spirit of God constantly resting upon him or her, never has any doubts about any principle that God has revealed. When the gathering was taught they were prepared for it; when the payment of tithing was taught they were prepared for it; . . . when celestial marriage was taught they were prepared for it . . . There was no doubt in their minds, because the same Spirit that taught them that this was the truth in the beginning, and that God had spoken from the heavens, taught them also that all these things were true. But when you have doubts respecting counsel given by the servants of God, then be assured, my brethren and sisters, there is room for repentance."[30]

After the announcement of the revelation of 1978, I inquired about the feelings of the members of the Church in southern Africa. There seemed to be surprise and joy throughout the mission. I heard of only one negative response, and it came from a brother who often complained about home teaching or other things he was asked to do.

One of our greatest and most important challenges is to see things as our Heavenly Father does. That is especially true when it comes to his revelations and his children. When a revelation of such magnitude comes, surely the Lord requires us to respond so that his purposes can be fulfilled.

Elder McConkie warned us: "We talk about the scriptures being unfolded — read again the parable of the laborers in the vineyard (Matthew 20) and remind yourselves that those who labor through the heat of the day for twelve hours are going to be rewarded the same as those who came in at the third and sixth and the eleventh hours. Well, it's the eleventh hour; it's the Saturday night of time. In this eleventh hour the Lord has given the blessings of the gospel to the last group of laborers in the vineyard. . . . All are alike unto God, black and white, bond and free, male and female."[31]

For many of us, first hearing the news of this revelation is a memory frozen in time, because of the deep feelings of joy and gratitude which it brought. President Gordon B. Hinckley observed: "I need not tell you of the electric effect that was felt both within the Church and without. There was much weeping, with tears of gratitude not only on the part of those who previously had been denied the priesthood and who became the immediate beneficiaries of this announcement, but also by men and women of the Church across the world who had felt as we had felt concerning this matter."[32]

Because of the tremendous significance of this revelation, it would be well for us to record our feelings and experiences for our posterity. Future generations may search our journals for our impressions of this marvelous revelation that occurred in our lifetime. It is important that we leave for our posterity a legacy of faith through our testimony of the Lord's prophets in our day.

It is my witness that the revelation on the priesthood came directly from God to his prophets and that this is one of the most significant revelations of this dispensation. I also testify that with this marvelous revelation came the responsibility to see and feel as the Lord does. It is required of each of us to have pure love towards all of our Father's children regardless of their country, culture, or color — for "all are alike unto God."

NOTES

1. Bruce R. McConkie, "The New Revelation on Priesthood," in *Priesthood* (Salt Lake City: Deseret Book Co., 1981), pp. 134–35.

2. Ibid., p. 131.

3. Spencer W. Kimball, "When the World Will Be Converted," *Ensign,* Oct. 1974, pp. 4–5.

4. McConkie, "New Revelation on Priesthood," p. 130.

5. See statement of the First Presidency of The Church of Jesus Christ of Latter-day Saints, 17 Aug. 1949, Archives, The Church of Jesus Christ of Latter-day Saints, Salt Lake City, Utah, as quoted in *"Neither White Nor Black": Mormon Scholars Confront the Race Issue in a Universal Church,* ed. Lester Bush and Armand Mauss (Midvale, Utah: Signature Books, [1984]), p. 221.

6. Spencer W. Kimball, "Revelation: The Word of the Lord to His Prophets," *Ensign,* May 1977, p. 78.

7. Spencer W. Kimball, *The Teachings of Spencer W. Kimball,* ed. Edward L. Kimball (Salt Lake City: Bookcraft, 1982), pp. 448–9.

8. Ibid.

9. Ibid.

10. See Martin Berkeley Hickman, *David Matthew Kennedy: Banker, Statesman, Churchman* (Salt Lake City: Deseret Book Co. with the David M. Kennedy Center for International Studies, 1987), pp. 343–44. See also address by David M. Kennedy to Religious Education faculty, Brigham Young University, Provo, Utah, 2 Oct. 1992.

11. McConkie, "New Revelation on Priesthood," p. 130.

12. Ibid., pp. 131–32.

13. In *Calgary Herald,* 12 Jan. 1985.

14. In *Daily Herald,* Provo, Utah, 30 Jan. 1987.

15. Loren C. Dunn, monthly letter to mission presidents and regional representatives in the Northern Plains Area. Copy in possession of the author.

16. In *Church News,* 6 Jan. 1979, p. 15.

17. Kimball, *Teachings of Spencer W. Kimball,* p. 451.

18. McConkie, "New Revelation on Priesthood," p. 127; Lucile C. Tate, *David B. Haight: The Life Story of a Disciple* (Salt Lake City: Bookcraft, 1987), p. 279.

19. Tate, *David B. Haight,* pp. 279–80.

20. McConkie, "New Revelation on Priesthood," pp. 128, 133–34.

21. Ibid., p. 135.

22. Gordon B. Hinckley, "Priesthood Restoration," *Ensign,* Oct. 1988, p. 70.

23. Tate, *David B. Haight,* p. 280.

24. McConkie, "New Revelation on Priesthood," p. 128.

25. Ibid., p. 134.

26. Ibid., pp. 132–33.

27. In *Church News,* 6 Jan. 1979, p. 15.

28. Pete Solomon letter, 8 June 1979, sent to the Church; copy in possession of author.

29. E. Dale LeBaron, ed., *"All Are Alike unto God"* (Salt Lake City: Book-craft, 1990), p. 21.

30. George Q. Cannon, in *Journal of Discourses* (London: Latter-day Saints' Book Depot, 1854–86), 13:375.

31. McConkie, "New Revelation on Priesthood," p. 137; see also 2 Nephi 26:33.

32. Hinckley, "Priesthood Restoration," p. 70.

14

THE "ELECT LADY" REVELATION: THE HISTORICAL AND DOCTRINAL CONTEXT OF DOCTRINE & COVENANTS 25

Carol Cornwall Madsen

Brigham Young University

In the last anxious hours before the Prophet Joseph Smith left for Carthage in June 1844, his wife, Emma, asked for a blessing. Unable to grant her wish at the time, Joseph instructed her to write out "the desires of her heart" and he would confirm the blessing by his signature upon his return. Among the desires she expressed in her short, self-inscribed blessing was her fervent wish "to honor and respect my husband as my head, ever to live in his confidence and by acting in unison with him retain the place which God has given me by his side."[1]

What unspoken thoughts moved Emma Smith to write those words? Could she have been affirming her belief that God had called her to be the wife and companion of a latter-day prophet? Might she have been thinking of the ordinances she had received with him in 1843, which promised her exaltation and a place by his side eternally? Or, after more than a year of anguishing over the principle of plural marriage, was Emma finally acknowledging that only by acting in concert with Joseph, even on this divisive issue, could she fulfill the revelation given to her fourteen years earlier through her prophet-husband?

These two spiritual documents, the 1830 revelation to Emma Smith, codified as Doctrine and Covenants 25, and her self-written 1844 blessing, of which the quoted passage is only a part, in many ways are companion pieces, each better understood in relation to the other. The enduring influence of the 1830 revelation to Emma is evident in the 1844 blessing, which carries strong echoes of the Lord's words to her fourteen years earlier. The later blessing illuminates not only the importance and reality of the 1830 revelation in Emma's life but also the timeless and universal quality of its content.

Doctrine and Covenants 25 has long been read primarily as a revelation commissioning a hymnbook for the newly organized Church. In recent years more attention has been given to the revelation's injunction to Emma "to expound doctrine and exhort the church" and to define Emma's role as an "elect lady."[2] Less examined have been its points of universal application and its correlation with the 1844 blessing, which this paper will address.

This sacred, personal communication embodies elements of a long tradition of women's personal theophanies. Dating back to the eleventh century, their spiritual autobiographies record these sacred moments. Some of them recount striking religious awakenings or a newly quickened sense of God's overarching love emerging from a variety of spiritual manifestations. These include visions of light in which God's presence is unmistakably felt and spiritual doubts are resolved.[3] Some recount long periods of spiritual struggle and study leading to "a divine change" and a discernment "of the fullness of God" and his divine power in all things.[4] One woman, after living a life of pleasure and luxury, felt her heart unaccountably pierced "by a sudden and immense love of God" which drew her away from her former life and set her on a path of total religious devotion manifest by her service to the sick.[5] An eighteenth-century American woman, Sarah Pierrepont, left no account of a miraculous vision or sudden revelation, but she wrote of occasions when the Spirit seemed to engulf her and she basked in "a glow of divine love" which came from "the heart of Christ into [her] heart in a constant stream, or pencil of light."[6]

Similar experiences, recorded by early Latter-day Saint women in their diaries and journals, also fall within this tradition, the pattern of spiritual enlightenment often the same. For instance, after weeks of fervent prayer to be led to the truth, Elizabeth Ann Whitney felt herself, one night, enveloped in the midst of a cloud from which a voice spoke, saying: "Prepare to receive the word of the Lord, for it is coming." Shortly thereafter Parley P. Pratt brought her the gospel message and she was baptized, becoming one of the earliest and most faithful members of the Church.[7] In a light that illuminated her mind while receiving a healing blessing, Jane Snyder Richards "saw as plainly as if a book was opened before me with it written in it, my need of baptism, if Christ who was sinless needed to be baptized should I hold myself as better than He."[8] Eliza R. Snow, on the night following her baptism, as she later recorded, felt an "indescribable, tangible sensation" that filled her with an "inexpressible happiness" as she saw in a vision a brilliant light from a candle blazing over her feet at the foot of her bed, which signified, she learned in the vision, that "the lamp of intelligence shall be lighted over your path."[9] And Mary Gibbs Bigelow, another early convert, sick and bedridden, thinking she was soon to die, received a vision in which the Savior promised her peace, health, and life long enough to complete the work she was still to do.[10] Such heavenly manifestations moved their recipients to conversion or confirmation of their faith and to lives of service and devotion to Christ.[11] Emma's revelation similarly confirmed her acceptance by God and showed her the way to service in his kingdom.

But the 1830 revelation for Emma was different from these personal communications from the heavens. Preceding the introduction of patriarchal blessings in the Church by three years, its form and content were very much their prototype. It was received through an intermediary, it declared to Emma that she was one of the elect, or of the Abrahamic covenant and lineage,[12] and its promises and foretellings were conditional on her faith and obedience. Why, then, we might ask, was this individual spiritual guide included in a book of scripture for all Latter-day Saints?

The answer might possibly lie in its distinctiveness from the patriarchal blessings it prefigured. First, Emma was the prophet's wife, and any blessing given to her was therefore distinctive. More specifically, like the other revelations that make up the Doctrine and Covenants, the revelation to Emma came directly from God through his prophet, not through a patriarch, bishop, or other ecclesiastical leader. Moreover, unlike personal revelations, patriarchal blessings, or even some of the other personally directed revelations in the Doctrine and Covenants,[13] it concludes with these significant words, which Joseph Smith repeated years later to the Relief Society in reference to the revelation: "And this is my word unto all."[14] Thus, in significant ways, it transcends the merely personal, fitting the parameters of scripture and thereby acquiring permanence, authority, and universality. While its specifics are addressed to Emma, its principles are applicable to all.

And what was God's message to Emma and, by implication, to the Church? The revelation's sixteen verses address four essential aspects of Emma's life: her actions and desires, her relationship to her prophet-husband, her responsibilities to the Church, and her relationship with the Lord.

In his consistent pattern of promise for performance, the Lord tells Emma in the revelation precisely what he expects of her as a Latter-day Saint and in return promises her aid in fulfilling those expectations. Though verses 4 and 10 appear to be mild rebukes, they could also be read as appeals for trust and faith in his divine will: "Murmur not because of the things which thou hast not seen, for they are withheld from thee and from the world, which is wisdom in me in a time to come" the Lord tells Emma in Doctrine and Covenants 25:4. He may have been referring only to Emma's regret at not having seen the gold plates, though she had held them, protected them, and acted as scribe in their translation, but he may also have been alluding to the tumultuous experiences Emma had endured since her marriage to Joseph three years earlier. The attempts by gold-seekers to wrest the plates from Joseph, the harassment during their translation, the mobs who interfered with Emma's baptism, the unwarranted arrest of Joseph the same night, as well as the alienation of her parents, the loss of home and roots, and the death of her first child, all gave Emma a harsh introduction to the life of a prophet's wife. An early lesson from these experiences was that only patience and trust in God's wisdom and often inscrutable purposes would sustain her through the difficult times. Then in verse 10 the Lord counsels Emma, in what certainly must be one of the most oft-repeated commands in Christian literature, to "lay aside the things of this world and seek for the things of a better," surely a call to keep perspective on the uncertainties her life offered. But her compliance to these two admonitions would not go unaided. "Lift up thy heart and rejoice," he encourages her in verse 13, "and cleave unto the covenants which thou hast made." Only a month earlier, Emma had entered into the covenant of baptism, which promised her that if she would "serve [the Lord] and keep his commandments," he would in turn "pour out his Spirit more abundantly upon [her]" (Mosiah 18:10). Furthermore, before another month passed, at her long-delayed confirmation she would receive the gift of the Holy Ghost, an additional source of solace and guidance.

At the time of the revelation Emma had just turned twenty-six and Joseph was not yet twenty-five. They were relatively inexperienced and unsophisticated young people who had been given momentous responsibilities. A supportive and trusting relationship would be crucial to the fulfillment of their respective callings. Its reciprocal nature is explained in verses 5 and 9 of the revelation. Emma was counseled to comfort and console her prophet-husband in his times of affliction and to continue to assist him when needed in his ecclesiastical duties as scribe (v. 5). In turn, she was promised Joseph's support with the Church, presumably to enable her to fulfill the mission to which the Lord had called her (v. 9). The import of this counsel became clear as circumstances challenged Joseph and Emma's efforts to fulfill their obligations to each other. While Joseph's support gave legitimacy and significance to Emma's assignments in the Church, her support of Joseph eased the burden of his calling. But the merging of their marital and ecclesiastical relationships often created an emotional kaleidoscope alternating joy with sorrow, peace with anxiety, trust with suspicion, and unity with doubt. For equilibrium, the Lord urged Emma to maintain her spirit of meekness and let her soul "delight in [her] husband, and the glory which [would] come upon him" (v. 14). To enjoy these blessings, he warned, she must "beware of pride" (v. 14).

The binding force of that counsel united Joseph and Emma in a supportive and truly complementary relationship for most of their seventeen years together. Joseph's letters to her express affection and confidence. Though few of Emma's letters to Joseph remain, the anxiety and urgency evident in her published letters to Illinois Governor Thomas Carlin, pleading against Joseph's extradition to Missouri, along with her boldness in daring to interfere with the processes of law, certainly testify of her willingness to be more than a comfort and consolation. One can only wonder why the strength of their union was not sufficient for Emma to accept plural marriage, a principle accepted in faith by so many other devoted couples. Perhaps, for Emma, it was *because* of that unity, the oneness that had so characterized their relationship, that she was unable to open it to others. Could Emma's reluctance to share her prophet-husband be a manifestation of the pride she had been warned against? Did her faith falter only in this final test when the sacrifice claimed too much of her own identity? The answers remain elusive.

But the revelation called for Emma to do more than support and assist Joseph. There were specific tasks for her to perform that would benefit the Church, in preparation for which her time was to be given "to writing, and to learning much" (v. 8). One assignment was "to make a selection of sacred hymns" (v. 11). By this mandate the Lord sanctioned music as an appropriate form of religious worship. Hymn texts have long been a medium to express religious thought and emotion, and the birth of Mormonism evoked a wide range of both, from the millennialist fervor of the poems of Parley P. Pratt and the doctrinal assertions of Eliza R. Snow to the joyous affirmations of W. W. Phelps. Now these and other poetic testimonies would become part of LDS worship.

It took two years for Emma to complete the hymn selection, and another three passed before the hymns were printed in a single volume. From July 1830 to April 1832, when the selection process was completed and W. W. Phelps was instructed to correct and publish the hymns, Emma worked despite a growing antagonism toward the Church in Kirtland and a series of personal tragedies. Through them all, she persisted in fulfilling this assignment of the Lord. Her mother-in-law observed that during this time "her whole heart was in the work of the Lord and she felt no interest except for the church and the cause of truth."[15]

Finally, in June 1832, *The Evening and the Morning Star* began printing Emma's selection of hymn texts described as "Hymns, selected and prepared for the Church of Christ, in the last days." The destruction of Phelps's press in 1833 suspended the printing of hymns and other Church publications. Until then, thirty-eight hymn texts had appeared in either the *Star* or its successor, the *Latter Day Saints' Messenger and Advocate*.[16] But in 1835 the Church council instructed Phelps to continue his work with Emma, and early in 1836, the first LDS hymnal finally came off the press, entitled *A Collection of Hymns for the Church of the Latter Day Saints*. The 127-page hymnal contained ninety hymns, approximately forty of them written by LDS authors, primarily Phelps himself. Emma's preface drew on the words of the 1830 revelation, affirming that "the song of the righteous" was "a prayer unto God" and suggesting that the hymnal was only a beginning effort "till more are composed or we are blessed with a copious variety of the songs of Zion."[17]

The idea that Emma Smith should be the sole compiler of the Church's hymnal emerged in 1839 when the high council authorized an expanded hymnbook. A New York convert, David Rogers, had previously published for the New York Saints a hymnal that had drawn heavily on Emma's 1835 selection, and Brigham Young had taken a collection of hymns to England with the intent of publishing a hymnal there. But the Nauvoo high council voted to destroy all copies of Rogers's hymnbook and to forbid Brigham Young to publish a British edition.[18] The prohibition evidently did not reach Young in time to prevent the publication of three thousand LDS hymnals in Manchester, England, in 1840. When he decided to revise the hymnal the next year, Brigham Young wrote to Joseph Smith for permission. Apparently the needs of the growing Church prompted Joseph to permit a second edition in England and a new, enlarged edition, under Emma's direction, in Nauvoo. Emma's exclusive stewardship over the church hymnal had been modified to allow the publication of a volume of hymns appropriate to the British Saints under Brigham Young's direction.[19]

A second, more problematic, commission of the Lord to Emma in the revelation was "to expound scriptures, and to exhort the Church, according as it shall be given thee by my Spirit" (v. 7). With only a few exceptions, no religious denominations at that time gave public platforms in mixed congregations to women. Tradition and contemporary ideals of feminine propriety were powerful agents in defining a woman's appropriate public behavior, and preaching in public was not a feminine occupation in the nineteenth century.[20] These social strictures, however, did not affect the small, informal Church meetings,

characteristic of LDS worship from its beginnings. In Nauvoo, women
regularly addressed the mixed Church gatherings in one another's home
for a Sunday or weeknight prayer, blessing, or cottage meeting. Along
with the men, they bore testimony, expounded doctrine, and read
scriptures to the assembled members. They prophesied, spoke in
tongues, and blessed one another.[21] Emma often accompanied Joseph
to such meetings.[22] Few could have been more conversant with Mormon
doctrine than Emma Smith or had more incentive to expound its truths.

The patriarchal blessings of other women during this period admonished them, also, to instruct one another, mentor the young in
gospel principles, and "encourage and strengthen" others in the faith.[23]
One so blessed was Phebe Woodruff before she left on a mission to
England with her husband, Wilford. Brigham Young promised her that
she would be "looked up to as A mother in Israel for council and for
Instruction." He granted her "power & wisdom to teach the truth to
thy friends and thy se[x]," and guaranteed that she would "not be at
a loss for Ideas & words in [her] teaching."[24]

The organization of the Relief Society in 1842 provided Emma
Smith with the public setting most conducive to the fulfillment of her
assignment. At its initial meeting, Joseph Smith proposed that the
sisters should "elect a president to preside over them." After Elizabeth
Ann Whitney nominated Emma, she was elected by the nineteen other
women present. Joseph then read the 1830 revelation, explaining that
at the time it had been given, Emma had been "ordained to expound
the scriptures to all and to teach the female part of the community."[25]
Though she met with the Society only from March to October in 1842,
when it adjourned for the winter months, and again for just four
meetings in March 1844, Emma was clearly its head and moving spirit.[26]

She took her calling to exhort the sisters seriously and immediately
set about instructing them to purify their own lives and help in creating
a virtuous community. She urged them to extend their compassionate
service to all distressed Saints and to draw around them protective
bands of unity. The Relief Society was to save souls as well as relieve
the poor, Joseph counseled, and Emma advised the sisters in this
important obligation. "Each member should be ambitious to do good,"
she urged, "deal frankly with each other, watch over the morals, and
be very careful of the character and reputation of the members of the
Institution etc."[27] To this end, Emma zealously acceded to Joseph's
charge to assist in "correcting the morals and strengthening the virtues
of the community" and "to reform persons . . . and by kindness sanctify
and cleanse [them] from all unrighteousness."[28] Ferreting out iniquity
was a delicate task, but Emma, with the help of her counselors,

endeavored to fulfill Joseph's charge. Like that of hundreds of female moral reform associations throughout the country, all bent on exposing evil, one of the Relief Society's aims was to cleanse the Church of any wrongdoing. Noting their reluctance to be moral caretakers, Emma lamented that "the sisters are not *careful enough* to expose iniquity; the time had been when charity had covered a multitude of sins," she said, "but now it is necessary that sin should be exposed."[29] Her commitment to "uphold virtue" and "put down transgression" dominated the final meetings of the Relief Society in March 1844 in which she used her authority as president to denounce the false doctrine of "spiritual wifery," a counterfeit of the revealed doctrine of plural marriage, and warn the sisters to guard against it and "any other improper practice."[30] That Emma used her position as Relief Society president and her commission to exhort the sisters as a license also to thwart the establishment of plural marriage is generally conceded.[31] The evidence shows that she did indeed attempt to mobilize overt action against the practice through the Relief Society, which numbered more than thirteen hundred by 1844. Moreover, the minutes of the final meetings of the Relief Society clearly indicate that she never questioned her right or her authority to instruct the sisters of the Church in their duties, as she saw them to be.

In contrast to the controversial nature of the Relief Society's moral purity campaign was Emma's equally emphatic desire that the sisters clothe themselves in Christian service. "Seek out and relieve the distressed," she urged, and she counseled them to give help and material aid to one another, invoking the Spirit by blessing one another when needed for healing, for comfort, for childbirth, and for spiritual support and guidance.[32] If the sisters needed a model of selfless service Emma could provide it. In this benevolent charge, Emma's actions far outweighed her words. From the Kirtland days, when she and Elizabeth Ann Whitney prepared a "love feast" for the poor, Emma, so often a beneficiary of the compassion of friends, was the first to extend it to others. Her compassion and hospitality in Nauvoo were legendary. Her home was often a sanctuary for the homeless, the orphan, the sick. Lucy Walker and her siblings were only a few of the dozens of individuals who came under her protective care. Virtually orphaned at their mother's death, because their father was abroad on a mission, the Walker children were offered a home with the Prophet and Emma. "Our own father and mother could scarcely have done more," Lucy noted when her younger sister died. "The Prophet and his wife introduced us as their sons and daughters. Every privilege was accorded us in the home. Every pleasure within reach was ours."[33]

Emma's counselors were also exemplars to the sisters. Elizabeth Ann Whitney, then a stranger to Emma, opened her home to Emma and Joseph when they arrived in Kirtland, almost destitute, and Sarah Cleveland, also a stranger at the time, gave Emma and her children refuge in Quincy when she fled from the Missouri persecutions, leaving her husband still imprisoned in Liberty Jail. It is little wonder that Emma turned to these women for her closest associates and advisers in the new organization.

Another persistent theme in Emma's exhortations to the Relief Society was her appeal for unity. "Measures to promote union in this society must be carefully attended to," she urged the members at the outset.[34] As the membership dramatically increased, Emma was even more urgent in her plea for unity. "We shall have sufficient difficulty from abroad," she presciently warned in August 1842, "without stirring up strife among ourselves and hardness and evil feelings, one towards another etc."[35] This call to "circle the wagons," she was saying, was to guard themselves more against an encroaching disloyalty to Joseph and disunion within the Church than against threats from the outside.

But, as is often the case, the principle of unity was easier for Emma to preach than to practice. Even as she pleaded for a united sisterhood, she was herself becoming a symbol of disunion. Both the 1830 revelation and her 1844 blessing centered on her unity with Joseph as the key to the success of her own calling. But in the end, unity gave way to doubt, and doubt invoked disloyalty. Her exhortations to the Relief Society in its final four meetings in March 1844 seemed frantic but futile. Immediately thereafter both the Relief Society and Emma's place as its "elect lady" abruptly ended. Emma's commitment to the 1830 revelation seriously faltered, and the consequences were monumental.

Finally, how did the 1830 revelation define Emma's relationship with the Lord? Was it unique, or can principles be extrapolated to all believers? The first three verses of the revelation set forth the primary elements of that relationship. First, the Lord claims Emma as a daughter because of her "willingness to accept the gospel," a condition applicable to all who desire to be sons and daughters of God.[36] Second, he covenants with her, promising her eternal blessings in return for obedience and faith, another universal principle. Finally, he forgives Emma her sins, personally validating the efficacy of her recent baptism, and receives her into the circle of the "elect," who are those, he explains elsewhere, who "hear my voice and harden not their hearts" (D&C 29:7).

Emma, like others of the elect, had proven her faithfulness even before mortality and through the "covenant of grace" was permitted to enter this life at a time and place that would bring her into contact with the gospel.[37] But being of the elect also carried responsibilities, foreordained missions that varied with each individual, according to God's purposes. A passage in Joseph Smith's private journal for 17 March 1842 affirms that definition: "*Elect* meant to be *Elected* to a *certain work*," a broad definition of the term. The Prophet then noted that Emma fulfilled this part of the 1830 revelation when she was elected president of the Relief Society, the specific work to which she had been "previously ordained."[38] In the Relief Society minutes of that date, however, he seemed to narrow the meaning, indicating that "elect lady" specifically meant "elected to preside," a term presumably applicable to any woman who presided. Certainly that was how the term was applied in later years. In that same meeting, John Taylor confirmed Emma's earlier blessing from Joseph, also declaring her to be "a mother in Israel" who was "to look to the wants of the needy, and be a pattern of virtue." In referring to the 1830 revelation, he said he "rejoiced to see this Institution organized according to the law of Heaven . . . according to the revelation" previously given to Emma "appointing her to this important calling."[39] His words suggest that the organization of the Relief Society facilitated the fulfillment of Emma's call as an elect lady.

One might wonder why it took twelve years for this part of the revelation to be realized. Perhaps Emma's service to the Church before 1842 was merely preparatory, although certainly falling within the range of Emma's special calling. The Lord evidently directed the proceedings of that organizational meeting, for there was a possibility for other women to be elected president, particularly Sarah M. Kimball, a logical choice, when Joseph opened the meeting for nominations. Elizabeth Ann Whitney, however, gave the nomination to Emma and her election by the women present ratified her call as the "elect lady."[40] From that time on, the title "elect lady" in reference to Emma Smith developed a mystique that curtailed its use for others until after her death, despite her dissociation with the Relief Society and the Church. Though Brigham Young authorized Eliza R. Snow to organize Relief Societies throughout the Church and direct its activities in 1868, she was not officially set apart "to preside" as the new "elect lady" until 1880, the year after Emma's death.[41]

The final element that defined Emma's relationship with the Lord is the fifteenth verse of the revelation. "Keep my commandments continually," he told her, "and a crown of righteousness thou shalt receive. And except thou do this," he cautioned, "where I am you cannot come" (D&C 25:15). In that passage Emma was taught a

fundamental principle of the gospel, that God's blessings are obtained
only by obedience to the laws upon which they are predicated (see
also D&C 130:20–21). This principle underlies every command and
blessing the Lord expressed to Emma in the revelation, which was as
complete and certain a personal guide to Emma Smith, the Latter-day
Saint, as it was a special calling to Emma Smith, the wife of the
Prophet.

Despite the years between them, the 1844 blessing reads, on several
points, like a reprise of the 1830 revelation. It repeats, expands, and
develops several of the themes introduced in the earlier document,
reflecting the seasoning of fourteen years. Perhaps more than her words
and actions in those final mercurial years before the Prophet's death,
the 1844 blessing is the best index to Emma's mind and spirit at that
time and the enduring effect of the 1830 revelation upon her.

Besides her "deepest desire to act in unison with Joseph and retain
her place by his side," a remarkable statement in view of the events
of the preceding months, Emma made several other self-revelatory
requests of the Lord in that 1844 blessing. She expressed a "craving
for wisdom" that she would not do or say anything she would regret;
she desired the Spirit of God and a fruitful mind that she would be
able "to comprehend the designs of God, when revealed through his
servants without doubting;" she sought wisdom to rear her children to
be "useful ornaments in the Kingdom of God;" and prudence to care
for her body that she would live to perform "all the work that [she]
covenanted to perform in the spirit world;" and, finally, she asked for
"humility . . . that she might rejoice in the blessings which God has
in store for all who are willing to be obedient to his requirements."

Were these the words of a prophet's wife hoping only to retain
her place with him, or could they have been a penitent's recovenant
with God? Perhaps they were both. As a glimpse into the heart of
Emma Smith on the eve of her husband's death, this final blessing, I
believe, expresses an intense desire to reconnect with the 1830 revelation that gave her a blueprint for her life. If the words of the blessing
can be taken as a measure of her soul at that moment, they testify of
Emma's longing to feel the approbation of the Lord and spiritual union
once again with Joseph.

What she was *then* willing to sacrifice to fulfill those longings,
however, will remain forever moot. The tragedy that followed closed
that chapter in Emma's life, even as it opened a new one in the life
of the Church.

Though documenting the spiritual journey of just one woman, the
1830 revelation and its companion blessing can well serve as spiritual

markers for all who seek to be in tune with the Lord and in harmony with the Church. "This is my voice unto all," the Lord said at the close of the revelation to Emma. Perhaps we should read it as God's voice to all.

NOTES

1. Typescript copy of blessing in Archives, The Church of Jesus Christ of Latter-day Saints, Salt Lake City, Utah; hereafter cited as LDS Church Archives.

2. See, for example, Linda Kay Newell and Valeen Tippetts Avery, *Mormon Enigma: Emma Hale Smith* (Garden City, N.Y.: Doubleday and Co., 1984) and Jill Mulvay Derr, Janath Russell Cannon, and Maureen Ursenbach Beecher, *Women of Covenant: The Story of Relief Society* (Salt Lake City: Deseret Book Co., 1992).

3. John Ferguson, ed., *An Illustrated Encyclopedia of Mysticism* (London: Thames and Hudson, 1976), s.v. "Catherine of Siena," p. 37.

4. Ibid., s.v. "Angela of Foligno," p. 13.

5. Ibid., s.v. "Catherine of Genoa," pp. 36–37.

6. Ibid., s.v. "Sarah Pierrepont," p. 145. See also Martin Buber, *Ecstatic Confessions,* trans. Esther Cameron, ed. Paul Mendes-Flohr (San Francisco: Harper and Row, 1985), and Walter Holden Capps and Wendy M. Wright, eds., *Silent Fire: An Invitation to Western Mysticism* (San Francisco: Harper and Row, 1978).

7. Edward Tullidge, *The Women of Mormondom* (New York: Tullidge and Crandall, 1877), p. 42.

8. Jane Snyder Richards, "Reminiscences of Jane Snyder Richards," typescript copy, LDS Church Archives.

9. Nicholas G. Morgan, Sr., ed., *Eliza R. Snow, an Immortal* (Salt Lake City: Nicholas G. Morgan, Sr., Foundation, 1957), p. 6.

10. Autobiography of Mary Gibbs Bigelow, 26 June 1809 to 19 Apr. 1858, typescript copy, LDS Church Archives.

11. Joseph Smith greeted with joy and thanksgiving this proliferation of spirituality that accompanied and indeed testified of the return of the gospel of Christ to the earth. "To witness and feel with our own natural senses, the like glorious manifestations of the power of the Priesthood, the gifts and blessings of the Holy Ghost, and the good and condescension of a merciful God," he wrote in 1830, "combined to create within us sensations of rapturous gratitude, and inspire us with fresh zeal and energy in the cause of truth." The dreams and visions of the Saints, he wrote, strengthened his faith and he welcomed them as evidence of the last days, "as foretold by the Prophet Joel." *History of The Church of Jesus Christ of Latter-day Saints,* 2d ed. rev., edited by B. H. Roberts (Salt Lake City: The Church of Jesus Christ of Latter-day Saints, 1932–51), 1:85–86. Besides the numerous manuscript accounts, Carol Lynn Pearson has collected reports of many of these experiences, most of them previously published, in a volume entitled *Daughters of Light* (Salt Lake City: Bookcraft, 1973).

12. See *Encyclopedia of Mormonism* (New York: Macmillan Co., 1992), s.v. "Elect of God," 2:448–49; see also LDS Bible Dictionary, s.v. "Election."

13. At least thirty-six other revelations are partially or fully addressed to individuals.

14. Minutes of the Female Relief Society of Nauvoo, 17 Mar. 1842, LDS Church Archives; hereafter cited as Nauvoo Minutes.

15. Lucy Mack Smith, "Biographical Sketches of Joseph Smith the Prophet and His Progenitors for Many Generations," original manuscript, LDS Church Archives, as quoted in Newell and Avery, p. 44.

16. For more details about the development of LDS hymnals, see Michael Hicks, *Mormonism and Music: A History* (Urbana and Chicago: University of Illinois Press, 1989), pp. 10–14, 18–34. A brief account is Karen Lynn Davidson, *Our Latter-day Hymns: The Stories and the Messages* (Salt Lake City: Deseret Book Co., 1988), pp. 7–13. An early account is E. Cecil McGavin, "Emma Smith's Collection of Hymns," *Improvement Era*, Jan. 1936, p. 38.

17. Hicks, *Mormonism and Music*, p. 20.

18. Ibid., pp. 25–27.

19. Ibid., pp. 26–27. Emma's second hymnal was published in 1841 by Ebenezer Robinson in the place of William Phelps, who was temporarily out of favor with Church leaders. Many of the borrowed hymn texts revised by Phelps for the 1835 edition were restored to their original form, giving the 1841 edition less of a restorationist tone than either the earlier edition or the British hymnbook, which contained many of the hymns of Parley P. Pratt. Emma expanded the collection one last time in 1843, but it was never printed. In 1860 Emma Smith was commissioned by the newly formed Reorganized Church of Jesus Christ of Latter Day Saints, which her son Joseph would lead, to make a selection of hymns. A number of RLDS publications deal with her contributions. See, for instance, Fred'k. M. Smith, "Emma Smith and Her Selection of Hymns," *The Saints' Herald* 52 (1905): 386–87; Audentia Smith Anderson, "Emma Smith and the Church Hymns," *The Saints' Herald* (6 May 1939): 553–54; Samuel A. Burgess, "Latter Day Saint Hymns, Emma Smith," *Journal of History*, 18 (July 1925): 257–60.

20. Lucy Mack Smith enjoyed the privilege once in 1845 in addressing the last conference of the Church before the departure of the Saints the following winter. See *History of the Church*, 7:470–72. For a complete version of her talk and commentary, see Ronald W. Walker, "Lucy Mack Smith Speaks to the Nauvoo Saints," *Brigham Young University Studies* 32 (Winter and Spring 1991): 276–84.

21. An interesting description of a cottage meeting is Charlotte Haven, "A Girl's Letters from Nauvoo," *The Overland Monthly*, Dec. 1890, p. 627.

22. Dean C. Jessee, ed., *The Papers of Joseph Smith* (Salt Lake City: Deseret Book Co., 1992), 2:58, 86, 123.

23. For more discussion of these early blessings, see Carol Cornwall Madsen, "Mothers in Israel: Sarah's Legacy," *Women of Wisdom and Knowledge*, ed. Marie Cornwall and Susan Howe (Salt Lake City: Deseret Book Co., 1990), pp. 191–92.

24. *Wilford Woodruff's Journal, 1838–1898*, typescript, ed. Scott G. Kenney, 9 vols. (Salt Lake City: Signature Books, 1983), 3:343.

25. Nauvoo Minutes, 17 Mar. 1842. This is a slight variation on the actual words of the revelation instructing Emma "to expound scriptures, and to exhort the Church" (v. 7). In earlier times, the terms "ordain" and "set apart" were often

used interchangeably, both asserting the delegation of authority. Thus Emma Smith was "ordained" to office, whereas twenty-four years later Eliza R. Snow was "set apart" to the same office. More recently, specific distinctions have been made between the two terms.

26. During its second year, because of the large enrollment, the Relief Society met as ward groups, each meeting conducted by Emma's counselors. There is no reference in the minutes to attendance by Emma at any of the meetings.

27. Nauvoo Minutes, 17 Mar. 1842.

28. Ibid.

29. Ibid., 18 May 1842.

30. Ibid., 9 and 16 Mar. 1842.

31. Newell and Avery equivocate on the issue. See *Mormon Enigma*, pp. 173–75. Derr, Cannon, and Beecher are more forthright. See *Women of Covenant*, pp. 61–62.

32. Nauvoo Minutes, 19 and 28 Apr. 1842.

33. "An Early Pioneer, Lucy Walker Kimball," in Kate B. Carter, *Our Pioneer Heritage* (Salt Lake City: Daughters of Utah Pioneers, 1976), 19:198.

34. Nauvoo Minutes, 24 Mar. 1842.

35. Ibid., 4 Aug. 1842.

36. Hyrum M. Smith and Janne M. Sjodahl explain that "all men and women are the children of God, through Adam, who 'was the son of God' (Luke 3:38); those who receive the gospel are sons and daughters in the Kingdom of God." *Doctrine and Covenants Commentary* (Salt Lake City: Deseret News Press, 1927), p. 173.

37. LDS Bible Dictionary, s.v. "Election."

38. Jessee, *Papers of Joseph Smith*, p. 371.

39. Nauvoo Minutes, 17 Mar. 1842.

40. Ibid.

41. *Woman's Exponent*, 9 (1 August 1880): 36.

15

THE RESTORATION OF ALL THINGS: WHAT THE DOCTRINE & COVENANTS SAYS

Robert J. Matthews

Brigham Young University

The "restitution of all things, which God hath spoken [of] by the mouth of all his holy prophets since the world began" (Acts 3:21) is a prominent theme of both ancient and latter-day scripture. It is to be accomplished through those who are called of God "as was Aaron," and who have the same holy calling and teach the same doctrines as the ancient prophets. The Restoration will eventually and permanently affect everybody and everything on the earth. That is the only true "new world order" because it is the gospel of Jesus Christ.

We live in the modern world of multiple inventions, labor-saving appliances, space travel, rapid earth-travel, and almost instant communication. It is a world of software, hardware, storage, memory, quick retrieval, and split-second timing. These things are all relatively new, and most have been developed in the past half century.

We also live in the dispensation of the fulness of times, which is the fulness of dispensations leading to a culmination of the Lord's work upon the earth. All previous dispensations were open-ended and will flow into this final dispensation like rivers into the seas. This dispensation is known as the time of "restitution of all things," when the covenants, promises, knowledge, doctrines, priesthood, and divine governing powers that were had by ancient prophets and seers will be established and organized again upon the earth for the benefit of mankind to bring about the purposes of God for the human family. The modern technological developments of travel, and so forth, are inspired by the Lord to assist in his work in this dispensation, which began with the First Vision to Joseph Smith in 1820 and will not end until the earth becomes celestial.

The Book of Mormon uses the concept of restoration (restore, restoring, restored) at least sixty-seven times, often with reference to the gathering and future glory of the house of Israel and also to the plan of salvation, the resurrection of the body, and the Lord's method of rendering a just verdict on the Day of Judgment. The Book of Mormon states that there is a "plan of restoration" which is "requisite with the justice of God; for it is requisite that all things should be restored to their proper order" (Alma 41:2).

Our subject today is what the revelations in the Doctrine and Covenants tell us about that restoration. We frequently talk about the restored gospel, the restored Church, and the restoration of all things, but what does all that mean? What will the Restoration eventually mean to the world? How much of the Restoration has already occurred? What does the future hold for us both in spiritual and in physical things because of the Restoration? How will libraries, schools, and study courses be changed? The Prophet Joseph Smith said: "I calculate to be one of the instruments of setting up the kingdom of Daniel by the word of the Lord, and I intend to lay a foundation that will revolutionize the whole world" (*Teachings of the Prophet Joseph Smith*, sel. Joseph Fielding Smith [Salt Lake City: Deseret Book Co., 1974], p. 366).

This is the kingdom of Daniel to which the Prophet Joseph Smith referred:

"And in the days of these kings shall the God of heaven set up a kingdom, which shall never be destroyed: and the kingdom shall not be left to other people, but it shall break in pieces and consume all these kingdoms, and it shall stand for ever.

"Forasmuch as thou sawest that the stone was cut out of the mountain without hands, and that it brake in pieces the iron, the brass, the clay, the silver, and the gold; the great God hath made known to the king what shall come to pass hereafter: and the dream is certain, and the interpretation thereof sure" (Daniel 2:44–45).

Since the restoration of all things is going to produce a revolution of worldwide proportions, it should be interesting to find out what is going to happen and what it will mean in our individual lives and activities.

The kingdom of God of which Daniel spoke is much more than a church in the usual sense, for it will replace the political kingdoms of the earth. This kingdom will have political, social, and economic, as well as ecclesiastical, aspects. When the kingdom of God is fully established in the earth, it will have all four of those dimensions. Today we are pleased to speak of The Church of Jesus Christ of Latter-day Saints as the kingdom of God on earth, and so it is, but the Church at this time functions primarily in its ecclesiastical dimension. With the restoration of the Aaronic and Melchizedek priesthoods, the authority was given to carry out all of the dimensions of the kingdom, and the doctrinal foundation was also made known. Each dimension was actually functional for a short time in the early days of the Church, but some aspects have been withdrawn from full, active operation until a more appropriate day. For example, the economic order was instituted in Ohio and Missouri under the principles of stewardship and consecration of property. These principles and the authority to implement them still exist in the Church, but the active organizational order has been temporarily discontinued. Likewise, the social order that focuses on a patriarchal family organization and celestial marriage (including plural marriage for some), has been temporarily modified. The authority to administer all aspects of the social order is still with the Church but is not completely active at present. The same is true of the civic or political dimension, which had a brief history and now is dormant. These things are not lost; they are simply not in active operation until the Lord commands that they be renewed at a more propitious time and circumstance. The power and authority for all of these activities reside in the keys held by the First Presidency and the Quorum of the Twelve Apostles.

What does the Doctrine and Covenants make known to us about the restoration of all things? The word *restoration* means that a previous order and system that was once in operation, but which has been lost to the world, shall be reinstituted and become functional again. The Doctrine and Covenants speaks much of a restoration, or the reestablishment of the ancient priesthood, ancient councils, ancient ordinances, and ancient doctrines.

THE WORDS OF THE PROPHETS SHALL BE FULFILLED

By reading the Doctrine and Covenants in a short span of time, there comes a growing awareness of the emphasis on ancient prophets, ancient prophecy, and ancient promises. No fewer than thirty-one times is mention made that the words of the "prophets of old" will be fulfilled and that faith such as that possessed by the prophets of old will again be had on the earth (see D&C 17:2; 20:4; 22:3; 27:6; 29:10–21; 33:8; 35:6; 35:23; 42:39; 43:30; 45:10, 15; 49:111–14; 52:9, 36; 58:8; 59:22; 61:13; 66:2; 76:7–8; 84:64, 108; 85:11, 12; 86:10; 98:32–33; 101:19; 109:23, 41, 45; 128:19). Likewise, there are several comparisons of the ancient Church with the modern Church, and the Lord explains the way that former prophets built up the Church in their day (D&C 64:8; 84:64, 108; 95:9). Declarations are made concerning Adam, Eve, Enoch, Noah, Gabriel, Raphael, Job, Melchizedek, Shem, Abraham, Sarah, Hagar, Isaac, Jacob, Joseph, Ephraim, Moses, Aaron, the sons of Levi, Pharaoh, David, Solomon, Nathan, Elijah, Elias,

Isaiah, Ezekiel, Malachi, Peter, James, John, Paul, and John the Baptist that implant an ancient character and flavor to the Doctrine and Covenants. These names are not simply mentioned and then forgotten, for in most instances personal, individual, and historical information is given that is relevant to the doctrine and practice of the restored Church.

The Doctrine and Covenants also discusses ancient artifacts, such as the gold plates, the breastplate, sword of Laban, the Urim and Thummim, the ball or director (Liahona), and other such very old items. It also speaks of the passing over of the destroying angel, the parting of the Red Sea, the travels of ancient Israel in the wilderness, the tabernacle, the circumstances of Abraham's offering his son Isaac, the Mount of Olives, the Mount of Transfiguration, the washing of the apostles' feet by Jesus, baptism, and other ancient practices. These are not stated merely as interesting items of history but are introduced as having relevance to activities to be performed in the latter-day Church. Furthermore, Oliver Cowdery was to have the "gift of Aaron" and also the same Spirit that inspired Moses (D&C 3:2–7, 11); and Joseph Smith was to receive revelations, "even as Moses" (D&C 28:2), and to be "like unto Moses" (D&C 107:91). The calling and the preaching of Peter (D&C 49:11–14) and of Paul (D&C 18:9) are specified. The ancient gospel of Jesus Christ that was taught by ancient prophets is to be preached by modern teachers through the instrumentality of the Book of Mormon (D&C 10:44–63).

THE FIRST VISION, SPRING 1820

In the First Vision the Father and the Son appeared personally to the boy Joseph Smith, and in response to his questions about which of the churches was right and which he should join, he was told to join none of them, for none, individually or collectively, was the Lord's authorized church. None was doing what the Lord wanted done in the earth among mankind in the last days. Because of the worldwide apostate condition, there needed to be a restoration of the ancient gospel, the ancient priesthood, the ancient covenants, and the ancient performances.

THE VISITS OF MORONI, 1823–1827

The angel Moroni, himself a resurrected ancient prophet, quoted to Joseph Smith many passages from the Old and New Testaments respecting the work of the Lord in the last days. Moroni cited passages from Isaiah, Joel, Jeremiah, Daniel, Malachi, Psalms, and Acts, which in every case deal with the reestablishment of the kingdom of God on the earth preparatory to the Savior's second coming (JS–H 1:36–41; *Messenger and Advocate,* 1835, vol. 1, nos. 5, 7, and 10, containing a letter of Oliver Cowdery; and *Encyclopedia of Mormonism* [New York: Macmillan, 1992], 1:355).

THE PROMISES MADE TO THE FATHERS

The angel Moroni, during a visit to Joseph Smith in September 1823, restated the words of Malachi as follows:

"Behold, I will reveal unto you the Priesthood, by the hand of Elijah the prophet, before the coming of the great and dreadful day of the Lord. And he shall plant in the hearts of the children the promises made to the fathers, and the hearts of the children shall turn to their fathers (D&C 2:1–2).

Malachi had lived about 400 B.C. Elijah had lived about 800 B.C. The fathers to whom the promises were made had lived even earlier, all the way back to Adam, Enoch, Abraham, Isaac, Jacob, and Joseph.

The promises spoken of are the covenants of the gospel of Jesus Christ, which are the promises of priesthood, salvation, and exaltation. All of them are contained in the Lord's covenant with Abraham. These ancient covenants were to be planted in the hearts of living persons on the earth in the last days — the children of the ancient prophets. These promises, in connection with the coming of Elijah, are mentioned three more times in Doctrine and Covenants 27:9; 110:14–15; and 128:17–18. Because the particular ancient prophets to whom these promises were made are not specifically named in these passages, it is instructive to note Doctrine and Covenants 27:10, in which it is stated in connection with Elijah's ministry that these prophets are "Joseph and Jacob, and Isaac, and Abraham, your fathers, by whom the promises remain."

Among the several provisions of the covenant of Abraham was the specific promise of a land inheritance to call their own, a fruitful land of milk and honey, which would be for an everlasting possession (Genesis 17:8; Acts 7:5). The restoration of all things has brought the renewal of this promise and will yet see the fulfillment of land inheritance. This promise will be defined more clearly below in my discussion of the role of the bishop.

THE RESTORATION OF ANCIENT RECORDS

The earliest evidence of a restoration of ancient records is the Book of Mormon, which is itself a collection of ancient documents, and it tells of other records that will come to light in the last days. These include the sealed portion of the plates that Joseph Smith obtained from the Hill Cumorah, which contain a revelation of "all things from the foundation of the world unto the end thereof" (2 Nephi 27:10). There will be a record of the ten tribes, including the Savior's visit to them. There will also be a complete record of the writings of John the Apostle (Ether 4:16). The Doctrine and Covenants begins the restoration of John's writing in Section 7, which is a translation of a parchment originally written and hidden up by John himself. Furthermore, the larger and more extensive original records of the Nephites and also the complete record of the Jaredites' twenty-four gold plates, are yet to be made known. Likewise, a translation of the brass plates of Laban will eventually go to all nations, kindreds, tongues, and peoples (1 Nephi 5:17–19; Alma 37:3–5).

While the translation of the Book of Mormon was still in progress in 1829, the Lord informed Joseph Smith and Oliver Cowdery that when they had finished with it, there were other records to be translated (D&C 8:11; 9:1–2). These other records included the Joseph Smith Translation of the Bible and also the book of Abraham (D&C 9:2, note a).

Doctrine and Covenants 93:6 and 18 speaks of the Church yet receiving the "fulness of the record of John." It is not completely clear whether this is a record of John the Baptist (that was the interpretation by President John Taylor, Elder Orson Pratt, and Elder Bruce R. McConkie[1]) or whether it is the writings of John the Apostle. It may very well mean both. In Doctrine and Covenants 107:57 the record of Enoch is spoken of with the promise that it will be available "in due time." Thus the Doctrine and Covenants gives great expectation for much additional reading of ancient documents in the future. None of these are new documents; they are ancient documents revealed anew.

The Book of Mormon makes clear that the Old Testament record once had more books than at present, and even the books it now contains have been reduced in size in some instances. In the restoration of all things these Old Testament books will be available in their original purity and correctness. A beginning has already been made with the Joseph Smith Translation of the Bible, which gives us a new glimpse of the writings of Enoch, Joseph, and Moses. We now have thirty-nine books in the Old Testament and twenty-seven in the New, making sixty-six books in all in the King James Version of the Bible. This will no doubt be enlarged in days to come.

In our present four-year cycle of Church Sunday School curriculum, we take one year each to study the Old Testament, the New Testament, the Book of Mormon, and the Doctrine and Covenants, and then we repeat the process. The Brigham Young University curriculum provides two semesters for Old Testament and two semesters for the New Testament, making a total of four semesters (eight credit hours) for study of the Bible on the undergraduate level. There are also graduate-level courses for another seven credit hours of Old Testament and six credit hours of New Testament.

With the restoration of ancient records it will someday require a much longer time to study the Bible, both in Sunday School and also in Church schools. I expect that at some future time the Brigham Young University religion curriculum for the Old Testament will contain not only the present courses but Brass Plates 303 (five hours) with an emphasis on the prophecies of Joseph and of Zenos. We now have a course specializing in Isaiah. When the brass plates are restored, we will need Old Testament 305, specializing in Zenock; 306, Zenos; 307, Neum and Ezias — each of these courses being three-credit hours each. At this rate, it could take a student four years just to study the beginning courses in the Old Testament alone. Instead of the current twenty-one hours in the Old Testament offering, there could easily be as many as forty hours. An equal enlargement would be necessary in the New Testament with additional courses on the teachings of Jesus, a course on the writings of John the Apostle, and another on the writings of John the Baptist. There would also have to be courses in Lost Tribes 101, 102, and 103, two hours each, using as the text the record yet to be revealed that is spoken of in 2 Nephi 29:7–14 and 3 Nephi 17:4.

The Book of Mormon curriculum will also have to be enlarged when the complete restoration finally descends upon us. In addition to the two beginning courses 121 and 122 now in the curriculum, there will have to be a 123, Readings from the 116 Lost Pages (two credit hours); Book of Mormon 124, The Twenty-four Gold Plates of Ether (four hours); and a special course for advanced students, Theology 500, The Sealed Plates (five hours, with labs and seminars). Advanced courses might also be given about the large plates of Nephi. For example, 501, The Book of Lehi; 502, Mosiah; 503, Alma; 504, Helaman, and so on through the entire collection. Today we offer a total of sixteen credit hours in Book of Mormon. In the time of restoration, there could be forty to fifty credit hours in Book of Mormon alone.

But that is not all. The restoration of ancient records will bring forth a large number of books that will be studied in Doctrine and Covenants and in Pearl of Great Price classes. These will include the Book of Remembrance, with the fulness of the writings of Adam, and of Enoch, and others. Furthermore, there will be the extended writings of Abraham and of Joseph of Egypt. The Book of Remembrance, which was started by Adam, will present not only historical items of great importance but also doctrinal and theological concepts that will require many scholars to revise their present viewpoints of the early patriarchs and concede that those patriarchs were indeed very knowledgeable and great. Abraham said he had records that contained marvelous things:

"But I shall endeavor, hereafter, to delineate the chronology running back from myself to the beginning of the creation, for the records have come into my hands, which I hold unto this present time. . . . [And] the records of the fathers, even the patriarchs, concerning the right of Priesthood, the Lord my God preserved in mine own hands; therefore a knowledge of the beginning of the creation, and also of the planets, and of the stars, as they were made known unto the fathers, have I kept even unto this day" (Abraham 1:28, 31).

There will be other wonderful things, for the Lord has said:

"Yea, verily I say unto you, in that day when the Lord shall come, he shall reveal all things — things which have passed, and hidden things which no man knew, things of the earth, by which it was made, and the purpose and the end thereof — things most precious, things that are above, and things that are beneath, things that are in the earth, and upon the earth, and in heaven" (D&C 101:32–34).

The documents containing such information will offer a comprehensive doctrinal perspective that will add a great deal to our understanding. Thus there could be information-packed courses in Revelation 501 — Enoch; Revelation 502 — Writings of John; and such other things as Book of Remembrance 503; Creation 504, and so forth.

We have so far spoken only of the manner in which the promised restoration of ancient records will affect the Sunday School curriculum and the BYU Religious Education curriculum; however, these additional records will shed light on all facets of life and learning, including mankind's origin and history and significant matters of human culture. These records will demonstrate mankind's high intelligence and civilization from the very beginning. The additional records will confirm what we already know from the scriptures we now have and will also give much more information. Hence, there will be a need for revised courses in ancient history, anthropology, biology, and all courses that deal with the origin of mankind, the origin of language, the origin of writing, and so forth. These subjects will then be looked upon with a new perspective. Present courses that teach that mankind is the product of organic evolution will no doubt be viewed as erroneous. It appears that almost all subject matter areas of the university curriculum will be shaken by the effects of the restoration of ancient records.

RESTORATION OF THE AARONIC PRIESTHOOD

The next topic, in order of sequence in the Doctrine and Covenants, is the restoration of the Aaronic Priesthood on 15 May 1829, as recorded in Section 13. The conferral was done by no less than John the Baptist, the greatest example of the powers of the Aaronic Priesthood of which we have record. John was, as we know from the New Testament, a direct descendant of Aaron of the tribe of Levi and thus a legitimate bearer of the Aaronic Priesthood and the requisite keys. When John conferred this priesthood on Joseph and Oliver, he spoke of its future relevance to the sons of Levi (D&C 13:1). Furthermore, the powers and prerogatives of this Aaronic Priesthood are repeated in subsequent revelations in the Doctrine and Covenants. For example, in Doctrine and Covenants 68:14–21, the Lord explains that the office of bishop is of the Aaronic order and rightly belongs to those who are literal, flesh-and-blood descendants of Aaron. It also indicates that at some future time, the literal seed of Aaron will function in that role in the Church.

A statement concerning the continuation of the Aaronic Priesthood from Aaron to John the Baptist (about thirteen hundred years) is given in Doctrine and Covenants 84:18–28, with an emphasis on the hereditary nature of this priesthood throughout all the generations of the seed of Aaron and also that the specific keys and powers associated with the Aaronic Priesthood are reserved for the firstborn among the sons of Aaron (D&C 68:14–21; 107:13–20). Aaron is mentioned twenty-four times in the Doctrine and Covenants, with considerable said about the hereditary nature of the priesthood that bears his name as well as that men must be called of God "as was Aaron" (D&C 132:59; see also 27:8; 28:3). The emphasis on the hereditary nature of the Aaronic Priesthood is not idle academic exercise. It will someday have very literal application in the Church and kingdom.

THE WORK OF THE BISHOP

The office of bishop was first made known in this Church, and the first bishop, Edward Partridge, was called in 1831. His duties were given in connection with the consecration of properties and the arranging of land inheritances (D&C 41:9–10). Of particular note is the declaration in Doctrine and Covenants 58:14, 17:

"Yea, for this cause I have sent you hither [to Missouri], and have selected my servant Edward Partridge, and have appointed unto him his mission in this land. . . . And whoso standeth in this mission is appointed to be a judge in Israel, *like as it was in ancient days,* to divide the lands of the heritage of God unto his children" (emphasis added).

By this statement we learn that the bishop has the same responsibilities in the fulness of time as in ancient times. The assignment given to Aaron and his sons was not for their day only or even for the duration of the Old Testament and law of Moses but was a perpetual role that will continue among the seed of Aaron, the sons of Levi, in the restoration of all things.

The Doctrine and Covenants leaves no doubt that the office of bishop belongs to the Aaronic Priesthood, that the bishop presides over the quorum of priests, and that he holds the keys of the Aaronic Priesthood. The Lord explains in some detail that the priests' office rightly belongs to the literal seed of Aaron and that the keys are held by the "firstborn among the sons of Aaron" (D&C 68:16). Because the Lord has not as yet designated to the First Presidency in this dispensation a specific person who is a literal descendant and firstborn of Aaron who should serve as the presiding bishop, the Lord has explained that a high priest of the Melchizedek Priesthood can function as a bishop. It is clearly stated, however, that the bishop's office is hereditary and someday will be filled by a literal descendent of Aaron when properly designated by revelation to the First Presidency (see D&C 68:15–21; 107:13–20; see also Smith, *Teachings of the Prophet Joseph Smith,* p. 112).

The role of bishop is to be a judge and also to be an administrator of the temporalities of the Church. He receives the sacred tithes and offerings and divides the inheritances of land and properties among families when the principles of consecration and stewardship are functioning. That is the economic dimension of the kingdom we spoke of earlier. When the laws of consecration and stewardship are again formally employed, and the Church is large, there will be need for many bishops engaged in the dividing of the lands of inheritance in Zion. It appears that they, at least the presiding bishop, will be literally descended from Aaron.

ETERNAL LAND INHERITANCES

It was noted earlier that the covenant to Abraham included the promise of a land inheritance to Abraham and to his seed for an everlasting possession. The Lord renewed this theme in several of the latter-day revelations as part of the restoration of all things. We read as follows:

"And I hold forth and deign to give unto you greater riches, even a land of promise, a land flowing with milk and honey, upon which there shall be no curse when the Lord cometh;

"And I will give it unto you for the land of your inheritance, if you seek it with all your hearts.

"And this shall be my covenant with you, ye shall have it for the land of your inheritance, and for the inheritance of your children forever, while the earth shall stand, and ye shall possess it again in eternity, no more to pass away" (D&C 38:18–20).

And also:

"And the earth shall be given unto them for an inheritance; and they shall multiply and wax strong, and their children shall grow up without sin unto salvation" (D&C 45:58).

And finally:

"But blessed are the poor who are pure in heart, whose hearts are broken, and whose spirits are contrite, for they shall see the kingdom of God coming in power and great glory unto their deliverance; for the fatness of the earth shall be theirs. . . .

"And their generations shall inherit the earth from generation to generation, forever and ever" (D&C 56:18, 20).

Title and possession of such lands for an everlasting possession are not for sale in the open market or at the real estate office but are obtained only by covenant, by consecration, and by obedience to the gospel of Jesus Christ (see Abraham 2:6). We learn from the Doctrine and Covenants that the arrangement of these inheritances is the work of the bishop.

THE RESTORATION OF THE MELCHIZEDEK PRIESTHOOD

Although the exact date of the restoration of the Melchizedek Priesthood by the ancient apostles Peter, James, and John is not given in the Doctrine and Covenants nor in Church history, it is known to have occurred within a few weeks after the restoration of the Aaronic Priesthood. With the Melchizedek Priesthood, the Prophet Joseph Smith could move ahead as he was directed and lay the foundation for the entire kingdom, in all of its social, ecclesiastical, economic, and political dimensions. Duties of the various priesthood offices, quorums, and councils are made known in Doctrine and Covenants 84 and 107. As a result of the restoration of the Melchizedek Priesthood, all of the ordinances and covenants that were ever made in ancient times could again be enjoyed on the earth. These are contained within the covenant of Abraham, which includes all of the ordinances and covenants necessary for the living to have full salvation as well as the performance of those same ordinances by proxy for the dead.

The ancient character of the priesthood is demonstrated by the statement that the modern Quorum of the Twelve Apostles and First Presidency hold the keys "in connection with all those who have received a dispensation at any time from the beginning of the creation; for verily I say unto you, the keys . . . have come down from the fathers" (D&C 112:31–32).

It becomes apparent from a chronological study of the Doctrine and Covenants that ofttimes doctrines and ordinances were made known to the Prophet Joseph for a considerable time before he was able to implement them in the Church. And as we have noted, some things are still held in abeyance even now, after more than a century and a half of this dispensation.

THE NEW AND EVERLASTING COVENANT

The new and everlasting covenant is the gospel of Jesus Christ. It is made up of a number of individual covenants such as baptism, priesthood, marriage, and so forth. Soon after the Church was organized in April 1830, some wanted to unite with the Church without new baptism. The Lord revealed that baptism was "a new and an everlasting covenant, even that which was from the beginning" (D&C 22:1). This language is consistent with the whole concept of restoration. Things are "new" to this dispensation but are everlasting and were in existence from the beginning.

The Lord said that authoritative baptism is required of all who join the Church (D&C 22:2–4). The Lord further clarified the meaning of the term "new and everlasting covenant," saying it was "the fulness of my gospel" (D&C 66:2) and that it has stringent laws, bounds, conditions, and covenants that were worked out, decided upon, and ordained by the Father and the Son before the foundation of the earth (D&C 132:5–12).

CELESTIAL MARRIAGE

We do not know the exact date on which the doctrine of celestial marriage (including plural marriage) was revealed to the Prophet Joseph Smith. It was sometime in 1831, although the written document, Doctrine and Covenants 132, was not composed until 12 July 1843 (see headnote to D&C 132). The eternal nature of the marriage relation and the sealing of children to parents in an eternal family is part of the social dimension of the kingdom. This family connection includes the nature of the marriage ceremony and the patriarchal order with the husband presiding in the home, the eternal nature of each family unit, and the sealing of generations together like links in a chain from Adam and Eve to the latest generation of their posterity on the earth.

The celestial marriage covenant is part of the covenant of Abraham. It is the type of marriage for eternity that Abraham had. Abraham himself is mentioned no fewer than twenty times in Section 132 alone and thirty-five times in the entire Doctrine and Covenants. The keys for instituting this type of marriage and family covenant were given in the Kirtland Temple, as recorded in Doctrine and Covenants 110:12, and are there called the "gospel of Abraham."

The temple endowment, the celestial marriage covenant, and the sealing of families and generations are interwoven in the plan of salvation and are all included within "the restoration of all things," which means that these very ordinances and promises were known and practiced by ancient prophets, beginning with Adam (see Abraham, facsimile 2, fig. 3). We note these particular phrases in the revelations:

Doctrine and Covenants 27:6. "And also with Elias, to whom I have committed the keys of bringing to pass the *restoration of all things* spoken by the mouth of all the holy prophets since the world began, concerning the last days."

Doctrine and Covenants 77:9. "And, if you will receive it, this is Elias which was to come to gather together the tribes of Israel and *restore all things.*"

Doctrine and Covenants 86:10. "Therefore your life and the priesthood have remained, and must needs remain through you and your lineage *until the restoration of all things* spoken by the mouths of all the holy prophets since the world began."

Doctrine and Covenants 124:28. "For there is not a place found on earth that he may come to and *restore again* that which was lost unto you . . . even the fulness of the priesthood."

Doctrine and Covenants 132:40, 45. "I am the Lord thy God, and I gave unto thee, my servant Joseph, an appointment, *and restore all things.* Ask what ye will, and it shall be given unto you according to my word. . . . For I have conferred upon you the keys and power of the priesthood, *wherein I restore all things* and make known unto you all things in due time."

The concept of restoration is firmly implanted in the Doctrine and Covenants, and because it states that "all things" will be restored, we must conclude that the restoration includes every eternal gospel doctrine, practice, ordinance, and facet of the kingdom of God that ever was upon the earth in any former dispensation. This restoration does not include some factors of the law of Moses, which were temporary in nature (see Smith, *Teachings of the Prophet Joseph Smith,* p. 173).

The Prophet was well aware of the difficulty that would arise in implementing the doctrine and practice of plural marriage. The following is from an account by Heber C. Kimball's daughter:

"[There was a] sensation caused in Nauvoo, one Sabbath morning [in 1840 or 41] . . . by a sermon of the Prophet's on 'the restoration of all things,' in which it was hinted that the patriarchal or plural order of marriage, as practiced by the ancients, would some day again be established. The excitement created by the bare suggestion was such that Joseph deemed it wisdom, in the afternoon, to modify his statement by saying that possibly the Spirit had made the time seem nearer than it really was, when such things would be restored" (Orson F. Whitney, *Life of Heber C. Kimball* [Salt Lake City: Stevens & Wallis, 1945], p. 328).

Because this earth will be a celestial kingdom, and Abraham, and others, including Joseph Smith, Brigham Young, and Heber C. Kimball, each of whom had plural wives, will live here, plural marriage will exist again on the earth in that kingdom. That does not mean that everyone will be required to live that law. It may not be for everyone.

THE TEMPLE ENDOWMENT

Concerning the endowment, which was given for the first time in this dispensation in the Red Brick Store in Nauvoo, Illinis, on 4 May 1842, the Prophet Joseph Smith explained:

"I spent the day in the upper part of the store, that is in my private office . . . in council with General James Adams, of Springfield, Patriarch Hyrum Smith, Bishops Newel K. Whitney and George Miller, and President Brigham Young and Elders Heber C. Kimball and Willard Richards, instructing them in the principles and order of the Priesthood, attending to washings, anointings, endowments and the communication of keys pertaining to the Aaronic Priesthood, and so on to the highest order of the Melchizedek Priesthood, setting forth the order pertaining to the Ancient of Days, and all those plans and principles by which any one is enabled to secure the fullness of those blessings which have been prepared for the Church of the Firstborn, and come up and abide in the presence of the Eloheim in the eternal worlds. In this council was instituted the ancient order of things for the first time in these last days" (*Teachings of the Prophet Joseph Smith*, p. 237).

It is to be noted that the Prophet Joseph Smith said that these things, which we recognize as the temple endowment, are the "ancient order of things" and pertain to the "Ancient of Days," who is Adam.

THE ROLE OF PRIESTHOOD QUORUMS AND COUNCILS

In the revelation on priesthood, also known as Doctrine and Covenants 107, priesthood councils or quorums are defined and set forth.
This revelation is dated 28 March 1835, but some of it was revealed
as early as November 1831 (see headnote to D&C 107).

Specifically mentioned are the Seventy, the Twelve, and the First
Presidency. The revelation explains that the unanimous decisions made
by each of these councils are binding (D&C 107:27–30). Of special
importance is the statement that the presiding quorums which are
established in the latter-day Church and kingdom are patterned after
ancient Melchizedek Priesthood quorums (D&C 107:29), not modern
inventions but part of the restoration of ancient things. Concerning
the order of ancient priesthood councils, the Prophet said:

"I had never set before any council in all the order in which it
ought to be conducted, which, perhaps, has deprived the councils of
some or many blessings. . . .

"In ancient days councils were conducted with such strict propriety,
that no one was allowed to whisper, be weary, leave the room, or get
uneasy in the least, until the voice of the Lord, by revelation, or the
voice of the council by the Spirit, was obtained, which has not been
observed in this Church to the present time. It was understood in
ancient days, that if one man could stay in council, another could;
and if the president could spend his time, the members could also; but
in our councils, generally, one will be uneasy, another asleep; one
praying, another not; one's mind on the business of the council, and
another thinking on something else" (*Teachings of the Prophet Joseph
Smith*, p. 69).

THE POLITICAL OR CIVIL DIMENSION OF THE KINGDOM

At present the priesthood of the Church functions as an ecclesiastical organization—that is, as a church. Nonetheless, the power is
inherent in the priesthood and the keys to function in a political manner
when circumstances permit. Such was the case with Adam, and Noah,
and with the Nephites, and with Moses. Concerning the children of
Israel under Moses, the Prophet Joseph Smith said:

"Their government was a theocracy; they had God to make their
laws, and men chosen by Him to administer them; He was their God,
and they were His people. Moses received the word of the Lord from
God Himself; he was the mouth of God to Aaron, and Aaron taught
the people, in both civil and ecclesiastical affairs; they were both one,
there was no distinction; so will it be when the purposes of God shall

be accomplished: when 'the Lord shall be King over the whole earth' and 'Jerusalem His throne.' 'The law shall go forth from Zion, and the word of the Lord from Jerusalem.'

"This is the only thing that can bring about the 'restitution of all things spoken of by all the holy Prophets since the world was' — 'the dispensation of the fullness of times, when God shall gather together all things in one' " (*Teachings of the Prophet Joseph Smith*, p. 252).

That is the civil or political dimension of the kingdom of God on earth, which is not operative at the present time.

The important distinction or separation that sometimes has to exist between civil and ecclesiastical matters was referred to by the Savior when he was questioned by Pilate about his kingship and his kingdom. Surely no believer can doubt Jesus' right to rule the world and the universe as Lord of lords and King of kings. The Jewish rulers, however, wanted to make trouble for Jesus in the eyes of the Roman Empire. They wanted Jesus to be charged with treason against Rome because he was the king of the Jews. A dialogue on this topic between the Roman governor Pilate and Jesus is found in John 18:33–38:

"Then Pilate entered into the judgment hall again, and called Jesus, and said unto him, Art thou the King of the Jews?

"Jesus answered him, Sayest thou this thing of thyself, or did others tell it thee of me?" [That is, Jesus asked, Are you speaking as a Roman official or citing what the Jews have said? Are you asking an ecclesiastical question or a political question?]

"Pilate answered, Am I a Jew? Thine own nation and the chief priests have delivered thee unto me: what hast thou done?" [Pilate's response, "Am I a Jew?" means, I am not asking as a Jew; I am asking politically as a Roman official.]

"Jesus answered, My kingdom is not of this world: if my kingdom were of this world, then would my servants fight, that I should not be delivered to the Jews: but now is my kingdom not from hence.

"Pilate therefore said unto him, Art thou a king then? Jesus answered, Thou sayest that I am a king. To this end was I born, and for this cause came I into the world, that I should bear witness unto the truth. Every one that is of the truth heareth my voice.

"Pilate saith unto him, What is truth? And when he had said this, he went out again unto the Jews, and saith unto them, I find in him no fault at all."

What all that means is, Yes, I am a king, and eventually my kingdom shall fill the whole earth, but not now. Therefore, I have not set up a kingdom that will rival or threaten the present Roman Empire.

We know that ultimately Jesus' kingdom *is* "of this world," for he said that the meek shall inherit the earth (Matthew 5:5; D&C 88:17), and in the Revelation of John the promise is made that the faithful shall become kings and priests unto God and "shall reign on the earth" (Revelation 5:10). The time will come when the kingdom spoken of by Daniel, and by Jesus, and by John, and by Joseph Smith, will fill the whole earth and will replace all the kingdoms of the earth. That is what the Twelve in Jerusalem had in mind when they asked Jesus, "Wilt thou at this time restore again the kingdom to Israel?" (Acts 1:6). Jesus answered, in effect, not at this time—but later (see v. 7). The time is not yet, even in 1992, but it will occur sometime in this dispensation. As expressed in Doctrine and Covenants 65:2, 5, 6:

"The keys of the kingdom of God are committed unto man on the earth, and from thence shall the gospel roll forth unto the ends of the earth, as the stone which is cut out of the mountain without hands shall roll forth, until it has filled the whole earth. . . .

"Call upon the Lord, that his kingdom may go forth upon the earth, that the inhabitants thereof may receive it, and be prepared for the days to come, in the which the Son of Man shall come down in heaven, clothed in the brightness of his glory, to meet the kingdom of God which is set up on the earth.

"Wherefore, may the kingdom of God go forth, that the kingdom of heaven may come, that thou, O God, mayest be glorified in heaven so on earth, that thine enemies may be subdued; for thine is the honor, power and glory, forever and ever. Amen."

And Doctrine and Covenants 87:6 indicates that the Lord has decreed eventually "a full end of all nations," to be replaced by the Lord's own kingdom.

THE GATHERING OF ISRAEL

A major accomplishment of the restoration of all things will be the literal gathering of the literal seed of Israel. It will be done because of the promise God made to the fathers that he would look after their posterity. Modern Israel has descended from ancient Israel, and are "lawful heirs, according to the flesh" (D&C 86:9). Special blessings were given to the sons of Jacob that have carried down through the years and will reach a fulfillment in the final gathering and restoration of Israel. Judah was given the scepter and the power to govern. From him came David the king, with a promise that from his seed would come the kings that would reign in Israel (Jeremiah 33:17; Psalms 89:3–4; 35–36; 132:11–12). The Doctrine and Covenants affirms that Jesus Christ came of that very lineage and is the Son of David, the stem of Jesse (Isaiah 9:6–7; 11:1; Luke 1:30–33; D&C 113:1). It was absolutely necessary that Jesus, as King of kings, come through the lineage of Judah and David, in addition to being the Son of God.

The sons of Levi, especially Aaron and his sons, have had a special role in earlier dispensations and will yet have a major role in the restoration of Israel and the consecration of properties, as we have already discussed. It is just as important that a future bishop be of the lineage of Aaron, as it was that Jesus be of the lineage of David. Likewise, the descendants of Joseph have the right to be the first to hear the gospel in the last days. Joseph's lineage has the Joseph-like responsibility to gather the tribes of latter-day Israel by giving them the "bread of life" similar to the way Joseph preserved his brothers anciently. Therefore Ephraim, who was given the birthright in ancient times, has the richer blessing and the particular responsibility to gather Israel (D&C 133:26–35). It is no accident or coincidence that Joseph Smith and most of the latter-day Saints are literal, blood descendants of ancient Joseph. That is part of the restoration of all things.

CHANGES IN THE EARTH ITSELF

If the covenant people are to be gathered, the land must become productive enough to sustain them. The Lord, through the prophets of old, spoke of the land becoming fruitful and the desert blossoming "as the rose" (Isaiah 35:1).

Genesis 10:24 states that at a certain time the land was physically divided and no longer remained as one land. Doctrine and Covenants 133:23–24 states that in the last days "the islands shall become one land . . . and the earth shall be like as it was in the days before it was divided."

If we contemplate the plan of God on the earth since the beginning and consider the importance of multiple witnesses, we can view the Bible, the Book of Mormon, and the record of the lost tribes as three major witnesses for the work of the Lord. These three separate testimonies came as the result of these peoples being separated by great distances of land and with the oceans as natural barriers. Who can say but that the division of the land into continents and islands separated by large oceans was done in the wisdom of God to bring about the condition in earlier dispensations whereby there would be separate witnesses, or records, from various branches of the house of Israel? Now, in the fulness of times, when the tribes of Israel are to be gathered and their records are also to be gathered — and since the rapid transportation of the last days makes the oceans no longer such major barriers — the need for separation is past. Therefore, as part of the restoration the land shall come together again, "like as it was before it was divided." The Lord has designed to "gather together in one all things, both which are in heaven, and which are on earth" (D&C 27:13; see also Ephesians 1:10).

Furthermore, the earth when created was paradisiacal, before the fall of Adam. The promise is that "the earth will be renewed and receive its paradisiacal glory" (Article of Faith 10). The Prophet Joseph Smith said the earth is to be renovated (*Teachings of the Prophet Joseph Smith,* p. 232).

This glorification of the earth is spoken of in the Doctrine and Covenants as follows:

"And the end shall come, and the heaven and the earth shall be consumed and pass away, and there shall be a new heaven and a new earth. For all old things shall pass away, and all things shall become new, even the heaven and the earth, and all the fulness thereof, both men and beasts, the fowls of the air, and the fishes of the sea; and not one hair, neither mote, shall be lost, for it is the workmanship of mine hand" (D&C 29:23–25; cf. 101:23–34).

Also:

"Nevertheless, he that endureth in faith and doeth my will, the same shall overcome, and shall receive an inheritance upon the earth when the day of transfiguration shall come. When the earth shall be transfigured, even according to the pattern which was shown unto mine apostles upon the mount; of which account the fulness ye have not yet received" (D&C 63:20–21).

THINGS NEVER BEFORE REVEALED

Not only will the ancient order be reestablished on the earth but the final dispensation will be given things never before revealed. We read in Doctrine and Covenants 121:26–28, 31–32:

"God shall give unto you knowledge by his Holy Spirit, yea, by the unspeakable gift of the Holy Ghost, that has not been revealed since the world was until now;

"Which our forefathers have awaited with anxious expectation to be revealed in the last times, which their minds were pointed to by the angels, as held in reserve for the fulness of their glory;

"A time to come in the which nothing shall be withheld. . . .

"All their glories, laws, and set times, shall be revealed in the days of the dispensation of the fulness of times —

"According to that which was ordained in the midst of the Council of the Eternal God of all other gods before this world was, that should be reserved unto the finishing and the end thereof."

When speaking of the restoration of all things, we must understand that it is the ancient promises, the ancient priesthood, and the doctrinal teachings that are to be renewed. The restoration does not mean that clothing styles, building construction, and traveling conveyances must revert to those of earlier times. We are not going to live in Abraham-style tents and travel by camel. The restoration is of eternal things, the promises of eternal glory and exaltation that were made to Adam and to Abraham, as well as the ordinances and covenants by which such blessings can be secured by individuals living today.

In preparation for the restoration, the Lord moved among the nations of the earth, causing the Renaissance and the Reformation and establishing the United States of America. All of this preparation and the modern inventions we now enjoy were inspired of God to assist in the restoration of all things. Because of the Restoration there has been as much improvement in doctrinal understanding over what churches believed 150 years ago as there has been in communication and travel over what people had 150 years ago.

God lives in a perfect, celestial society with all the advantages and enjoyments of perfect intelligence, rapid communication, rapid travel, and the very best in building construction and utility. The high state of twentieth-century technology, which exceeds anything this earth has ever known, is very primitive compared with what is yet to be revealed when the earth becomes a celestial world. Because of both present and future technological development, we in this dispensation will be able to do a great many things not possible in earlier times.

True prophets of every dispensation have been working hand-in-hand with each other and with the Lord Jesus Christ in the same cause, as explained by the Prophet Joseph Smith:

"The building up of Zion is a cause that has interested the people of God in every age; it is a theme upon which prophets, priests and kings have dwelt with peculiar delight; they have looked forward with joyful anticipation to the day in which we live; and fired with heavenly and joyful anticipations they have sung and written and prophesied of this our day; but they died without the sight; we are the favored people that God has made choice of to bring about the Latter-day glory; it is left for us to see, participate in and help to roll forward the Latter-day glory, 'the dispensation of the fulness of times, when God will gather together all things that are in heaven, and all things that are upon the earth,' 'even in one,' when the Saints of God will be gathered in one from every nation, and kindred, and people, and tongue, when the Jews will be gathered together into one, the wicked will also be gathered together to be destroyed, as spoken of by the prophets; the

Spirit of God will also dwell with His people, and be withdrawn from the rest of the nations, and all things whether in heaven or on earth will be in one, even in Christ. The heavenly Priesthood will unite with the earthly, to bring about those great purposes; and whilst we are thus united in one common cause, to roll forth the kingdom of God, the heavenly Priesthood are not idle spectators, the Spirit of God will be showered down from above, and it will dwell in our midst. . . . [We are laying the foundation of] a work that God and angels have contemplated with delight for generations past; that fired the souls of the ancient patriarchs and prophets; a work that is destined to bring about the destruction of the powers of darkness, the renovation of the earth, the glory of God, and the salvation of the human family" (*Teachings of the Prophet Joseph Smith*, pp. 231–32).

SUMMARY

The Prophet Joseph Smith said that the work the Lord called him to do would revolutionize the world. The Lord called his work "my act, my strange act" (D&C 101:95; see also 95:4; Isaiah 28:21). He also called it "a marvelous work and a wonder" (2 Nephi 25:17). The Restoration is strange to those not of the Church, and it is marvelous to those who are of the Church. Even so, most of us have perhaps had but peripheral comprehension of the marvelous changes that will yet take place in the earth and in the Church in order to bring about the restoration of all things spoken of by the mouths of all the holy prophets since the world began. Such is the role of this dispensation. The restoration of all things is a reality. It has begun, and much has been revealed. There is still much to be implemented that has already been revealed, and there is more yet to be revealed.

NOTE

1. See also John Taylor, *The Mediation and Atonement of Our Lord and Savior Jesus Christ* (Salt Lake City: Deseret News Press, 1882); Orson Pratt, in *Journal of Discourses* (London: Latter-day Saints' Book Depot, 1854–86), 16:58 (18 May 1873); Bruce R. McConkie, *Doctrinal New Testament Commentary* (Salt Lake City: Bookcraft, 1965), 1:70–71. A discussion of this subject is also found in Robert J. Matthews, *A Burning Light* (Provo, Utah: Brigham Young University Press, 1972), pp. 79–81.

16

PROTECTION AGAINST DECEPTION

Leaun G. Otten

Brigham Young University

Satan's motives are to deceive and destroy. He has been actively engaged in this endeavor since the Garden of Eden. The Savior's word provides detection and deliverance from the evil one for the Lord's children. Through living prophets, the Lord has revealed sufficient knowledge that would protect us from being deceived, and revealed warning and counsel about avoiding deception is recorded in the Doctrine and Covenants.

LIVING PROPHETS

Modern prophets have warned and counseled us about avoiding deception. President Harold B. Lee counseled the Latter-day Saints to be aware of being deceived not only by some not of the faith but also by some within the kingdom:

"We pray for our Saints everywhere, pray that they will hold steadfast. But, some of the greatest of our enemies are those within our own ranks. It was the lament of the Master, as he witnessed one of those chosen men, who under inspiration he chose as one of the Twelve, betray him with a kiss and for a few paltry pieces of silver turn him over to his enemies. Judas then stood by and, realizing the enormity of what he had done, took the only escape out to sacrifice himself. And Jesus could only explain that of the Twelve, meaning Judas, he had a devil."[1]

Then President Lee quoted from Doctrine and Covenants 71:9–11, in which the Lord informs us that no weapon formed against his church will prosper and that our responsibility is to keep his commandments. Commenting on that instruction from the Lord, President Lee said: "What he is trying to have us understand is that he will take care of our enemies if we continue to keep the commandments. So, you Saints of the Most High God, when these things come, and they will come, this has been prophesied—you just say,

" 'No weapon formed against the work of the Lord will ever prosper, but all glory and majesty of this work that the Lord gave will long be remembered after those who have tried to befoul the name of the Church and those of its leaders will be forgotten, and their works will follow after them.'

"We feel sorry for them when we see these things happen."[2]

Some time after the Saints arrived in the Great Basin, President Heber C. Kimball foresaw the very conditions we find ourselves in now. Although his words were directed to the Saints in the valleys of these mountains, they are applicable to all those who believe in Jesus Christ. President Kimball said: "We think we are secure here in the chambers of the everlasting hills, where we can close these few doors of the canyons against . . . the wicked and the vile, . . . but I want to say to you, my brethren, the time is coming when we will be mixed up in these now peaceful valleys to that extent that it will be difficult to tell the face of a Saint from the face of an enemy to the people of God."[3]

Another warning from President Harold B. Lee: "We may well expect to find our Judases among those professing membership in the Church, but, unfortunately for them, they are laboring under some kind of evil influences or have devious motives."[4]

President Spencer W. Kimball's counsel to us has broadened our understanding of the many avenues used by the evil one to deceive us. One quotation from President Kimball illustrates the scope of Lucifer's efforts:

"Voices again! Rasping voices proclaiming 'doctrines of devils,' saying there is no sin; there is no devil; there is no God. Saying that we will 'eat, drink, and be merry' like the antediluvians who never believed that the flood would really come.

"Many voices of seducing spirits advocate carnal pleasures and unrestrained physical satisfactions. Our world is now much the same as it was in the days of the Nephite prophet who said: ' . . . if it were not for the prayers of the righteous . . . ye would even now be visited with utter destruction. . . .' (Al. 10:22.) Of course, there are many many upright and faithful who live all the commandments and whose lives and prayers keep the world from destruction. . . .

"Many voices, loud and harsh, come from among educators, business and professional men, sociologists, psychologists, authors, movie actors, legislators, judges, and others, even some of the clergy, who, because they have learned a little about something, seem to think they know all about everything.

"This egotism and pride is prompted by the cunning father of lies. Hear the voice of a Nephite prophet describing their acceptance of the 'cunning plan of the evil one':

" ' . . . to be learned is good if they hearken unto the counsels of God.' (2 Ne. 9:29.)

" ' . . . When they are learned they think they are wise . . . supposing they know of themselves, wherefore their wisdom is foolishness. . . . And they shall perish.' (2 Ne. 9:28.)"[5]

THE DOCTRINE AND COVENANTS

I would now like to turn to the Lord's book we call the Doctrine and Covenants. In his goodness to us, the Lord has counseled, instructed, given directions, and revealed commandments to protect us from deception. Because it is impossible to discuss here all that the Lord has revealed on this subject, I will discuss only eight specific areas of counsel.

Recognizing the Lord's Authorized Mouthpiece

If it is not the major source, certainly "false revelation" coming from those not authorized by Jesus Christ would rank high on Lucifer's list of methods of deception. So there would be no misunderstanding about who is the authorized source of revelation coming from the Lord, the Savior defined the relationship that exists between himself and his prophet. Speaking to Joseph Smith, the Lord said: "Thou shalt be called a seer, a translator, a prophet, an apostle of Jesus Christ, an elder of the church through the will of God the Father, and the grace of your Lord Jesus Christ" (D&C 21:1).

Joseph Smith's appointment and calling was not of men nor of any organization of men. It was of Jesus Christ. This concept is reinforced in the same verse when the Savior declared that Joseph's calling was the will of the Father as well as of the Son. Further, the Lord directed that the prophet's calling should be recorded in the history of the Church. Therefore, every member of the church, from that day forward, should be aware of the relationship existing between the prophet and the Savior. No one should misunderstand the sacred responsibility of the prophet, for the Lord declared: "His word [the prophet's] ye shall receive as if from my own mouth" (D&C 21:5).

The Lord has made it equally clear that a relationship exists between the members of the Lord's church and the Lord's prophet: "Wherefore, meaning the church, thou shalt give heed unto all his words and commandments which he shall give unto you as he receiveth them, walking in all holiness before me; for his word ye shall receive as if from mine own mouth, in all patience and faith" (D&C 21:4–5).

When the Lord said "all his word," we are left to conclude there are no exceptions.

Blessings are promised to faithful members who heed the Lord's counsel:

1. The gates of hell shall not prevail against them,

2. The Lord God will disperse the powers of darkness from before them,

3. The Lord God will cause the heavens to shake for their good and his name's glory,

4. The Lord God will give a special witness to them that the prophet's words are given to him by Jesus Christ (see D&C 21:6, 9).

If we will follow this divine counsel, we will not be deceived about the source of revelation.

Five months after the Church was organized, Lucifer sought to deceive some Church members by giving a so-called revelation through one of the members, Hiram Page. Again the Savior reviewed the order of his Church pertaining to revelation for the Church:

"Behold, I say unto thee, Oliver, that it shall be given unto thee that thou shalt be heard by the church in all things whatsoever thou shalt teach them by the Comforter, concerning the revelations and commandments which I have given.

"But, behold, verily, verily, I say unto thee, no one shall be appointed to receive commandments and revelations in this church excepting my servant Joseph Smith, Jun., for he receiveth them even as Moses. . . .

"And if thou art led at any time by the Comforter to speak or teach, or at all times by the way of commandment unto the church, thou mayest do it.

"But thou shalt not write by way of commandment, but by wisdom;

"And thou shalt not command him who is at thy head, and at the head of the church. . . .

"And, again, thou shalt take thy brother, Hiram Page, between him and thee alone, and tell him that those things which he hath written from that stone are not of me and that Satan deceiveth him. . . .

"For all things must be done in order and by common consent in the church, by the prayer of faith" (D&C 28:1-2, 4-6, 11, 13).

Five months after Doctrine and Covenants 28 was received, a female member of the Church by the name of Hubble claimed to have received revelation for the Church. The Lord again reiterated the basic principle upon which revelation is conveyed from the Divine and gave two more principles to protect us from deception by revealing "the law of revelation to his church" and by identifying the "special gate" through which the Lord's mouthpiece must come:

"For behold, verily, verily, I say unto you, that ye have received a commandment for a law unto my church [D&C 42], through him whom I have appointed unto you to receive commandments and revelations from my hand.

"And this ye shall know assuredly—that there is none other appointed unto you to receive commandments and revelations until he be taken, if he abide in me.

"But verily, verily, I say unto you, that none else shall be appointed unto this gift except it be through him; for if it be taken from him he shall not have power except to appoint another in his stead.

"And this shall be a law unto you, that ye receive not the teachings of any that shall come before you as revelations or commandments;

"And this I give unto you that you may not be deceived, that you may know they are not of me.

"For verily I say unto you, that he that is ordained of me [that is, to be the Lord's mouthpiece] shall come in at the gate and be ordained as I have told you before, to teach those revelations which you have received and shall receive through him who I have appointed" (D&C 43:2–7).

To protect us from deception by way of false revelation, the Savior has given a law to all members of the Church to accept only authorized revelation from one man on this earth—that is, his mouthpiece, the prophet. To afford us further protection, the Savior has revealed that his authorized mouthpiece must come through a special gate, which is becoming president of the Quorum of the Twelve Apostles. For a more clear understanding of this concept, I quote President Joseph Fielding Smith:

"Some Latter-day Saints, because of their lack of knowledge, have been deceived into following false teachers and 'prophets' because they have never learned the simple truth which the Lord makes so plain in this revelation:

" 'For verily I say unto you, that he that is ordained of me shall come in at the gate and be ordained as I have told you before, to teach those revelations which you have received and shall receive through him whom I have appointed' [D&C 43:7]. This commandment is the key by which the members of the Church are to be governed and protected from all those who profess to be appointed and empowered to guide the Church. . . .

"We frequently hear discussions in our classes and between brethren to the effect that any man could be called, if the authorities should choose him, to preside over the Church and that it is not the fixed order to take the senior apostle to preside, and any member of that quorum could be appointed. The fact is that the senior apostle automatically becomes the presiding officer of the Church on the death of the President. If some other man were to be chosen, then the senior would have to receive the revelation setting himself aside. President John Taylor has made this very plain. (See 'Succession In the Priesthood,' chapter 17, 'The Gospel Kingdom.') Says President Taylor, speaking of the time following President Young's death: 'I occupied the senior position in the quorum, and occupying that position which was thoroughly understood by the quorum of the twelve, on the death of President Young, as the twelve assumed the presidency, and I was their president, it placed me in a position of president of the Church, or, as expressed in our conference meeting: "As president of the quorum of the twelve apostles, as one of the twelve apostles, and of the presidency of the Church of Jesus Christ of Latter-day Saints." In this manner, also, was President Brigham Young sustained, at the general conference held in Nauvoo, in October following the martyrdom of the Prophet Joseph Smith.' ('Gospel Kingdom,' p. 192.) The counselors in the presidency cease to be counselors when the President dies and take their regular place among their brethren."[6]

Through the giving of this law, the Lord has established a means of protection for the Saints that they might never be deceived (see D&C 43:6). Any revelation that comes from the Lord to his church will always come through the one man who has come through the gate and is the senior apostle of Jesus Christ. He will be the one who presides over the Lord's kingdom. That is the law of revelation to the Lord's church.

Understanding the Proper Relationship between the Living Word and the Written Word

The Prophet Joseph Smith taught: "That which is wrong under one circumstance, may be, and often is, right under another."[7] The living word thus takes precedence over the written word. Many of our Father's children have been deceived by accepting dead prophets' words and failing to accept the living word. That is particularly true when "that which is wrong under one circumstance, may be, and often is, right under another." Speaking of dead prophets and the keys they held, Elder Boyd K. Packer told of an experience he had with President Kimball:

"In 1976 an area general conference was held in Copenhagen, Denmark. Following the closing session, President Kimball expressed a desire to visit the Vor Frue Church, where the Thorvaldsen statues of the Christus and of the Twelve Apostles stand. . . .

" . . . I stood with President Kimball, Elder Rex Pinegar, and President Bentine, the stake president, before the statue of Peter. In his hand, depicted in marble, is a set of heavy keys. President Kimball pointed to them and explained what they symbolized. Then, in an act I shall never forget, he turned to President Bentine and with unaccustomed sternness pointed his finger at him and said with firm, impressive words, 'I want you to tell every Lutheran in Denmark that they do not hold the keys! I hold the keys! We hold the real keys and we use them every day.' . . .

"We walked to the other end of the chapel where the rest of the group were standing. Pointing to the statues, President Kimball said to the kind custodian who was showing us the building, 'These are the dead Apostles. Here we have the living Apostles.' Pointing to me he said, 'Elder Packer is an Apostle.' He designated the others and said, 'Elder Monson and Elder Perry are Apostles, and I am an Apostle. We are the living Apostles. You read about seventies in the New Testament, and here are the living seventies, Brother Pinegar and Brother Hales.'

"The Custodian, who to that time had shown no particular emotion, suddenly was in tears.

"As we left the little chapel where those impressive sculptures stand, I felt I had taken part in an experience of a lifetime."[8]

The relationship of the living word to the written word was revealed by the Lord in Doctrine and Covenants 46. The historical setting for this revelation is as follows:

"With reference to the matters mentioned in verses 1–7 in this revelation, John Whitmer writes: 'In the beginning of the Church, while yet in her infancy, the disciples used to exclude unbelievers, which caused some to marvel and converse of this matter because of the things written in the Book of Mormon [3 Nephi 18:22–34]. Therefore the Lord deigned to speak on this subject, that His people might come to understanding, and said that He had always given to His Elders to conduct all meetings as they were led by the Spirit.' "[9]

Now listen to the Lord's answer,

"Hearken, O ye people of my church; for verily I say unto you that these things were spoken unto you for your profit and learning.

"But notwithstanding those things which are written, it always has been given to the elders of my church from the beginning, and ever shall be, to conduct all meetings as they are directed and guided by the Holy Spirit. . . .

"But ye are commanded in all things to ask of God, who giveth liberally; and that which the Spirit testifies unto you even so I would that ye should do in all holiness of heart walking uprightly before me, considering the end of your salvation, doing all things with prayer and thanksgiving, that ye may not be seduced by evil spirits, or doctrines of devils, or the commandments of men; for some are of men, and others of devils.

"Wherefore, beware lest ye are deceived; and that ye may not be deceived seek ye earnestly the best gifts, always remembering for what they are given" (D&C 46:1–2, 7–8).

The Lord here reminds us of the importance of modern-day revelation. Though instruction had been given and recorded in an ancient scriptural text (the Book of Mormon), the way it was to be applied in a modern setting was not clear. The Lord instructed the brethren that the guidance of the Spirit was the way by which the program of his Church should be conducted and problems should be solved. In other words, handbooks of instruction, important though they may be, will never contain all the answers to all the problems. We must always rely upon spiritual guidance, coupled with that which has been previously given, to do that which is right in the sight of the Lord.

Detecting Hypocrisy within the Church

Hypocrisy within the Savior's church has been exploited by Lucifer to deceive many. The Savior has therefore given us counsel and revelation that afford us protection. The Prophet Joseph Smith taught about Doctrine and Covenants 50: "Soon after the Gospel was established in Kirtland, and during the absence of the authorities of the Church, many false spirits were introduced, many strange visions were seen, and wild, enthusiastic notions were entertained; men ran out of doors under the influence of this spirit, and some of them got upon the stumps of trees and shouted, and all kinds of extravagances were entered into by them; one man pursued a ball that he said he saw flying in the air, until he came to a precipice, when he jumped into the top of a tree, which saved his life; and many ridiculous things were entered into, calculated to bring disgrace upon the Church of God, to cause the Spirit of God to be withdrawn, and to uproot and destroy those glorious principles which had been developed for the salvation of the human family."[10]

Joseph Fielding Smith made the following observations about Section 50:

"If the members of the Church will carefully consider the word of the Lord and follow the precepts here given they will not be deceived by the evil spirits of man or devils. The promise is made in a positive manner that all 'who buildeth upon this rock shall never fall.' Yes, sad to say, there are members of the Church who are ready to follow any theory, philosophy, or strange doctrine especially if with it there is something mysterious.

"Even in that day there were hypocrites and deceivers drawn into the Church and with them they brought their abominations which had to be speedily eliminated by the Lord making known their evil practices."[11]

The Lord's counsel to us as recorded in Section 50 affords us great protection from hypocrisy:

"Hearken, O ye elders of my church, and give ear to the voice of the living God; and attend to the words of wisdom which shall be given unto you, according as ye have asked and agreed as touching the church, and the spirits which have gone abroad in the earth.

"Behold, verily I say unto you, that there are many spirits which are false spirits, which have gone forth in the earth, deceiving the world.

"And also Satan hath sought to deceive you, that he might overthrow you.

"Behold, I, the Lord, have looked upon you, and have seen abominations in the church that profess my name.

"But blessed are they who are faithful and endure, whether in life or in death, for they shall inherit eternal life.

"But wo unto them that are deceivers and hypocrites, for, thus saith the Lord, I will bring them to judgment.

"Behold, verily I say unto you, there are hypocrites among you, who have deceived some, which has given the adversary power; but behold such shall be reclaimed;

"But the hypocrites shall be detected and shall be cut off, either in life or in death, even as I will; and wo unto them who are cut off from my church, for the same are overcome of the world.

"Wherefore, let every man beware lest he do that which is not in truth and righteousness before me" (D&C 50:1–9).

Sometimes a member of the Church has difficulty staying active and faithful in the Church. Such difficulty sometimes arises from acts of hypocrisy and the resulting negative influence seen in the lives of some members of the Church. When such an individual allows hypocrisy in the lives of others to justify his own failure to perform according to his covenants, he is doing so because he has not come to an understanding of the Lord's counsel. He has been deceived. As early as 1831, the Lord revealed that there were deceivers and hypocrites in the Church and warned of the possible destructive influences such people might have in the lives of the members (see D&C 50:4-7).

As members of the Church, we ought to be wise enough to understand the problem and heed the counsel of the Lord. There are hypocrites in the Church, and the Lord said so. The Lord also said that when such conditions exist, he will deal with the hypocrite in this life or in the next. Church action may need to be taken in mortality, or the hypocrite may find himself shut out of the Lord's presence in eternity. Either way, it is the Lord's prerogative to take action. Furthermore, Church members are counseled to do what is right before the Lord and to refrain from justifying their own inappropriate action because of the unrighteousness of others (see D&C 50:8-9). No one needs to be deceived by the hypocritical actions of some who have membership in the Church but whose motives are not pure when they fail to live by the standards of the Church.

Receiving Edification through the Spirit

The gospel was restored to people who received it from authorized servants of the Lord. When the gospel message was presented to them, it was by the power and influence of the Spirit of the Lord. They were acquainted with the correct method of teaching. To emphasize this correct method, the Lord asked the following question:

"Wherefore, I the Lord ask you this question—unto what were ye ordained?

"To preach my gospel by the Spirit, even the Comforter which was sent forth to teach the truth" (D&C 50:13-14).

Then another question follows—knowing the approved method of teaching, why are you confused and why are you unable to detect false actions and behavior?

"And then received ye spirits which ye could not understand, and received them to be of God; and in this are ye justified?" (D&C 50:15).

Repeating this principle several times, the Lord summarized his counsel to Church members as follows: "And that which doth not edify is not of God, and is darkness" (D&C 50:23).

Edification uplifts both spiritually and morally. That which doth not edify is not of God and is darkness. In all facets of life, we can be afforded protection from deception by simply asking, "Is this uplifting me spiritually and morally? Is this edifying me?" If so, it is of God. If not, it is darkness. That is true of movies, teachers, books, television programs, doctrine, theories, and so on. All of us are afforded protection against deception if we will heed this counsel of the Master.

Gaining Adequate Knowledge and Understanding

We have been taught that there is a right and a wrong to every question. But our knowledge and understanding are not always sufficient to accurately identify truth from error. In Doctrine and Covenants 50, the Lord described our inadequacies when he said: "But no man is possessor of all things except he be purified and cleansed from all sin" (v. 28). There are many situations when our knowledge, intellect, and experience are insufficient to make wise and proper decisions. When such situations arise, divine help is available. The Lord said:

"And if ye are purified and cleansed from all sin, ye shall ask whatsoever you will in the name of Jesus and it shall be done. . . .

"Wherefore, it shall come to pass, that if you behold a spirit manifested that you cannot understand, and you receive not that spirit, ye shall ask of the Father in the name of Jesus; and if he give not unto you that spirit, then you may know that it is not of God.

"And it shall be given unto you, power over that spirit; and you shall proclaim against that spirit with a loud voice that it is not of God" (D&C 50:29, 31–32).

The prerequisite for obtaining divine guidance is cleanliness of soul, obtained by repentance and obedience to the commandments of the Lord. When a person is free from sin, he is invited to ask for information that will enable him to separate truth from error. The Lord promised to provide such insights from on high. No one needs to be deceived on account of lack of knowledge and understanding. Keeping oneself clean before the Lord opens the windows of heaven, which are revelation. By gaining divine knowledge, one walks in the Spirit of truth.

Observing the Lord's Pattern in All Things

At a gathering of missionaries who had been called to a special meeting in Kirtland, Ohio, on 7 June 1831, the Lord revealed through the Prophet Joseph Smith the following: "And again, I will give unto you a pattern in all things, that ye may not be deceived; for Satan is abroad in the land, and he goeth forth deceiving the nations" (D&C 52:14).

The Lord provided a description of a person whose actions and attributes are acceptable to him. This pattern is as follows (see D&C 52:15–21):

1. One who prays,
2. One whose spirit is contrite and humble,

3. One who receives the Lord's ordinances and keeps the cove-nants,

4. One whose language is meek and uplifting,

5. One who receives and recognizes the Lord's power, and

6. One whose works and teachings reflect the truths given by rev-elation of the Lord through his authorized mouthpiece.

Why should we be deceived by anyone within or without the Church? Applying the Lord's pattern will protect us from the teachings of all men and women who are not acceptable before the Lord. If those teachings are not acceptable to him, then certainly they should not be acceptable to us.

Keeping with the Majority of the Saints

In a sermon delivered in the Salt Lake Tabernacle on 5 May 1870, Elder Orson Hyde of the Council of the Twelve Apostles said: "Joseph the Prophet . . . said, 'Brethren, remember that the majority of this people will never go astray; and as long as you keep with the majority you are sure to enter the celestial kingdom.' "[12]

On another occasion, the Prophet Joseph Smith declared: "Fac-tions and parties will arise out of this Church, and apostates will lead away many. But in the midst of all this, keep with the majority, for the true leaders of God's people will always be able to have a majority, and the records of the Church will be with them."[13]

Elder Andrew Jenson, for many years assistant historian of the Church, wrote in a pamphlet called The Infancy of the Church:

"At the time of the martyrdom of the Prophet Joseph, the Saints were gathered and were building a Temple, baptizing for the dead, etc., which work unceasingly has been kept up by those who under the leadership of the Twelve came to the Rocky Mountains notwith-standing the various factions which have separated themselves from the true Gospel tree. The writer [Elder Stevenson] heard the Prophet say on a stand at the east end of Nauvoo Temple, that the time was coming when there would be many dissensions from the Church. 'But,' said he, 'I now see the time which I have long desired to see. Let me go where I may, the Gospel tree is planted never more to be rooted up, for there are those present who are prepared to carry on the Gospel, whatever may become of me.' He also said: 'I WILL GIVE YOU A KEY BY WHICH YOU MAY NEVER BE DECEIVED, IF YOU WILL OBSERVE THESE FACTS: WHERE THE TRUE CHURCH IS, THERE WILL ALWAYS BE A MAJORITY OF THE SAINTS, AND THE RECORDS AND HISTORY OF THE CHURCH ALSO.' "[14]

Determining True Authority

Knowing that authority is needed from God for acts of men pertaining to their salvation to be valid in the sight of God, Lucifer has deceived many by suggesting to them several avenues by which they may claim authority from God. One method he exploits is the visitation of angels. To counterfeit the Lord's method, Lucifer has inspired some to claim they have been ordained by angels.

The Prophet Joseph Smith himself bore testimony that such could not be. He said angels would restore the priesthood only once. They restored the priesthood to him, and anyone who claims that an angel has come and given the priesthood subsequent to the time that Joseph Smith received his priesthood is "a liar":

"No true angel from God will ever come to ordain any man, because they have once been sent to establish the priesthood by ordaining me thereunto; and the priesthood being once established on earth, with power to ordain others, no heavenly messenger will ever come to interfere with that power by ordaining any more. . . .

"If any man comes to you professing to be ordained by an angel, he is either a liar or has been imposed upon in consequence of transgression by an angel of the devil, for this priesthood shall never be taken away from this church."[15]

SUMMARY

As we walk by faith through mortality, a kind Father has extended his love to us by revealing vital safeguards to protect us from deception:

1. Recognizing the Lord's authorized mouthpiece.

2. Understanding the proper relationship between the living word and the written word.

3. Detecting hypocrisy within the Church.

4. Receiving edification through the Spirit.

5. Gaining adequate knowledge and understanding.

6. Observing the Lord's pattern in all things.

7. Keeping with the majority of the Saints.

8. Determining true authority.

NOTES

1. Harold B. Lee, in Conference Report, Oct. 1973, pp. 166–67.

2. Ibid., p. 167.

3. Orson F. Whitney, *Life of Heber C. Kimball*, 2d ed. (Salt Lake City: Bookcraft, 1945), p. 446.

4. Harold B. Lee, *Stand Ye in Holy Places: Selected Sermons and Writings of President Harold B. Lee* (Salt Lake City: Deseret Book Co., 1974), p. 21.

5. Spencer W. Kimball, in Conference Report, Apr. 1971, pp. 7–8.

6. Joseph Fielding Smith, *Church History and Modern Revelation* (Salt Lake City: The Council of the Twelve Apostles, 1946), 1:172–73.

7. Joseph Smith, *Teachings of the Prophet Joseph Smith*, sel. Joseph Fielding Smith (Salt Lake City: Deseret Book Co., 1938), p. 256.

8. Boyd K. Packer, *The Holy Temple* (Salt Lake City: Bookcraft, 1980), pp. 83–84.

9. Joseph Smith, *History of The Church of Jesus Christ of Latter-day Saints*, 2d ed. rev., edited by B. H. Roberts (Salt Lake City: The Church of Jesus Christ of Latter-day Saints, 1932–51), 1:163 n.

10. Smith, *History of the Church*, 4:580.

11. Smith, *Church History and Modern Revelation*, 1:184.

12. Orson Hyde, in *Journal of Discourses* (London: Latter-day Saints' Book Depot, 1854–86), 13:366.

13. *Millennial Star*, 45 (1883): 389.

14. Andrew Jenson, *The Infancy of the Church* (Salt Lake City, 1889), p. 5, letter 2.

15. *Millennial Star*, 8 (1846): 139.

17

GOD TAILORS REVELATION TO THE INDIVIDUAL

Jerry Perkins

Brigham Young University

Our Eternal Father knows us as individuals, and he tailors his revelation to us as individuals. In the October 1978 general conference of the Church, Elder John H. Groberg, of the Seventy, shared a story that dramatically emphasizes those two important concepts. A young Tongan child, Felila, had been diagnosed as having hydrocephalus. Without help, she would die. Felila's parents, who were Latter-day Saints, went to the district president, who contacted Elder Groberg, the mission president in Tonga at the time. Elder Groberg said that the plight of this child united men and women, member and non-member, American and Tongan in seeking a way for her to be treated at Primary Children's Hospital in Utah. Many sacrifices were made, and all arrangements were settled, but at the very time the goal was to be realized, the little girl died. The faith of many was tried, including the faith of Elder Groberg. He said: "I was left alone, or so it seemed. I moved slowly and heavily down that dusty trail. Why? Why? After all that work and that strong faith of so many and those impressions [of the Spirit], why?"

This mission president honestly asked the God of the universe what the purpose was of this little girl's death. And our Father in Heaven tailored a revelation to this individual situation of sorrow being experienced by one of his sons. Elder Groberg continued:

"I was overcome by the Spirit. . . . And I heard a voice. . . . [It said,]

" 'Come home Felila, my daughter. Come home to the care your loved ones have sought for you. . . . You have finished your mission in life. Hearts have been softened; souls have been stretched; faith has been increased. Come home now, Felila.' "

The Lord touched the individual life of this son. Brother Groberg exclaimed:

"He knew her! He knew her name. He knew all about her and about all those others. How perfect our Father's love! . . . In some

257

marvelous way, which is beyond our mortal comprehension, he knows and understands all things."[1]

In addition to knowing Felila, the Lord also knew John H. Groberg. An experience that could have perhaps crushed the faith of many was tailored for Elder Groberg to increase his faith, his love for his Savior, and his awe of this God who so gently cared for a little child.

THE GREAT PARENT OF THE UNIVERSE

The Lord is a God who desires to be personally close to each of his children. He is, as the Prophet Joseph taught, "the Great Parent of the universe [who] looks upon the whole of the human family with a fatherly care and paternal regard."[2] He loves us. He cares for us. Why would we not want to seek assistance from this great God? His care and regard can be sensed, for instance, as he communed with his Saints in tones of encouragement when his Church was still in its infancy. The Lord stated:

"Verily, verily, I say unto you, . . . where two or three are gathered together in my name, . . . behold, there will I be in the midst of them—even so am I in the midst of you. Fear not to do good, my sons. . . . Therefore, fear not, little flock; do good; let earth and hell combine against you, for if ye are built upon my rock, they cannot prevail" (DC 6:32–34).

He is a God of mercy, a God of love. When he says that we are his sons and daughters, his friends, his children, and his little flock, he communicates to us the relationships that are most important to him. As a Father, a Friend, a Shepherd, he desires to bless us with spiritual gifts that will be individually significant and designed to bring each of his children perfection and eternal life. President George Q. Cannon testified of the importance of this truth:

"I feel to bear testimony to you, my brethren and sisters, . . . that God is the same to-day as He was yesterday; that God is willing to bestow these [spiritual] gifts upon His children. . . . [This] is the design of God concerning His Church. He wants His Saints to be perfected in the truth. For this purpose He gives these gifts, and *bestows them upon those who seek after them*, in order that they may be a perfect people upon the face of the earth, . . . because God has promised to give the gifts that are necessary for their perfection."[3]

If we but seek, if we but ask, each individual son and daughter of God can receive the gifts of the Spirit promised by an Eternal Father and subsequently use those gifts to become "perfected in the truth."

GOD WILL REVEAL TO THE INDIVIDUAL

God knows each of his children individually. He is seeking to help each of us perfect our life as individuals, and he will reveal specific truths, direction, guidance, and love to each of us. He has promised it. It is true. Revelation and spiritual gifts await the child who will earnestly ask and seek.

Great leaders pleadingly strive to motivate us to seek "for the power of God," receive "the precious promises," and "avail ourselves of the privileges which God has placed within our reach."[4] Our leaders keep emphasizing that revelation is a means for a loving Father to communicate with each of his children. Joseph F. Smith sought to heighten our understanding of personal revelation. He stressed how individualistic revelation is:

"The gift of revelation, does not belong to one man solely; . . . it belongs to every individual member of the Church. . . . It is the privilege of every individual member of the Church to have revelation for his own guidance, for the direction of his life."[5]

Elder James E. Faust asked how we, as members of the Church, could make decisions about important individual concerns without seeking revelation: "Members of the Church know that the promptings of the Spirit may be received upon all facets of life, including daily, ongoing decisions (see D&C 42:61). How could anyone think of making an important decision such as 'Who is to be my companion?', 'What is my work to be?', 'Where will I live?', and 'How will I live?', without seeking the inspiration of Almighty God?"[6]

Prophet after prophet has made declarations to drive home the concept that the Lord wants to talk with his children. He wants to reveal truth to them. He wants to guide and direct them as they make decisions, as they fall in love, as they face heartrending problems, as they seek to bless the lives of their family, their friends, their associates, and even the entire world. And, the Lord wants to do it individually, with each son and each daughter. Great leaders of the latter day have emphasized this idea of individual revelation.

President Joseph Fielding Smith taught: "We believe that our Eternal Father is just as ready to converse with *those who seek him now* as he was in ancient days."[7]

President Lorenzo Snow said: "The spirit of revelation . . . will reveal [to every man and woman], even in the simplest matters, what they shall do, by making suggestions to them."[8]

Brigham Young declared: "*Every member* has the right of receiving revelations *for themselves*, both male and female. It is the very life of the Church of the living God. . . . It is the right of an *individual* to get revelation to guide *himself*. It is the right of the head of a family to get revelations to guide . . . his family."⁹

Elder Bruce R. McConkie told us: "Revelation is something that should be received by every individual. . . . I think our concern is to get personal revelation, to know for ourselves, independent of any other individual or set of individuals, what the mind and the will of the Lord is . . . as pertaining to us in our individual concerns. . . . The fact is that every person should be a *prophet for himself* and in his own concerns and in his own affairs."¹⁰

THE LORD SEEKS TO REVEAL TO US AS INDIVIDUALS

The Lord is willing, waiting, and wanting to reveal his will to each of his children, but in order for that to occur, we must be individually prepared. Church leaders from Joseph Smith's era to the present have expressed great concern about the Latter-day Saint who is not prepared to receive the revelations of God.

The Prophet Joseph Smith cautioned: "Tell the people to be humble and faithful, and be sure to keep the Spirit of the Lord and it will lead them right. Be careful and not turn away the still small voice."¹¹

President Brigham Young feared that the Latter-day Saints would "have so much confidence in their leaders" that they would "settle down into a state of blind self-security," abandoning the responsibility to obtain their own revelation. He commanded: "Let every man and woman know, by the whispering of the Spirit of God to themselves, whether their leaders are walking in the path the Lord dictates or not."¹²

President Joseph Fielding Smith said, "The Lord withholds much that he would otherwise reveal if the members of the Church were prepared to receive it."¹³

President Spencer W. Kimball explained why the Lord withholds revelations: "The Lord will not force himself upon people, and if they do not believe, they will receive no revelation. If they are content to depend upon their own . . . calculations and interpretations, then, of course, the Lord will leave them to their chosen fate."¹⁴

Elder Richard G. Scott spoke of missed revelation by saying, "I believe that we often leave the most precious personal direction of the Spirit unheard."¹⁵

And finally, President Ezra Taft Benson put this entire issue into perspective: "The Spirit is the most important matter in this glorious work."¹⁶

HOW AND WHY CAN I RECEIVE
INDIVIDUAL REVELATION?

Because "the Spirit is the most important matter in this glorious work," how do we gain that Spirit so revelation is a part of our individual daily lives, as the Lord and his prophets envisioned?

Jay Jensen, now of the Seventy, indicated that gaining revelation and knowing the workings of the Spirit of God are some of the greatest challenges in life. When does one know one has received revelation?

At the Missionary Training Center, Brother Jensen often counseled with young missionaries who, in their opinion, had never received revelation. They had felt the Spirit rarely, if ever, in their lives. After Brother Jensen spoke with them for just a few minutes, asking gentle yet probing questions, he realized that the missionaries "had, in fact, had a number of spiritual experiences but had not realized it before."[17] They were not aware of how the Spirit works.

Why is that so? Why do some of the greatest gifts of God, those involving the Spirit and personal revelation, go unnoticed by his children to whom he gave the gifts? And why do they go unnoticed, especially when those children need the gifts so urgently and are, in their view, actively seeking those gifts? Apparently, many of us do not understand the gifts of revelation offered by God, and so we ask, How does one receive revelation?

We need to understand the workings of the Spirit; we need to have confidence that the Lord knows his children's names and that he loves us individually; and we need to realize that there are many ways the Lord can communicate with us and that he tailors revelation to the individual.

UNDERSTAND THE WORKINGS OF THE SPIRIT

In relating his experiences regarding the revelation that all worthy males were now eligible to receive the priesthood of God, Elder Bruce R. McConkie pointed out one significant reason that Latter-day Saints miss the prompting of the Spirit directed their way by the Lord. He stated: "Latter-day Saints have a complex" in regard to the things of the Spirit.[18] He explained that we want more than what actually happens. Elder McConkie observed that many Latter-day Saints were disappointed with the revelation given to President Spencer W. Kimball and the Quorum of the Twelve Apostles: "Many of them [Latter-day Saints] desire to magnify and build upon what has occurred, and they delight to think of miraculous things. And maybe some of them would like to believe that the Lord himself was there, or that the

Prophet Joseph Smith came to deliver the revelation . . . Well, these things did not happen."[19]

President Kimball reminded us that "the burning bushes, the smoking mountains, . . . the Cumorahs . . . were realities; but they were the exceptions." He taught us that the great volume of revelation comes in less spectacular ways. Finally, this prophet helped explain why many of us miss the revelations of God: "Always expecting the spectacular, many will miss entirely the constant flow of revealed communication."[20]

Elijah was reminded that the Lord was in the still small voice (1 Kings 19:11–12). We are reminded in Alma that "miracles [are] worked by small means" (Alma 37:41). The Doctrine and Covenants testifies that "a marvelous work is about to come forth among the children of men" (4:1), yet this work was so small at the outset that the Lord referred to the participants in it as his "little flock" (6:34).

Elder Graham Doxey of the Seventy addressed the issue of how personal revelation is missed by many: "On religious matters, too many of us are saying, 'What did you say? Speak up; I can't hear you.' And when he doesn't *shout* back, or cause the bush to burn, or write us a message in stone with his finger, we are inclined to think he doesn't listen, doesn't care about us. Some even conclude there is no God. . . .

"The questions are not 'Does God live? Does God love me? Does God speak to me?' The critical question is 'Are you listening to him?' . . . It is the same for *you* as it was for Elijah, as it is with the modern-day prophets: *The still, small voice is still small.*"[21]

Jay Jensen offered a similar explanation of why so many of us are unaware of how the Spirit of the Lord works. He felt that perhaps it was because there were so many references to "spectacular" revelation in Church talks, magazines, lesson manuals, testimony meetings. He said, "Frequent exposure to such experiences may lead some to believe that if they haven't experienced some similar kind of outpouring or manifestation, they haven't had a spiritual experience."[22]

Modern-day prophets and apostles, including Richard G. Scott, Bruce R. McConkie, Spencer W. Kimball, Boyd K. Packer, Ezra Taft Benson, Thomas S. Monson, and Gordon B. Hinckley have stressed that the revelations from the Lord usually come in simple, quiet ways. The passages of the Doctrine and Covenants that seem to be quoted most often by the Brethren as they seek to explain revelation are "enlighten thy mind" (6:15); "peace to your mind" (6:23); "I will tell you in your mind and in your heart" (8:2); "study it out in your mind" and "cause that your bosom shall burn" (9:8); and "enlighten your mind" and "fill your soul with joy" (11:13).

Though visions and audible voices are ways the Lord reveals his truth, more commonly he whispers to the mind and the heart. One key to recognizing the Spirit is to realize that it influences the mind and the feelings at the same time. The Spirit gives us ideas in our minds that we feel good about in our hearts, or feelings in our hearts that are reasonable to our minds. There is an interaction of reason and emotion that the scriptures underscore.

The Brethren also emphasize this interaction in their writings. Elder Boyd K. Packer emphasized feelings: "I have come to know that inspiration comes more as a feeling than as a sound."[23]

Elder Richard G. Scott emphasized the interrelationship of mind and emotions in revelation: "When we receive an impression in our *heart*, we can use our *mind* either to rationalize it away or to accomplish it. Be careful what you do with an impression from the Lord."[24] President Benson stressed the role of emotions in receiving revelation: "We hear the words of the Lord most often by a feeling. If we are humble and sensitive, the Lord will prompt us through our feelings. That is why spiritual promptings move us on occasion to great joy, sometimes to tears. . . . The Holy Ghost causes our feelings to be more tender. . . . We have a greater capacity to love. People want to be around us because our very countenances radiate the influence of the Spirit."[25]

Elder Dallin Oaks stressed the role of the mind when he emphasized the sequential relationship of reason and revelation: "In the acquisition of knowledge about the things of God, reason is not an alternative to revelation. Study and reason can *find* the truth on many of these subjects, but only revelation can *confirm* it. Study and reason are a means to an end, and the end is revelation from God."[26]

For revelation to occur, the individual child of God must understand how the Spirit works. Several important teachings about the workings of the Spirit are that we as Latter-day Saints "have a complex" about the revelations of God and we "delight to think of miraculous things" (McConkie); we miss revelation because "we're always expecting the spectacular" (Kimball); and "the still small voice is still small" (Doxey) as it speaks to the mind and the emotions in an interrelated way (Packer, Scott, Benson, Oaks).

THE LORD KNOWS HIS CHILDREN'S NAMES

The evidences of how our Father specifically helps his children are abundant in scripture, Church history, in testimony meetings, and in the lives of God's children. In the story of the little Tongan girl who needed help, Elder Groberg realized that the Lord knew Felila's name and loved her individually.

The Book of Mormon prophet Enos was also known by name to the Lord, and He knew exactly what His son needed. When Enos wrestled before God for a remission of his sins, a voice came to him and called him by name, "Enos" (Enos 1:5). Just as the little Tongan girl was known by her individual name, "Felila," so also was Enos known by name. Just as the Lord knew Felila's mission in life, so did he know the potential mission of Enos, this great, struggling soul before him. The Lord knew Enos was on the verge of a significant change in his life. Therefore, he touched Enos' life deeply with statements such as "thy sins are forgiven thee" (Enos 1:5), "thou shalt be blessed" (Enos 1:5), "because of thy faith in Christ" (Enos 1:8), and "thy faith hath made thee whole" (Enos 1:8). The Lord knew Enos well. He knew change was imminent: "And after I, Enos, had heard these words, my faith began to be unshaken in the Lord" (Enos 1:11). The time was right. The Lord knew it. An individual life was changed forever because of a revealed spiritual gift to an individual son by a Father who knew precisely what His son needed.

Joseph Smith was another son whom the Father knew by name. In April of 1830, Joseph was in Colesville, New York, at the home of Joseph Knight, Sr. Newel Knight, Joseph Knight's son, had been plagued by evil spirits, and Joseph Smith cast out the spirits. The result of this miracle divided the people of Colesville. Many were converted, but opposition to the Church also increased. Baptisms were interfered with, and the Prophet was involved in troublesome lawsuits that delayed the work the Lord had for him. Joseph had much to do. He was behind in the great work of the Restoration. He had to counsel and guide and direct this infant Church. Yet he also had the responsibility of caring for his family and tending to the farm—chores that would not wait. Into this scene of conflicting responsibilities and overwhelming duties entered a loving Lord, who reduced tension by reminding Joseph that God was with him:

"Behold, thou wast called and chosen to write the Book of Mormon, and to my ministry; and I have lifted thee up out of thine afflictions, and have counseled thee, that thou hast been delivered from all thine enemies, and thou hast been delivered from the powers of Satan and from darkness!" (D&C 24:1).

In the next verse, the Lord told Joseph to avoid sin. Then He told Joseph to "magnify thine office." One could imagine the pangs of guilt this admonition could cause the Prophet; so much to do, so many responsibilities left unattended. But the Lord understood, and so he got very specific. He relieved Joseph of immediate responsibility by giving him some priorities: "After thou hast sowed thy fields and secured them" (D&C 24:3), *then* go forth and serve the Lord. The Savior's individual counsel to Joseph shows how much our Lord is concerned with the problems of our day-to-day life. The tender, all-knowing Father realized the turmoil in Joseph's heart caused by being caught between dedication to family and dedication to the Lord's service. In kindness and love, the Lord resolved the conflict by saying, in effect, "Joseph, my son, take care of your fields and your family first; then, go 'speedily' back to my work."

Another Joseph was individually known to God. He was not a prophet and not well-known by mankind, but he was known to our magnificent God of love and goodness. The Lord stated that he is "no respecter of persons" (D&C 1:35), and the fact that he knows a Joseph Millett as well as a Joseph Smith indicates that he truly is "no respecter of persons." Joseph Millett is known to us because he kept a journal. In that journal he recorded his Church mission experiences. Elder Millett served a mission in Nova Scotia and in New England. He was faithful. He sacrificed much. He brought many into the true church of Christ.

Joseph Millett was given permission by Orson Pratt, his mission president, to seek a wife among the eastern Latter-day Saints. He then met and married Sarah Elizabeth Glines. The young couple traveled to Boston and bolstered the Saints there, went on to upstate New York and to Vermont and taught eleven converts, and then helped a group of Saints from Nova Scotia prepare to move west. Finally, Joseph and Elizabeth made their own way west, first by train to Chicago and then on foot. On their way "they stopped to work and prepare for the journey across the plains and to give rest to Sarah, who was pregnant and ill during the spring and summer [Joseph's journal reads]: 'She [Elizabeth] was confined on the 28th of June, 1855. For months I hardly got an hour's sleep in 24. Our little boy Artemus died [on the] 7th of August 1855. The Saints did all they could for us.' "[27]

A simple journal statement fraught with the tender sacrifice of the Milletts. The Millett family then began their journey in earnest and arrived in Utah in 1856. They faithfully responded to the calls of Brigham Young to help settle Manti, Sevier Valley, Dixie, and finally, in 1868, the extremely harsh Spring Valley in Nevada.

One of Joseph Millett's sons stated:

"[My father] lived a faithful life, was kind and benevolent to all, full of charity and sympathy, ever seeking where he might do good to the poor and fatherless and those in need, denying himself the comforts he might have enjoyed had not his means been spent helping others."[28]

Now comes the most important part of this story of an ordinary man known by the Lord. In 1871 in Spring Valley, Nevada, the situation was difficult for all the Saints. Joseph and Elizabeth had lost their oldest daughter to typhoid, and the entire family had suffered great sickness and hunger. The entire valley was in desperate straits. Joseph Millett wrote in his journal:

"One of my children came in, said that Brother Newton Hall's folks were out of bread. Had none that day. I put . . . our flour in sack to send up to Brother Hall's. Just then Brother Hall came in. Says I, 'Brother Hall, how are you out for flour.' 'Brother Millett, we have none.' 'Well, Brother Hall, there is some in that sack. I have divided and was going to send it to you. Your children told mine that you were out.' Brother Hall began to cry. Said he had tried others. Could not get any. Went to the cedars and prayed to the Lord and the Lord told him to go to Joseph Millett. 'Well, Brother Hall, you needn't bring this back if the Lord sent you for it. You don't owe me for it.' You can't tell how good it made me feel to know that the Lord knew that there was such a person as Joseph Millett."[29]

The Lord knows our names. He knows our needs and concerns and the challenges of our daily lives. He wants to help us, and so he has promised to reveal his will to those who earnestly seek and ask.

THE LORD TAILORS REVELATION TO THE INDIVIDUAL

Personal revelation cannot be vicarious. Joseph Smith emphasized the importance of the personal experience of revelation: "Reading the experience of others, or the revelation given to *them*, can never give *us* a comprehensive view of our condition and true relation to God. Knowledge of these things can only be obtained by experience through the ordinances of God set forth for that purpose [i.e., personal revelation]."[30]

Just as the Lord was revealed to the individual Joseph Smith with this statement, "This is My Beloved Son. Hear Him!" (JS–H 1:17), so does He also desire to reveal Himself to each of us.

Joseph Smith taught: "By learning the Spirit of God and understanding it, you may grow into the principle of revelation."[31] That is an interesting phrase, "grow into the principle of revelation." It indicates that our capacity for revelation changes. As that capacity changes, God will tailor revelation to that new capacity, both as to the message and to the mode of delivery.

During a Doctrine and Covenants class at Brigham Young University, I asked the students to explain how the Lord gave revelation. With rare exception, the explanation focused on Doctrine and Covenants 9, with special emphasis upon the phrase "and if it is right I will cause that your bosom shall burn within you" (D&C 9:8). I then asked if someone could explain this burning, and it was very difficult for any of us to do so.

A concern and some questions came to me after this experience. Are we defining revelation in terms that are too narrow? Does the acceptance of this narrow definition of spiritual matters cause us not to fully understand revelation? If we do not understand revelation and the workings of the Spirit, can we understand when we have received revelation?

Robert Millet, dean of Religious Education at Brigham Young University, cautioned:

"It would be a mistake for the Latter-day Saints to suppose that answers and confirmations come only in one way — as a burning of the bosom, for example. The Lord desires to communicate with his children and will choose the means which will most clearly and persuasively convey his holy words and his perfect will to those who seek him diligently."[32]

A teacher who only lectures runs the risk of diminishing communication. That teacher does not take into account the individual learning styles of the students, nor the specific nature of the subject matter being taught, nor the special circumstances of the day, the season, the mood of the class, or the situation in which the teacher and the students find themselves.

The Lord, however, is a Master Teacher. He is not solely a lecturer. He fully understands his students, and therefore he uses a vast array of ways to communicate with them. Most of the time, revelation comes in very simple ways, touching our feelings, enhancing our thoughts; however, the specific manner by which revelation is given is as varied as our Father's children.

A great seminary teacher I know, Brother Ted Gibbons, has wrestled often with the question, How does the Lord reveal his will to his children? Though the Spirit of revelation is stressed in the phrase "tell you in your mind and heart" and that is the Lord's main emphasis when he seeks to help us understand how he communicates with us, Brother Gibbons's findings[33] indicate how many different ways the Lord can tell us in our minds and hearts:

Audible voice. See 1 Samuel 3:4, 5, 10.

Still small voice. See 1 Kings 19:12.

God gives understanding. See Job 32:8.

Heart burns when you open the scriptures. See Luke 24:32.

Feel love, joy, gentleness, peace. See Galatians 5:22.

Led by Spirit, not knowing. See 1 Nephi 4:6.

Spirit constraineth. See Alma 14:11.

Lord's voice in the mind. See Enos 1:10.

Peace to your mind. See Doctrine and Covenants 6:23.

Burning in the bosom. See Doctrine and Covenants 9:6–9.

Spirit leads to do good, to do justly, to walk humbly, to judge righteously. See Doctrine and Covenants 11:12.

Spirit enlightens mind and fills soul with joy. See Doctrine and Covenants 11:13.

Spirit occupies mind with an issue, concept, idea, etc. See Doctrine and Covenants 128:1.

Write by the Spirit of inspiration. See Moses 6:5.

From the still small voice of Elijah to the open visions of the Prophet Joseph Smith, the Lord has unlimited ways to communicate spiritually with those who seek revelation. As we grow into the principle of revelation, the Lord will tailor that revelation to our capacity and situation along that pathway of growth.

After considering the ways revelation is granted unto mankind, this statement of Robert L. Millet becomes quite appropriate: "The nature of the occasion, as well as the readiness and need of the recipient, dictates how a message from God may be communicated. Certain situations require a message which pierces to the very soul, others where that voice, although still and small, makes 'the bones to quake' while it makes manifest the mind of the Lord (D&C 85:6; see also Helaman 5:30; 3 Nephi 11:3). . . .

" . . . The Lord desires to communicate with his children and will choose the means which will most clearly and persuasively convey his holy words and his perfect will to those who seek him diligently."[34]

In Doctrine and Covenants 56:4, the Lord states, "Wherefore I, the Lord, command and revoke, as it seemeth me good." That is not capriciousness on the part of the Lord. Joseph Smith explained: "That which is wrong under one circumstance, may be, and often is, right under another.

"God said, 'Thou shalt not kill;' at another time He said, 'Thou shalt utterly destroy'. This is the principle on which the government of heaven is conducted—by revelations adapted to the circumstances in which the children of the kingdom are placed."[35]

Revelation is dynamic. The Lord, knowing the specific needs of his children, not only reveals specific messages for the individual but chooses the most appropriate way to reveal the message.

We can see how the Lord varied both the message and the means of revelation as Joseph Smith "grew into the principle of revelation." Joseph received the First Vision. The message was basic—the churches of the earth had gone astray, and the Lord would restore the true church of Christ upon the earth. The means of this revelation was a personal visitation. All of Joseph's senses were attuned to the message, making the revelation poignant and powerful. God the Father and Jesus the Christ lived. They knew his name! And Joseph was now called.

Three years later, Moroni appeared to Joseph. Still the mode of communication was personal visitation. The angel Moroni visited three times that night and then again the next morning. There was no conceivable way that the young man could doubt what was happening to him. The revelation was designed specifically — tailored — to cast out all doubt. The message was much more complex than that of the First Vision. One part of the message could very possibly have sent the youth's head whirling with thoughts such as: "God is going to reveal the priesthood? By the hand of the Old Testament prophet Elijah? Why Elijah? And when is the great and dreadful day of the Lord? What exactly is Moroni talking about, 'plant in the hearts of the children the promises made to the fathers'? Why would the earth be utterly wasted?" Joseph must have been overwhelmed. He knew the message was real, because he saw and heard it so many times. But what did it mean? Perhaps this message was tailored to the thoughts of a deep-thinking boy to challenge him, to prepare him for what was to come, to let him know there was to be a restoration in the fulness of times.

Joseph's capacity with revelation increased; he was growing into the principle. The Urim and Thummim were next given to Joseph Smith along with the plates from which the Book of Mormon was translated. Joseph used the Urim and Thummim to translate, or, in other words, to receive revelation. The mode of revelation was no longer personal visitation, but a tangible instrument of revelation was still being used.

In addition to translating the Book of Mormon, Joseph used the Urim and Thummim to receive revelation in behalf of others who would make inquiries of the Lord through him. The Lord also communicated directly with Joseph by means of the Urim and Thummim. For instance, when Martin Harris lost the 116 pages of the Book of Mormon manuscript, the following "tailored" message was revealed to Joseph Smith:

"For although a man may have many revelations, and have power to do many mighty works, yet if he boasts in his own strength, and sets at naught the counsels of God, and follows after the dictates of his own will and carnal desires, he must fall and incur the vengeance of a just God upon him" (D&C 3:4).

That was exactly what Joseph needed to hear. He had "feared man more than God," and if the direction of Joseph's allegiance was not immediately changed, he would be in danger of the prophecies of Moroni coming true—that Joseph would be destroyed by the Lord's enemies (JS–H 1:42). One can imagine how grateful Joseph was that the means of this revelation was the Urim and Thummim. Imagine what it would have been like to stand before the Lord and receive such a direct and powerful message from the Master himself.

Elder John A. Widtsoe made the following comments regarding the Urim and Thummim: "It must be concluded that the stones were essential to the work of translation.

"Though the Urim and Thummim was necessary, it need not be concluded that it relieved the person who used it of effort on his part. . . . It required great concentration of desire and thought, even with the Urim and Thummim, to secure the sought-for results in translation or revelation. At the best, this instrument served as an aid to the Prophet's natural senses."[36]

Soon, however, the Prophet no longer used the Urim and Thummim. Brother Richard Cowan, professor of Religious Education at Brigham Young University, estimates that one-half of all the revelations the Prophet received before the Melchizedek Priesthood was restored were received through the Urim and Thummim.[37] After he received the Melchizedek Priesthood, he no longer used the device. Elder Widtsoe explained why: "The Prophet did not always receive revelations by the aid of the Urim and Thummim. As he grew in spiritual power, he learned to bring his mind into such harmony with divine forces that it became, as it were, itself a Urim and Thummim to him; and God's will was revealed without the intervention of external aids; that is, truth may become known without outside help when one is in harmony or in full tune with the requirements of the subject in hand."[38]

Joseph had continued to grow into the principle of revelation. To assist in that growth and help get Joseph in "harmony or in full tune," the Lord gave a special assignment to the Prophet when He revealed to Joseph information about His millennial reign. Suddenly, in the midst of teaching the Prophet, the Lord stopped and said:

"And now, behold, I say unto you, it shall not be given unto you to know any further concerning this chapter, until the New Testament be translated. . . . Wherefore I give unto you that ye may now translate it, that ye may be prepared for the things to come. For verily I say unto you, that great things await you" (D&C 45:60–62; emphasis added).

The Lord continued increasing the spiritual maturity of the Prophet. As Joseph translated the New Testament, no longer did he need the Urim and Thummim, for his mind was in harmony with the Divine and had become, as it were, a Urim and Thummim unto itself. Joseph continued to increase his capacity for revelation, and by so doing he was becoming eligible for what the Lord said were "the great things to come."

In Doctrine and Covenants 73, the Lord said to Joseph, "It is expedient to translate again" (v. 3). That was 10 January 1832. A little more than a month later, the Prophet and Sidney Rigdon mentally wrestled with the concept of the resurrection of the just and unjust, which was triggered by their study of John 5:28–29. Great things were in store for the Prophet. He had so fully grown into the principle of revelation and had come into harmony with the Lord that he qualified to receive one of the greatest revelations ever given to mankind. God tailored this revelation to Joseph's heightened capacity. "The Vision," the personal witness of Christ, a view of Lucifer's designs upon mankind, the three degrees of glory — all were seen by Joseph and Sidney. Wilford Woodruff said of this great vision: "[It] gives more light, more truth, and more principle than any revelation contained in any other book we ever read."[39] The magnitude of the revelation was also indicated in the way it was given: a series of visions of God the Father and his Son Jesus Christ; a vision of Satan and his designs upon the world; a vision regarding the ultimate destiny of the just and the unjust who are resurrected. A further indication of the individual capacity of different people for receiving revelation is in this observation: "Joseph sat firmly and calmly all the time in the midst of a magnificent glory, but Sidney sat limp and pale, apparently as limber as a rag, observing which, Joseph remarked, smilingly, 'Sidney is not used to it as I am.' "[40]

Joseph's progression in revelation continued, and another site of advancement in spiritual maturity was Liberty Jail. Joseph cried: "O God, where art thou? . . . How long shall thy hand be stayed . . . ? Yea, O Lord, how long shall they suffer these wrongs and unlawful oppressions, before thine heart shall be softened toward them . . . ? O Lord God Almighty, maker of heaven, earth, and seas . . . stretch forth thy hand. . . . Let thine anger be kindled against our enemies. . . . Remember thy suffering saints, O our God" (D&C 121: 1–6).

When the heart of Joseph was sufficiently prepared, the Lord tenderly replied: "My son, peace be unto thy soul . . . thine afflictions shall be but a small moment; and then, if thou endure it well, God shall exalt thee on high; thou shalt triumph over all thy foes. . . . Know thou my son, that all these things shall give thee experience, and shall be for thy good" (D&C 121:7–8; 122:7).

The teachings of Elder Neal A. Maxwell indicate the deepening changes to Joseph's spirit that were occurring. Many of the revelations the Lord had prepared for Joseph could not be given until after the Prophet had endured what the Lord termed adversity and afflictions, which would be "but a small moment" (D&C 121:7). Elder Maxwell stated:

"The whole experience in Liberty Jail, as Joseph indicated, was such that without it he could not possibly have understood certain dimensions of suffering. It was just as promised in an 1834 blessing given him by his father: 'Thy heart shall meditate great wisdom and comprehend the deep things of God.' . . .

"Thus at the very time he was suffering telestial abuse and oppression from secular authorities . . . Joseph was instructed on the completely opposite manner, the celestial way, in which the Lord's priesthood leaders are to lead!

" 'No power or influence can or ought to be maintained by virtue of the Priesthood, only by . . . gentleness and meekness' [D&C 121:41]. . . .

"In the timing and wisdom of the Lord, the schooling revelations of March 1839 [D&C 121–23] were given when the Prophet was fully ready to receive them. They were not given just after the First Vision, or . . . during Joseph's remarkable translation of the Book of Mormon. Schooling has its seasons, even for prophets."[41]

The Prophet had changed within the walls of this prison, never to be the same. He understood, to a greater degree than almost any other man, what the Savior had done for him as an individual. When the Lord said, "The Son of Man hath descended below them all. Art thou greater than he?" (D&C 122:8), a powerful union had been forged. To be mentioned in the same verse with the Christ in the context of suffering indicates the depths of suffering Joseph had experienced. How pensive Joseph must have felt as the Lord expressed: "Thy days are known and thy years shall not be numbered less; therefore fear not what man can do, for God shall be with you forever and ever" (D&C 122:9).

The individuality of the message indicates God's knowledge of Joseph. The Lord knew Joseph Smith. The Lord loved him. The Lord revealed life and the eternities to his son. The Prophet had spiritually matured and had "grown into the principle of revelation." Though excruciatingly hard on Joseph at times, the Lord had consistently tailored revelation to the individuality of his son, the Prophet.

CONCLUSION

The principle of personal, individualized revelation is not one of past ages, reserved solely for the Elijahs, the Almas, or even the Joseph Smiths. It is a vibrant principle that daily influences God's "friends," "his sons and daughters," "his little flock." The well-worn phrase, God "is the same yesterday, to-day, and forever" (1 Nephi 10:18) is made even more vivid by understanding the dynamic nature of personal revelation. God's children learn that he really is the same today because he continues to bless the lives of his children with revealed messages designed specifically for them.

Revelation is between the Father and his children. For Elder Richard G. Scott, son of God, revelation is real, it is powerful, it is individual. When he was on a Church assignment in Mexico City, he attended a priesthood meeting taught by a humble, unschooled priesthood leader. This teacher struggled in his efforts to teach principles that had obviously changed his life. Elder Scott noted how desperately this humble teacher wanted to teach the gospel of the Savior. The love the teacher expressed for the Savior and his teachings was obvious, and the teacher's spirit "permitted a spiritual strength to envelop the room." Elder Scott was so touched by this spirit, he began to receive strong impressions or revelation "as an extension of those principles taught by the humble instructor." Elder Scott testified, "These impressions were intended for me *personally* and were related to my assignments in the area." The overall message the Lord was communicating to his son was, "You are to continue to build the Church on the foundation of true principles, but with an increased expression of love and appreciation . . . for the great Lamanite people." Elder Scott knew this message was tailored specifically for him, and it was uniquely designed to help him serve the Mexican people. He said, "Specific directions followed, instructions and conditioned promises that have altered the course of my life."[42]

The Lord reveals messages designed for the situation at hand. On 4 April 1974, the general authorities and Church leaders from around the world came to Salt Lake City to be instructed in the ways of God. President Lee had died, and, according to Elder W. Grant Bangerter, the thoughts of many were " 'How can we proceed without our great leader?' 'How can President Kimball fill the empty space?' And again the prayers went forth: 'Please bless President Kimball.' "[43]

President Kimball perhaps had been perceived as a kindly servant of God who would probably never be the prophet because of age and health problems. Perhaps he was viewed as a gentle yet not overly dynamic leader noted more for his love and humility rather than his power. The thought hung heavily, "We will miss President Lee."

When President Kimball began to speak, however, Elder Bangerter noted: "The Spirit of the Lord was upon President Kimball and it proceeded from him to us as a tangible presence, which was at once both moving and shocking. He unrolled to our view a glorious vision. . . . He showed us how the Church was not fully living in the faithfulness that the Lord expects of His people. . . . We had settled into a spirit of complacency. . . . It was at that moment that he sounded the now famous slogan, 'We must lengthen our stride.' . . .

"President Kimball spoke under this special influence for an hour and ten minutes. It was a message totally unlike any other in my experience. I realized that it was similar to the occasion on the 8th of August, 1844, when Brigham Young spoke to the Saints in Nauvoo following the death of the Prophet Joseph. . . . Many people testified, however, that as Brigham Young arose, the power of the Lord rested upon him to the extent that he was transfigured before them, with the appearance and the voice of Joseph Smith. That moment was decisive in the history of the Church, and the occasion of April 4, 1974, is parallel.

"When President Kimball concluded, President Ezra Taft Benson arose and with a voice filled with emotion, echoing the feeling of all present, said, in substance: 'President Kimball, through all the years that these meetings have been held, we have never heard such an address as you have just given. Truly, there is a prophet in Israel.' "[44] The Lord was seeking to reveal to the united leadership of the Church — a message tailored for the situation — that "truly, there is a prophet in Israel."

Revelation, however, does not belong only to the realm of leaders wrestling with important issues at decisive junctures in history. It is accessible to all of God's sons and daughters. A young man, returning home at Christmas to give an engagement ring to his sweetheart, heard the Spirit whisper, "Pull over into the far right lane and slow down." His life was saved because he followed these instructions of personal revelation.[45]

A doctor, who wept because of the suffering of a dying patient, asked God if there was anything else that the medical profession could do to help the family. He said, "At that moment, a thought came forcefully into my mind. The only way [she] could be restored to her full capacity was to leave her disabled, diseased body behind and move on to the next life. . . .

"My grief was gone. I felt only joy — the unmistakable joy and peace that only the Holy Ghost can bring. I remembered the Lord's words, 'I will impart unto you of my Spirit, which shall enlighten your mind, which shall fill your soul with joy' [D&C11:13].

"I left the doctors' lounge with peace in my heart. A few hours later [she] died quietly and peacefully."[46]

A woman swept out to sea on an outrigger canoe near the Philippines heard a voice that told her, "Don't leave the boat." Obedience to that voice saved her life.[47]

A schoolteacher in 1970 read the tragic tale of a black officer in the United States cavalry who had been improperly court-martialed in 1881. The teacher was so deeply moved by the injustice that he spent the next eight years clearing the lieutenant's name. When the teacher's spirits drooped or his efforts lagged, he would dream of the officer, who came to him in his dreams and said, "What have you done for me today?"[48]

Truly, God tailors revelation to the individual needs and capacities of his children. He waits to bless all of his children who will simply seek his counsel. He waits to instruct his "friends," his "little flock," his "sons and daughters."

NOTES

1. John H. Groberg, in Conference Report, Oct. 1978, pp. 94–95.

2. Joseph Smith, *Teachings of the Prophet Joseph Smith,* sel. Joseph Fielding Smith (Salt Lake City: Deseret Book Co., 1976), p. 218.

3. George Q. Cannon, in *Millennial Star,* 56 (1894): 260–61; emphasis added.

4. Ibid., p. 260.

5. Joseph F. Smith, *Gospel Doctrine: Selections from the Sermons and Writings of Joseph F. Smith* (Salt Lake City: Deseret Book Co., 1963), p. 34; emphasis added.

6. James E. Faust, in Conference Report, Apr. 1980, p. 16.

7. Joseph Fielding Smith, *Doctrines of Salvation,* comp. Bruce R. McConkie (Salt Lake City: Bookcraft, 1954–56), 1:274; emphasis added.

8. Lorenzo Snow, in Conference Report, Apr. 1899, p. 52; emphasis added.

9. Brigham Young, in Conference Minutes, Oct. 1844, *Times and Seasons,* 5 (1844): 683, as quoted in Wilburn D. Talbot, *The Acts of the Modern Apostles* (Salt Lake City: Randall Book Co., 1985), p. 89; emphasis added.

10. Bruce R. McConkie, *How to Get Personal Revelation,* Brigham Young University Speeches of the Year (Provo, 11 Oct. 1966), pp. 2–4.

11. "History of the Church," *Juvenile Instructor,* 8 (1873): 114, as quoted in Jay E. Jensen, "Have I Received an Answer from the Spirit?" *Ensign,* Apr. 1989, p. 21.

12. Brigham Young, in *Journal of Discourses* (London: Latter-day Saints' Book Depot, 1854–86), 9:150.

13. Smith, *Doctrines of Salvation*, 1:283.

14. Spencer W. Kimball, in Conference Report, Apr. 1977, p. 114.

15. Richard G. Scott, "Spiritual Communication," in proceedings of the 1985 Sperry Symposium, *Principles of the Gospel in Practice* (Salt Lake City: Randall Book Co., 1985), p. 8.

16. Ezra Taft Benson, Mission Presidents' Seminar, Salt Lake City, Utah, 1975, 1986, 1987, as quoted in Jensen, "Have I Received an Answer from the Spirit?" p. 21.

17. Jensen, "Have I Received an Answer from the Spirit?" p. 21.

18. Bruce R. McConkie, "The New Revelation on Priesthood," in *Priesthood* (Salt Lake City: Deseret Book Co., 1981), p. 135.

19. Ibid.

20. In Munich Germany Area Conference Report, 1973, p. 77, as quoted by Graham W. Doxey, in Conference Report, Oct. 1991, pp. 32–33.

21. Doxey, in Conference Report, Oct. 1991, p. 33.

22. Jensen, "Have I Received an Answer from the Spirit?" p. 21.

23. Boyd K. Packer, in Conference Report, Oct. 1979, p. 28.

24. Richard G. Scott, in Conference Report, Oct. 1989, p. 39.

25. As quoted in Robert L. Millet, "Learning the Spirit of Revelation," in *Insights into the Doctrine and Covenants, the Capstone of Our Religion*, ed. Robert L. Millet and Larry E. Dahl (Salt Lake City: Bookcraft, 1989), p. 49.

26. Dallin H. Oaks, *The Lord's Way* (Salt Lake City: Deseret Book Co., 1991), p. 65.

27. Eugene England, *Why the Church Is As True As the Gospel* (Salt Lake City: Bookcraft, 1986), p. 29.

28. Ibid., p. 30.

29. Ibid.

30. Joseph Smith, *History of The Church of Jesus Christ of Latter-day Saints*, 2d ed. rev., edited by B. H. Roberts (Salt Lake City: The Church of Jesus Christ of Latter-day Saints, 1932–51), 6:50.

31. Ibid., 3:381.

32. Millet, "Learning the Spirit of Revelation," p. 50.

33. Ted L. Gibbons, Pleasant Grove Seminary lesson plan for 1 Samuel 3, Jan. 1992.

34. Millet, "Learning the Spirit of Revelation," pp. 49–50.

35. Smith, *Teachings of the Prophet Joseph Smith*, p. 256.

36. John A. Widtsoe, *Joseph Smith, Seeker after Truth, Prophet of God* (Salt Lake City: Deseret News Press, 1951), pp. 266–67.

37. Richard O. Cowan, *The Doctrine and Covenants, Our Modern Scripture* (Salt Lake City: Bookcraft, 1985), p. 3.

38. Widtsoe, *Joseph Smith*, p. 267.

39. Wilford Woodruff, in *Journal of Discourses*, 22:146.

40. Philo Dibble, in *Juvenile Instructor*, May 1892, p. 304.

41. Neal A. Maxwell, *"But for a Small Moment"* (Salt Lake City: Bookcraft, 1986), pp. 7, 10, 13.

42. Scott, "Spiritual Communication," pp. 6–8; emphasis added.

43. W. Grant Bangerter, in Conference Report, Oct. 1977, p. 38.

44. Ibid., pp. 38–39.

45. Terry J. Moyer, "A Voice in the Fog," *New Era,* Dec. 1989, p. 12.

46. Stanton McDonald, "A Blessing Fulfilled," *Ensign,* Mar. 1988, pp. 42–43.

47. Michelle Hamilton, "Swept to Sea," *Reader's Digest,* Aug. 1992, p. 128.

48. David Maraniss, "Justice for a Buffalo Soldier," *Washington Post Magazine,* 20 Jan. 1991, as quoted in *Reader's Digest,* May 1991, p. 90.

18

TRIALS AND TRIBULATIONS IN OUR SPIRITUAL GROWTH: INSIGHTS FROM DOCTRINE & COVENANTS 121 AND 122

Keith W. Perkins

Brigham Young University

One of the age-old questions of the world is "Why do the wicked seem to prosper and the righteous suffer?" Great literary masterpieces, such as the book of Job, deal with this question. Examples from the lives of many individuals illustrate it. But perhaps no better answer to the question of suffering can be found than in the words of the Lord to Joseph Smith while the Prophet lay imprisoned in Liberty Jail.[1]

Trials and tribulations can make people more kind, gentle, and loving, or they can make people bitter. An example of this tendency is found in Alma 62:41: "But behold, because of the exceedingly great length of the war between the Nephites and the Lamanites many had become hardened, because of the exceedingly great length of the war; and many were softened because of their afflictions, insomuch that they did humble themselves before God, even in the depth of humility."

The life of the greatest Being who ever lived on this earth, the Lord Jesus Christ, illustrates this tendency more than that of any other being. What Christ suffered is beyond our comprehension. He, the greatest of all, cried out in the Garden of Gethsemane: "O my Father, if it be possible, let this cup pass from me: nevertheless not as I will, but as thou wilt" (Matthew 26:39). And on the cross he further cried out, "Eli, Eli, lama sabachthani? that is to say, My God, my God, why hast thou forsaken me?" (Matthew 27:46). Yet he accepted the will of the Father and suffered for our sins, pains, temptations, sicknesses, and afflictions. Thus his love and understanding increased (Alma 7:11). His love is so great that when the prophets speak of the ultimate love, they call it the "pure love of Christ" (Moroni 7:47).

In this dispensation, the best contrast between the potential good and the potential ill effects of trials and tribulations is found in the cases of Joseph Smith and Sidney Rigdon. In the dark days of betrayal and apostasy, these two men, along with others, were illegally thrown into the foul jails of Richmond and Liberty, Missouri. They spent almost four long months in Liberty Jail, a "Temple Prison."[2] Here they suffered all kinds of abuse. They were poisoned three or four times and fed human flesh. Their food was brought to them in a basket which still had on it the droppings of chickens who had roosted on it the night before.[3] They had been sentenced to be shot and were saved only because a brave man, General Alexander Doniphan, refused to carry out the order. They had listened to the guards' foul oaths and boasting of their terrible deeds of murder, rape, and abuse. "We are compelled to hear nothing but blasphemous oaths, and witness a scene of blasphemy, and drunkenness and hypocrisy, and debaucheries of every description," wrote the Prophet Joseph Smith.[4] They had learned from the visits of family members and friends to their prison of other atrocities committed against the Saints. Besides the terrible conditions under which the prisoners suffered, at times Joseph was also very sick with a toothache and a terrible pain in his face from a severe cold.[5]

Sidney Rigdon was released from jail after a few months, but before leaving he declared that "the sufferings of Jesus Christ were a fool to his."[6] After this experience he was no longer the great leader in the Church that he had been. Joseph Smith rejected him as a counselor because of his unfaithfulness.[7] The Prophet later remarked that if Sidney led the Church, he would lead the Church to destruction in less than five years.[8] After the death of the Prophet Joseph Smith, Sidney returned to Nauvoo from Pittsburgh, where he had gone in spite of the Lord's counsel (D&C 124:108). Sidney claimed he should be the guardian for the Church. When he secretly began plotting against the Twelve, after originally agreeing to support them, he was excommunicated.[9] These events show that Sidney Rigdon chose to allow his trials and tribulations to make him a bitter man, finally losing his testimony, faith, and honor.

If we say that suffering and trials were the ruin of Sidney Rigdon, we could say that tribulations were the making of Joseph Smith. We learn the most about the Prophet's positive response to trials and tribulations from letters he wrote while in Liberty Jail.

A heartrending letter from the Prophet's wife, Emma, was the specific catalyst for Joseph's epistles. Emma told not only of her personal suffering but of the suffering of all the Saints: "The daily sufferings of our brethren in traveling and camping out nights, and those on the other side of the river would beggar the most lively description."[10] She also apprised him of the growth and progress of his family, especially their baby son, who was growing and learning to walk without his father there to enjoy those precious moments. "We are all well at present, except Fredrick, who is quite sick. Little Alexander who is now in my arms is one of the finest little fellows, you ever saw in your life, he is so strong that with the assistance of a chair he will run all round the room."[11] This news must have torn at the heartstrings of this tender, loving man, making his imprisonment even harder to bear. Yet Joseph reveals his understanding of the purposes of pain in a message to the Church, which he sent with his response to Emma's letter.

This epistle to the Church has become a classic in Latter-day Saint literature. Portions were selected by Elder Orson Pratt when he was assigned to prepare the 1876 edition of the Doctrine and Covenants and have become sections 121, 122, and 123 in our present edition. These are some of the finest words of counsel on the purpose and benefits of trials and tribulation. They give us answers to these perplexing questions and comfort to those who strive to understand the precious truths. Truly the Lord fulfilled his promise that he would reveal those things "that [have] not been revealed since the world was until now; which our forefathers have awaited with anxious expectation . . . a time to come in the which nothing shall be withheld" (D&C 121:26–28; see also Matthew 13:21; D&C 28:7; 42:61; 90:14; 101:32–33). Certainly the age-old question of why the righteous suffer and the wicked seem to prosper was one of the "mysteries" to be revealed.

Now let us look at Joseph's epistle to the Church. Some of the best answers to the question at hand were not mined by Elder Pratt and have been left like golden nuggets for us to find ourselves.

Joseph Smith first reminds the Saints of the characteristics they must have if they are going to grow from the trials they have recently experienced. "May faith and virtue, and knowledge and temperance and patience and godliness, and brotherly kindness and charity be in you and abound, that you may not be barren in anything, nor unfruitful."[12]

Then he shares with them some of the most intimate and heart-rending prayers that he had uttered while in prison: "O God, where art thou? And where is the pavilion that covereth thy hiding place?

"How long shall thy hand be stayed, and thine eye, yea thy pure eye, behold from the eternal heavens the wrongs of thy people and of thy servants, and thine ear be penetrated with their cries?

"Yea, O Lord, how long shall they suffer these wrongs and unlawful oppressions, before thine heart shall be softened toward them, and thy bowels be moved with compassion toward them?

"O Lord God Almighty, maker of heaven, earth, and seas, and of all things that in them are, and who controllest and subjectest the devil, and the dark and benighted dominion of Sheol—stretch forth thy hand; let thine eye pierce; let thy pavilion be taken up; let thy hiding place no longer be covered; let thine ear be inclined; let thine heart be softened, and thy bowels moved with compassion toward us.

"Let thine anger be kindled against our enemies; and, in the fury of thine heart, with thy sword avenge us of our wrongs.

"Remember thy suffering saints, O our God; and thy servants will rejoice in thy name forever" (D&C 121:1–6).

We do not know how long Joseph Smith must have prayed, whether hours, weeks, even months; but finally the loving answer from his Heavenly Father came. Joseph describes the important spiritual effects of this period of supplication in his preliminary remarks: "The floodgates of our hearts were lifted and our eyes were a fountain of tears, but those who have not been enclosed in the walls of prison without cause or provocation, can have but little idea how sweet the voice of a friend is; one token of friendship from any source whatever awakens and calls into action every sympathetic feeling; it brings up in an instant everything that is passed; it seizes the present with the avidity of lightning; it grasps after the future with the fierceness of a tiger; it moves the mind backward and forward, from one thing to another, *until finally all enmity, malice and hatred, and past differences, misunderstandings and mismanagements are slain victorious at the feet of hope; and when the heart is sufficiently contrite, then the voice of inspiration steals along and whispers,* My son, peace be unto thy soul; thine adversity and thine afflictions shall be but a small moment; and then if thou endure it well, God shall exalt thee on high; thou shalt triumph over all thy foes; thy friends do stand by thee, and they shall hail thee again, with warm hearts and friendly hands; thou art not yet as Job; thy friends do not contend against thee, neither charge thee with transgression, as they did Job; and they who do charge thee with transgression, their hope shall be blasted and their prospects shall melt away as the hoar frost melteth before the burning rays of the rising sun."[13]

Note that the answer to even the Prophet's prayer does not come until finally "all enmity, malice and hatred . . . are slain victorious at the feet of hope." Then, and only then, does it come, and so it is with all of us. We cannot have hatred and malice and have the Spirit of the Lord.

We also learn from this portion of the letter that our life on this earth is very short—the Lord calls it "a small moment." Elder Neal A. Maxwell has given us some excellent insights into this portion of the Lord's revelation to Joseph Smith: "In the Apocryphon of James, Jesus reportedly told an afflicted Peter and James, 'If you consider how

282 KEITH W. PERKINS

long the world existed before you, and how long it will exist after you, you will find that your life is one single day and your sufferings one single hour.' ('The Apocryphon of James,' in *The Nag Hammadi Library in English*, ed. James M. Robinson, San Francisco: Harper and Row, 1978, p. 31.)

"How like what the Lord told suffering Joseph in jail: 'My son, . . . thine adversity and thine afflictions shall be but a small moment.' (D&C 121:7.)

"One's life, therefore, is brevity compared to eternity — like being dropped off by a parent for a day at school. But what a day!"[14]

In addition to Elder Maxwell's insights into this revelation, President Marion G. Romney's comments help us appreciate the tremendous growth that came to Joseph Smith during this "brief moment" of suffering in Liberty Jail and help us gain appreciation for the Prophet's greatness as a result of this experience. President Romney said: "Speaking for himself and his fellow prisoners, he [Joseph] said: ' . . . in His Almighty name we are determined to endure tribulation as good soldiers unto the end.' (DHC, Vol. 3, p. 297.) And counseling the Saints to do likewise, he said: ' . . . let thy bowels . . . be full of charity towards all men. . . . ' (DHC, Vol. 3, p. 300.)

"This admonition, considered in light of the circumstances under which it was given, seems to me to almost equal the Master's statement from the cross: 'Father, forgive them; for they know not what they do.' (Luke 23:34.) . . .

"No wonder the Lord could say to him, as he did, ' . . . I seal upon you your exaltation, and prepare a throne for you in the kingdom of my Father, with Abraham your father.

" 'Behold, I have seen your sacrifices, and will forgive all your sins; I have seen your sacrifices in obedience to that which I have told you. . . . ' (D&C 132:49–50.)"[15]

In his letter from Liberty Jail, Joseph Smith demonstrated his understanding of the principle of growth through trial. He taught the Saints that their sufferings in Missouri were the crucible of the Lord to refine them into pure gold. Joseph wrote: "And now, beloved brethren, we say unto you, that inasmuch as God hath said that He would have a tried people, that He would purge them as gold, now we think that this time He has chosen His own crucible, wherein we have been tried; and we think if we get through with any degree of safety, and shall have kept the faith, that it will be a sign to this generation, altogether sufficient to leave them without excuse; and we think also, it will be a trial of our faith equal to that of Abraham, and that the ancients will not have whereof to boast over us in the day of judgment, as being called to pass through heavier afflictions; that we may hold an even weight in the balance with them; but now, after having suffered so great sacrifice and having passed through so great a season of sorrow, we trust that a ram may be caught in the thicket speedily, to relieve the sons and daughters of Abraham from their great anxiety."[16]

It may sound strange to us for the Prophet Joseph Smith to state that this trial of their faith would be equal to Abraham's (compare D&C 132:49–50). We remember that in the case of Abraham, the ultimate sacrifice was not required, only asked; but many of the Saints had sacrificed their very lives and the lives of their loved ones. The Prophet spoke of that issue on another occasion: "And again the affliction of my Brethren reminds me of Abraham offering up Isaac his only son, but my Brethren have been called to give up even more than this, their wives and their children, yea and their own life also. O Lord what more dost thou require at their hands before thou wilt come and save. . . . Lord thou wilt save them out of the hands of their enemies. Thou hast tried them in the furnace of affliction, a furnace of thine own choosing, and couldst thou have tried them more than thou hast? O Lord then let this suffice and from henceforth let this be recorded in heaven for thine angels to look upon and for a testimony against all those ungodly men who have committed those ungodly deeds [forever and] ever."[17]

The purposes and benefits of our trials and tribulations begin to be revealed, like the hidden treasure in this epistle from the Lord's prophet. First, we learn from the Lord that suffering refines us into purer, more perfect people. Just as refined gold is more brightly beautiful than contaminated ore, so do we become more loving, kind, and considerate and thus more beautiful to the Lord. Second, by suffering we are able to "hold an even weight in the balance with [the ancient Saints];"[18] that is, we are worthy of the same reward they received because we paid the same price they did. Third, the Prophet tells us that after our tribulations, "God shall give unto [us] knowledge by His Holy Spirit, yea by the unspeakable gift of the Holy Ghost, that has not been revealed since the world was until now; which our forefathers have waited with anxious expectation to be revealed in the last times, which their minds were pointed to by the angels, as held in reserve for the fulness of their glory; a time to come in the which nothing shall be withheld" (D&C 121:26–28). Thus one of the greatest gifts that God can give us, the gift of the Holy Ghost, comes as a direct result of our trials and tribulations.

The Lord also told the Prophet Joseph Smith: "If thou art called to pass through tribulation; if thou art in perils among false brethren;

if thou art in perils among robbers; if thou art in perils by land or by sea;

"If thou art accused with all manner of false accusations; if thine enemies fall upon thee; if they tear thee from the society of thy father and mother and brethren and sisters; and if with a drawn sword thine enemies tear thee from the bosom of thy wife, and of thine offspring, and thine elder son, although but six years of age, shall cling to thy garments, and shall say, My father, my father, why can't you stay with us? O, my father, what are the men going to do with you? and if then he shall be thrust from thee by the sword, and thou be dragged to prison, and thine enemies prowl around thee like wolves for the blood of the lamb;

"And if thou shouldst be cast into the pit, or into the hands of murderers, and the sentence of death passed upon thee; if thou be cast into the deep; if the billowing surge conspire against thee; if fierce winds become thine enemy; if the heavens gather blackness, and all the elements combine to hedge up the way; and above all, if the very jaws of hell shall gape open the mouth wide after thee, *know thou, my son, that all these things shall give thee experience, and shall be for thy good.*

"The Son of Man hath descended below them all. Art thou greater than he?

"Therefore, hold on thy way, and the priesthood shall remain with thee; for their bounds are set, they cannot pass. Thy days are known, and thy years shall not be numbered less; therefore, fear not what man can do, for God shall be with you forever and ever" (D&C 122:5–9; emphasis added).

For the most part this excerpt is not a prediction to the Prophet of what could or would happen but a rehearsal of his history. The six-year-old son mentioned in the passage, Joseph Smith III, relates what the experience referred to was like:

"I remember vividly the morning my father came to visit his family after the arrest that took place in the fall of 1838. When he was brought to the house by an armed guard I ran out of the gate to greet him, but was roughly pushed away from his side by a sword in the hand of the guard and not allowed to go near him. My mother, also, was not permitted to approach him and had to receive his farewell by word of lip only. The guard did not permit him to pass into the house nor her to pass out, either because he feared an attempt would be made to rescue his prisoner or because of some brutal instinct in his own breast. Who shall say?"[19]

The Lord told Joseph the ultimate reason for trials and tribulations: "All these things shall give thee experience, and shall be for thy good."

"What an experience!" we say and hope it never happens to us. But when we know that our suffering will give us experiences necessary for our exaltation and will ultimately be for our good, then such experiences become easier to bear. And, as the Lord said to Joseph, no matter how hard our trials and tribulations have been, we still know there is One who has suffered far more than we. Because of his sufferings, he bears our infirmities, our pains, and our sicknesses (Alma 7:11–12). He knows what we are going through, for "the Son of Man hath descended below them all" (D&C 122:8).

Now we can see why Joseph Smith understood so much about suffering. Very early, the Lord had told him: "Be patient in afflictions, for thou shalt have many; but endure them, for, lo, I am with thee, even unto the end of thy days" (D&C 24:8). And near the end of Joseph's life the Prophet could, like Paul (2 Timothy 4:7), report how he had finished the course which the Lord had laid out for him: "And as for the perils which I am called to pass through, they seem but a small thing to me, as the envy and wrath of man have been my common lot all the days of my life; and for what cause it seems mysterious, unless I was ordained from before the foundation of the world for some good end, or bad, as you may choose to call it. Judge ye for yourselves. God knoweth all these things, whether it be good or bad. But nevertheless, deep water is what I am wont to swim in. It all has become a second nature to me; and I feel, like Paul, to glory in tribulation; for to this day has the God of my fathers delivered me out of them all, and will deliver me from henceforth; for behold, and lo, I shall triumph over all my enemies, for the Lord God hath spoken it" (D&C 127:2).

Orson F. Whitney said of Joseph Smith: "It remained for the Prophet Joseph Smith to . . . set forth the why and wherefore of human suffering; and in revealing it he gave us a strength and power to endure that we did not before possess. For *when men know why they suffer*, and realize that it is for a good and wise purpose, they can bear it much better than they can in ignorance. . . .

" . . . It is for our development, our purification, our growth, our education and advancement, that we buffet the fierce waves of sorrow and misfortune; and we shall be all the stronger and better when we have swam the flood and stand upon the farther shore. . . .

" . . . When we want counsel and comfort, we do not go to children, nor to those who know nothing but pleasure and self-gratification. We go to men and women of thought and sympathy, men and women who have suffered themselves and can give us the comfort that we need. Is not this God's purpose in causing [allowing] his children to suffer? He wants them to become more like himself. God has suffered far more than man ever did or ever will, and is therefore the great source of sympathy and consolation: 'Who are these arrayed in white, nearest to the throne of God?' asked John the Apostle, wrapt in his mighty vision. The answer was: 'These are they who have come up through great tribulation, and washed their robes and made them white in the blood of the Lamb.' [Revelation 7:14]

"There is always a blessing in sorrow and humiliation. They who escape these things are not the fortunate ones. 'Whom God loveth he chasteneth.' When he desires to make a great man he takes a little street waif, or a boy in the back woods, such as Lincoln or Joseph Smith, and brings him up through hardship and privation to be the grand and successful leader of a people. Flowers shed most of their perfume when they are crushed. Men and women have to suffer just so much in order to bring out the best that is in them."[20]

No wonder Brigham Young said that Joseph Smith became more nearly perfect in the almost thirty-nine years he lived with persecution than he could have in a thousand years without the trials that he faced.[21]

When he was a member of the Quorum of the Twelve, Spencer W. Kimball gave one of his finest talks on the subject of growth through trial. He entitled his discourse, "Tragedy or Destiny?" A few brief excerpts from this masterful address help us to answer the question of the ages concerning suffering:

"Is there not wisdom in his giving us trials that we might rise above them, responsibilities that we might achieve, work to harden our muscles, sorrows to try our souls? Are we not exposed to temptations to test our strength, sickness that we might learn patience, death that we might be immortalized and glorified? . . .

"I like also the words of these verses, the author of which I do not know:

> "Pain stayed so long I said to him today,
> " 'I will not have you with me any more.'
> "I stamped my foot and said, 'Be on your way,'
> "And paused there, startled at the look he wore.
> " 'I, who have been your friend,' he said to me,
> " 'I, who have been your teacher—all you know
> " 'Of understanding love, of sympathy,
> " 'And patience, I have taught you. Shall I go?'
> "He spoke the truth, this strange unwelcome guest;
> "I watched him leave, and knew that he was wise.

"He left a heart grown tender in my breast,
"He left a far, clear vision in my eyes.
"I dried my tears, and lifted up a song—
"Even for one who'd tortured me so long."[22]

Sometimes sufferings, trials, and afflictions come upon us because of our own sins and transgressions. Such was the case with the Saints who were driven out of Jackson County, Missouri, in 1833. Even though they had been driven out, the Lord still held out the promise of eternal life, *if* they repented: "Verily I say unto you, concerning your brethren who have been afflicted, and persecuted, and cast out from the land of their inheritance—I, the Lord, have suffered the affliction to come upon them, wherewith they have been afflicted, in consequence of their transgressions; yet I will own them, and they shall be mine in that day when I shall come to make up my jewels" (D&C 101:1–3).

President Kimball gave us a fourth reason why people suffer: accidents. They are a part of mortality. The Lord sends his rain upon the just and the unjust (Matthew 5:45). After relating a number of tragic accidents, President Kimball asked, "Could the Lord have prevented these tragedies? The answer is, Yes. The Lord is omnipotent, with all power to control our lives, save us pain, prevent all accidents, drive all planes and cars, feed us, protect us, save us from labor, effort, sickness, even from death, if he will. But he will not.

"We should be able to understand this, because we can realize how unwise it would be for us to shield our children from all effort, from disappointments, temptations, sorrows, and suffering.

"The basic gospel law is free agency and eternal development. To force us to be careful or righteous would be to nullify that fundamental law and make growth impossible."[23]

We have reviewed from scriptures and from living prophets the four major reasons for suffering: (1) experience, (2) our good, (3) our own sins, and (4) accidents. It is important for our spiritual growth that we recognize the validity of these reasons. Regardless of how our trials, tribulations, and sufferings come upon us, however, it is our attitude toward them that will determine whether they become stumbling blocks or stepping-stones. We need to remind ourselves of the promises the Lord made to the Prophet Joseph Smith as he neared the end of his months of ordeal in the jails in Missouri: "And although their influence shall cast thee into trouble, and into bars and walls, thou shalt be had in honor; and but for a small moment and thy voice shall be more terrible in the midst of thine enemies than the fierce lion, because of thy righteousness; and thy God shall stand by thee forever and ever. . . . Therefore, hold on thy way, and the priesthood shall remain with thee; for their bounds are set, they cannot pass. Thy days are known, and thy years shall not be numbered less; therefore, fear not what man can do, for God shall be with you forever and ever" (D&C 122:4, 9).

From these examples we can see that when we handle the trials, tribulations, and suffering as we should, then we will be able to claim the blessings the Lord has in store for us. He tells us of them in Doctrine and Covenants 58:3–4, saying, "Ye cannot behold with your natural eyes, for the present time, the design of your God concerning those things which shall come hereafter, and the glory which shall follow after much tribulation. For after much tribulation come the blessings. Wherefore the day cometh that ye shall be crowned with much glory; the hour is not yet, but is nigh at hand."

NOTES

1. Elder Neal A. Maxwell has written a great deal about tribulation, especially that of Joseph Smith in Liberty Jail. Some of his best works on this subject are *All These Things Shall Give Thee Experience* (Salt Lake City: Deseret Book Co., 1979), *"But for a Small Moment"* (Salt Lake City: Bookcraft, 1986), and *Meek and Lowly* (Salt Lake City: Deseret Book Co., 1987).

2. Elder B. H. Roberts called Liberty Jail the "Temple Prison" and said: "It was more temple than prison, so long as the Prophet was there. It was a place of meditation and prayer. A temple, first of all, is a place of prayer; and prayer is communion with God. It is the 'infinite in man seeking the infinite in God.' Where they find each other, there is holy sanctuary—a temple. Joseph Smith sought God in this rude prison, and found him." B. H. Roberts, *A Comprehensive History of The Church of Jesus Christ of Latter-day Saints* (Salt Lake City: Deseret News Press, 1930), 1:526.

3. See Joseph Smith, *History of The Church of Jesus Christ of Latter-day Saints*, 2d ed. rev., edited by B. H. Roberts (Salt Lake City: Deseret Book Co., 1957), 3:420, 448.

4. Ibid., p. 290.

5. Ibid., p. 418.

6. Ibid., p. 264; see also *Times and Seasons*, 5 (1 October 1844): 666.

7. Smith, *History of the Church*, 6:47–49.

8. Ibid., pp. 592–93.

9. Ibid., 7:268–69.

10. *Doctrine and Covenants, Section 1 through Section 102*, Gospel Doctrine Teacher's Supplement (Salt Lake City: The Church of Jesus Christ of Latter-day Saints, 1978), p. 59.

11. Ibid.

12. Smith, *History of the Church*, 3:290.

13. Ibid., p. 293; emphasis added.

14. Neal A. Maxwell, "Premortality, a Glorious Reality," *Ensign*, Nov. 1985, p. 17.

15. Marion G. Romney, in Conference Report, Oct. 1969, pp. 58–59.

16. Smith, *History of the Church*, 3:294.

17. Dean C. Jessee, *Personal Writings of the Prophet Joseph Smith* (Salt Lake City: Deseret Book Co., 1971), p. 284; spelling and punctuation standardized.

18. Smith, *History of the Church*, 3:294.

19. *The Saints' Herald*, 6 Nov. 1934, p. 1414.

20. Orson F. Whitney, *Improvement Era* 22 (November 1918): 5–7; emphasis added.

21. Brigham Young, in *Journal of Discourses* (London: Latter-day Saints' Book Depot, 1854–86), 2:7.

22. Spencer W. Kimball, *Faith Precedes the Miracle* (Salt Lake City: Deseret Book Co., 1973), pp. 97, 99.

23. Ibid., p. 96.

FROM KIRTLAND TO COMPUTERS: THE GROWTH OF FAMILY HISTORY RECORD KEEPING

Kip Sperry

Brigham Young University

From 1831 to 1838 The Church of Jesus Christ of Latter-day Saints had its headquarters in Kirtland, Ohio, a rural village located in the Western Reserve in northeastern Ohio some thirty miles east of Cleveland. Spiritual experiences and events took place there which would have a substantial effect on the LDS Church and on the world for generations to come. Even though the Mormons were not received well by all local residents, the Church continued to grow, and eventually the Saints built their first temple in Kirtland.[1] While Church members sacrificed for the building of the temple, they were being prepared to receive heavenly manifestations. It was a period of pentecostal events and a time of rejoicing when the heavens were opened to the Latter-day Saints.[2]

The importance of the Kirtland experience in Church history cannot be underestimated. The 1830s was a period of growth, spiritual manifestations, missionary service, and persecution of Church leaders and members. Almost one-half of the sections of the Doctrine and Covenants were received in the Kirtland area. The First Presidency, the Quorum of the Twelve Apostles, and other major Church offices and priesthood leadership positions were organized in Kirtland. During the first half of 1836 more visions of heavenly beings were recorded than during any other period in Church history, as recorded in the Doctrine and Covenants and other Church sources.

The first meetings in the Kirtland Temple began in January 1836 and were followed by glorious spiritual experiences and visions.[3] The dedication of the Kirtland Temple occurred on 27 March 1836. The historic events which happened there have had a profound influence on family history and genealogical record keeping. The Kirtland Temple dedicatory prayer is included in Doctrine and Covenants 109, and visions manifested to the Prophet Joseph Smith are recorded in Section

110. On Easter Sunday, 3 April 1836, one week after the temple's dedication, Elijah the prophet appeared to Joseph Smith and Oliver Cowdery; this was a most significant event in Church history. The Prophet Joseph wrote:

"After this vision had closed, another great and glorious vision burst upon us; for Elijah the prophet, who was taken to heaven without tasting death, stood before us, and said:

"Behold, the time has fully come, which was spoken of by the mouth of Malachi — testifying that he [Elijah] should be sent, before the great and dreadful day of the Lord come —

"To turn the hearts of the fathers to the children, and the children to the fathers, lest the whole earth be smitten with a curse —

"Therefore, the keys of this dispensation are committed into your hands; and by this ye may know that the great and dreadful day of the Lord is near, even at the doors" (D&C 110:13–16).[4]

That appearance fulfills the often-quoted prophecy of Malachi in the Old Testament: "Behold, I will send you Elijah the prophet before the coming of the great and dreadful day of the Lord: and he shall turn the heart of the fathers to the children, and the heart of the children to their fathers, lest I come and smite the earth with a curse" (Malachi 4:5–6).

Malachi described Elijah's mission to establish a bond between present and past generations. The Prophet Joseph Smith explained, "the word *turn* here should be translated *bind,* or seal."[5] From the secular standpoint, Elijah's task is "defined as settling various disputed questions, in particular involving genealogy."[6] For Latter-day Saints, the authority to perform sacred temple ordinances in the restored Church centers upon the restoration of the priesthood and the restoration of the keys held by Elijah. Concerning the mission of Elijah, the Prophet Joseph Smith taught: "Elijah was the last Prophet that held the keys of the Priesthood, and who will, before the last dispensation, restore the authority and deliver the keys of the Priesthood, in order that all the ordinances may be attended to in righteousness."[7]

Those people who do family history and seek out their ancestry have the spirit of Elijah as they turn their hearts to their ancestors and seal children to their parents. Thus, Elijah's mission is fulfilled through the temple ordinances and priesthood authority to do this work. As Richard O. Cowan stated, "Through the sealing keys restored by Elijah, priesthood ordinances performed on earth can be 'bound' or 'sealed' in heaven; also, Latter-day Saints can perform saving priesthood ordinances in behalf of loved ones who died without the opportunity of accepting the gospel in person. In this way the hearts of the children are turning to their fathers."[8]

The spirit of Elijah is a moving, powerful force which motivates people to seek out their heritage. Elder Boyd K. Packer indicates, "When that spirit comes, somehow we desire to know more about those forebears—we desire to *know* them."[9] It is this spirit which compels Church members to go to the temple to do the sacred ordinances for themselves and for their deceased ancestors. President Joseph Fielding Smith summarized the power and purpose of Elijah when he wrote:

"Who are the fathers spoken of by Malachi, and who are the children? The fathers are our dead ancestors who died without the privilege of receiving the gospel, but who received the promise that the time would come when that privilege would be granted them. The children are those now living who are preparing genealogical data and who are performing the vicarious ordinances in the temples.

"The turning of the hearts of the children to the fathers is placing or planting in the hearts of the children that feeling and desire which will inspire them to search out the records of the dead."[10]

The sacred ordinances for the dead were not revealed to members until the Church had gathered at Nauvoo, Illinois, in the 1840s. The first baptisms for the dead took place in Nauvoo in 1840, and endowments for the living began there in 1842.[11] Proxy endowments for the dead began in 1877 in the St. George Temple. Elder Mark E. Petersen summarized the consequences of Elijah's appearance in these words:

"So we have great twofold activity in the earth as a result of Elijah's modern mission. On the one hand there is world-wide activity in the preparation of family histories and pedigrees, providing the necessary identification for those who have lived on the earth and are now dead.

"On the other hand is the intense activity of the members of The Church of Jesus Christ of Latter-day Saints in building temples and performing in them the sacred ordinances of the gospel that all who come unto Christ may be saved in his kingdom."[12]

INTEREST IN FAMILY HISTORY OUTSIDE THE CHURCH

Widespread interest in family history has occurred since the momentous events in Kirtland, Ohio. Civil registration of births, marriages, and deaths began in England on 1 July 1837, one year after the appearance of Elijah in Kirtland. Many states in America began keeping vital records in a manner patterned after English civil registration. In 1841 Massachusetts became the first state in America to pass legislation requiring the keeping of statewide vital records.[13]

The New England Historic Genealogical Society (NEHGS), the oldest genealogical organization in the western hemisphere, was founded in Boston, Massachusetts, in 1845, the year after the martyrdom of the Prophet Joseph Smith in Carthage, Illinois, on 27 June 1844.[14] NEHGS began publication of *The New England Historical and Genealogical Register* in January 1847; it is the oldest genealogical periodical and one of the most scholarly. With more than thirteen thousand members, NEHGS is one of the largest genealogical societies in the world and houses a library of more than 140,000 volumes, more than 10,000 rolls of microfilm, and thousands of genealogical manuscripts.

The creation of other large genealogical societies in America and elsewhere followed. The New York Genealogical and Biographical Society was organized in New York City in 1869. This society has published *The New York Genealogical and Biographical Record* quarterly since January 1870. The National Genealogical Society (NGS) was founded in Washington, D.C., in 1903 and currently has more than eleven thousand members. NGS began publishing the *National Genealogical Society Quarterly* in 1912. The scholarly periodicals published by these societies include compiled genealogies of early American families and methodology articles. Both NGS and NEHGS will lend selected volumes to their members through the mail from their lending libraries — a helpful service for those living some distance from a library with genealogical holdings.

The growth of genealogical and family history societies since the restoration events in Kirtland, Ohio, has been phenomenal. Today, there are about two thousand genealogical societies in North America, and many more are found in foreign countries, most notably Great Britain.[15] In addition, compiled genealogies (family histories), local histories, biographical compendiums, atlases, and other sources used by family historians have been published in large numbers since the coming of Elijah. The keeping of family Bibles, diaries, and other family sources has been evident since the early nineteenth century.

Although the first federal census in the United States began in 1790, it was not until 1850 that names of all family members were listed, along with age, birthplace (state or country), and other personal details. Photography, especially individual and family photos, has been popular since the middle of the nineteenth century.

Patriotic and lineage societies have been popular in America since the late nineteenth century. Foremost among these are the National Society, Daughters of the American Revolution (DAR), Sons of the American Revolution (SAR), and the General Society of Mayflower

Descendants, to name just a few. The Society of Genealogists (SOG) in London was founded in 1911 and has more than twelve thousand members; SOG publishes the quarterly *Genealogists' Magazine*. Studies in other associated fields have also increased in interest since the nineteenth century: local and community history, ethnic history, social history, heraldry and coats-of-arms, biography, and related disciplines.

The interest in family history continues to grow throughout the twentieth century. Two recent events have made tracing one's roots one of the most popular hobbies ever: the nation's Bicentennial celebration in 1976 when many local histories appeared and an abundance of national pride was felt, and then came the publication of Alex Haley's *Roots* and the subsequent television series.

Other physical witnesses of increased interest in family history have been the growth in the number of libraries housing genealogical collections; the growth of genealogical and historical societies, lineage and hereditary societies, surname associations, and family organizations; the increase of interest in family reunions and family newsletters; the granting of pioneer certificates to those showing descent from early pioneers in a specific area; the number of genealogical periodicals, newsletters, and genealogical columns published in newspapers; the growth of ethnic and religious organizations; the number of compiled genealogies (family histories) published; the volume of records which have been preserved in microform (microfilm and microfiche); the increasing abundance of indexes to records—genealogical records, newspapers, local histories, etc.; the use of computers to organize and index genealogical data has increased; computer interest and users' groups are abundant; the number of genealogical software programs and utilities for personal computers is increasing; the growth of interest in restoring cemeteries and transcribing gravestones; the preservation of historical sites; the restoration of old photographs and documents; the use of videotaping of oral history interviews and family reunions; and the publishing of genealogical accounts, local records and methodology books and articles in periodicals.

INTEREST IN FAMILY HISTORY WITHIN THE CHURCH

LDS Church members throughout the nineteenth century kept journals, diaries, letters, and other personal papers which offer primary evidence of their conversion to the gospel, their testimony, and their pioneering experiences. In addition, the Church kept records of minutes of local meetings, Church members' vital statistics, immigration information, the Journal History of the Church, patriarchal blessings, biographical sketches, and other records.[16]

The Genealogical Society of Utah (GSU) was founded 13 November 1894 under the supervision of the First Presidency of the Church as an organization and a genealogical library to acquire records and help Church members and others with ancestral research. Founded on the concept of the eternal nature of the family, the library underwent several name changes from the Genealogical Society Library and Genealogical Department Library to, in 1987, the Family History Library.

From a modest beginning of some 100 books in 1894, the Family History Library in Salt Lake City today houses the largest collection of genealogical records in the world.[17] Its collection contains more than 1.8 million rolls of microfilm from throughout the world, more than 300,000 microfiche, and more than 225,000 published volumes. The microfilm collection contains the equivalent of 6 million 300-page volumes consisting of nearly 2 billion names. The collection grows at the rate of about 5,000 rolls of film and about 1,000 books per month. Open to the public, the Family History Library is located in a modern five-story building and serves more than 800,000 patrons annually (about 2,500 people per day). Beginning in 1993, the public will be able to use computers and other genealogical sources in the former Hotel Utah, now known as the Utah Building, where a model FamilySearch Center will be located.

The Family History Library's rapid, continuous growth can be seen in many areas. The largest collections are genealogical records from the United States, Great Britain, Canada, Latin America, and various continental European countries. States with the largest collections include New York, Massachusetts, Pennsylvania, North Carolina, Ohio, Tennessee, Illinois, Kentucky, Georgia, New Jersey, and Iowa. Canadian provinces with the largest collections include Ontario, Québec, and Nova Scotia.

Examples of microfilmed records include civil vital records (births, marriages, and deaths), census schedules, church records, military records, passenger lists and immigration records, naturalization records, gravestone inscriptions, land and probate records, and many others. Microfilming of pre-1900 European records has included mostly ecclesiastical (parish) registers containing christenings, marriages, deaths, and burials. While most microfilmed records are of originals, some compiled genealogies, manuscript collections, and published sources are filmed as well.[18]

The Church has generated many thousands of names in computer format to aid family historians in their research. Elder M. Russell Ballard has stated that advanced technology, such as satellite communications, computerized typesetting in many languages, is being used more all the time. "I happen to believe these things have been inspired and created for the building of the kingdom of God. If others use them, that's fine, but their basic purpose is to help spread the gospel."[19]

FamilySearch is the Church's automated system of family history information. This system has been developed to simplify family history research. Information in these files is available in computer form at the Family History Library, the Harold B. Lee Library at Brigham Young University, family history centers, the Library of Congress, and some public libraries.

FamilySearch consists of the following computer files (as of 1992):[20]

1. Ancestral File (more than 12 million names linked together by family groups and pedigrees, along with names and addresses of submitters and other information).

2. International Genealogical Index (more than 184 million names of deceased individuals for whom temple ordinances have been cleared or already performed). The IGI helps members avoid duplicating temple ordinances.

3. Social Security Death Index (39.5 million names of deceased people who had Social Security numbers and whose deaths were reported to the Social Security Administration between 1962 and 1988, with some names as early as 1937 and some as late as 1989).

4. Military Index (individuals in the U.S. military service who died in Korea or Vietnam from 1950 to 1975).

5. Family History Library Catalog (an automated edition of the catalog which describes records at the Family History Library in Salt Lake City).

6. TempleReady (a computer program that helps Church members prepare names of ancestors for temple ordinances and take the names to the temple).

Of special interest to many Latter-day Saints, TempleReady is the Church's new program for submitting names for proxy temple ordinances. By using diskettes, Church members are able to take their ancestors' names directly to the temple so that sacred ordinances can be performed for them.

Other FamilySearch computer files and indexes are forthcoming: the 1880 United States census, the 1881 English census, names of American Civil War soldiers, and others. Indexing and name extraction from original records, such as vital and church records, will continue to expand these databases.

The Family History Department has developed the Personal Ancestral File (PAF), a useful genealogy software program for personal computers. PAF is designed to simplify genealogical record keeping and help to organize family records. It is one of the most popular genealogical software programs in use. PAF is easy to use and inexpensive; it can be used to submit names for temple ordinances and to the Ancestral File.

The Family History Library began a system of branch genealogical libraries in 1964, now known as family history centers, and today has more than 1,800 centers in fifty-five countries where copies of most microfilms can be lent for a modest fee to cover postage and handling. This lending system gives thousands of members and other family historians access to the Library's microfilmed collections. An estimated 2 million patron visits are recorded annually in the family history centers, with about 70 percent from individuals who are not members of the Church. It is estimated that 16,000 volunteers serve in family history centers.[21]

Working with the National Genealogical Society in Arlington, Virginia, the Family History Department has developed the Genealogical Projects Registry, a cooperative effort to share information about in-progress indexing and other genealogical projects. It is designed to prevent duplication of genealogical projects.

The Genealogical Society of Utah (now the microfilming arm of the Family History Department) has been microfilming records in many countries of the world to preserve records since 1938. Today there are more than 200 microfilming projects in 45 countries, with some 40 cameras filming records in the United States and Canada. The names of about 500 million people are filmed annually. Just recently microfilming began in what was formerly the Soviet Union. Extensive microfilming of local records in areas where the Church is prominent in American history has been undertaken: Geauga and Lake counties, Ohio; Hancock County, Illinois; Jackson County, Missouri; and in many Utah counties.

Examples of recent acquisitions for the United States include the 1920 United States census and related indexes, 24 million World War I draft registration cards, passport applications from the National Archives, naturalization records from many federal and local courts, Canadian Border Crossings (St. Albans, Vermont, District Manifest records), city directories for many cities and time periods, military records and indexes from the National Archives, family and local histories from the Library of Congress and elsewhere, Native American records for many areas of the country, Russian consular records, state census schedules for various years and localities, vital records and related indexes for some cities and states, church records for various denominations, and many other genealogical records.

In addition to compact disc, the Family History Library Catalog (FHLC) and International Genealogical Index (IGI) are also available on microfiche. The FHLC identifies the Library's holdings by author, title, locality, surname, and subject. The compact disc version of the IGI is easier to use than the microfiche edition. Both of these microfiche files can be purchased by libraries and individuals.

Temple attendance has also increased since the early days of the Church. Latter-day temples are necessary to perfect the Saints and to redeem the dead. We are now in a temple-building era; today there are forty-five operating temples. The increase in the number of temples dedicated since Kirtland and the increase in temple attendance attest to the compelling force of the spirit of Elijah. Archibald F. Bennett, then secretary and librarian of the Genealogical Society in Salt Lake City, discussed the importance of temples and acquiring records: "A paramount duty of Latter-day Saints, who are of Israel, is to build temples, wherein saving ordinances can be administered. In preparation for such holy ordinances, ancestral records must be gathered. Since the coming of Elijah it seems as though the whole world is committed to aid us in the compiling and gathering of records. . . . This gathering of records is destined to grow and increase beyond the limits of the most ardent imagination."[22]

In addition to temple service, countless thousands of hours are spent by Church members in extracting and indexing names from parish registers and other records. The Family Record Extraction Program focuses on the family and helping to build the Church's computer databases. All of these activities are necessary for the building of the kingdom of God on earth.

CONCLUSION

There was very little interest in family history in the western world before the sacred events in Kirtland, Ohio, in April 1836. Since then, there has been worldwide interest in family history and genealogy. "The priesthood keys restored that day in the Kirtland Temple have blessed multitudes of mankind, both in mortality and in the spirit world. These blessings have not come because of the powers of mortal men. They are the result of the concern of the Lord for His children."[23]

Family history and genealogy in The Church of Jesus Christ of Latter-day Saints since the appearance of Elijah in the Kirtland Temple has grown from modest means to the largest genealogical organization in the world. The Family History Department is a professional and well-respected organization which microfilms and preserves records and makes them available to the public. The department's mission statement is "The Family History Department enables church members to readily identify, link, and provide temple ordinances for their ancestors, and preserves the official temple record."[24]

Since 1836, there has been unprecedented growth in genealogical societies and in family histories and other publications, as well as an increase in genealogical interests. The growth of patron usage at the Family History Library in Salt Lake City, family history centers, and other genealogical libraries has been phenomenal in recent years. Thrilling discoveries await the serious reseacher.

Modern computer technology has been inspired for the building of the kingdom of God on earth, including FamilySearch and other computer files. The use of computers to aid family history partially fulfills the revelation given to Joseph Smith in Nauvoo, Illinois, in 1842: "Let us, therefore, as a church and a people, and as Latter-day Saints, offer unto the Lord an offering in righteousness; and let us present in his holy temple, when it is finished, a book containing the records of our dead, which shall be worthy of all acceptation" (D&C 128:24).

Everyone is encouraged to submit accurate and well-documented genealogies to the Ancestral File so that others may benefit from their research efforts. More than 9,000 diskettes containing more than 9 million names were received last year by the Ancestral File Unit at the Family History Department. The Church's genealogy databases are constantly growing. Perhaps this interest was foreseen in an epistle from Joseph Smith in 1842: "And again, let all the records be had in order, that they may be put in the archives of my holy temple, to be held in remembrance from generation to generation, saith the Lord of Hosts" (D&C 127:9).[25]

NOTES

1. Anne B. Prusha, A History of Kirtland, Ohio (Mentor, Ohio: Lakeland Community College Press, 1982). In addition to the Mormon experience in Kirtland, Prusha discusses the growth of the community and the relationship of the Mormons to the non-Mormons. See also Mrs. Peter S. Hitchock, "Joseph Smith and the Kirtland Temple," The Historical Society Quarterly, Lake County, Ohio 7 (Nov. 1965): 127–32. The Mormon experience in the Kirtland area is recorded in various issues of the Painesville Telegraph and in local histories of Western Reserve counties, although not always favorably. The Kirtland Temple is now owned and maintained by the Reorganized Church of Jesus Christ of Latter Day Saints, with headquarters in Independence, Missouri.

2. Karl Ricks Anderson, Joseph Smith's Kirtland: Eyewitness Accounts (Salt

Lake City: Deseret Book Co., 1989), pp. 169–77. See also Milton V. Backman, Jr., *The Heavens Resound: A History of the Latter-day Saints in Ohio, 1830–1838* (Salt Lake City: Deseret Book Co., 1983), pp. 302–9.

3. Richard O. Cowan, "The House of the Lord in Kirtland: A 'Preliminary' Temple," *Regional Studies in Latter-day Saint Church History: Ohio*, ed. Milton V. Backman, Jr. (Provo, Utah: Department of Church History and Doctrine, Brigham Young University, 1990), pp. 105–22.

4. See also Joseph Smith, *History of The Church of Jesus Christ of Latter-day Saints*, 2d ed. rev., edited by B. H. Roberts (Salt Lake City: Deseret Book Co., 1948), 2:435–36.

5. Smith, *History of the Church*, 6:183–84; see also D&C 2.

6. Jacob Neusner, ed., *Judaisms and Their Messiahs at the Turn of the Christian Era* (Cambridge: Cambridge University Press, 1987), p. 274. To quote further, "The resurrection of the dead comes through Elijah" (p. 273).

7. Joseph Smith, *Teachings of the Prophet Joseph Smith*, sel. Joseph Fielding Smith (Salt Lake City: Deseret Book Co., 1976), p. 172; see also pp. 337–38.

8. Richard O. Cowan, *Temples to Dot the Earth* (Salt Lake City: Bookcraft, 1989), p. 32.

9. Boyd K. Packer, *The Holy Temple* (Salt Lake City: Bookcraft, 1980), p. 210.

10. Joseph Fielding Smith, *Doctrines of Salvation*, comp. Bruce R. McConkie (Salt Lake City: Bookcraft, 1954–56), 2:127–28.

11. Larry C. Porter and Milton V. Backman, Jr., "Doctrine and the Temple in Nauvoo," *Brigham Young University Studies*, 32 (1992): 51–53.

12. Mark E. Petersen, "Why Mormons Build Temples," *Temples and the Latter-day Saints* (Salt Lake City: Mutual Improvement Associations of The Church of Jesus Christ of Latter-day Saints, 1967), p. 16.

13. The years that civil registration of vital records began in the following states are examples: Massachusetts, 1841; New Jersey, 1848; Rhode Island, 1853; Michigan and Ohio, 1867; to name just a few. Throughout the nineteenth century and into the early twentieth century, other states passed legislation requiring the recording of vital records.

14. See D&C 135 and Smith, *History of the Church*, 6:629–31.

15. Addresses and information regarding genealogical and historical societies, libraries, vital record offices, ethnic archives and societies, periodicals and newsletters, etc., can be found in Elizabeth Petty Bentley, *The Genealogist's Address Book* (Baltimore: Genealogical Publishing Co., 1991).

16. The largest repositories of LDS Church records for genealogical use are the Historical Department, in the east wing of the Church Office Building, Salt Lake City; Harold B. Lee Library, Brigham Young University; and the Family History Library, Salt Lake City. Other large libraries, such as the Library of Congress and Yale University, also collect Mormon Americana.

17. The Family History Library is located at 35 North West Temple Street, Salt Lake City, UT 84150 (telephone 801–240–2331).

18. Many of the Family History Library's resources are described in Johni Cerny and Wendy Elliott, eds., *The Library: A Guide to the LDS Family History Library* (Salt Lake City: Ancestry Publishing, 1988). The most up-to-date listing

of Library holdings, however, is the Family History Library Catalog (FHLC) on microfiche, on compact disc, and on-line.

19. M. Russell Ballard, in *Church News*, 8 Mar. 1980, p. 4.

20. For example, Sidney Branton Sperry appears in the Ancestral File, International Genealogical Index, and the Social Security Death Index. Born 26 December 1895 in Salt Lake City, Utah, he was the son of Harrison Sperry, Jr., and Josephine Titcomb Sperry. The Ancestral File traces his ancestry to Richard Sperry, an immigrant who resided in New Haven, Connecticut. Dr. Sperry died on 4 September 1977 in Provo, Utah. The Sidney B. Sperry manuscript collection is housed in the Department of Archives and Manuscripts, Harold B. Lee Library, Brigham Young University, Provo, Utah (see "Register of the Sidney B. Sperry Collection," compiled by Dale Lyons and Brian Cannon, UA 618). (N.B. The author is also a descendant of Richard Sperry, the immigrant.)

21. Family History Department, Member Services Division, statistical sheet (Salt Lake City, 1992).

22. Archibald F. Bennett, *Searching with Success: A Genealogical Text* (Salt Lake City: Deseret Book Co., 1962), pp. 82–83.

23. Leaun G. Otten and C. Max Caldwell, *Sacred Truths of the Doctrine and Covenants*, 2d ed. (Springville, Utah: LEMB, 1983), 2:249.

24. Family History Department Mission Plan, 4 July 1990.

25. Since this presentation was made at the Sidney B. Sperry Symposium on 26 September 1992, Susan Easton Black gave a lecture entitled "The Spirit of Elijah" at the Tenth Annual Harman Lecture, Division of Continuing Education, Brigham Young University, in January 1993.

20

THE WEAK THINGS OF THE WORLD

Brett P. Thomas

Brigham Young University

The weak and simple who come unto Christ will break down the strong and mighty. By proclaiming the commandments of God and thrusting in their sickle with all their might, they will confound the wise, thrash the nations by the power of God's Spirit, and lay up for themselves treasures in heaven and salvation to their souls (see D&C 1:18–23; 4:4; 133:59; 1 Corinthians 1:27).

Such power and salvation will come not because their weaknesses have been wrapped up, shelved, and forgotten, but rather because Christ has promised that the light of the gospel will reveal their weaknesses. If these servants respond by turning unto Christ in humility and faith, the sculptor of souls will endow them with his grace and will mold, shape, and transform these weaknesses into divine strengths (see Ether 12:27–37; 2 Corinthians 12:9–10).

This divine process, however, is absolute foolishness to the world and is often enigmatic to the Saint. The purpose of this paper is to examine the paradox of human frailty as a divine vehicle which testifies to the world of the grandeur and perfection of God. These frailties are not a deterrent to heaven, but rather an integral part of the pilgrimage to God and his glory.

In Doctrine and Covenants 1, the Lord cites four reasons why he has chosen the weak and simple to proclaim the fulness of his gospel to the ends of the world:

1. "The weak things of the world shall come forth and break down the mighty and strong ones, that man should not counsel his fellow man, neither trust in the arm of flesh — but that every man might speak in the name of God the Lord, even the Savior of the world" (vv. 19–20).

2. "Faith also might increase in the earth" (v. 21).

3. "[God's] everlasting covenant might be established" (v. 22).

4. The commandments of God would be "given unto [his] servants in their weakness, after the manner of their language, that they might come to understanding" (v. 24).

THE WEAK BREAK DOWN THE STRONG

The weak and simple break down the strong and mighty by teaching the truth by the power of the Holy Ghost. "Wherefore, I the Lord ask you this question—unto what were ye ordained? To preach my gospel by the Spirit, even the Comforter which was sent forth to teach the truth" (D&C 50:13–14). This truth teaches that Jesus is the Christ, the literal son of God, and "that he came into the world, even Jesus, to be crucified for the world, and to bear the sins of the world, and to sanctify the world, and to cleanse it from all unrighteousness; that through him all might be saved" (D&C 76:41–42). The salvation of souls is his work and his glory. In short, the truth teaches the glory of God.

Those who emulate the Savior through obedience to the commandments receive light and truth and come to know of God's glory (see D&C 93:28, 36). Because "light and truth forsake that evil one" (D&C 93:37), they lose every desire to be supported by the strength of the world; indeed, the strength of the world holds no appeal. A classic example of that is Moses' dramatic encounter with the glory of God and the glory of the world. On an "exceedingly high mountain," Moses talked with God and "the glory of God was upon Moses; therefore Moses could endure his presence" (Moses 1:1–2). The Lord taught: "I have a work for thee, Moses, my son; and thou art in the similitude of mine Only Begotten; and mine Only Begotten is and shall be the Savior, for he is full of grace and truth; but there is no God beside me, and all things are present with me, for I know them all" (Moses 1:6). Moses was then shown a marvelous vision of the "world and the ends thereof, and all the children of men which are, and which were created; of the same he greatly marveled and wondered" (Moses 1:8).

But then the lights went out:

"And the presence of God withdrew from Moses, that his glory was not upon Moses; and Moses was left unto himself. And as he was left unto himself, he fell unto the earth.

"And it came to pass that it was for the space of many hours before Moses did again receive his natural strength like unto man; and he said unto himself: Now, for this cause I know that man is nothing, which thing I never had supposed.

"But now mine own eyes have beheld God; but not my natural, but my spiritual eyes, for my natural eyes could not have beheld; for I should have withered and died in his presence; but his glory was upon me; and I beheld his face, for I was transfigured before him.

"And it came to pass that when Moses had said these words, behold, Satan came tempting him, saying: Moses, son of man, worship me.

"And it came to pass that Moses looked upon Satan and said: Who art thou? For behold, I am a son of God, in the similitude of his Only Begotten; and *where is thy glory*, that I should worship thee?" (Moses 1:9–13; emphasis added).

Satan was stuck by that question, and he knew it. His glory was nothing compared to God's. Moses continued with this stark juxtaposition:

"For behold, I could not look upon God, except his glory should come upon me, and I were transfigured before him. But I can look upon thee in the natural man. Is it not so, surely?

"Blessed be the name of my God, for his Spirit hath not altogether withdrawn from me, or else where is thy glory, for it is darkness unto me? And I can judge between thee and God; for God said unto me: Worship God, for him only shalt thou serve.

"Get thee hence, Satan; deceive me not; for God said unto me: Thou art after the similitude of mine Only Begotten.

"And he also gave me commandments when he called unto me out of the burning bush, saying: Call upon God in the name of mine Only Begotten, and worship me.

"And again Moses said: I will not cease to call upon God, I have other things to inquire of him: for *his glory has been upon me, wherefore I can judge between him and thee*. Depart hence, Satan" (Moses 1:14–18; emphasis added).

Because Moses knew he was the son of God after the similitude of Jesus Christ and that "man is nothing" or powerless without the sustaining grace and glory of the Savior, he was able to clearly discern the weakness of the world. The power of truth exposes the shallowness of the world's strength. The world's glory simply cannot compare. Therefore, the power of the truth breaks down the "mighty and strong" by revealing the glory of God.

Jesus Christ shatters the world's stereotype of strength. The strength of Christ is the antithesis of the arm of flesh. His mission is to reveal his perfect attributes unto man and to invite them to be like him through his atonement. These truths expose the utter futility in trusting in the arm of flesh. For example, his attributes of faith, hope, and charity are eternally stronger than doubt, despair, and pride; and his attributes of meekness, purity, and mercy are infinitely superior to the raging destructiveness of anger and the spiritual atrophy of bitter, torn, and unforgiving relationships. His perfect mastery of power shows clearly by contrast the corrupt nature of mankind's power, which throughout history has trampled and enslaved their fellowman. In short, he teaches the terrible weakness of sin and that only through him and by him can mankind be saved. He invites the world to a greater strength—a complete submissiveness unto the will of the Father and a perfection in righteousness.

"But wait a minute!" the weak and simple exclaim: "How can we with our finite tongues possibly do justice to God's infinite glory? And how can we in our imperfections possibly testify of Jesus Christ and his divine nature?" The answer, of course, is we can't—but God can, through us. When Enoch received his call from God he queried: "Why is it that I have found favor in thy sight, and am but a lad, and all the people hate me; for I am slow of speech; wherefore am I thy servant? And the Lord said unto Enoch: Go forth and do as I have commanded thee, and no man shall pierce thee. *Open thy mouth, and it shall be filled, and I will give thee utterance,* for all flesh is in my hands, and I will do as seemeth me good" (Moses 6:31–32; emphasis added). The salient testimony of the scriptures is that God and his Spirit support those who faithfully obey him and keep his commandments, "for I will go before your face. I will be on your right hand and on your left, and my Spirit shall be in your hearts, and mine angels round about you, to bear you up" (D&C 84:88).

The weak and simple are to "speak in the name of God the Lord, even the Savior of the world" (D&C 1:20). Those who speak in the name of Jesus Christ express their willingness by covenant to take upon themselves his name. They represent him, act, speak, and do as the Savior would do if he were present. No mortal, of course, can possibly do that alone, so God promises the companionship and power of the Holy Ghost through the ordinances of the gospel (D&C 39:4–12). This grace, or enabling power, remits sins, heals souls, empowers to do the works of Christ, and, if individuals are proven faithful, will one day, after they pass through the veil, endow them with the very attributes of Christ. Therefore, by "speak[ing] in the name of God the Lord, even the Savior of the world," the weak and simple speak with the power of the Holy Ghost and invite all to come unto Christ and to learn of him. This invitation, of course, begins with faith.

THAT FAITH MIGHT INCREASE IN THE EARTH

The apostle Paul has given us an important insight into why God has chosen the simple and weak to help faith increase in the earth: "And I, brethren, when I came to you, came not with excellency of speech or of wisdom, declaring unto you the testimony of God. For I determined not to know any thing among you save Jesus Christ, and him crucified. And I was with you in weakness, and in fear, and in much trembling. And my speech and my preaching was not with enticing words of man's wisdom, but in demonstration of the Spirit and of power: *That your faith should not stand in the wisdom of men, but in the power of God*" (1 Corinthians 2:1–5; emphasis added).

Paul's phrase "your faith should not stand in the wisdom of men, but in the power of God" points to the problem of mankind's tendency to lean on the ways of the world and their difficulty in developing faith in the ways of God. An illustration of this principle is found in God's choosing of his prophets. When President David O. McKay died, a Church member approached Elder Harold B. Lee and questioned him about the prospect of Joseph Fielding Smith, president of the Quorum of the Twelve Apostles, becoming the next prophet. Elder Gene R. Cook described the dialogue as follows:

" 'Is it correct what I have heard that they're going to make Joseph Fielding Smith the President of the Church?'

" . . . Elder Lee answered politely and confirmed that he thought that would be the case.

"But the man persisted and said, 'How can that be? I can't believe that. How can we sustain Joseph Fielding Smith? He's ninety-three years old. Why, he's so old I'm not sure he is really quite with it.' The man continued developing this point—how could a man of that age, his body weak and worn down, still direct this Church?

"President Lee listened for a while, but his sharp mind was spinning. He responded, 'My good brother, do you know what it takes to be a prophet of the Lord?'

"The man said, 'Well, I guess I really don't know exactly.'

" 'Well,' said Elder Lee, 'what do you think it would take?'

"The fellow then said, 'Well, I suppose he'd have to know all about genealogy, the missionary program of the Church, and all the missionaries and what they're doing and how to supervise them. He would need to know about the Primary and the Relief Society and the building and construction programs.' He named quite a few other major functions of the Church.

"When he finished Elder Lee said, 'That's all wrong.' He could sometimes say that quite pointedly. The man was taken back a bit. Then Elder Lee answered his question by stating, 'Shall I tell you what it takes to be a prophet? There's only one capacity; just one. And that is to be able to hear the voice of the Lord. That's all. He's got all the rest of us to do the work. He just has to do one function. Do you suppose that this great living Apostle, who has been sustained a prophet for six decades, longer than any other man on earth, might be able to do that?' "[1]

Surely, "as the heavens are higher than the earth, so are [God's] ways higher than [our] ways" (Isaiah 55:9). These heavenly ways include the intentional transmission of divine truths through the mouths of the weak and simple so that we will be directly confronted with the issue of faith (see D&C 21:4–5). Those who learn to embrace this principle of faith, cleave and draw near unto God by trying the virtue of his word. Striving to become acquainted with his voice, they search the scriptures and immerse themselves into the words of his servants. Indeed, they begin to testify that "these words are not of men nor of man, but of [God]" (D&C 18:34). Thus, as they begin to treasure these words and hearken unto them, their faith is increased in Jesus Christ, the Savior of the world, and they are enabled to "let the solemnities of eternity rest upon [their] minds" (D&C 43:34).

THAT GOD'S EVERLASTING COVENANT MIGHT BE ESTABLISHED

Hearkening unto the words of eternal life through the weak and simple leads us to the ordinances of God. The Prophet Joseph Smith taught: "Reading the experience of others, or the revelation given to *them,* can never give *us* a comprehensive view of our condition and true relation to God. Knowledge of these things can only be obtained by experience through the ordinances of God set forth for that purpose."[2] Through the ordinances of the gospel and the authority of the priesthood, the powers of godliness are manifest unto men in the flesh (see D&C 84:21). Thus, through the weak and simple whom God has authorized to act in his name, God and man enter into an everlasting covenant, even the fulness of the gospel (see D&C 66:2). This covenant promises to sanctify mortal man, make him holy, and enable him to dwell in God's presence and live as he lives. Jesus Christ has promised: "Unto as many as received me gave I power to do many miracles, and to become the sons of God; and even unto them that believed on my name gave I power to obtain eternal life. And even so I have sent mine everlasting covenant into the world, to be a light to the world, and to be a standard for my people" (D&C 45:8–9).

This standard is a great strength to those who strive to follow him. God sustains those who bind themselves to him through holy and sacred covenants. When the weak and simple repent and worthily renew those covenants, the Savior empowers them unto righteousness, the powers of heaven pour down upon them, the doctrine of the priesthood distills upon their souls, and, ultimately, they are promised that "the Holy Ghost shall be [their] constant companion, and [their] scepter an unchanging scepter of righteousness and truth; and [their] dominion shall be an everlasting dominion, and without compulsory means it shall flow unto [them] forever and ever" (D&C 121:46).

THAT THEY MIGHT COME TO UNDERSTANDING

Finally, God has given his commandments unto his servants "in their weakness, after the manner of their language, that they might come to understanding" (D&C 1:24). Understanding comes by receiving the Spirit of God as it is preached by the Spirit of God through God's servants (see D&C 50:16–22) and by living and applying the truth (see Mosiah 12:27; Proverbs 9:10; John 7:15–19). The weak and simple will learn the truth line upon line, precept upon precept, and grace for grace as they learn to emulate the truth — even the Savior of the world (see D&C 93:20; 98:12–14). Paradoxically, as we are confronted with our own weaknesses and the weaknesses of others, we learn to apply our hearts to understanding and coming to know the strengths of our Savior, Jesus Christ.

Confronting Weakness "after the Manner of Their Language"

On 1 November 1831, ten elders met in conference to discuss the publication of revelations given to the Prophet Joseph Smith. The compilation of these revelations would be titled "The Book of Commandments." So important was this event that the heavens were opened, and God endowed Joseph with one of the greatest revelations ever given to man. It is known today as Section 1 of the Doctrine and Covenants, the Lord's Preface. Not all of the elders present at the conference were enthusiastic about this new revelation, however. William E. McLellin felt that the language of it was inferior and needed to be improved. In response to his complaint, McLellin received through Joseph the following revelation from the Lord:

"Your eyes have been upon my servant Joseph Smith, Jun., and his language you have known, and his imperfections you have known; and you have sought in your hearts knowledge that you might express beyond his language; this you also know.

"Now, seek ye out of the Book of Commandments, even the least that is among them, and appoint him that is the most wise among you;

"Or, if there be any among you that shall make one like unto it, then ye are justified in saying that ye do not know that they are true;

"But if ye cannot make one like unto it, ye are under condemnation if ye do not bear record that they are true" (D&C 67:5–8).

In other words, the Lord was challenging anyone present at the conference to write a revelation. William McLellin, who had boasted of his literary prowess, accepted the challenge and left the room to try. After a period of time, he returned to the conference in tears without a single written word. Instead of drinking deeply from the fountain of living waters, McLellin, when confronted with "weakness, after the manner of [Joseph Smith's] language" (D&C 1:24), saw only the weakness — which cost him the Spirit and crippled his ability to see the grandeur of this glorious revelation.

King Benjamin spoke on this issue. Keenly aware of his weak and trembling mortal frame (see Mosiah 2:26–30), Benjamin introduced his great sermon with these cautionary words: "I have not commanded you to come up hither to *trifle* with the words which I shall speak, but that you should hearken unto me, and open your ears that ye may hear, and your hearts that ye may understand, and your minds that the mysteries of God may be unfolded to your view" (Mosiah 2:9; emphasis added). The Spirit pours down upon the souls of those who are prepared to hear. Trifling with words or focusing unduly on the weakness of God's servants inhibits that divine outpouring.

President Heber J. Grant shared the following testimony:

"I call to mind one incident . . . when I was a young man, probably seventeen or eighteen years of age. I heard the late Bishop Millen Atwood preach a sermon in the Thirteenth Ward. I was studying grammar at the time, and he made some grammatical errors in his talk.

"I wrote down his first sentence, smiled to myself, and said: 'I am going to get here tonight, during the thirty minutes that Brother Atwood speaks, enough material to last me for the entire winter in my night school grammar class.' We had to take to the class for each lesson two sentences, or four sentences a week, that were not grammatically correct, together with our corrections.

"I contemplated making my corrections and listening to Bishop Atwood's sermon at the same time. But I did not write anything more after that first sentence — not a word; and when Millen Atwood stopped preaching, tears were rolling down my cheeks, tears of gratitude and thanksgiving that welled up in my eyes because of the marvelous testimony which that man bore of the divine mission of Joseph Smith, the prophet of God, and of the wonderful inspiration that attended the prophet in all his labors.

"Although it is now more than sixty-five years since I listened to that sermon, it is just as vivid today, and the sensations and feelings that I had are just as fixed with me as they were the day I heard it. Do you know, I would no more have thought of using those sentences in which he had made grammatical mistakes than I would think of standing up in class and profaning the name of God. That testimony made the first profound impression that was ever made upon my heart and soul of the divine mission of the prophet. I had heard many testimonies that had pleased me and made their impression, but his was the first testimony that had melted me to tears under the inspiration of the Spirit of God to that man."³

"Remember that which cometh from above is sacred, and must be spoken [and received] with care, and by constraint of the Spirit" (D&C 63:64). This principle has tremendous ramifications. Ordinary Latter-day Saints preach sermons, teach lessons, administer ordinances, and covenant to act as representatives of Jesus Christ. Some Saints feel overwhelmed, nervous, and insecure. Others may be overbearing, smug, and dogmatic. None of us bears one another's burdens without our own debilitating blemishes. It matters not where the weakness lies, be it our own or another's; rather, the test is how we respond to the weakness — the condition of our hearts.

Succor the Weak

Lehi's dream teaches us that hard hearts and blind minds fail to see God's hand in his work. They scoff, mock, and point their fingers toward those who struggle to press forward in Christ (see 1 Nephi 8:27– 28). The pure in heart, however, "succor the weak, lift up the hands which hang down, and strengthen the feeble knees" (D&C 81:5). Modern revelation instructs: "If any man among you be strong in the Spirit, let him take with him him that is weak, that he may be edified in all meekness, that he may become strong also" (D&C 84:106). It would be arrogant and presumptuous for one member to categorize himself or herself as the strong and label someone else as the weak. Equally erroneous would be members wallowing in self-pity, seeing themselves only as the weak and others as the strong. There is a divine mixture of weakness and strength in all of us, and so much of our probation rests on our willingness to see each other and help each other as God does — in other words, with faith, hope and charity. In this holy process we are edified together, not in spite of each other, but because of each other.

Anciently, when Israel was fighting the Amalekites, Joshua's army was strengthened as long as Moses could hold up his arms with the rod of God. The record reads: "And it came to pass, when Moses held up his hand, that Israel prevailed: and when he let down his hand Amalek prevailed. But Moses' hands were heavy; and they took a stone, and put it under him, and he sat thereon; and Aaron and Hur stayed up his hands, the one on the one side, and the other on the other side; and his hands were steady until the going down of the sun" (Exodus 17:11–12).

In other words, when his arms dropped because of fatigue, so did the strength of Israel's armies and they began to fall back. At length, when Aaron and Hur sustained the arms of Moses, Israel was empowered to victory. Note the interrelationship of strengths and weakness. As we sustain the servants of God, we are strengthened from on high. Both prophet and servant are edified together through their strengths and their weaknesses. In a very real way, we can sustain one another in our hearts, thoughts, prayers, and actions. Indeed, we are commanded to strengthen one another in "all [our] conversation, in all [our] prayers, in all [our] exhortations, and in all [our] doings" (D&C 108:7). As Jesus taught Peter, the true test of conversion is whether we strengthen one another. Charity is born of such conversion, enabling us to see the good, or "god," in our fellowman. We will then see no ordinary people; rather, as C. S. Lewis has written, we will see the glory of God:

"The load, or weight, or burden of my neighbour's glory should be laid on my back, a load so heavy that only humility can carry it, and the backs of the proud will be broken. It is a serious thing to live in a society of possible gods and goddesses, to remember that the dullest and most uninteresting person you can talk to may one day be a creature which, if you sa[w] it now, you would be strongly tempted to worship, or else a horror and a corruption such as you now meet, if at all, only in a nightmare. All day long we are, in some degree, helping each other to one or other of these destinations. It is in the light of these overwhelming possibilities, it is with the awe and circumspection proper to them, that we should conduct all our dealings with one another, all friendships, all loves, all play, all politics. There are no *ordinary* people. You have never talked to a mere mortal."[4]

Because Thou Hast Seen Thy Weakness, Thou Shalt Be Made Strong

It is precisely in the process of shouldering our neighbor's glory and bearing his burdens that they may be light that we begin following in the footsteps of Jesus Christ — a path which is laden with the promise: "If men come unto me I will show unto them their weakness. I give unto men weakness that they may be humble" (Ether 12:27). This promise, to put it mildly, is a painful one. C. S. Lewis likened it to suddenly opening the door to a cellar and seeing rats scurrying to safety. The sudden light from above did not create the rat, or, symbolically, the sin or weakness; it simply exposed it.[5] In a like manner, when we come unto Christ, we will discover our own rats in the cellar which the light of the gospel will continue to reveal unto us, demanding that we deal with them, despite our natural inclination to turn our heads and look the other way. For example, only those who desire humility discover the powerful pull of pride, only those who strive to be submissive discover how dearly they like hanging onto their own will, and only those who truly desire repentance discover the seriousness of sin. We can learn a great deal from the prophets, who, when given additional light that exposed their weaknesses, didn't close the door to their cellar and bolt it shut. On the contrary, in humility they approached the Lord and learned difficult but vital lessons, repented, and received line upon line, precept upon precept, and gradually became pillars of strength, not in spite of their weaknesses, but because of them.

Consider Joseph Smith. Early in his ministry he learned the folly of trusting in the arm of flesh. After the loss of 116 pages of manuscript he was chastised: "You should not have feared man more than God. . . . Behold, thou art Joseph, and thou wast chosen to do the work of the Lord, but because of transgression, if thou art not aware thou wilt fall" (D&C 3:7, 9). The Prophet pleaded for forgiveness, and he learned an invaluable lesson. He learned to do the will of God at all costs. His watchword became, "Whatever God requires is right, no matter what it is"[6] and "I made this my rule: *When the Lord commands, do it.*"[7] Because Joseph continually turned to the Lord in humility, the Lord continually turned his weaknesses into strengths.

The natural man has a terrible time acquiring that eternal yet elusive attribute of humility. Without weakness, humility seems almost impossible to obtain (at least during this mortal probation). Paul shared with the Corinthians: "Lest I should be exalted above measure through the abundance of the revelations, there was given to me a thorn in the flesh. . . . For this thing I besought the Lord thrice, that it might depart from me. And he said unto me, My grace is sufficient for thee: for my strength is made perfect in weakness. Most gladly therefore will I rather glory in my infirmities that the power of Christ may rest upon me. . . . For when I am weak, then am I strong" (2 Corinthians 12:7–10).

The power of Christ rests upon us when we partake of his atonement. Only through the atonement of Christ can we acquire his attributes, such as humility, submissiveness, patience, brotherly kindness, long-suffering, and charity (see Mosiah 3:19; Alma 7:23; 2 Peter 1:2–8). Nevertheless, even those who appear to have mastered these attributes and have seemingly arrived at an apex of righteousness — even they — still acknowledge the vital role of weakness in their lives.

The prophet Jacob testified: "Our faith becometh unshaken, insomuch that we truly can command in the name of Jesus and the very trees obey us, or the mountains, or the waves of the sea. Nevertheless, the Lord God showeth us our weakness that we may know that it is by his grace, and his great condescensions unto the children of men, that we have power to do these things" (Jacob 4:6–7).

The prophets can inspire us to stretch ourselves to reach their heights. Indeed, some of the greatest souls who have ever graced this earth have been the prophets of God. Yet, even though we stand in awe of a Nephi's faith, an Alma's conversion, or a Joseph Smith's visionary communion with God, we can also gain needed hope from their weaknesses as well. The scriptures are amazingly candid concerning the personal struggles of the servants of God. Like Paul, all the prophets seemed to have their particular "thorn in the flesh."

At the conclusion of general conference on 3 April 1977, a prophet, seer, and revelator arose and spoke with a raspy voice. That unique, endearing voice was that of President Spencer W. Kimball. Twenty years earlier, as an apostle of God, he had undergone surgery in which one vocal cord and part of another were completely removed. It had not been easy for this apostle to return to the pulpit. Six months after the surgery, he was asked by Elder Harold B. Lee to speak in a stake conference. Edward Kimball records:

"He stood and 'made the most terrible sound you can imagine' until finally he found his voice and gave his sermon. Then he sat down, buried his head in his hands and mourned. 'I was crying gallons of tears inside. I don't think they showed. But I really thought I was through, that I'd never preach again, that I wouldn't even try.' "[8]

But try he did, and this humble, voiceless man from Arizona became a prophet among prophets, a voice of God. This "weak" voice declared on that conference day in April 1977:

"I say, in the deepest of humility, but also by the power and force of a burning testimony in my soul, that from the prophet of the Restoration to the prophet of our own year, the communication line is unbroken, the authority is continuous, and light, brilliant and penetrating, continues to shine. The sound of the voice of the Lord is a continuous melody and a thunderous appeal. For nearly a century and a half there has been no interruption."[9]

Who can doubt that the afflictions of Spencer W. Kimball were crucial in the development of his humility, which in turn helped him

BRETT P. THOMAS

become so acquainted with God's voice that he would describe that voice as "a continuous melody and a thunderous appeal."

Those who come unto Christ will become "stronger and stronger in their humility, and firmer and firmer in the faith of Christ" (Helaman 3:35). When we humble ourselves before God and have faith in him, we are in effect saying: "O Lord, thou art our father; we are the clay, and thou our potter; and we all are the work of thy hand" (Isaiah 64:8). This divine sculpting of souls will produce extremes in experience. At times we will "glory in that which the Lord hath commanded me; yea, and this is my glory, that perhaps I may be an instrument in the hands of God to bring some soul to repentance; and this is my joy" (Alma 29:9), but at other times, the glory and the joy will not be so apparent as we agonize over our discipleship because "we behold our weakness, and stumble" (Ether 12:25). But wherever we are in the spectrum of these experiences, we can be assured that God is near, that he cares deeply, and that he will succor us perfectly. "Yet thou art there," Enoch testified, "and thy bosom is there; and also thou art just; thou art merciful and kind forever" (Moses 7:30). Descending into the depths of all human experience, Jesus Christ took upon himself not only our sins but our afflictions of every kind "that his bowels may be filled with mercy, according to the flesh, that he may know according to the flesh how to succor his people according to their infirmities" (Alma 7:12). Who can measure the depth and breadth of his grace?

The Lord revealed to Moroni: "My grace is sufficient for all men that humble themselves before me; for if they humble themselves before me, and have faith in me, then will I make weak things become strong unto them. Behold, I will show unto the Gentiles their weakness and I will show unto them that faith, hope and charity bringeth unto me — the fountain of all righteousness" (Ether 12:27–28).

CONCLUSION

Christ is the fountain of all righteousness. He has promised the faithful: "Because thou hast seen thy weakness thou shalt be made strong, even unto the sitting down in the place which I have prepared in the mansions of my Father" (Ether 12:37). Beholding our weaknesses teaches us to see with the "eye of faith," which drives us to our knees, in humility "relying wholly upon the merits of him who is mighty to save" (2 Nephi 31:19). Through sacred and holy covenants we express our willingness to take upon ourselves the name of Christ and to take upon ourselves the burdens of one another, "to mourn with those that mourn," to "comfort those that stand in need of comfort, and to stand as witnesses of God at all times and in all things, and in all places" (Mosiah 18:9).

Such emulation of the Savior prepares us to receive grace for grace. That is to say, we receive grace as we give grace to others by blessing their lives. The fountain of all righteousness endows us with his grace by pouring his Spirit upon us in abundance and filling us with a "more excellent hope" (Ether 12:32) and a "perfect love" (Moroni 8:26). These tender mercies assure us that Heavenly Father loves us and that his Son loves us, even to the laying down of his Son's life for us (see Ether 12:32–34). As we embrace this charity and "seek this Jesus of whom the prophets and apostles have written" (Ether 12:41), we shall be redeemed by him, and strengthened by him, to be in the presence of him:

"[They] shall be in the presence of the Lamb. And the graves of the saints shall be opened; and they shall come forth and stand on the right hand of the Lamb, when he shall stand upon Mount Zion, and upon the holy city, the New Jerusalem; and they shall sing the song of the Lamb, day and night forever and ever. And for this cause, that men might be made partakers of the glories which were to be revealed, the Lord sent forth the fulness of his gospel, his everlasting covenant, reasoning in plainness and simplicity—to prepare the weak for those things which are coming on the earth" (D&C 133:55–58).

Surely, preparing to be "in the presence of the Lamb" and to "be made partakers" of his glory is a strength worth striving for.

NOTES

1. L. Brent Goates, ed., *He Changed My Life* (Salt Lake City: Bookcraft, 1988), pp. 32–33.

2. Joseph Smith, *Teachings of the Prophet Joseph Smith,* sel. Joseph Fielding Smith (Salt Lake City: Deseret Book Co., 1976), p. 324.

3. Heber J. Grant, *Gospel Standards: Selections from the Sermons and Writings of Heber J. Grant,* ed. G. Homer Durham (Salt Lake City: Improvement Era., 1969), pp. 294–95.

4. C. S. Lewis, *The Weight of Glory and Other Addresses* (New York: Collier Books, 1980), pp. 18–19.

5. C. S. Lewis, *Mere Christianity* (New York: Macmillan, 1960), pp. 164–65.

6. Smith, *Teachings of the Prophet Joseph Smith,* p. 256.

7. Joseph Smith, *History of The Church of Jesus Christ of Latter-day Saints,* 2d ed. rev., edited by B. H. Roberts (Salt Lake City: The Church of Jesus Christ of Latter-day Saints, 1932–51), 2:170.

8. Edward L. Kimball and Andrew E. Kimball, Jr., *Spencer W. Kimball: Twelfth President of The Church of Jesus Christ of Latter-day Saints* (Salt Lake City: Bookcraft, 1977), p. 312.

9. Spencer W. Kimball, "Revelation: The Word of the Lord to His Prophets," *Ensign,* May 1977, p. 78.

INDEX

317